T4-ADN-282

P.F.M. FONTAINE

THE LIGHT
AND
THE DARK

A CULTURAL HISTORY OF DUALISM

VOLUME XV

J.C. GIEBEN, PUBLISHER
AMSTERDAM

THE LIGHT AND THE DARK

P.F.M. FONTAINE

THE LIGHT AND THE DARK

A CULTURAL HISTORY OF DUALISM

VOLUME XV

IMPERIALISM IN MEDIEVAL HISTORY I

DUALISM IN BYZANTINE HISTORY 476 - 638
AND
DUALISM IN ISLAM 572 - 732

J.C. GIEBEN, PUBLISHER

AMSTERDAM 2000

No part of this book may be translated or reproduced in any form, by print, photoprin microfilm, or any other means, without written permission from the publisher.

© by P.F.M. Fontaine / ISBN 90 5063 208 4 / Printed in The Netherlands

CONTENTS

Preface		xxi
Manual		xxiii
I	THE GREAT DUALISTIC THEMES OF ANTIQUITY	1
PART I	INTRODUCTORY	1

PART II   ON DUALISM AS SUCH 3
1. What is dualism? 3
2. And what dualism is not 5
3. Dualism and monism 6
4. A perfect world not possible 7
5. Anomalies and contradictions 8
6. War and death 9
7. A hierarchy of dualism 9

PART III   HORROR MATERIAE 11
1. Societies that did not despise the material world 12
2. Indian abhorrence of existence 13
3. An inferior world 14
4. Plato 15
5. Xenocrates 15
6. Neopythagoreanism 16
7. The dualism of Numenius 16
8. Plato's heritage in Middle Platonism 17
9. Plato's heritage in Neoplatonism 18
   a. Plotinus 18
   b. Porphyry 19
   c. Iamblichus 20
10. Philo 20
11. The Essenes 21
12. The Corpus Hermeticum 22
13. The Gnosis 22
   a. The earliest Gnostics 23
   b. The Sethians and Ophites 23
   c. The Barbelo-Gnostics 24
   d. The Basilidians 24
   e. The Valentinians 25

	f. The most successful Gnostic communities	25
14.	Christian Theology	27
	a. The Docetist position	28
	b. The Adoptionist position	28
	c. Ascetic positions	30
	d. The Arian position	32
	e. The nature(s) of Christ	34
	f. Horror materiae as a widespread phenomenon	35

PART IV TWO-WORLDS DUALISM   36
1. In Iranian religion   37
2. The Presocratics   37
3. Fear of chaos   38
4. The spiritual world denied   39
   a. The Stoa   40
   b. Greek atomism   40
   c. Lucretius and the nature of things   41
   d. Roman philosophers and moralists   41
5. In Neoplatonism   42
6. The Gnosis   43
7. In Christian theology   44

PART V KNOWLEDGE   45
1. About knowledge   45
2. The Aristotelian ideal of knowledge   46
3. Gnostic Knowledge   49

PART VI TWO RACES OF MEN   50
1. The Pythagorean fraternity   51
2. Philosophical élitism   51
3. Gnostic élitism   52
4. Second-rank Christians   53
5. Attitudes to women   54
6. Fear of sexuality   56
7. The 'others'   60
8. Slavery   61

PART VII IMPERIALISM   62
1. Imperialism in Mesopotamia and Asia Minor   62
2. The Persian Empire   64
3. The Macedonian Empire   64
4. The Roman Empire   65

CONCLUSION   66
Notes to Chapter I   67

II	UNIVERSALISM CONTRA PARTICULARISM: THE BYZANTINE RECONQUEST OF THE WEST	74

PART I A NEW CAPITAL AS THE SEAT OF A NEW IMPERIALISM 74
1. A new capital 74
2. Imperialistic claims 75
3. The extent of Zeno's Empire 76
4. Theodora 78
5. The grand design 81

PART II THE CONQUEST OF NORTH AFRICA 82
1. Mounting tension 82
2. The decision to fight 82
3. The landing in North Africa and the chances of war 83
4. The end of the Vandal kingdom 84
5. The fighting goes on 85
6. Byzantine misrule 86
7. The final victory 87

PART III THE CONQUEST OF ITALY 88
1. Justinian's second target 88
2. The Ostrogothic kingdom in Italy 88
3. Problems about the succession of Theodoric 89
4. The successful phase of the Italian campaign 90
5. The Ostrogothic counter-offensive 93
6. A Frankish intervention 94
7. The reduction of the Ostrogothic kingdom 95
8. New hopes for the Ostrogoths 97
9. The final phase 99
10. The end of the grand design 100

PART IV THE FRAGMENTATION OF ITALY 101
1. A sequel to the story of the Byzantine conquest 101
2. The Gepids 101
3. Enmity between Lombards and Gepids 102
4. The Lombard-Avar alliance 102
5. The Lombards invade Italy 103
6. Conclusion 104

Notes to Chapter II 104

III	THE SLAV THREAT AND AVAR IMPERIALISM	110

PART I THE SLAV THREAT 110
1. War on many fronts 110
2. An old presence 111
3. Opening the sluices 111

PART II	AVAR IMPERIALISM		112
1.	The coming of the Avars		112
2.	What the Avars wanted		112
3.	The capture of Sirmium		113
4.	Avar insolence		114
5.	An imperial counter-offensive		115
6.	An Avar embuscade		115
7.	A double attack on the capital		116
8.	The arrival of ever more Slavs		117
9.	Evaluation		117
	Notes to Chapter III		118

IV	TWO MIGHTY IMPERIALISMS IN CONFLICT: THE STRUGGLE BETWEEN BYZANTIUM AND PERSIA		120
1.	Persian imperialism as an old problem		120
2.	First clashes with the Byzantine Empire		121
3.	The cardinal error of Justinian I		121
4.	The 'eternal peace'		123
5.	Five years of warfare		123
6.	War in the Caucasus region		125
7.	How long is a century?		127
8.	War in Syria		128
9.	Fighting in Persarmenia		129
10.	Successful operations		129
11.	A disputed succession in Persia		130
12.	The fall of Maurice and of Narses		132
13.	Chosroes II attacks		133
14.	The fall of Phocas		134
15.	No counter-offensive yet		134
16.	The Persians march on		137
17.	The great counter-offensive		138
	a.	Triumph in Cappadocia	138
	b.	Persia invaded	140
	c.	In the winter quarters	141
	d.	Uneventful years	141
	e.	Chosroes' master stroke	143
	f.	The Turkish allies	144
	g.	A battle on hallowed ground	145
	h.	After Chosroes	146
	j.	Chosroes' fall	148
	k.	Peace concluded	149
18.	The final result		150
	Notes to Chapter IV		150

V	BYZANTINE HOOLIGANISM	155
1.	Popular amusement	155
2.	A solemn occasion	155
3.	The charioteers	157
4.	Fan clubs	157
5.	What united the two parties	159
6.	A dualistic situation	160
7.	Rioting Blues and Greens	161
8.	The Nika revolt	163
	a. A shouting-match in the Hippodrome	163
	b. A bungled hanging	164
	c. A hot night and a hot day	164
	d. A show of force and its consequences	165
	e. A counter-Emperor	165
	f. The rebellion smothered in blood	167
	g. The revenge	167
9.	The aftermath	167
10.	The new Aya Sofia	168
11.	The struggle of order and disorder	168
Notes to Chapter V		169

VI	RELIGIOUS DISSENSIONS	171
PART I	SAMARITANS AND JEWS	171
1.	The overall situation of the Jews	171
2.	Samaritan revolts	172
3.	The Jewish policy of Byzantium	174
	a. Anti-Jewish measures of Justinian I	174
	b. Heraclius I and his fear of the Jews	176
	c. Jewish reactions	177
PART II	INTERLUDE ON CAESAROPAPISM	178
1.	Commingling of the secular and religious spheres in the pagan world	178
2.	The anti-political stance	179
3.	Christian universalism and the Christian Empire	180
4.	Differing developments in West and East	181
5.	Caesaropapism	182
6.	Justinian's caesaropapist policy	183
PART III	RELIGIOUS POLICY WITH REGARD TO PAGANS AND THE HETERODOX	184
1.	Imperial policy regarding pagans	184
2.	Imperial policy regarding the heterodox	185
	a. The Manichaeans	185
	b. The Montanists	186
	c. The Donatists	186

PART IV	RELIGIOUS POLICY REGARDING THE MONOPHYSITES	187
1.	What is Monophysitism?	187
2.	The theology of Nestorius	188
3.	The Nestorian Church	189
4.	The road to Monophysitism	190
5.	Eutyches	191
6.	Continuing opposition	191
7.	The influence of the monks	192
8.	The overall situation in the middle of the fifth century	193
9.	Vehemence in Egypt	194
10.	The Emperor Leo I manoeuvring	194
11.	A caesaropapist intervention	195
12.	'A doctrinal aberration'	197
13.	The Henotikon	198
14.	An anti-Chalcedonian backlash	200
15.	The star of Chalcedon rising again	200
16.	The Rome-Byzantium schism	201
17.	The action of Severus	202
18.	On the brink of victory?	205
19.	The new Emperor	205
20.	Uproar in the Aya Sofia	207
21.	The popular demands ratified	208
22.	The schism healed	209
23.	Action against the anti-Chalcedonians	210
24.	A Pope visits Constantinople	211
25.	All heretics condemned	211
26.	Justinian's position	212
27.	A period of quiet	213
28.	A second papal visit	214
29.	Justinian tackles the Egyptian problem	214
30.	The structuring of the Monophysite Church	215
31.	Monophysite kingdoms	215
32.	Under Justinian's successors	216
Notes to Chapter VI		217
VII	ARABIA BEFORE ISLAM	223
1.	The land	223
2.	The inhabitants	224
3.	Pre-Islamic Arab history	224
4.	Social relations	225
5.	Pagan Arab religion	227
6.	'Fatalism'	228
Notes to Chapter VII		229

VIII	MOHAMMED	232
1.	History and legend	232
2.	Mohammed's early years	233
	a. His descent, parents, and family	233
	b. The young orphan	234
	c. The legend of the opening of Mohammed's breast	234
3.	His marriage with Khadija	235
4.	Mohammed as a visionary	237
	a. On the way to monotheism	237
	b. The revelation	237
	c. What did Mohammed really experience?	238
	d. Later visions	239
5.	'The years of ridicule'	240
	a. The first converts	240
	b. Public preaching	241
	c. The public enemy	242
6.	No more success in Ta'if	243
7.	Converts from Yathrib	244
	a. Interested pilgrims from Yathrib	244
	b. The 'first *'Aqaba*'	244
	c. The 'second *'Aqaba*'	245
8.	A change of heart	245
9.	The *Hidjira*	246
	a. The Muslims leave Mecca	246
	b. An attack on Mohammed planned	246
	c. The migration to Yathrib	247
10.	A new era	248
11.	Mohammed makes himself at home in Medina	249
12.	The foundation of a Muslim state	250
	a. The Medinan Muslim community	250
	b. The Medinan Jews	251
	c. A totally new community	251
	d. The breach with the Jews	252
	e. The Medinan city-state	253
13.	A plethora of world-historical events	253
14.	Mohammed's last years	254
	a. His later career	254
	b. His wives	254
	c. His children	255
	d. His death and burial	255
Notes to Chapter VIII		255

IX	ISLAM AS A RELIGION	263
1.	Credal formulas	263
2.	Islamic monotheism	263

3.	The nature of Allah	264
	a. God not the Father	264
	b. The unitarian concept	264
	c. The old problem of the One and the Many	265
	d. The attributes of God	265
4.	Allah and love	266
	a. Allah's concern for mankind	266
	b. The distant God	267
	c. Love of the neighbour	267
	d. Whom Allah does not love	268
	e. Disbelief	268
5.	Articles of the Muslim creed	269
	a. Angels and devils	269
	b. The prophets	269
	c. The hell	270
	d. The joys of heaven	270
6.	The duties of the Muslim	271
	a. The five pillars of Islam	271
	b. Confessing and praying	271
	c. Giving alms and fasting	272
	d. The pilgrimage to Mecca	272
7.	Islamic law	273
	a. The *shari'ah*	273
	b. The ban on alcohol	273
	c. Women	274
8.	Islamic 'fatalism'	274
9.	Determining the place of Islam	275
	a. Natural religion	275
	b. The analogy of being	277
10.	Is Islam dualistic?	278
	a. A declaration of intent	278
	b. Utterly opposed poles or not	279
	c. Conclusion	282
Notes to Chapter IX		283

X	MUSLIMS, JEWS, AND CHRISTIANS	287
1.	Schoeps' opinion	287
2.	Mohammed's irritation with the Medinan Jews	288
3.	The first blows	289
4.	The growing distance	289
5.	Mohammed takes action against the Banu Quanuqa'	290
6.	The murder of the Jewish poet Ka'b	291
7.	The fate of the an-Nadir Jews	291
8.	The ordeal of the Qurayza Jews	292
9.	The liquidation of Khaybar	294
10.	The *dhimma*	295

11.	Muslim objections against Judaism	296
12.	Dualism?	297
13.	Schoeps' opinion reconsidered	298
14.	Mohammed and the Christians of Mecca and Medina	299
15.	Mohammed and Jesus	299
16.	Mohammed and Mary	301
17.	Jesus' life in the Koran	302
18.	The Koran and the death of Jesus	302
19.	First encounters with Christians	304
20.	Mohammed's attitude towards Christians	305
21.	The effects of islamization	306
Notes to Chapter X		308

XI 'RELIGIOUS IMPERIALISM'   312

1.	Muslim imperialism	312
2.	The Holy War concept	312
3.	The 'two worlds'	313
4.	Mohammed's struggle with the Meccans	315
5.	The capture of Ta'if	317
6.	Byzantine nervousness	318
7.	Mohammed's death causes a crisis	319
8.	Arabian unity	319
9.	War on two fronts	320
10.	The Persians lose their capital	321
11.	Jerusalem in Muslim hands	322
12.	Egypt conquered	322
13.	The end of the Sasanian Empire	323
14.	The organization of the Muslim Empire	323
15.	Problems of the succession	324
16.	Peace with Byzantium	326
17.	North Africa conquered	326
18.	New succession problems	326
19.	Fresh conquests in the East	327
20.	Conquests in the West	328
21.	The results	329
Notes to Chapter XI		330

Chronologies   333

Bibliography   337

General Index   346

Maps
I	The Byzantine Empire anno 476	opposite p. 76
II	The Byzantine Empire in 563	opposite p. 90

20. Buddhism
    Vol. V. Ch. II.23
21. Confucianism
    Vol. V, CH. III.16-21, 23-24
22. Mohism
    Vol. V, Ch. III.22
23. Daoism
    Vol. V, Ch. III.25
24. The Gnosis
    Vol. VI, Ch.IV
    Vol. VII, Chs. I-III
    Vol. VIII, Chs. III-IX
    Vol. IX
25. The Christian Church and the Jews
    Vol. XII, Ch. II
26. The Christian Church and Judaizing
    Vol. XII, Ch. III
27. Christian theology in the first centuries
    Vol. XIII
28. The new religions of Late Antiquity
    Vol. XIV, Ch. II

VI   PHILOSOPHY

1. Pythagoreanism
   Vol. I, Ch. I
2. Ionic and Eleatic philosophy
   Vol. I, Ch. II
3. Sophists and Socrates
   Vol. III, Ch. II
4. Plato and Aristotle
   Vol. III, Ch. III
5. Hellenistic philosophy
   Vol. VI, Ch. III
6. Indian philosophy
   Vol. V, Ch. II.16
7. Chinese philosophy
   Vol. V, Ch. III.15
8. The philosophy of Philo
   Vol. VIII, Ch. I
9. The Philosophy of Late Antiquity
   Vol. XIV, Ch. I

VII   LITERATURE

1. Greek epics and lyrics
   Vol. I, Ch. III
2. Greek tragedy and comedy
   Vol. III, Ch. I

11.	Muslim objections against Judaism	296
12.	Dualism?	297
13.	Schoeps' opinion reconsidered	298
14.	Mohammed and the Christians of Mecca and Medina	299
15.	Mohammed and Jesus	299
16.	Mohammed and Mary	301
17.	Jesus' life in the Koran	302
18.	The Koran and the death of Jesus	302
19.	First encounters with Christians	304
20.	Mohammed's attitude towards Christians	305
21.	The effects of islamization	306
Notes to Chapter X		308

XI   'RELIGIOUS IMPERIALISM'   312

1.	Muslim imperialism	312
2.	The Holy War concept	312
3.	The 'two worlds'	313
4.	Mohammed's struggle with the Meccans	315
5.	The capture of Ta'if	317
6.	Byzantine nervousness	318
7.	Mohammed's death causes a crisis	319
8.	Arabian unity	319
9.	War on two fronts	320
10.	The Persians lose their capital	321
11.	Jerusalem in Muslim hands	322
12.	Egypt conquered	322
13.	The end of the Sasanian Empire	323
14.	The organization of the Muslim Empire	323
15.	Problems of the succession	324
16.	Peace with Byzantium	326
17.	North Africa conquered	326
18.	New succession problems	326
19.	Fresh conquests in the East	327
20.	Conquests in the West	328
21.	The results	329
Notes to Chapter XI		330

Chronologies   333

Bibliography   337

General Index   346

Maps
I	The Byzantine Empire anno 476	opposite p.	76
II	The Byzantine Empire in 563	opposite p.	90

III	Italy after the Lombard invasion	opposite p. 102
IV	Avars and Slavs	opposite p. 114
V	Byzantines and Persians	opposite p. 128
VI	Mohammed's Arabia	opposite p. 224
VII	Arab conquests 632-732	opposite p. 318

PREFACE

Allow me to plagiarize myself by beginning this preface and this volume with the phrases that I opened Volume XII with; what I wrote there also applies to the present volume. Each of the fifteen volumes of this series, together comprising the whole of Antiquity, including the Middle East, India, and China, can be read independently of the others. However, I may expect of nobody that he or she will read all those volumes from cover to cover. Therefore, I attach to this book a Manual. On the premise that no overburdened scholar will read this work *in toto*, I can at least guide scholars and other interested readers to their fields of study and interest. In the Manual these fields are tabulated, with reference to the corresponding volumes, chapters, and sections. Yet, with this much conceded to my overburdened reader, permit me to state that this series forms a whole, with all the parts interconnecting and interrelated. It has one all-comprising and over-arching theme, that of dualism.

Throughout this volume I use the same definition of dualism as in all former ones. There is dualism when we are confronted with two utterly opposed conceptions, systems, principles, groups or kinds of people, or even worlds, without any intermediate terms between them. They cannot be reduced to one another; in some cases one is not even dependent on the other. The opposites are considered to be of different quality, so much so that one of them is always seen as being distinctly inferior and hence must be neglected or even destroyed.

XX

I found an interesting discussion of what dualism is in a book by Helen Haste, *The sexual metaphor* (Harvester Wheatsheaf, Hemel Hampstead, Hertfordshire GB, 1993). In this book the author pleads for a fundamental change in the man-woman relationship. She states that "real changes occur only when there is a profound change in the underlying metaphor of gender;" this is what she calls 'the sexual metaphor', 'the *metaphor* [her italics] of masculinity versus femininity'. If we want to change these metaphors, and especially that 'versus' in them, "as we apply them to stereotypes of human behaviour and attributes, we have also to challenge the principles of dualism on which so much of our thinking rests." She then makes the intriguing remark that "we construct 'either-or' categories not just for convenience, but by defining one pole as the negation of the other, we assert not only what is, but also what is *not* [her emphasis]."

She goes on to say that this 'either-or' is not only there for its 'conceptual usefulness'; quite the contrary, it is always disturbing and divisive. Haste demonstrates this by applying it to the man-woman-relationship; this is, she states, the masculine-feminine polarity, often an area of anxiety and uncertainty. "Masculinity and femininity themselves are problematic and fraught." Often indeed, but not always. For in my opinion the man-woman relationship is basically not antagonistic but complementary. Yet it can easily become antagonistic to the point of dualism. In this series I demonstrated this in the light of the position of women in Greece and India.

Haste mentions (p. 15) as 'either-or' metaphors: active-passive, public-private, rationality-chaos, which all have something to do with the idea of gender. The public sphere is often seen as the male domain, whereas the women have to tend the home, or the man is the rational one, whereas the woman is naturally irrational. The two main metaphors, however, of the man-woman relationship are hierarchy and functional complementarity; the latter one is not dualistic. "Functional complementarity means the coexistence of two parallel but interwoven sets of characteristics, each necessary for effective polarity." This is how it should be [and let me add: as it, thank heavens, often is]. Hierarchy means that one part lords it over the other, mostly the man over the woman, but it can also be the other way round. In these cases the relation comes close to being dualistic or is actually so. This is relative dualism, since the stronger party assumes that the other is defective in some or even in many respects - calling women 'the weaker sex' - and has to be helped and sustained so that she, or perhaps he, is made dependent on the other half.

I find it very helpful what Helen Haste says, but it is a pity that she sometimes confuses dualism with duality. "Polarity or dualism is a common principle for categorisation: light versus dark, public versus private, mind versus body, rational versus intuitive, black versus white [p. 44]." I should not use the word 'dualism' for these oppositions. She herself, somewhat further on, speaks of 'dualism' as the most appropriate term. However, take for instance the polarity 'rational-intuitive'. They are different things, of course. Yet every scientist knows that the best discoveries are often made intuitively, through a sudden flash of insight and not through rational reasoning.

As for all foregoing volumes of this series, I have to thank some people who helped me. First of all, there is my eldest daughter, Dr. T.A.M. Smidt van Gelder-Fontaine - Resianne to me -, who found the time to read almost the whole present volume. She provided me with a number of very useful remarks and comments, which led to alterations in the text. Then comes my able corrector Dr. Jo Swabe, who carefully corrected the English of the Preface and all the chapters. She was followed by my dear wife Anneke, who corrected the one but last version on typing errors. I want to stress, however, that all of it is my own responsibility, the scholarship, the English, and the layout.

It is with a sad feeling that I mention my publisher J.C. Gieben. I am grateful for his seeing this volume through the press. However, what saddens me is that he is going to close down his publishing firm. I came to him for the first time in December 1985. Since then he has published fifteen volumes of 'The Light and the Dark'. Believe me or believe me not, in all those fifteen years we never had one cross word; everything always went as smoothly as possible. I have to be and I am indeed very grateful for this, and I wish Mr. Gieben, Han to me since long, all the best.

This leaves me with a problem, of course. I have not yet decided what to do. For a sensible decision I need a lot of information, which I do not yet have at this moment of writing. One thing is certain, however, I intend to go on writing. I do not know whether I will look for another publisher. It is also quite conceivable that I will continue on Internet. The next volume, Volume XVI, will be on the western imperialism of the Middle Ages.

Piet F.M. Fontaine
Amsterdam (NL)

MANUAL

This manual is designed for those readers who do not want to read the whole work, but, instead, want to see what is said in it about the subject(s) they are interested in.

I   ON DUALISM AS SUCH

         Prefaces of Vols. I, VI, IX,
         Vol. IV, Ch. IV.4

II   PERIODS AND CIVILIZATIONS

         1. Greece
            Vol. I Archaic and early classical periods
            Vol. II and III Fifth and fourth centuries B.C.
            Vol. VI The Hellenistic world
         2. Egypt
            Vol. IV, Ch. I
         3. Mesopotamia and Anatolia
            Vol. IV, Ch. III
         4. Israel
            Vol. IV, Ch. II
         5. Iran
            Vol. IV, Ch. IV, Vol. V, Ch. I
         6. India
            Vol. V, Ch. II
         7. China
            Vol. V, Ch. III
         8. Roman history
            Vols. X, XI,
            XII, Ch. I,
            XIII

III   POLITICAL HISTORY

         1. Greece
            Vol. II
            Vol. VI, Chs. I and II

2. Rome
   Vol. X
   Vol. XI, Chs. I, II, III, IV
3. Egypt
   Vol. IV, Ch. I.1-4
4. Mesopotamia and Anatolia
   Vol. IV, Ch. III.1-9.
5. Israel
   Vol. IV, Ch. II.14
   Vol. VI, Ch. II.11
6. Iran
   Vol. IV, Ch. IV.1-3
   Vol. V, Ch. I.1-3
7. India
   Vol. V, Ch. II.1-11
8. China
   Vol. V, Ch. III.1-5

IV SOCIAL HISTORY

1. Greece
   Vol. II, Ch. III.3
   Vol. II, Ch. IV.4
2. India
   Vol. V, Ch. II.13-15
Since esoteric religious movements are socially distinct from the rest of the population, we may subsume these too under this heading :
3. The Pythagoreans
   Vol. I, Ch. I
4. Eleusinian mysteries and Orphics
   Vol. I, Ch. IV
5. Yoga
   Vol. V, Ch. II.21
6. Jainism
   Vol. V, Ch. II.22
7. Dao
   Vol. V, Ch. III.25
8. The Essenes
   Vol. VIII, Ch. V
9. Almost all Gnostic movements
   Vol. VII, Ch. III, Vols. VIII and IX
10. The subjected peoples of the Roman Empire
    Vol. XI, Ch. IV
11. The Jews of the Roman Empire
    Vol. XI, Ch. V
12. The Greeks of the Roman Empire
    Vol. XI, Ch. VI
13. The Roman Empire and the Christian Church
    Vol. XII, Ch. I

14. Attitudes to the body and sexuality in the Graeco-Roman world
    Vol. XIV, Ch. III
15. Christian and classical culture
    Vol. XIV, Ch. IV

V HISTORY OF RELIGIONS

1. Pythagoreanism
   Vol. I, Ch. I
2. The Olympian religion
   Vol. I, Ch. IV.1-8
3. The Eleusinian mysteries
   Vol. I, Ch. IV.8
4. The cult of Dionysus
   Vol. I, Ch. IV.9
5. Orphism
   Vol. I, Ch. IV.10
6. Greek shamanism
   Vol. I, Ch. IV.11
7. Egyptian religion
   Vol. IV, Ch. I.5-7
8. The religion of Israel
   Vol. IV, Ch. II
   Vol. VII, Ch. VI
9. Religions of the Middle East
   Vol. IV, Ch. III.10
10. Iranian religion
    Vol. IV, Ch. IV.4-12
    Vol. V, Ch. I.4-5
11. Mazdakism
    Vol. V, Ch. I, Appendix
12. The New Testament
    Vol. VII, Ch. IV
13. The Essenes
    Vol. VII, Ch. V
14. Hermetism
    Vol. VIII, Ch. II
15. The Veda
    Vol. V, Ch. II.17
16. Brahmanism
    Vol. V, Ch. II.18-19
17. Hinduism
    Vol. V, Ch. II.20
18. Yoga
    Vol. V, Ch. II.21
19. Jainism
    Vol. V, Ch. II.22
20. Buddhism

20. Buddhism
   Vol. V. Ch. II.23
21. Confucianism
   Vol. V, CH. III.16-21, 23-24
22. Mohism
   Vol. V, Ch. III.22
23. Daoism
   Vol. V, Ch. III.25
24. The Gnosis
   Vol. VI, Ch.IV
   Vol. VII, Chs. I-III
   Vol. VIII, Chs. III-IX
   Vol. IX
25. The Christian Church and the Jews
   Vol. XII, Ch. II
26. The Christian Church and Judaizing
   Vol. XII, Ch. III
27. Christian theology in the first centuries
   Vol. XIII
28. The new religions of Late Antiquity
   Vol. XIV, Ch. II

VI PHILOSOPHY

1. Pythagoreanism
   Vol. I, Ch. I
2. Ionic and Eleatic philosophy
   Vol. I, Ch. II
3. Sophists and Socrates
   Vol. III, Ch. II
4. Plato and Aristotle
   Vol. III, Ch. III
5. Hellenistic philosophy
   Vol. VI, Ch. III
6. Indian philosophy
   Vol. V, Ch. II.16
7. Chinese philosophy
   Vol. V, Ch. III.15
8. The philosophy of Philo
   Vol. VIII, Ch. I
9. The Philosophy of Late Antiquity
   Vol. XIV, Ch. I

VII LITERATURE

1. Greek epics and lyrics
   Vol. I, Ch. III
2. Greek tragedy and comedy
   Vol. III, Ch. I

VIII   HISTORIOGRAPHY

       1. Greek historiography
          Vol. III, Ch. III.1
       2. Old Testament
          Vol. IV, Ch. II.1-6
       3. New Testament
          Vol. VII, Ch. IV.1-2.

CHAPTER I

THE GREAT DUALISTIC THEMES OF ANTIQUITY

PART I INTRODUCTORY

The Roman Empire of the West disappeared from the historical scene in 476, *sang- und klanglos*, as the Germans would say. Though this is one of the greatest events in history, its exact date is not known. But was it really an event? Or rather a non-event? Even the traditional date '476', that everyone learns at school, is not wholly undisputed. The last Emperor, Romulus Augustulus, was still a child, when he acceded to the throne in 475. His name reads as a pun on the legendary founder and first king of Rome and its first Emperor, but this 'Augustulus', 'little Augustus', is not a flattering diminutive. No revolution brought the end of his reign, no invading barbarian army swept him away, nor did he fall a victim to a plot. He was simply deposed leaving no trace in the annals of history after his enforced abdication.

That the Empire of the West no longer existed is shown by the fact that the man who deposed Romulus Augustulus did not style himself 'Emperor', but contented himself with the title 'King of the Germans in Italy'. He was Odoacer. a man of about forty, a Germanic general in the Roman army, who belonged to the tribe of the Sciri; he could count on the loyalty of the Germanic troops in Roman service.

Did the Western Empire have no heirs? Was there no heritage? I feel that there is little sense in mentioning the very last remnant of the Empire, the so-called 'Realm of Syagrius', a Roman general who after 476 held out in the region between the Loire and the Somme, until his domain was overrun by the Franks in 486. It is far more important that Odoacer acknowledged the suzerainty of the Emperor of the East, Zeno, to whom he sent the imperial insignia. The Roman Senate wrote a letter to the Byzantine Emperor in which it expressed its unanimous opinion that the West no longer needed an Emperor of its own; one ruler for both East and West was sufficient. By common consent the seat of the universal Empire was transferred from Rome to Constantinople. In this way the Byzantine Empire became the heir of the western imperial tradition. Zeno rewarded Odoacer by giving him the title of *patricius*. In practice the transfer of imperial rights to the East meant nothing at all as yet, but it presented the Byzantine rulers with a claim of which they later would take advantage.

As a result of the Germanic invasions of the fifth century the territory of the *ci-devant* Western Empire had divided into a number of Germanic kingdoms : the Anglo-Saxon ones in Britain, that of the Franks in the southern half of the Netherlands, Belgium and Luxemburg, northern France and south-western Germany, that of the Burgundians in eastern France and Switzerland, of the Alemanni in Austria, of the Visigoths in southern France and in the Iberian peninsula, and of the Vandals in North Africa. Finally, there was that Kingdom of the Germans in Italy. But not one of their kings, not even Odoacer, got it into his head to proclaim himself Emperor, either of the whole West or of his own particular realm. This did, however, not mean that the imperial idea - what the Germans call the *Kaiseridee* - was dead and buried. For the time being it seemed to play no role, but it lived on and would be transformed by the Frankish rulers some centuries later.

Apart from the *Kaiseridee*, the Roman heritage contained some other elements which for centuries on end would continue to influence European civilization : the Latin language, Roman Law, bureaucratic expertise, Roman architecture. Then, of course, there was also that all-embracing structure, the Roman Catholic Church, that had inherited the Roman Empire's claim to universality. Yet however formative these elements were for the development of European culture, it is not these that interest us most within the context of this series. For our subject, our overall theme, is dualism, and the question now is whether the Middle Ages, to which we now turn, also inherited the dualistic elements that we have discovered in the fabric of the societies of the ancient world.

PART II ON DUALISM AS SUCH

1. What is dualism?

Although dualism is a phenomenon as old as the world, the specific terms 'dualism' and 'dualist' are of fairly recent origin. 'Dualist' was the first to appear, in a book published in 1700 by Thomas Hyde, professor of Hebrew in Oxford University. Since this book dealt with the ancient Persian religion, the term 'dualist', and also 'dualism', was from the very first thought to mean Iranian dualism.[1] It became widely known when Pierre Bayle inserted it into an article on 'Zoroaster' in the second edition (1702) of his famous dictionary. The term 'dualism' proper was used for the first time by Christian Wolff in his *Psychologia rationalis* of 1702. Wolff transferred the concept from the sphere of religion to which it had been restricted by Hyde, Bayle, and also Leibniz in his *Theodicy* of 1710, to that of philosophy, by stating that dualism also denoted the substantial difference of the spiritual and the corporeal, the immaterial and the material.[2]

Since it is perfectly possible that there are readers of this volume for whom this is the first one of the series they have seen, it is necessary, and at any rate not superfluous, to repeat the definition of dualism I presented in the Preface to Volume I and which is to be found in all the Prefaces since then. I have never seen reason to change it.

There is dualism when we are confronted with two utterly opposed conceptions, systems, principles, groups or kinds of people, or even worlds, without any intermediate terms between them. They cannot be reduced to each other; in some cases the one is not even dependent on the other. The opposites are considered to be of different quality, so much so that one of them is always seen as distinctly inferior and hence must be neglected, repudiated, or even destroyed. Using on the shortest possible formula, one could say that dualism is about unbridgeable oppositions.

More than once in the foregoing volumes I argued against two frequent misunderstandings, the first being that dualism has its origin in Iran, in the Zoroastrian religion; Iranian dualism is only one case among many. The second is that it is to be found mainly in the domain of religion, with an annex in philosophy. I have characterized dualism as an anthropological phenomenon, as something that is common to all mankind, without a specific historical or ethnic origin. And there is absolutely no reason why unbridgeable oppositions would occur only in religion or philosophy. Everyone is able to detect such oppositions in politics, in social life, and even in the personal sphere. I feel that I have to repeat here the warning of Samuel Laeuchli; [3] I wholeheartedly agree with it and will confront those of my critics with it who doggedly accuse me of overstepping my mark when I, in my treatment of dualism, go beyond the confines of religion and philosophy. This scholar says that "the dualistic problem has been confused by two rigid assertions. The first limits dualism to an extreme of an Iranian type of two gods, one good and one evil. The second limits dualism to only the metaphysical, religious, or philosophical aspects of such duality. This narrow conception prevents the observer from grasping the dualistic problem in the ancient world." [4]

The problem with dualism is that it is something disruptive, something that causes fissions, that pushes apart. For this reason it can never be a positive element in societies and civilizations; nothing definite or stable can be based on it. But on the other hand, no human community, no culture is wholly without it; there is always some dualistic element, and more often a few. The dominating trend of mankind is to be 'social', to come together and to hold together; we strive after peace and harmony. In one word, we want to be constructive and not disruptive. But at the same time there also is always an urge operative towards radicalizing oppositions, an urge that can have disastrous consequences. When there is such an urge, we are speaking of dualism.

Dualistic elements are erratic blocks, appearing now and again. Sometimes they do not pose much of a problem, although they are never harmless; sometimes they present a very great danger, threatening to destabilize or even to destroy the social fabric. Nonetheless, even if a society is riddled with dualistic elements, the urge towards organic unity remains the domineering one, or else there would be no society. Even philosophical or religious systems can hardly be basically dualistic, for if they were, they would destroy themselves; there is always a point where they hang together, or a solid ground upon which they are built. The one exception to this rule is the Gnosis, to which we shall have to return.

I feel that it is, on the whole, not so difficult to detect dualistic phenomena or to distinguish them from non-dualistic ones. It might be a help to discover them in the mass of meanings and opinions, if we pay attention to the following elements : vegetarianism, esotericism, dogmatism, the authoritarian attitude, élitism, the tragic sentiment, pessimism, fatalism, shamanism, gnosticizing, magic, puritanism, machism. None of these is necessarily dualistic, but the more of them come together in one system of thought, acting, or living, the nearer we are to a full-grown dualism.

2. And what dualism is not

I feel that a few caveats are in place here. First, there is the tendency to call every opposition dualistic. If this were true, I would not have begun this work, for the simple reason that there are countless oppositions of every kind, most of them without much signifance, certainly not enough to devote scholarly treatises to them. For these we should be content with the term duality. The word 'dualism' should be used only for unbridgeable oppositions, which excludes the large majority of oppositions.

My second caveat is that dualism is not an intellectual system; neither is it an ideology, a philosophy or a religion; instead, it is a mental phenomenon. It exists, like beauty, in the beholder's eye (or mind). For this reason we cannot compare it to non-dualistic systems, because a dualistic complex and a non-dualistic system are things of a different order. Although I am using the term 'dualistic system' myself, I am doing so with a bad conscience; it is basically a *contradictio in adiecto*.

In spite of this, there have been a number of attempts to create dualistic systems. There were not many of them in Antiquity, almost all of which remained restricted in membership. Presenting a short catalogue of them, we must mention the following systems : the Pythagorean fraternity, [5] the Orphic religion, [6] the philosophies of Empedocles, Heraclitus, and above all Parmenides, [7] those elements in Plato's teaching that show a strong tendency towards dualism, [8] and those systems of Late Antiquity that are dependent on Plato's heritage, Neopythagoreanism, [9] Middle Platonism, [10] and Neoplatonism, especially Plotinus, [11], further outside the Graeco-Roman world Zoroastrianism, [12] and still more Iranian Zervanism, [13] in India Yoga in particular, [14] and Chinese Daoism. [15]. The most characterically dualistic systems, although existing within the orbit of the Graeco-Roman civilization, yet standing apart from it, are the Gnostic ones as decribed in Volumes VII, VIII, and IX.

3. Dualism and monism

The domineering trait of all civilizations. societies, religions, and systems of thought is that they are basically non-dualistic (with the one exception mentioned). The history of dualism is not the history of the world. But it should be remarked, in the same breath, that they are not monistic either. It is not correct to assume that monism and dualism are oppositions, something in the sphere of 'either-or'; they are chips of the same block, products of a somewhat defective view of the world. What the 'holistics', with whom the concept of monism is very much in favour, tend to forget is that, by positing the opposition monism-dualism as an 'either-or', they are turning it into a dualistic opposition.

As I wrote in the Preface to Volume IX (p. XVII), monism can generate dualism. It is not possible to place all metaphysical, cosmic, social, and human phenonema under one heading; rests and remnants will always remain that refuse to fit into the monistic pattern. Such remnants will 'rebel' against the monistic monopoly, leading to a dualistic situation, since all kinds of reality cannot be forced into one single straightjacket. A case in point is pantheism, for instance, to which many people in all centuries have paid homage. It literally means that the godhead is fully identical with the order of creation. It then becomes indistinguishable from it; we may say then that all is matter, just as we are entitled to say that all is god. And if the godhead remains distinct from the created order, however slightly, then pantheism is not complete; in that case it is not what it pretends to be.

Often, indeed, we see that a system, philosophical or religious, begins with a monistic starting-point, but becomes dualistic one stage lower. A good example of this is Stoic philosophy. Zeno and his school maintained that the universe is an entirely physical system; this is an instance of monistic materialism. But the Stoics also acknowledged incorporeal elements, like Time and Space. Although the godhead of the Stoa is purely physical, he is also everlasting and the artificer of all that is - which means that the eternal Creator is clearly distinct from the matter on which he is working. [16]

An example from the religious field is Zoroastrianism which is commonly decried as thoroughly dualistic. It begins, however, with a monistic dogma. There is only one god to be venerated, Ahura Mazda or the Wise Lord. This supreme godhead brings forth a number of *spentas*, a word that literally means 'working'; a *spenta* is an effect. It is a holy and immortal being; the principal one is Spenta Mainyu, the Holy Spirit. But Zoroaster's system is not as monistic as it seems. For there is also Angra Mainyu, the Hostile Spirit, who is of old the enemy of Ahura Mazda. Since the good supreme spirit could not be made into the origin of evil, an evil spirit was needed to create what is bad. In this way Zoroaster succeeded in combining his monotheistic (or monistic) starting-point with his dualistic views. [17]

4. A perfect world not possible

Let me quote again what Karen Blixen said in her novel *Out of Africa* (1937) : "The world, after all, is not a regular or calculable place". Making the world into such a place is beyond our human feasibilities; conceiving it as such a place is an optical illusion which will cause deep disappointment. Systems which, like communism, pretended to create a perfect world of perfect people, all broke down, leaving nothing behind them but despair and ruins. It should be remarked that it is not the aim of Christianity, and in particular not of the

Roman Catholic Church, to bring about a sinless world without wrongdoers. The Church is first and foremost an instrument for the forgiving of sins, but she knows only too well that people will continue to sin.

5. Anomalies and contradictions

In the Preface to Volume IX I spoke at length of the anomalies and contradictions with which our world - or must we say : our conception of it - is riddled. We are unable to view it as a whole. I began with pointing to the existence of unsolvable paradoxes among which I mentioned those of Grelling and Russell. Their unsolvability shocked the very fabric of logic. In order to get rid of them a totally new system of logic would be necessary; such a system has not been developed so far.

Still greater misery was caused in scientific circles by the publication of Gödel's theorem in 1930, known as the 'incompleteness theorem'. The intrinsic or fundamental incompleteness of a logico-mathematical system consists of the fact that in the last resort it is undecidable, which means that it is neither provable nor disprovable, or in other words, that it is not possible to state whether it is true or untrue. What Gödel's theorem says is that no system of formal logic promises perfect consistency. Faultless deduction from first principles is not possible; since there is no absolute coherence, some elements will not fit. This is another way of saying what I so often argued in foregoing volumes and also here : that monistic systems are logically impossible. Thomas Kuhn, in his book *The Scientific Revolutions* (1970, 1962[1]), widened the scope of the consequences the theorem has by stating that no paradigm that provides a basis for scientific research ever completely resolves all its problems. There will always remain contradictions, inconsistencies, and anomalies.

A perfect example of inconsistency is the indubitable fact that the first and second laws of thermodynamics contradict each other. The first law is well-known. It is the law of the conservation of energy : the total amount of energy remains constant. But the second law is far less known. It is the law of entropy, which says that there is a constant loss of energy. The consequence scientists have to face is that an entirely coherent description of the field of nature is impossible; there is a flaw, a fundamental contradiction.

The German physician Werner Heisenberg was wholly in line with these ideas when he introduced his concept of 'uncertainty relations'. This is shorthand for what quantum mechanics teaches us : that nothing definite can be stated of the particles of an atom, neither of their respective places in it nor of the velocity with which they move. No atomic model is possible. This has important philosophical consequences. We have a world we can observe, understand, and describe, and there is a world that is beyond all description, comprehension, and imagination. The bad thing is that this second world is the basic one on which all reality rests. But, when speaking of two opposed and unrelated worlds, we are speaking of dualism.

6. War and death

There are more dualistic elements to which attention should be paid in coming volumes. One of the most important is the occurence of war. Antiquity bore witness to endless wars. The Roman Empire would be nowhere without its never-ending warfare; Roman society was wholly geared to war, as its *raison d'être*. Another subject to be studied in later volumes.

Finally, there is the opposition of life and death, one of the most vicious. In all ages people have found it very hard to cope with it. How much of a problem was it during the Middle Ages?

7. A hierachy of dualism

It might be possible, in an overview of the ancient world, to draw up a hierarchy or a scale on which we place the civilizations of that world according to the degree of dualism and the number of dualistic oppositions found in them. As I wrote above, no civilization is wholly exempt from them. I presented this hierarchy already in the Preface to Volume XI; here I must be short on it. The least dualistic of all societies in Antiquity was ancient Israel. Based as it was on an intimate relationship between God and his people, dependent on the unity of creed and cult, and conducted through life by the stipulations of Mosaic Law, it took an essentially optimistic and harmonious view of human existence. But this society also had its loose ends. There was the visceral fear of idols against whom the prophets conducted a running fight; it was sometimes difficult to resist the lure of magic. In the secular field we see the rivalry of the two kingdoms, Israel and Juda, which led to internecine warfare. Later, after the Captivity, there was the enmity of Jews and Samaritans.

Egyptian society was, on the whole, non-dualistic. But it knew, and still knows, the difference of the north and the south, of the Delta and the Valley of the Nile. Very pregnant was the opposition of the desert and the fertile land along the Nile, of red and black. Egyptians were not the only people in history to find themselves superior to all other nations : they were the 'true men', the others were less than human. We detect the same feeling of superiority in the Chinese. They, and they alone, are in harmony with heaven; here too, the others are denied a truly human existence.

The two most dualistic societies of Antiquity were Greece and India. The Greek nation was politically fragmented into innumerable entities, the *poleis*, most of them small, which conducted interminable destructive wars against each other. This put them at a disadvantage, for instance, to the Persian Empire, but in spite of this, they boasted that they were the only ones possessing *paideia*, the proper way of being human. Within Greek society we find the dualistic opposition of the free and the slaves, who were not considered human. Greek philosophy knew many dualistic elements to which we shall have to return.

Ancient Indian society had its origin in conquest; the invading Aryans subjected the autochthonous population, which was kept at a very inferior position. This probably supplied the dualistic pattern that we find back in so much of Indian history. The Aryans were a *macho* race, filled with a deep contempt of, and a visceral fear, of women. This is particularly evident in Hindu religion. In Indian mythology we find the opposition of the powers of Above (the benevolent) and Below (the malicious). In their philosophy there are the oppositions of Unity and Diversity, Male and Female, Matter and Spirit.

The Brahmanic religion propagated the superiority of the Brahmans, the guardians of the truth; they kept themselves aloof from human society. All Indian religions, especially Buddhism, are built on the fundamental dualism of personal existence, selfish and thoughtless as it is, and the state of unworldly contemplation that leads to the final loss of all that is self. All these subjects have been treated at length in the foregoing volumes to which I may refer the reader.

In the course of their long history the Romans, so to speak, took over the whole of the ancient world. With their claim to universalism they were the successors to the much older oriental empires and that of the Macedonians. Further on in this chapter I shall come back to this. Here it must be stated that this reign of law and order also knew its dualisms, exemplified in the struggle of opposing social and political groups that resulted in a century of bloody civil wars. Rome had also its problems with the large slave element, while the much vaunted *Pax Romana* was often hardly more than an illusion, what with the never-ending rebellions of the subjected nations and tribes. The Roman government and the general public too found it hard to cope with the Jewish element and still more with the Christian community. All this was discussed at length in Volumes X and XI.

PART III HORROR MATERIAE

I devoted much thought to the question of which of the great dualistic themes of Antiquity was the most conspicuous and important. Knowledge perhaps? The idea that there might exist a kind of higher Knowledge, not to be divulged to the profane, and invested with peculiar proprieties? This was certainly an important element in the mental make-up of the ancient world. But finally I came to the conclusion that *horror materiae* was something still more decisive, that vague, but sometimes vehemently outspoken abhorrence of what is physical, material, and bodily. The Graeco-Roman world never managed to cope in a balanced way with the difference between what is spiritual and what is material. Their relationship often assumed dualistic traits, so that the spiritual was glorified and the material despised.

1. Societies that did not despise the material world

Judaism remained curiously free of this. The Old Testament literally starts from the premise that creation is good. The material world was to the Jews a world created by God and bearing the mark of his hands. Jewish life was built on the intimate relation of God and his people, often compared to the love relation between man and wife. Later, in Christianity, we find the idea that the spiritual and material worlds came close together in the person of Jesus of Nazareth, the God-Man, in whom heaven and earth, divine and human, were united.

A good second is Egyptian society. As every other society in this world, this too had its dualistic tensions, but we cannot detect that *horror materiae*. The Egyptians enjoyed life. It is true that they were obsessed with death and in all possible manners attempted to triumph over it. Yet this is not the same as having an abhorrence of what is material and physical. Rather the contrary, for they wanted, for instance by mummifying, to stop the process of decaying that is the inexorable consequence of death. The nearest the ancient Egyptians came to that fear of matter is that they were afraid of Chaos. They felt that their well-ordered society was posed between Chaos and Order. Everything had begun with a 'not-yet', with non-existence. A dualistic division between Chaos and Order dominated the Egyptian vision of the world. Order reigned but Chaos always seemed near. [18]

A third in this rather short series is Chinese society. We need not idealize it; it too knew its tensions. As always and everywhere, there was a certain distance between ideal and reality. But *idealiter* this society was all for agreement and harmony. The most conspicuous dualistic elements that dominated the ancient western world, those of Pure and Impure and Good and Bad, do not occur in Chinese thought. The distinction *par excellence* was that between *Yin* and *Yang*. Since westerns use to think conceptually, they assume that this is a pair of philosophical or intellectuals concepts. But *Yin* and *Yang* are material entities, albeit of the most ethereal sort. They are not dualistically opposed but, instead, complementary. From their interaction all things proceed, for instance winter and summer. This excludes every possibility of the existence of the *horror materiae*. [19]

2. Indian abhorrence of existence

We get a totally different picture when we turn to ancient India. For millennia Indian thought has been dominated by the opposition of Spirit and Matter or of Spirit and Nature; these are totally different elements. It was a dualistiuc opposition. Spirit is always superior and prior. Even the human person does not escape from this opposition, because the elements of which he is composed, body and soul, are of an opposed and different (in quality) kind. There were several schools of thought, differing considerably among themselves, but they all agreed on the dualistic opposition of body and soul according to which the body was the inferior and often even contempible part. The true philosophical Hindu sage keeps himself as far apart from this world as possible; he follows the *via negativa*, which means abstinence from the pleasures ordinary human existence has to offer. Renouncement of the world is the catchword. Everything that is changeable and perishable is inessential and false.

We find this abhorrence of 'the world' in a particularly strong form in Yoga systems. According to the most radical of them matter has no divine origin; it produces nature and the universe, all of itself, but there is no soul in them, only mechanical movement. 'Soul' is something totally different. The consequence is that man is composed of utterly different and irreconcilable elements. [20] Perhaps the abhorrence of what is material is nowhere so conspicuous as in Jainism. Jainists, the members of a sect that survives today, live a life of ascetiscism and meditation. They are strict vegetarians. The most radical of them shun everything that the senses offer them. They abhor comfort and want to 'kill' the body. Only so the road upwards can be trodden. [21]

The ultimate aim of the Buddhist is to get rid of this fleeting world. Orthodox Buddhism takes an extremely pessimistic view of human existence. It only brings us suffering and death; even the very fact of having been born is something negative. The universe is something transient; there is nothing definite in it. The human self, the individuality, is hopelessly wrong, full as it is of egotism, greed, ambition, and all possible vices. The Buddhist who wants to free himself of this transient and material world will have to erase his individuality. Different roads may be followed to attain this, but they all end in Nirvana, the state of rest that is the absolute opposite to actual existence; it is the only stable entity.

Indian religions differ in many respects from each other, but they all acknowledge the same basic tenets. To all of them there is an almost unbridgeable distance between actual life and the ultimate state of rest. Our present world is seen as something absolutely negative; it is full of flux, unrest, change, and suffering. The dominating idea is to get off the wheel of life; this is possible, but mostly more than one life is necessary to attain this end. All Indian religions are basically built on a dualism between personal existence, fundamentally selfish and thoughtless as it is, and the state of unworldly, absolutely immaterial and spiritual contemplation that leads one to the final loss of all that is self. [22]

3. An inferior world

Returning now to the West, we will not find such rabid contempt of existence in its ancient societies (with the notable exception of the Gnosis). Nonetheless, as I wrote above, the Graeco-Roman world had its problems in finding a balance between spirit and matter. There is in Greek philosophy a hardly disguised *horror materiae*, an abhorrence of all that is physical. The idea that this world, which is also that of mankind and its history, is something inferior in fact and hardly worth being considered and discussed, is fairly common in ancient philosophy. From the very beginning of Greek philosophy the status of existents had been weak, with a correspondingly high status for what is called *to on*, Being, that what is invariable and never changes.

This basic idea had several consequences, to which we shall have to return. It led to élitism, the idea that the physical world was that of ordinary people, a world that the philosophers shunned. Another consequence is that the chasm between Being and existence is often made so wide that we may speak of dualism, the dualism of two different and opposed worlds.

4. Plato

To Plato body and soul did not constitute an harmonious and complementary pair; he never really felt at ease whith what is bodily and physical. It is true that he recognizes the *cosmos* as substantially one, but is also true that he distinguishes a higher and a lower creation in it; there are a (world-)soul and a (world-)body. The soul is perfect and pure and therefore good; the body, the physical reality, consists of chaotic and unspecified primordial matter that is brought into shape by *Nous*, the superior reason of the world-soul. But the result is not a perfect balance of soul and body; the fundamental principles of the universe are opposed and tend to move into different directions. [23]

Since Plato was the greatest and most influential ancient philosopher, we may expect that important elements of his ideas will continue to resurface in later centuries. The philosophical schools of Antiquity have by and large preferred to follow Plato rather than Aristotle and his realism. These schools are mainly Platonist and Neoplatonist. This means than many a later thinker will not show a great regard for what is material.

5. Xenocrates

This began already with Xenocrates, a contemporary of Alexander and known as the systematizer of Platonic thought. He was, in all probability, the father of an idea that had a great future before it, namely the concept of the 'chain of being', which means that created entities are hierarchically ranged on a scale that we may conceive of, metaphorically, as the ascending (or descending) steps of a ladder. The term 'hierarchically' implies that the lower stages may be evaluated as being of a lower order. In Xenocrates' opinion this is really so since the physical world is that of perception by the senses, and the senses are prone to error and false judgments. [24]

6. Neopythagoreanism

The overstrung attention for Being, for Nous, for Spirit, with the accompanying underrating of what is material, even of what is human, was bound to provoke a reaction. This reaction came in the period of Greek materialism. The position of Spirit was taken by that of Matter. This does not necessarily mean that materialist thinkers glorified Matter to the detriment of Spirit; many of them were just as pessimistic about the material world (and human existence) as the spiritualists. We shall yet come back to this.

A reaction to this materialism, which often assumed very crude forms, did not fail to appear. It came in the shape of Neopythagoreanism and Neoplatonism. This does not mean that the prevailent dualism of Spirit and Matter was overcome; ancient philosophy never found a satisfying answer to it. After a long eclipse Pythagoreanism once again appeared on the scene. The original Pythagoreanism was known to have been mystical and spiritual, ascetic and vegetarian, but also élitist and esoteric; it enjoyed the reputation of having been profoundly religious. Yet it cannot be said to have been affected by the *horror materiae*; in the famous list of Pythagorean opposites that of Spirit and Matter does not occur.

Neopythagoreanism became popular, especially in Rome, in all probability because of its tendency to mysticism. To many people it seemed more truly religious than the official Roman cult. [25] Many adherents thought they were harking back to the original teachings of Pythagoras himself, but since the sixth century B.C. many new elemenst had found their way into it, borrowings of Plato, Aristotle, and the Stoa. [26] Just as Plato had been influenced by Pythagoreanism, he in turn influenced Neopythagoreanism which means that we must expect dualistic elements in it.

7. The dualism of Numenius

Nobody doubts that Numenius was a dualist, with Matter in the dock. True to original Pythagoreanism, he acknowledges two principles, the Monad and the Dyad, that exist side by side and independently from each other. Matter is the Dyad, or duality; it can impossibly originate from the Monad = God, for it is fundamentally and irremediably evil. All that is wrong in the world must be attributed to the workings of Matter. This is an undiluted *horror materiae*. Since creation consists of Matter, its creator cannot be the monadic God. Numenius therefore needs a second god for the creational work, the Demiurge. The same dualistic split is to be found in the human person in whom two souls cohabit, a rational and an irrational one, 'opposed for battle'. They never fuse into a unity. [27]

8. Plato's heritage in Middle Platonism

Plato continued to exercize a great influence on philosophers, especially in the later centuries of the Roman Empire. Now a thinker who wants to be a true Platonist can hardly be anything else than a dualist, since the great master himself was an out and out dualist. [28] According to the philosophy of Alcinous, the precise aim of philosophizing is to set the soul free from the body. All thought should be directed to non-material things; the true lovers of wisdom shall finally ascend to the realm of the gods leaving their bodies (and the whole material world) behind. [29]

The most important and influential thinker in this line was doubtless Plutarch. As an enemy of the crude Greek anthropomorphism he wanted to give a new face to the godhead, but in doing so, he presented him (or it) as an abstraction, wholly impersonal. It were only the prophets of Israel who were able to present God as a personal and approachable being, a God *non des philosophes*. What we also find in Plutarch is the unbridgeable opposition of the One and the Many, in which the One is identical with Being and the Many with non-being. Only the One is pure; the Many is impure, that is the consequence. Many signifies a heterogenous collection of different factors, combined in a haphazard way; this even applies to human beings.

Plutarch's philosophical position is that of a metaphysical dualist, which entails a fair measure of *horror materiae*. There are two first principles, the One and the Infinite Dyad. The Dyad means formlessness and disarrangement but is ruled over by the One. This author most graphically expressed this in his most famous and very influential treatise *De Iside et Osiride*. Osiris is the personification of all that is pure, because he is immaterial. Unlike the Judaeo-Christian God he keeps himself apart from matter which would defile him. Plutarch's godhead is so absolutely transcendent that people can at best have only a dim vision of him. Those who do not philosophize will not be aware of his real nature at all. This god is no creator, of course. The human person is a ramshackle mixture of spiritual and material elements. Man's real identity resides in the *Nous*, the Mind, that coexists uncomfortably with the body; it is only the *Nous* that may go up to higher spheres. [30]

We find the same metaphysical dualism, with its *horror materiae*, in the philosopher Atticus. In his system Matter is pre-existent to the *cosmos*. It is disorderly and in constant movement; this movement is caused by a maleficent soul that is the source of all evil. Order is brought about by a well-intentioned Demiurge, but irrationality never wholly disappears from the universe; disorder remains active. It is the same in the human being in whom there is also an irrational substratum. [31]

9. Plato's heritage in Neoplatonism

a. Plotinus

After Plato Plotinus is without any doubt the greatest philosopher of Antiquity, one with a very great influence, this in spite of the fact that he was and is often found incomprehensible, the Martin Heidegger of ancient philosophy, if I may say so. But when all is said and done philosophy was not his greatest occupation. It was a means to an end, and this end was the complete unification of the human soul with the godhead. The tenor of his thought was, therefore, theological, or must we say mystical, rather than metaphysical.

Dualism becomes evident in his description of the human person. The human soul belongs to the All-Soul and through it to the One, the Supreme Good. Yet the body is the brute part that tries to drag the higher part down. Plotinus is so explicit on this that we can speak of there being two beings in man who is a 'dual' thing, in his terms. What here rears its head is the *horror materiae*. This philosopher has a very low opinion of Matter. We should not think of it as something physical; it comes close to non-being. Matter is the Primal Evil to him, but evil is not a quality (Matter has no qualities); rather, it is a lack, an 'absolute lack'. It needs no further explanation that, when a purified human being surges upwards to the higher spheres to be united there with the godhead, it does not take the body with it. [32]

b. Porphyry

Porphyry, Plotinus' best-known disciple, was not an original thinker but rather a transmitter of Neoplatonic thought. This makes him important within this context, for what was it that he transmitted to later generations? He thinks of the human race in a dualistic way; he distinguishes those who are striving upwards and those who are not. There is a domain of the soul and a domain of the body, and too many people remain in the physical domain. He does not say that the body is bad, but there is a tendency in man towards acquiescing to inferior passions. The starting-point for the upward journey is an ascetic life. As so many an ancient thinker Porphyry was a vegetarian. A very telling phrase of his is that consuming meat is 'a distinctive sign of human nature', of the all-too-human, by way of speaking. Abstaining from meat makes a man more than human; it brings him closer to the gods who do not eat at all. One should not even partake in sacrificial meals, because this meant eating meat. The true lover of wisdom is totally different from the common run and keeps himself apart from it.

Porphyry's metaphysical ideas do not differ from those of his Master : there is a gradual descent from the One to Matter, and an ascent of the soul to the One. The aim of philosophy is the purification of the soul, but it is hindered in this process by the body and its demands. The soul is, therefore, always balancing between the way on high and the way down; in his view also the body is left behind at the moment of death. [33]

c. Iamblichus

It will not surprise us that we find in Iamblichus, a disciple of Plotinus, a dualism that is just as outspoken as that of his master. The spiritual and material spheres are sharply separated, with the inevitable consequence that the body will not follow the soul, when it ascends to the higher spheres. Iamblichus is incapable of telling us why there is a material world at all; it is useless and without any significance. [34]

10. Philo

We should also pay a moment of attention to Philo, the Jewish philosopher who lived in Alexandria in the first century A.D. Above I wrote that Jewish society did not share the contempt and abhorrence of all that is material that was common with the thinkers of the ancient world. Philo is an exception to the rule in this respect, deeply influenced as he was by Greek and Hellenistic philosophy.

In his philosophial theology a chasm between God and the created world, can be detected, a chasm so wide that we may speak of metaphysical dualism. It seems impossible to bring God into direct contact with Matter, as though this would defile him. His God is not the real creator. Philo's depreciation of Matter is so great that he even speaks of it as 'non-existent'. Matter is confused and chaotic; it is ruled by the principle of disorder. The world, created out of Matter, is not something admirable in his view; it is always changing and in constant flux.

As a Jew, Philo could not take the Gnostic line that somebody or something other than God himself would have created the world. There is also a principle of order at work in the world, indicated by the philosopher as 'cause' and 'mind'. This principle is behind the creation of the *cosmos*, which, highly organized as it is, could not come into being without the action of God; it is much more than Matter, but since it contains Matter, it is tainted by the negativity of Matter. He does not want his God to occupy himself directly and personally with the creation of the *cosmos*. For the creational work he introduces a great number of intermediaries, powers and ideas, angels and *logoi*, and the *Logos*. Probably, although Philo does not say so in as many words, the Ideas or Forms, are the real creators of the world. He needs all these intermediaries, because God must be kept at an immeasurable distance from the created, actual world; it is as if he were erecting a shield between God and the world, the thicker the better. Philo is here much closer to ancient philosophy than to biblical theology. [35]

11. The Essenes

The Essenes were a Jewish sect that kept itself apart from ordinary Jewish social and liturgical life; this was even geographically so since their main establishment, a kind of monastery, was to be found on a lonely site, Qumran, on the shores of the Dead Sea. Since the sect was Jewish and based itself on the Old Testament, we do not find a wholesale condemnation of the created world. God is its Creator; there is no evil-intentioned Demiurge. Yet there can be no doubt that the brethern living in the Qumran monastery considered the ordinary world - and to them that was the Jewish society - was wicked; they practised *apartheid* with regard to it.

There are certainly dualistic elements in their attitude toward the material and physical world. Their misogyny is conspicuous. We know that for orthodox Jews the rules of purity and impurity were and are of the utmost importance. But the Essenes, in their cult of purity, went far beyond them. One gets the impression that they hated the idea that they had a body with material and physical needs. They almost excused themselves for the fact that they had to eat. They did not dine before they had bathed and draped themselves in white garments. It seems likely that, although we have no indication that they followed a vegetarian diet, their meals would have been extremely frugal; everyone received no more than an allotted portion. They ate in the deepest silence. All this was done to prevent the deplorable habit of eating defiling them. [36]

12. The *Corpus Hermeticum*

The *Corpus Hermeticum* is a collection of writings that originated in Egypt; this anonymous body of revealed wisdom was ascribed to various famous sages, to Iranian *Magi* like Zoroaster, to some Hellenic sage like Pythagoras, or to Toth-Hermes, an Egyptian divinity whose name it bears. [37]

The attitude these writings take with regard to Matter and the created world is not uniform. There is an optimistic line and there is a pessimistic line : the world is good and the world is bad. Ten of these treatises are in the optimistic vein; this non-dualistic stream is by far the strongest. But the *Corpus* also contains four pessimistic tracts. [38]

The most important of these tracts is the *Poimandres*, the 'Shepherd of Men'. It sees Matter as a serpent-like, unspecified mass; there is not the slightest connection between it and the primal God. It does not make any difference that its author does not speak of Matter but of 'Nature'. This is dark, horrifying, and tortuous. [39] Here too God is solidly screened off from creation and therefore from mankind also; several creational stages are interposed between him and the actual, physical world. [40]

Yet another of these hermetic tracts, the *Korê Kosmou*, the 'World Girl', does not take a pessimistic view of the world; the earth is declared sacred. But man is an exception to this; he really is a *Fremdkörper* on the face of the earth. Body and soul hardly belong to each other, the body being far inferior to the soul. The soul lives in it as if it were imprisoned. [41]

13. The Gnosis

Nowhere in the ancient world was the contempt of Matter so outspoken as in the Gnostic ideologies, and not only of Matter as such, but of all that is material, physical, bodily, even of sexuality, often also of women.

a. The earliest Gnostics

There can be no doubt that the earliest Gnostics, Simon the Magus, Menander, Saturnilos, and Cerinthus, took a very pessimistic view of the material world. But since they were no philosophers, they did not express their contempt of this world in metaphysical terms. The nearest we come to this is with Cerinthus, who taught that God and the world were radically different; God had nothing to do with creation. [42] In a collection of texts probably dating from the second century A.D. and known as the *Pseudo-Clementina*, we find the doctrine of two opposed worlds according to which our human world is the inferior one; it is the realm of evil, doomed to destruction. [43] According to the ideology of another early Gnostic sect, the Carpocratians, who flourished in Egypt during the second century A.D., the situation of mankind is absolutely hopeless; only a few souls will be able to return to God. The human soul comes from above, a thing most people conveniently forget. The soul lives in the body as in a prison. Here too the body will be left behind when the soul finally surges upwards. [44]

b. The Sethians and Ophites

We begin to feel the full blast of Gnostic contempt of what they dub 'the lower world' when we come to the Egyptian sect of the Sethians. This lower world is that of Darkness; it is disorderly, crooked, and ignorant. 'Nature' is not exactly the same as Darkness, but is almost just as bad. For both Darkness and Nature, the constitutive elements of the lower regions, Sethian texts abound in pejorative terms. It is also seen as feminine. [45] The creational process is sketched in negative terms. Nature and Darkness copulate with each other in an unchaste way; this is the origin of all that exists in the lower world. Mind and Nature are unbridgeably opposed. [46]

There exist several reports of the creation of man in Sethian scripture, but they all agree that humanity cannot boast of a distinguished pedigree. In one report mankind has a dark, chaotic, and uncouth origin. In another its origin is wholly from below; he is no more than a purely natural being without a divine origin. His parents are wind and water. In a third, man is fundamentally ignorant of the things on high and occupies himself only with 'dead things', the worthless things from here below. [47]

With regard to the *cosmos* and its origin the Sethian tracts differ somewhat, but they agree that it is something evil. According to an influential text, it was dark powers that brought the world into being. Especially the body is evil. In another text the *cosmos* is the realm of wicked powers, the *archons*; the super-archon is the *Cosmocrator*, who is nobody else than the Jewish God. All the Sethian texts express nothing but contempt for earthly existence and for humanity as such; sexuality and femininity also come off very badly. The world is destined for destruction, of course; only the souls of the elect will ascend on high. [48]

The opinions of the Ophites and related sects do not significantly differ from those of other Gnostic sects. There is always a nether, material world, that is utterly objectionable, and the dualistic opposition of soul and body in which the body without exception is the deeply inferior part for which there is no place in heaven. [49] According to Ophian ideology, the Father is completely indifferent to the created world; he loathes it so deeply that he does not take any interest in it. Only a few privileged persons will be able to escape from this doomed and wicked world. [50]

c. The Barbelo-Gnostics

The mythology of the Barbelo-Gnostics is complicated to a degree; I described it in full detail in a former volume. [51] There is no need to go into this once again. What stands out is that the world is utterly bad. Creation is blind so that it cannot know God. It is a world of utter depravity and must be rejected as such by those who have insight.

d. The Basilidians

It is somewhat of a problem that we have two versions of Basilidian ideology, but these versions are not essentially different. In the first version the First

Principle (not called God) is hermetically sealed off from mankind; in no other system is the distance so great. The body is good for nothing; salvation is possible, although only for a few elect, but the body will have no part in it, as it is 'by nature corruptible'. [52] In a second version, the Supreme One is not so hermetically sealed off from the world, but his part in the creational work is made infinitesimally small; the larger the distance is that separates it from a world that is not good, the better. Here also we find an incredible number of intermediate stages. The terrestrial world, our world, is a material world, utterly objectionable and only fit to be rejected. It is the domain of darkness and ignorance. As in all other Gnostic systems, only a few elect will be able to escape from it. [53]

e. The Valentinians

Valentinians see the present world as a 'deficiency', a place where there is envy and strife. The cause of this deficiency is ignorance. Its fate is hopeless, for it can never be enlightened. Another thing that is wrong with the world is that it is multiple; this is not only a fundamental imperfection but even an impurity. 'Dark' and 'dead' are also words used for it. Matter had its inception from ignorance, suffering, and fear. There is simply no good in it. Not God the Creator but a Demiurge made man, and he fashioned him from the material and devilish essence. Valentinians have a deep contempt for the body, and in fact for all that is material and physical. Man has a soul, but soul and body are dualistically kept apart, so that the body can have no part in salvation. Valentinianism seems to have been fairly successful and have numbered many adherents. [54]

f. The most successful Gnostic communities

The three most successful and long living Gnostic sects were the Marcionite Church, the Mandaeans, and Manichaeism. The latter had an exceptionally long spell of life, while Mandaeans exist even today.

The founder of the Marcionite Church, Marcion, acknowledged three primal principles, God, or the Supreme Good, the Demiurge, and Matter. As is usual in Gnostic ideology, the Supreme Good has no relation whatsoever to the creation. The creational work is done by the evil-intentioned Demiurge who is identical with Jahve, the God of Israel. Matter is unbegotten and uncreated; out of this the Demiurge fashioned the world. The Demiurge is fundamentally bad, and Matter is evil; the consequence is that the world and all that it contains is something repellent.

The Demiurge is also the creator of man; a human being is feeble, helpless, mortal, and prone to sin. He is a complete failure. As a product of the malicious Demiurge mankind is merely a sorry lot. Marcion loathed sexuality and procreation; marriage is an evil thing. For when man becomes creative himself, the result can only be disastrous. Marcion rejected the whole of religious history, with both the Old and New Testaments; real religion had begun with him. In fact he dualistically and radically rejected all history.

Marcion's ideology is one of the most radical dualisms of Antiquity. His two gods, the Supreme One and the Demiurge, have nothing to do with one another; the Supreme One is utterly unknowable. The distinction between the divine and physical principles which also led to the opposition of soul and body, together with the rejection of procreation, is crucial. Marcionite ideology was one of the most pregnant cases of the *horror materiae*. [55]

The Mandaeans, the only Gnostic sect that survives, live mainly in the marshy southern regions of Iraq. Their mythology is incredibly complicated and, to western eyes, often confused. There is a higher and a lower world that are strictly separated from each other (although there is one version in which the two worlds are not so sharply kept apart). The lower world is that of death, darkness, and evil. Mankind has a double origin. The body is something negative, lifeless and powerless; the soul comes from above and is alien to this world. This world is something to be despised; its influence on man is bad. The female sex is not highly valued. [56]

The most successful, wide-spread and long-lasting Gnostic sect of Antiquity was Mani's Church of Justice. It was also one of the most dualistic. The true Manichee was an out and out dualist. In his view the upper and nether worlds were totally different and radically separated from each other. The nether world is that of Matter, of mankind and its history. It is a world of darkness, in constant movement, disorderly and uncoordinated. There is nothing but strife, discord, and uproar. It is ruled by *archons*, all of them evil-intentioned. Their vices are found back in mankind among which sexual lust and the desire to copulate are the most conspicuous. Man has a strong taste for the bad; it forces him to do evil. The female sex is extremely weak; always allured by evil as woman is, she is a great danger to men. There is indeed a possibility that the man can be saved, but the position of woman is clearly hopeless.

Abhorrence of all that is material and physical are characteristic features of every Gnostic system, but nowhere did it have such radical consequences as in Manichaeism. Almost everything is utterly condemnable : work, touching things, treading the earth, food and in particular meat, wine, social intercourse with non-Manichees, marriage, procreation, and sexuality. Nothing on earth had any meaning or value to the Manichees. My conclusion was that they simply hate life. [57]

14. Christian theology

On the face of it it is not to be expected that this *horror materiae* would also be found in Christian theology. It was God who, directly and personally, created the world and mankind, and saw that 'it was good'. God the Creator is also the Providence who watches over his handiwork and is present in it. Christianity has this view in common with Judaism. Yet it also presented the concept of the God-Man, in the person of Jesus of Nazareth, in whom heaven and earth, divinity and physicality, were organically united. However, as we have already seen, a Jewish thinker like Philo, who professed himself to be a believer, was nonetheless deeply influenced by pagan thought. It might be possible that the same influence would be found in Christian theologians. We shall see that the centuries-long theological debate centred mainly on the status of Jesus : was he divine or was he human? Or was he both?

a. The Docetist position

According to the adherents of Docetism, Jesus was human only in appearance; in reality he was exclusively divine. Insofar as Gnostic sects were interested in the theological status of Jesus, they were invariably Docetist. Yet many non-Gnostics were of the same opinion. That Jesus would have been a being of flesh and blood seemed to them too earthly an idea, too common, too coarse. There is more than a shimmer of the *horror materiae* in this. Did the Docetists realize the consequences of their position? If Jesus was not human, then his death on the cross would have occurred only in appearance and the Redemption would not have taken place. Heaven and earth, divinity and physicality, would have remained dualistically separated. [58]

b. The Adoptionist position

Adoptionists saw the problem from a different angle. Here Jesus was not exclusively divine, but an earthly being was 'adopted' by the Father and raised to a higher status. A forerunner was Hermas, the author of the *Pastor*, a second-century work. In this work, the Son is not the second person of the Holy Trinity, but the Holy Ghost. The Incarnation did not mean that the Son took on a human form, but that the Holy Ghost descended on or into a human being. [59]

Adoptionism took on several forms. One of these was Monarchianism; this meant that God was unitary, so that there is no Trinity. The consequence is that there can also be no Son who became man. This position was vigorously defended by Noetus arond 200. The curious consequence of his theology is that, if Christ was God, he must be the Father, and that it was the Father who had suffered on the cross. This dealt a heavy blow to the position of the Father; it was as though his place in heaven had become empty. The connection between the supernatural and the natural was thus endangered. [60]

Another form of Adoptionism was Modalism. Modalists held that God was unitary, but their problem was that the Gospels also spoke clearly and unambiguously of the Son. Therefore, they declared that Father and Son were two 'modes' of being in God, not two different persons. The prophet who went about on earth might, in consequence, be called either Father or Son. Then we have the 'Alogoi', a term used to designate those who rejected the *Logos*-doctrine and would have nothing of the Fourth Gospel in which this doctrine is forcefully propounded. In their view there is no preexistent *Logos* who became man in the person of Jesus of Nazareth. Jesus was just a man, an extremely pious man who was transformed from on high into the Christ. This did not mean that he was a God during his lifetime; he was raised to the status of a God only when he rose from the dead. All those Adoptionists shied away from the idea that somebody could be wholly God and wholly man at the same time. They kept the divinity and humanity of Jesus carefully apart, because they did not want to bring them into too intimate a contact. [61]

The position of Paul of Samosata deserves special attention, because his influence was great. He spoke of Christ as being only a man; the *Logos* did not dwell in him. He did not recognize the Trinity; one might speak of Father, Son, and Holy Ghost, but these were only three names for the same God, not three persons. His theological concept was wholly unitarian. Christ, having only a human nature, acted as the mouthpiece of the Father who made his will known through him.

The problem for all the Adoptionists and Monarchists and also for the Paulinians was that Christ had to be the Redeemer. To deny this would have meant to reject the whole of the New Testament. If they had done so, Jesus would have been no more than a teacher of wisdom, somebody like Pythagoras or Socrates; they were not ready to do this. In consequence, Jesus could not be an entirely ordinary human being. And indeed, it was stated that he was different from all others, because Wisdom (supernatural Wisdom) had taken its abode in him; but Jesus and that Wisdom were two, they did not have the same substance. [62]

I have characterized the positions of all these Adoptionists, Monarchianists, Modalists, and Paulinians as nominalism *avant la lettre*. This term 'nominalist' comes to mind when we hear one of them, Praxeas, state "what is a word, ... something empty and inane and insubstantial." To Paul the words Father, Son, Holy Ghost was 'no more than contentless appellations for one and the same being, appellations to which no reality corresponds.' This is the sheerest dualism, for this nominalism denotes the split between reality and the way we speak of it. In nominalism, the general is severed from the particular and the individual, which makes it hard to understand how they are connected with each other. Reality is fragmented in this way. [63]

If God is absolutely unitary, complete and enclosed in himself, without properties, it will become very hard to see how he communicated himself to the world. Since the *Logos* is also no more than a name, there is no longer an essental link between heaven and earth. God and man seem to be separated by an unbridgeable chasm. Haunted as they are by the idea that the supreme God should not be brought into too close a contact with the world, the physical and natural world, with mankind, they land themselves into insuperable difficulties. [64]

c. Ascetic positions

The Roman Catholic Church has always pleaded for asceticism and has always had room for ascetics. However, in Antiquity there were movements that went far beyond a moderate ascetiscism, so much so that their attitude came very near to a deep contempt for the world that God created. There were, for instance, the Encratists who condemned all forms of sexual intercourse, and especially those in marriage, as *porneia*. Often meat and wine were considered as kinds of food and drink one should abstain from. Encratists were the strictest of vegetarians; the most radical practised total sexual abstinence. If this would spell the end of the human race, so much the better. [65]

The great spokesman of the Encratist movement was Tatian who, by the way, was also wholly adverse to pagan philosophy; there existed only one true philosophy, the Christian doctrine, he taught. Tatian stressed God's transcendence so strongly that no room is left for his immanence, his being present in the world. The spirit that is present in the *cosmos* is another than the divine; here too the supernatural and the natural are carefully kept apart.

No wonder that he nowhere mentions Jesus of Nazareth. Nor does he speak of the Redemption. [66]

In Tatian's anthropology there is, as in all Encratist ideology, an unmistakable *horror materiae*. This explains the rigorism of the Encratists; they have a very high idea of what man had to be as the image of God, but felt that actual man fell dualistically short of this. Mankind lay so low that it could not be saved, not even by Jesus' death on the cross. It is only through his own freedom, that is through a radically ascetic way of life, that one might be saved. [67]

The influence of Tatian and Encratism does not seem to have been great; Montanism became far more popular. It originated in Phrygia, a province of Asia Minor. According to Montanus and his followers the coming of the New Jerusalem was at hand; Christians had to be ready for this. Marriage had become a quite unnecessary institution; it happened that marriages were dissolved. The temperament of the Montanist movement was rigorist and exalted. The role of the Holy Ghost was heavily accentuated; dreams, visions, and prophecies were highly valued. The consequence was that Christ and his teachings were pushed into the background. The Montanist movement tried to reach far beyond the human, the all-too-human in their view. What counted was not ordinary human existence but only the world that was to come. [68]

Yet another rigorist and ascetic movement was that of the Donatists in North Africa. Donatists held that the ideal Christian was the martyr. They felt a deep contempt for ordinary Christians who were not really prone to die for the faith. The movement did not possess much of a theology of its own, but their viewpoints and their actions led to endless trouble in North Africa. It judged itself to be more pure, more unwordly, more ascetic, more averse to the things of this world, than the main Church. [69]

A third rigorist and ascetic movement was Priscillianism, founded by Priscillian in Northern Spain. Priscillian took a very sombre view of the world and of mankind; it was the domain of Satan, and man was a child of perdition. The true Christian should keep him- or herself as far apart from the world as possible, for it is made of matter, and matter is evil. Only the spirit is good. Priscillianists should abstain from meat and alcohol; their preference is for the celibate state, marriage being no more than a concession for the weak. This movement too is puritanical and élitist.

d. The Arian position

Arianism is a heterodox movement that became extremely popular and won countless adherents in the Church of the fourth and fifth centuries. The originator of this movement was Arius, an Alexandrian presbyter who was active in the beginning of the fourth century A.D. It is a point of discussion whether or not he was directly influenced by Origen, but he certainly had some things in common with him. The most important of these is that both stressed the *aseitas* of God, his absolute transcendance, leaving little room for his immanence. It is evident that this must have had consequences for the person of Jesus Christ. At the background of this opinion we may detect the anti-materialism that we discover in so many theological writers of the first centuries. They seem instinctively averse to any suggestion that God could bring forth something that might be dubbed material or phsyical, and sometimes even exclude the possibility that God would bring forth a Son who would assume the flesh. Arius disagrees with Origen in this respect that to Origen the Son has no origin in time and that he is coeternal with the Father. Arius held that the Son is part of creation. [70]

In Arian theology Jesus Christ is a human person, but not an ordinary one. He does not share the nature of the Father nor is he perfect, but he stands in a very special relationship to the Father, not by his own merits, but by grace and adoption. Arius situates his ineffable godhead at an immeasurable distance from creation. During the first centuries of the Church the *Logos*-doctrine, with its starting-point in the Fourth Gospel and fully developed by Origen, had been steadily gaining ground. Yet Arius did not accept it. His Christ is not the Second Person of Holy Trinity who did become the God-Man, but a strange hybrid, neither God nor really man, and at any rate not the *Logos*. With his rejection of the *Logos*-doctrine he was widening the gap between God and creation further. [71]

Arius hated the idea of the Multiple; in his view the Many was of a lower and subordinate order. Therefore, he could not stand the idea that God is Three-in-One; he found that this was introducing Multiplicity in the godhead who had to be and remain absolutely One. Arius did not use the terms One and Many; instead, he spoke of the Monad and the Dyad; the Monad is eternal and unbegotten, it is God; the Dyad does not exist in God but only in the temporal world and is made. By denying the concept of the Trinity he tore apart the essential and existential connection of the One and the Many, of unicity and multiplicity, in the bosom of the godhead. It banished the world and mankind from the realm of the divine. Arian theology was utterly unable to answer the question how mankind could be redeemed, since his Jesus, being human, was incapable of doing this. [72]

Doctrinally the question was decided once and for all by the Council of Nicaea in 325. Its most important canon fully restored the *Logos*-doctrine. It defined as the creed of the Christian Church that Jesus was truly and unequivocally the God-Man, just as much God as the Father. With this statement the Roman Catholic Church assumed an undualistic and anti-dualistic position from which it would never waver again. It acknowledged the essential and existential connection between God and man, who came together in the person of Jesus Christ, and implicitly rejected any idea of contempt for what is created, for matter, for mankind. [73]

That the Church had pronounced itself in an authoritative manner did not mean at all that the troubles were now over. In the aftermath of Nicaea several theologians began to object to the term *homoiousios* = consubstantial, that the Fathers had used for the relationship between the Father and the Son. Some would prefer the term *homoousios*, which does not mean 'consubstantial' but 'similar'. It meant that Jesus was not essentially of the same nature as the Father but only similar to him. [74] The question divided the Church for a long time; attempts at a compromise formula were mostly doomed to failure. Many bishops sought a substitute for Nicaea. [75]

Events took a new and more radical turn in the middle of the fourth century. Some theologians then began to propagate a new form of Arianism that goes by the name of 'Neo-Arianism'. They postulated God's absolute *aseitas*; they held it for ontologically impossible that he would communicate himself to something or somebody else; this meant that there could be no consubstantiality with the consequence that Jesus is not the Son. The hallmark of Neo-Arianism is its essentialism (in which there is much Aristotelian philosophy) : God is entirely cut off from the work of creation which he left to the Son. God is not the Father nor is he the Providence. The dualistic chasm that was already apparent in Arius's theology becomes far more conspicuous here. [76]

In view of the continuing turmoil, a second Ecumenical Council was held, this time at Constantinople in 381. This reaffirmed all the canons of Nicaea. After this Arianism was moribund in the Roman Empire. [77]

e. The nature(s) of Christ

The struggle over the nature or natures of Christ, that was just as long and arduous as that over Arianism, began with the theology of Apollinaris fils. He was unable to accept that there were two natures in Christ, a human and a divine one, both perfect and complete. He sharply distinguished between the human and divine natures. According to him, these subsisted side by side, apart from each other; what belonged to the one did not belong to the other. In this concept Christ's physical nature was far inferior to the divine. [78] This is a consequence of Apollinaris' anthropology that was quite common at the time. The human person was seen as composed of two imperfect and not comfortably cohabiting parts, the body and the soul. The soul, superior and spiritual as it is, is the guiding element, whereas the body is the material and wholly terrestrial part. What Apollinaris professes is a dichotomy of body and soul that comes very close to dualism. [79] At the background of his theology we can detect that *horror materiae* that prevented him from acknowledging two organically connected natures in Christ.

We find the same underrating of Jesus' humanity in the theology of Theodore of Mopsuestia. His ideas were a reaction against those of Apollinaris (which in turn were a reaction against Arianism). He gladly accepted that Jesus was perfectly divine and perfectly human. But both his body and his soul had a different origin : the soul came from God but the body from Mary. Therefore, Jesus was not the preexistent *Logos*, for the Logos only descended on him at the moment of his conception. The two natures (which he acknowledged) never fused wholly together; there was never more than a cohesion, but not one essence, not one identity. The human element is clearly inferior to the divine one. The *Logos* did not use the body as his natural home, but rather as his instrument. Theodore was one of the many theological thinkers who was uncomfortable with the idea that the godhead could have something to do with the material, the physical, the body. [80]

Nestorius, who became bishop of Constantinople in 428, took a somewhat different line. He objected to giving Mary the title of *theotokos*; he preferred the *Christotokos*. He found it smacking of Greek paganism if Jesus would have had a human mother; this would make him too human to his taste. He seems to have felt that a divinity that came to Jesus through Mary was of a lower quality than if a divine status was accorded directly to him by the Father. [81] He too could not conceive of an organic fusion of the divine and the human in Christ. [82]

Somewhat later, around 450, a monk in Constantinople, Eutyches, began a full-scale attack on the concept of the two natures in Christ. He emphatically declared that there was only one nature; this nature was the divine one, for he did not believe that Christ is consubstantial with mankind through his human nature. This is the beginning of what is called Monophysitism. [83] Eutyches' intervention led once again to great disturbance in the oriental Church. The question was doctrinally decided by the Council of Chalcedon in 451. It condemned every form of Monophysitism. It declared the person Jesus to be complete with regard to his divinity and complete with regard to his humanity. Two natures, with all their proprieties, were stated to subsist in one single person. [84]

f. *Horror materiae* as a widespread phenomenon

The background of all these discussions was a repugnance felt by many theological scholars, to all that is material, physical, bodily. This *horror* materiae is not only found in parts of Christian theology, but also in the Gnosis and in pagan philosophy. It was widespread and a constitutive element of the mental make-up of the Later Roman Empire. There was a general tendency to 'spiritualize', to extol what is spiritual to the detriment of what is terrestrial and physical. This tendency was far stronger in the East than in the West. In the end the orthodoxy of the Roman Catholic Church triumphed over all deviant and heterodox opinions. In the context of my overall theme this means that the Church firmly repudiated all forms of dualism.

However, although the heterodox theologies may have differed significantly from each other, in none of them the divine and the human go together harmoniously. If two natures were assumed indeed, then it seemed as though the divine nature was superimposed on the human one. We are always close to dualism and often in the middle of it. This dualism was the great temptation of Late Antiquity; many great minds, pagan as well as Christian, were leaning towards it. Many dualistic sects, such as the Gnostic ones, enjoyed great success.

The Roman Catholic Church overcame this temptation through two great anti-dualistic statements. The Creed of Nicaea, in 325, by stating that God is the Creator of all things visible and invisible, distanced itself once and for all from the *horror materiae*. It did more so still when it declared that Jesus was just as much God as he was man. The second great doctrinal statement was that of the Council of Chalcedon in 451. It repeated that Jesus is truly God and truly man, and that his two natures cohabit harmoniously in one organic unity, in one single person, in whom heaven and earth, divine and human, spiritual and physical came together. On this rock medieval civilization would be built. [85]

PART IV TWO-WORLDS DUALISM

From contempt for the material world, for Matter, to a two-worlds dualism it is only a small step. This step was often made indeed. There are two kinds of such dualism. The first is a radical dualism in which there are two worlds that in no way are connected with each other; they exist totally apart from each other. This kind of dualism is rare but it occurs. Far more frequent is a relative dualism in which there are also two worlds. But one of these worlds, the inferior one, is dependent on the other, the superior world. That the step from contempt for the material and human world to a two-worlds dualism must not be necessarily made becomes apparent in ancient India where that *horror materiae* was a constitutive element in all Indian religions; the conclusion that there were, therefore, two worlds, was, as far as I know, never expressly drawn.

1. In Iranian religion

The classical example of a two-worlds dualism is the Zoroastrian religion of Iran. However, this religion, as I wrote above, starts from a monistic premiss : there is only one god to be venerated, Ahura Mazda, the Wise Lord. The dualism sets in one stage lower. One of his spirits, his *spentas*, is the *Spenta Mainyu*, the Holy Spirit; this spirit has a twin brother, the *Angra Mainyu* or *Ahra Mainyu*. Ahura Mazda is principally the guarantee of the unity of the world, but *Angra Mainyu* wants to have a world of his own, a world of Evil, of Lies, of Deceit, of Misgovernment, and of Death. [86]

This idea of an incipient two-worlds dualism becomes more explicit in Zervanite ideology, considered as a heresy by orthodox Zoroastrians. It is here that we find the irreconcilable enmity of Ormuzd and Ahriman, the good and the bad gods. Yet even here there is some sort of monistic starting-point because these two gods have a common father, Zervan, who is Time. But this Zervan does not have a great significance in Zervanite theology; it is all about Ormuzd and Ahriman, the inexorable enemies, who are fighting one another for the possession of the world; both of them account for one half of the universe. We are here very close to a radical dualism. [87]

2. The Presocratics

We do not know enough of the ideas of most Presocratics to determine whether or not they professed a two-world dualism. The first great philosopher of whom we know more than almost nothing is Anaximander who held that there are two worlds indeed, that of the *apeiron*, the boundless, which is eternal and immortal, and the universe, which is movable, changeable, and perishable. [88]

The one who really set the tone was Parmenides. This sixth-century Greek philosopher distinguished two worlds, that of Being and that of Seeming, called by him the Ways of Being and of Seeming. There is only one right way, that of Being. Being is uncreated, imperishable, unique, and complete. It has no past and no future, it is always present, it is unending and does contain everything. This short description is already sufficient to show that there is no room for anything else outside Being. This is the only real world. The other world, that of Seeming, is inferior and deceptive; from a philosophical point of view it has no right to exist. That second world is our world, the world of mankind, the historical world. Parmenides has nothing but contempt for it. A truly philosphical mind should not occupy itself with it.

This is one of the crassest instances of metaphysical dualism to be encountered in Antiquity. What we see here is a division of all that exists into two opposite and mutually independent systems. [89]

3. Fear of chaos

It is necessary to say something about the Greek fear of chaos, for this too conceals a sort of two-worlds dualism. Modern people feel uneasy when they are confronted by such basic concepts of physics as Heisenberg's uncertainty relation. There is fear of chaos behind this. The reader will probably object that these developments were utterly unknown to the ancient world, even to its greatest thinkers. True, of course! That is, as long we stick to terms as atomic physics and quantum mechanics. However, the sentiment of fear that the developments denoted by these terms cause was known to the ancients also. The *cosmos*, they thought, could end catastrophically; the gods might not be eternal, and humanity might be wiped out. [90] They also recognised that visceral fear that people feel when they hear what quantum mechanics means. But they had another term for the opposition order-disorder, namely *peras-apeiron*. *Peras* signifies Limit, *Apeiron* the Unlimited.

The Greeks, those great lovers of order and regularity, were afraid of the Unlimited. It was holy and mysterious indeed, it might contain the beginnings of all that is, but in its indefinite state it was also terrifying. To remedy this, but perhaps without being wholly successful, *Peras* must be laid on the Unlimited and delimit it, at least part of it. To the Greek mind the *cosmos* was all order and beauty with a definite purpose. But it has a *peras*. It is limited and final, it moves or hangs in the Unlimited. Obviously the *cosmos* does not contain the whole of reality; there is something else beyond and around it, something unmixed and undefined from which another *cosmos* might spring.

At the back of the Greek mind was the image of the *polis*, of their sociopolitical community, with its well-delineated territory. Beyond that, perhaps six miles farther on already, the uncontrollable world began, alien, not to be trusted, maybe inimical; in this also it was an image of the *cosmos*. The Romans had the same idea of their Empire, although this was incomparably much larger than a *polis*. Within its well-defended frontiers law and order reigned, the *Pax Romana*. The lands on the other side of the frontier were the domain of lawless barbarians or, in the East, of a competing, strange, and dangerous realm.

The opposition *Peras-Apeiron* was discussed in ancient philosophy from the first moment to the last. Limit-Unlimited was the first item in Pythagoras' list of dualistic oppositions, with the *Apeiron* somewhat more primary than the *Peras*. A thousand years later it still meant something to the last great philosopher of Antiquity, Proclus. We shall have to see what was done with it in the Middle Ages.

4. The spiritual world denied

We may consider the two-worlds dualism as an attack on reality, reality such as ordinary people know it, their reality, that of the world in which they live. The Hellenistic thinkers of the centuries between Alexander and the beginning of our era did not adhere to a two-worlds dualism as a philosophical concept.

Yet this does not mean at all that, in their view, the higher and the lower worlds organically belonged together as differing parts of the same universe. They solved the problem of the two opposed worlds by simply denying one of them. Thus with them too the attack on reality continued relentlessly, because no spiritual world exists.

a. The *Stoa*

The Stoics were not pessimistic about the *cosmos* at all. Quite the contrary, the *cosmos* was utter perfection to them, 'the best of all possible worlds'. But all that exists, the whole universe with all that it contains, is matter and nothing more (although Stoic thought smuggled some incorporeal elements into their system). That there is no creator does not mean that the *cosmos* is without design. The Stoic universe has been dubbed as 'a self-directing physical system'. May we speak of an attack on reality then? Apparently not. But the problem is in this 'self-directing'. For the Stoic world is not directed by any moral principle but by Fate and necessity, by the 'necessity of Fate'. Mankind simply has to follow, to obey Fate; even the future is determined. So, when all is said and done, the Stoics take a very pessimistic view of reality and of human existence. [91]

b. Greek Atomism

There is a certain resemblance between the *Stoa* and Greek Atomism. Both are basically materialistic, Atomism perhaps more radically so, since all that is spiritual and non-material has no place in it; it is perfectly atheistic. It may be seen as the exact counterpart of Parmenides' essentialism, since there is no Being in it; Being is not even seeming, it is nothing. Everything consists of atoms, which Democritus calls *ta onta*, the real things, which form configurations. It is a mechanistic system operating mechanically, but there is no finality in it; there is no reason why specific atomic collocations are formed. But they are not the products of chance; it is necessity that brings them into shape.

I call this an attack on reality, because it puts it beyond human ken. The atomist system is profoundly anti-scientific and even a-rational. It separates the human mind from reality. [92] The great problem is that in Stoic thought the mind can only enter by the back-door, whereas in Atomism it is completely absent. Since there is only matter, there can be nothing spiritual and, in consequence, also not an independent mind. This means that the mind is entirely part of the observed. 'Observed' is not the appropriate term in this context, since there is no observer. Both systems, that of the *Stoa* and Atomism, may be seen as reactions to, on the one hand, the impossibilities of the Olympian religion and, on the other, the iron essentialism of the Eleatic school. However, as such they are overreactions in which the philosophical idea defeats itself. The utterly reduced idea they have of reality makes it impossible to study it.

c. Lucretius and the nature of things

It was the basic Hellenic belief that the universe is a *cosmos*, a well-ordered whole, and that it is purposeful and meaningful. Greek Atomism, purely materialistic as it is, and according to which the world is a product of chance and devoid of any divine design runs counter to this Hellenic notion. Nonetheless, it became the widespread conviction of countless intellectuals. Cicero tried in vain to counter the trend with his *De natura deorum*. After him came Lucretius with his *De natura rerum*, of things (matter) instead of gods. He made no room for the traditional gods but followed Democritus in his materialism, teaching in a poetic form that the world and all that it contains consists of atoms that move about in empty space. [93]

d. Roman philosophers and moralists

Seneca was not a very religious man; theology was a branch of philosophy in his opinion. And philosophy was what he sorely needed, for he did not feel really at ease in a world in which the universe and nature and God and *Fatum* were all one, at least almost indistinguishable. He does not acknowledge a creator who can exist without the created world. In this respect he is a materialist in the line of the *Stoa*. We find in him the same psychological dualism that is so conspicuous in Plato's thought; body and soul cohabit uncomfortably and unwillingly, as he sees it. I called this viewpoint 'existential dualism', because, as the fundamental dualist he is, he does not recognize a supernatural, metaphysical world. [94]

Epictetus confesses the same materialism, monistic in nature. When he speaks of the *pneuma*, the mind or the *Logos*, he is speaking of something material. He too does not acknowledge a metaphysical world. Yet although he was a materialist, he does not celebrate the body and all that is bodily. The body is not the source of pleasure and happiness. He speaks with contempt of it, so that there is a soul-body dualism in his work. [95]

The philosopher on the imperial throne, the Emperor Marcus Aurelius, was also a Stoic, which means that he too was a monistic materialist, although not consequently so. Marcus Aurelius shares with Seneca and Epictetus the soul-body dualism. He teaches that man should live in harmony with the universe of which he forms a part. But the body does not fully participate in this harmony; it is somewhat of a *Fremdkörper* in the universe. [96] All three are at a loss with what to do with mind or spirit; their materialism teaches them to deny it, but it keeps knocking on the back-door. It is obviously hard to be a convinced materialist. Monistic systems use to be just as inconsequential as dualistic ones. [97]

5. In Neoplatonism

The two Neoplatonic philosophers in whose work a two-worlds dualism is most clearly apparent are Plotinus and Proclus. Although in Plotinus' view the *cosmos* is by no means integrally bad, one sometimes gets the impression that there seem to be two *cosmoi*, a lower and a higher one. The latter is the ideal *cosmos* with the *Nous* as its model, while the lower *cosmos* is a battlefield of conflicting elements and not a true unity. It can never be perfect since Matter is one of its constitutive elements. The philosopher says in as many words that there are two extremes : Matter and Divine Reason. [98]

The last great philosopher of Antiquity was Proclus; he was the head of the Academy in Athens, where he died in 485, that is, after the fall of the Western Roman Empire. His system is monistic in principle; all that existed is contained in the One and proceeds from it. One should think that a human thinker can start from the existents and climb up to the One along them. But this is absolutely impossible. For the One cannot be known; it is ineffable. Nothing can be postulated of it; it is beyond all knowledge. This creates an unbridgeable distance between the multiple and the One. In the same vein Proclus makes a distinction between eternity and time which is so sharp that we must call it dualistic; it divides the universe into two separate realms that stand in opposition to each other. This is not radical dualism since there is a unifying principle that unites both realms with each other. [99] Since with Proclus we are already reaching into the Middle Ages, and since he too adheres to the a thousand years old tradition of the two-worlds dualism, the question is justified whether we will also discover it in medieval ideology.

6. The Gnosis

Above we saw how abysmally deep the contempt, even the hatred, was that the Gnostics felt for Matter, for all that is material, physical, bodily, or in general, human. It goes without saying that their systems will also contain the two-worlds dualism and even be built on it. This is the case indeed. Gnostic systems, how different from each other they may be, have this in common that they divide the universe into an upper and a nether part. The upper part is usually called the *Pleroma*, the Fullness. It is the realm of the divine, the spiritual; there is nothing physical in it. The nether part is the created world; it is material and deeply inferior. This is where mankind dwells. The two realms are screened from each other by an almost impenetrable shield - almost, because a few privileged human beings may pass through it; the passport they need is called Knowledge.

The supreme principle does not even form part of the *Pleroma*; he is beyond and above it. In every system he (or it) has another name : prime principle, the unknown God, the Majesty, the Father of All, the Monad, the

Depth, but he is never the biblical Creator-God. He is totally uninterested in creation, in the human world, that is. The lower world is mostly the product of an evil-intentioned Demiurge; he is often equated with the Jahve of the Old Testament. What he has made bears the stamp of his being, which means that it is fundamentally evil. This world is doomed to destruction. Its main characteristic is ignorance, invincible ignorance, except for those few, who are blessed with the redeeming Knowledge. [100]

7. In Christian theology

It is an intriguing question whether we can discover this two-worlds dualism in early Christian theology also. On the face of it this seems impossible. Neither in the Bible nor in orthodox ecclesiastical doctrine is there only a trace of such dualism. The decisive pronouncement is that of Nicaea in 325 that God is the Creator of *visibilium et invisibilium*, of all things visible and invisible. This excludes every idea of there being two opposed worlds. However, taking into account that this two-worlds dualism has an extremely long history in Antiquity and that many great minds recognized it, the possibility exists at least that we may find a shade of it in this or another Christian theologian.

Already with Justin the Martyr, in the middle of the first century A.D., we come dangerously close to this kind of dualism. Justin's Supreme Being is the Creator, but he does not actually create; he is a creator in potency but not in act. Therefore, Justin needs an agent who actually creates; this agent is the *Logos*. Since creation is obviously something of a lower order, which does not concern the Father, this *Logos*, the actual creator, is also of a lower order. In the background we detect the figure of a Demiurge who is different from (although in this case not opposed to) the Supreme God.

A special case in this respect is Origen, important because he was such an influential author. His cosmology bears a remarkable resemblance to that of the Gnosis, which is all the more remarkable because Origen was out to combat it. He in fact acknowledges a 'double creation'; he took the two versions of the creational work in Genesis as reports of two different creations.

First there was a spiritual creation and after that a physical one. The second creation took place on the basis of a primordial Fall or 'antecedent fault'. This idea can also be found in the work of Gregory of Nyssa. Man existed first as a spiritual entity without a body and only later received a physical shape. The first creation is in the image of God, but the second creation being material is not. This creation is not really a creation but rather a *ktisis*, no more than a derivation from the true and original creation, or as Origen called it, a *katabolê*, a 'foundation'. This term is used in a pejorative sense. If this is not two-worlds dualism, we are very near to it.

We should keep an eye on this two-worlds dualism in order to see whether we also find it in the Middle Ages.

PART V KNOWLEDGE

1. About Knowledge

Without any doubt one of the most dualistic elements, present in Antiquity, was connected with the word 'knowledge'. We should rather write 'Knowledge' with a capital, for we are not speaking about knowledge acquired by learning through experience, which everyone does, or through professional training, nor of knowledge as the result of study and scientific investigation. We are referring to a higher sort of knowledge, something of a very peculiar, we might even say, of an esoteric character.

The Greek language had several words for 'to know', all with different functions. [101] But of these stands apart from all the others, namely *gi(g)nooskein* (the substantive *gnoosis* only came later). The meaning of this verb gradually developed from 'to realize, to get to know' to 'realize inwardly, personally', as different from knowing factually or intellectually. Already in Homer *gignooskein* is used specifically; it may denote distinction, discernment, or recognition, but nowhere has it the meaning of 'carnal knowledge'.

It is possible to trace the history of *gignooskein* and later of *gnoosis* throughout Greek literature in its entirety before our era. Almost in every author (the exceptions being the historians and the doctors) I found that the verb as well as the substantive has a specific meaning, that of a higher knowledge, which is present only in the wise. Epicurus even went so far as to state that without *gnosis* there is no salvation. Probably the word 'Gnosis', with a capital, and all that it implies, will now come to the reader's mind. And rightly so! But this subject will have to wait for a moment.

2. The Aristotelian ideal of knowledge

Firstly something must be said of the typically Greek ideal of purely theoretical knowledge, that is, of knowledge that is not useful, not applicable in science or technology. Rudolf Boehm, to whose work [102] I am indebted for this section, rightly remarks that Aristotle, when speaking of knowledge of this kind, does not employ the word 'philosophy'. Philosophy may be a good thing and is often necessary, but in connection with what the wise man should strive after it is rather superfluous.

The very first words of the *Metaphysica* are that "all men naturally desire knowledge." [103] This is a truism, of course, but the philosopher immediately after states that there are 'degrees of knowledge', to borrow a phrase of Jacques Maritain. The senses provide a form of knowledge that, however, is not different from the knowledge animals have. The sensations are stored in the memory. Human beings, far more than animals, learn through experience. But art is a higher form of knowledge than experience, for this remains restricted to individuals, whereas art is concerned with universals. "Artists know the wherefore and the cause." [104] However, in this context Aristotle does not understand by 'artist' the same as we do. His word for art is *technê*, a certain skill; his 'artist' is rather an artisan. The hallmark of artists is that they can teach. In view of this, it should not surprise us that to Aristotle mathematics is also a *technê*. [105]

In the *Nicomachean Ethics* the philosopher explains that art, in the sense of technical skill, is a means to achieve truth, be it as an affirmation (true) or a denial (not true). However, scientific knowledge is a still higher form of knowledge. Objects of this kind of knowledge exist of necessity, that is, they cannot vary and are eternal. A person who possesses scientific knowledge possesses knowledge that rests on first principles (*archai*). [106]

Aristotle can now present an order of the possessors of knowledge : those who have only the faculty of sensation - the man of experience - the artist (artisan) - the master craftsman - the man of productive science - the man of speculative science, of the 'theoretical sciences'. Now we are where Aristotle wants to have us : in the realm of Wisdom (*sophia*), for Wisdom is knowledge of certain principles (*archai*) and causes. [107] The term 'theoretical' means that this supreme form of knowledge can only be acquired by *theoria*, by contemplation. Attention should be paid to the fact that Aristotle does not speak of *philosophia* at all, of the study of philosophy, but only of *sophia*.

Wisdom has no practical end; it must be loved for what it is. The philosopher states that "that science which is desirable in itself is more nearly Wisdom than that which is desirable for its results." [108] A gap is here opening between the theoretical and the practical; *theoria* is rated very much higher than all forms of practice, even than science aiming at practical results. "The man who desires knowledge for its own sake will desire the most perfect knowledge, and this is the knowledge of the knowable, and the things which are most knowable [= worthy of knowing] are first principles and causes," for it is "through these and by these that other things come to be known." [109] This is "the only independent science since it exists for itself." [110]

We are now in a lofty region of thought. Are we not reaching beyond what is humanly possible? This is an objection that Aristotle makes himself. He quotes the poet Simonides who says ; "God alone can have this knowledge;" man should only seek the knowledge that is within its reach. And indeed, if the gods were jealous, the one who excels in knowledge would be unfortunate. But no! Aristotle's Deity is not jealous; the man of the highest knowledge runs no risk. [111] And it is true, this supreme knowledge is really divine. It is divine for two reasons : it is peculiarly the possession of God, and it is concerned with divine matters. "Although other sciences are more necessary [i.e. in a practical respect] than this, none is more excellent." [112] It is so excellent because it brings us close to the godhead.

Aristotle defined, in this line of reasoning, a kind of knowledge far superior to any other kind. he admits that it is not typically human but essentially divine; it is true wisdom, God's wisdom. This does not mean that it is not attainable for a human being, but it will remain the privilege of a few. This creates a gap, a probably unbridgeable gap, between the lovers of Wisdom and the more practically disposed.

There is still more to this. We should not forget that Aristotle, in this context, uninhibitedly uses the terms 'eternal, divine, independent, and free (*eleutheros*)'. Such terms all point to what is more than human, for he knows perfectly well that "in many respects human nature is servile." [113] But *theoria* raises man above himself and liberates him from his own nature. The greatest man can do is to cultivate his intellect and pursue intellectual activity; such a man is most beloved by the gods and, in consequence, the most happy. [114]

In the *Nicomachean Ethics* Aristotle introduces the term *energeia* that means 'activity'. Activity may cause pleasure, and different forms or degrees of pleasure correspond to different activities. The most pronouncedly human pleasure is that caused by the *energeia*, the occupation, of the perfectly and supremely happy man, that is, of the lover of Wisdom. [115] This is something sought for its own sake, with complete disregard for anything else. [116] The activity the philosopher is thinking of is the activity of contemplation, of *theoria*. The great advantages of this form of activity are spelled out as follows. It is the most continuous activity, "for we can reflect more continuously than we can carry on any other form of action." It is also the most pleasant, for philosophy (here Aristotle actually uses the word) "contains pleasures of marvellous purity and permanence." It is also self-sufficient; "the wise man can contemplate by himself, he is the most self-sufficient of men. It produces no result beyond the actual act of contemplation." It is the true leisure, the true *scholê*; it provides such freedom from fatigue as is possible for a human being, 'and all the other attributes of blessedness.' [117]

Are we still speaking of what is human? No, we are not! "Such a life as this will be higher than the human level : not in virtue of his humanity man will achieve it, but in virtue of something that is divine - something that is superior to his composite nature ... The life of the intellect is divine in comparison with human life." And since we are distancing ourselves from what is human, we are also getting beyond mortality, for to be human is to be mortal. A mortal has thoughts of mortality; "but we [the lovers of Wisdom] ought so far as possible to achieve immortality." One who lives in this way lives according to his true self, according to his 'dominant and better part.' "He lives not his own life but the life of some other than himself." [118] Once again a gap opens up, that between the ordinary self and the true self, between mortal and immortal. I feel that Rudolf Boehm is quite correct in concluding that what Aristotle really wants is immortality. When he urges us 'to live in accordance with the highest thing in us,' he is in reality fleeing from death. [119]

I dwelled so long on this subject for two reasons. The first is that the Aristotelian ideal of knowledge contains several dualistic elements; the reader will have noticed them. The second is that we must pursue this quest now that we are entering the domain of the Middle Ages. Did the Schoolmen too, the great thinkers of this period, know this ideal? And those of later ages? Is medieval theology a *scientia divina*? Is modern science something more than human? Questions that will continue to occupy us.

3. Gnostic Knowledge

Nowhere else in Antiquity did Knowledge (with a capital) play so great and so decisive a role as in the Gnosis. The very word *gnoosis* signifies knowledge. It is true that not all Gnostic sects actually called themselves 'Gnostic', but this does not detract from the fact that Knowledge was a primary and constitutive element in all systems. An ideology is to be characterized as 'Gnostic', when it presents two dualistic elements : a horizontal dualism with which is meant that the *Pleroma* and the nether world are hermetically sealed off from each other, and a vertical dualism, that of a division of mankind into those who know and those who do not know (and do not care to know either). As I wrote above, it is only given to a few privileged persons to penetrate into the *Pleroma*; they are able to cross the dividing line with the help of Knowledge.

On this point an unsolvable opposition to Christian doctrine becomes apparent. According to Gnostic ideology some people are saved through the possession of Knowledge, whereas in Christian teaching all men may be saved by the merits won by Jesus Christ through his death on the cross.

Gnostic *gnosis* is a special and very peculiar sort of knowledge, something religious that is indispensable for 'redemption', for eternal salvation. Often this Gnosis is redemption itself : whoever possesses it is saved. This Knowledge is not given to everyone, by no means; it has a secret, an élitist character. It is only the happy few who possess it; they are proud of it and look down in contempt on those who do not know.

This indispensable Knowledge can only be acquired by revelation, not by the so to speak public revelation we find in the Bible; it is a personal communication, an inner illumination received by a privileged person. The source of this Knowledge is, therefore, to be found in the individual person himself.This leads us to the doctrine of the 'sovereign spirit', that is, of the independent human mind that in perfect freedom decides on matters of truth - with the consequence that everybody possesses his or her own truth. The place, the *locus*, where truth is to be found is in man himself.

PART VI TWO RACES OF MEN

The famous opening phrase of the Declaration of Independence : "All men are born equal', was not written for Antiquity. Nowhere in the whole ancient world did the belief exist that all people are fundamentally equal. It was quite the contrary : the basic idea was that human beings are not equal at all, that a better and a lesser sort of them existed . This led to dualism, of course, to the contempt, or worse, of certain groups of people who were considered inferior. It was only with the coming of Christianity, and also in the *Stoa*, that a different idea was introduced. According to Christian doctrine all human beings are children of Adam and have sinned in him; in consequence, all people without exception are in need of redemption.

1. The Pythagorean fraternity

Everywhere in the ancient world we find fraternities with a private and more or less secret character, societies with religious and mystical features, élitist clubs that admitted new members only after the strictest balloting. They kept their teaching to themselves and did not divulge it to outsiders, which means that they belonged to 'esoteric' associations.

The 'model' of these associations was the Pythagorean fraternity. High demands were made upon the character and behaviour of the candidates; they had to show self-control and be taciturn. They had to remain silent on the mysteries that the Master had taught them. A strict separation between the sacred and the profane becomes apparent here : the rituals of the fraternity were not destined for the ears and eyes of the uninitiated. They lived a very frugal existence and were vegetarians. As much as they could they avoided contact with 'common' people. However much the Pythagoreans may have talked of fraternity and love of mankind, their way of life betrays a certain contempt for people and an unmistakable self-exaltation. [120]

2. Philosophical élitism

The great majority of ancient philosophers felt they were a different sort of people, just because they were uninterested lovers of Wisdom. This idea led to élitism. They conceived of themselves as being superior to the common run of people, to the unthinking masses. Many tried to keep apart from 'the others' as though contact with them would defile them; they tended to seek one another's company. We may think here of Plato's Academy [121] and of Epicurus' 'School of the Garden'. [122]

Almost all philosophers of Antiquity distinguished two sets of people, that of the wise and that of the banal people who are not interested in Wisdom. This sort was looked down upon as being contemptible. The wise are always few in number; the philosopher in question and his followers always belong to them. By living according to philosophical precepts, often ascetically, they felt able to reach the summits of thought and even to some extent to be made divine. Philosophical societies were esoteric, which means that they had their own lifestyle and their own way of thought. We shall have to see whether such élitism and esoterism (with vegetarianism) also existed in the Middle Ages.

3. Gnostic élitism

It is as if the dualistic elements of Antiquity achieve their most rabid and radical forms in the Gnosis. This also applies to the idea of élitism, even of being chosen, found in its most potent form in the Gnosis. Above I spoke of the vertical dualism that is one of the great hallmarks of the Gnosis : the division of mankind into two parts, a small one and a much larger one, namely of those who know and the unknowing.

The sentiment of being elected was one of the solid pillars on which Gnostic movements rested. Gnostics were separate, they were chosen, they were elected. And they, they alone, would be saved. They kept very much to themselves and did not show the slightest interest in the rest of mankind. The seal of election was the acceptance of the Knowledge. They held the great majority of human beings in the deepest contempt because they were utterly incapable of seeing the unique significance of this redeeming Knowledge or were indifferent to it. In consequence, they could not be saved. Our human world is destined for destruction; all those who remain unknowing will perish in its final ruin. [123]

Although modern scholars speak of a 'Christian Gnosis', [124] the Gnostics themselves did not share this opinion. Special targets of their hatred were the Jews and the Christians. They polemized against Judaism and Christianity in the bitterest of tones. Orthodox Christians stand on the side of darkness, death, ignorance, and pollution. Since the Church does not reject the world, it forms part of it and will go down with it. [125]

4. Second-rank Christians

We do not find this dualistic contempt for part of humanity in the theology of Origen, but nonetheless, we discover a certain duality of the simple and the perfect. The simple are ordinary believers who come no further than the material significance of scriptural texts, their direct sense. These faithful are quite content with an elementary knowledge of the faith. Origen does not see them as doomed; they have the faith that will save them. However, the perfect aspire to more; their understanding of biblical texts and their interpretation of the dogmas of the creed lead them to a wisdom that is the true knowledge. Their faith is based on the contemplation of higher things. Naturally, this smacks somewhat of Gnostic ideology. In another respect too he came dangerously close to the Gnosis. For he held that there was an 'eternal Gospel', which surpasses the New Testament just as much as the New Testament surpasses the Old. Origen here comes close to the Gnostic idea of a secret and esoteric Knowledge. [126]

The idea of élitism is strongly present in some deviant sects. The Encratite heresiarch Tatian clearly acknowledged two races of men. God's spirit, he taught, is not given to all (to all Christians, he means). There are souls that are obedient to wisdom (*sophia*) - to Encratite wisdom, that is - and souls that are disobedient and reveal themselves thereby as the enemies of God. [127]

Montanists and Donatists despised ordinary Christians; these were not ascetic, not spiritual enough to their taste, and above all, they did not aspire to martyrdom. The Donatists were particularly harsh to Christians who had lapsed in times of persecution and later wanted to return to the fold. The Montanists venerated the Holy Ghost more than the Father and the Son. Their prophets claimed to receive revelations and visions that were given to the rank and file who had to be content with the Bible and what the Church taught them. Ordinary Christians were second rank at best. [128]

Another prophet of asceticism, Priscillian, distinguished gradations in perfection among the faithful. Many of them were too attached, he found, to 'the flesh' and the world. He did not see them as 'sons of perdition', but he also had his chosen, faithful so inspired by the divine spirit that they had become 'sons of God'; these were the truly elected. He also acknowledged a 'hidden wisdom' that was destined only for the chosen, not for the mass of the ordinary faithful. This hidden wisdom contained teachings that were not to be found in the Gospels. [129]

5. Attitudes to women

Almost all ancient societies showed a tendency to consider women as the lesser breed. It would not be the slightest exaggeration to say that the situation of women in ancient societies was bad; it varied from rather bad through bad to very bad. But there are a few exceptions. In ancient Israel the situation of women was reasonably good. Genesis 1 had categorically stated that man and woman were equals; in Genesis 2 the marital bond of these two equals was made a divine institution. There is no depreciation of women in the Old Testament. The ones who come in for criticism, often of a very severe kind, are the men. There is an endless procession of males, beginning with the kings, who were no good, whereas Scripture reveals quite a number of women with flawless characters. [130]

In Egypt too the women were by no means badly off. Juridically they were the equals of the men and were considered as adult and free persons with a status of their own. We find the same satisfying position of women in ancient Crete, at least until the middle of the second millennium, when the island was conquered by invaders coming from Mycene. All the same, these three societies were patriarchical, in the sense that all the ruling positions were occupied by males. A patriarchate does, however, not necessarily, mean that the women are oppressed.

Nowhere in the ancient world was the situation of the women so bad as in ancient India, with perhaps the exception of Athens. Here the women were definitely the lesser sort. The Aryans who had conquered India were a *macho* race of warriors who held women in contempt. In the families pride of place was given to the sons; girls were not welcome. Although wives were supposed to remain content with one husband, the men were often polygamous, especially when their wives had no offspring or bore them only daughters. Men and women were not on the same footing, and the women were the losers. The fate of widows was far from enviable; they were doomed to a very frugal life in practical isolation. Sometimes widows followed their deceased husbands on the funeral pyre. Widows were the lowest of the lesser breed. Sons were favoured, but girls were property, first of their fathers, later of their husbands. They did not receive much of an education.

Indian men did not see their wives as persons of the same worth and value as themselves. Ancient Hindu texts abound with deprecatory remarks about women. Buddhism, when it came, did nothing to ameliorate the position of women. The Buddha himself did not think too highly of them. In this religion the women are also inferior to the men; misogynist tendencies can be found in Buddhist literature. [131]

It must be admitted that, with respect to the situation of women, there is only one section of ancient Greek society about which we are reasonably well informed; this section is Athenian high society. There the position of the women was extremely poor. Athens may have had an exceptionally high culture, but the part women played in it was infinitesimally small. A difference to Indian society is perhaps that Athenian girls from well-to-do families received some sort of education, which probably means that they learned to read and write. But they were not welcome; their fathers preferred sons. Daughters grew up with the well-founded idea that they were second choice.

Juridically they were the property of their fathers and passed from his hands into those of the husband. Girls were married young (too young) to a man who was usually much older than herself. She played no part at all in Athenian society, did not go out, and spent most of her life behind the walls of her home, weaving and caring for her household. The attitude of the husband towards his wife was normally characterized by condescension and paternalism. [132]

Roman society was a *macho* society if there ever was one. It was a society that I have described as one 'geared to war'. For endless centuries the Romans fought wars and conquered. This inevitably meant that the soldier was the most valued individual in Roman society. Since women did not become soldiers, we may suppose that they would compare very unfavourably with the men. But this picture is perhaps not wholly correct. It must be said that we know next to nothing or nothing at all of the lives of the overwhelming majority of the women in Roman history. We know something more of those women who lived within the range of attention of Roman historians, mostly society women that is.

Roman women were dependent on a male tutor, when they were still unmarried on their fathers or brothers, and later on their husbands. They had no rights of their own, and they had one primary task : to bear soldiers. True as this is, they were somewhat freer than their Athenian sisters, for they could go out and were not restricted to the confines of their homes. Another important point is that they had to transmit the values of the Roman state to their sons and daughters; these values were those of a patriarchical and profoundly military society. This means that Roman women, at least Roman *matronae*, shared the concepts the men had of their role in society.

6. Fear of sexuality

The deprecatory tone ancient texts so often employ with regard to women often conceals a certain male fear of them. And behind this fear that of sexuality lurks, for women were often seen as fundamentally erotic beings. And as such woman is regarded a threat to the males. The tone was set once and for all by Hesiod who presented his Pandora as a disaster contrived by a vindictive godhead, but nevertheless as an attractive disaster. He called her the *kalon kakon*, the beautiful evil. The passage where Hesiod expresses this view shows a deep distrust of women, of erotics in fact. [133]

Hindu society was extremely negative about female erotic power; there is a barely concealed fear of women as sexual beings. They were considered the 'roots of evil'. Their erotic radiance inspired fear, for their desire was impure. They were out to seduce the males and rob them of their manly force; they sucked away the men's vitality and strength. [134]

When it came to despising sexuality (and procreation), Gnostic ideology topped everything; here the contempt developed into hatred. We find this already in a non-Gnostic author like Philo who held that everything went astray when woman was created. For the already existing man desired her sexually, and that was bad, even the origin of evil. To Philo the original sin was one of a sexual nature. What he shares with the Gnostics is a deep distrust of femininity and sexuality. [135] There is also a Hermetic text, in the *Poimandres*, that says that "the cause of death is love", with which sexual intercourse is meant. [136]

Many Gnostic systems use sexual imagery in order to describe the creational process; this is invariably done in negative terms. This negativity is in accordance with the fact that Gnostics hold creation, matter, the world, in very low esteem; sexuality is a part of that doomed world. [137] An important Sethian text, when discussing the part of sexuality in the origin of mankind, does not refer to the males but rather to femininity that is obviously the source of all erotic desire. [138] One of the most radical in these matters was the little known sect of the Severians. Their rejection of women and sexuality could not be more radical. Women are the work of Satan, and marrying a woman is fulfilling the work of Satan. All people are half of God and half of the devil : the upper half of their bodies is created by God and the lower half, with the sexual organs, by the evil power. [139]

In Barbelo-Gnostic ideology sexual desire is the hallmark of man's fallen state; this forces people to have sexual intercourse so that they beget offspring; in doing this they are subject to the bad Demiurge. [140] The Gnostics deplored that there were two sexes. In some texts the first human being was androgynous, but later Eve, the female principle, was separated from him which became the cause of death. For as soon as man and woman were separated everything went wrong. There was, in Gnostic opinion, an essential difference between androgynity and bisexuality. The first is an expression of oneness and as such it is a pleromatic phenomenon, whereas bisexuality denotes multiplicity, which is seen as fundamentally wrong. [141]

There is one Gnostic text, the Gospel of Philip, that does not speak wholly negatively of marriage. A sacramental marriage is an image of the celestial union in the *Pleroma*. But by no means are all marriages good! The author makes a sharp distinction between defiled and undefiled marriages.

The former are characterized by desire and are, in consequence, 'fleshly' and impure, and belong to darkness and night, while the latter are dominated by the will and are therefore pure and belonging to the day and the light. [142]

A basic Gnostic text like *On the Origin of the World* takes a very low view of sexuality. Sensual pleasure in the end leads to death; procreation means destining human beings to die. [143]

The idea the more important and better known Gnostic sects have of sexuality is little more optimistic. Marcion, for instance, found sexuality the most reprehensible of all the Demiurge's institutions. Man should not attempt to be creative himself, for the results would be deplorable. Marriage is something evil, it is simply unchastity. He would have nothing of procreation, of child-bearing, and rearing babies. [144] In consequence, no marriages were contracted in the Marcionite Church; only celibates and eunuchs were baptized. Marcionites should not carry on the work of the Demiurge. [145]

According to the Mandaeans the female sex exists because there is no order in the world. Their ideas of women and sexuality are negative and dualistic. Marriage is not a sacrament to them. [146]

The Manichaeans had a very low idea of Eve, that is, of women. They are dark beings in whom few particles of light are to be found. Weak as they are, they are not resistent against evil and are a constant danger to the men. Mankind should be redeemed, but the existence of sexuality and the urge to procreate considerably hinder the work of redemption; they compared sexual intercourse to cannibalism. [147]

Many non-Gnostic Greek and Roman pagan authors express an evident reticence with regard to sexuality. It is possible, and even probable, that that *horror materiae*, which I have already mentioned several times, played a role in this. [148] The sexual morals of ancient republican Rome were extremely austere. Although the general attitude with regard to sex was positive - for the Republic needed soldiers -, we see nowhere that sexuality was celebrated as something joyful or as a liberating power. It had to be kept under strict control, because it could easily become a destabilizing force. [149]

A side-effect of the tumultuous end of the Republic was that the sexual mores were loosened. In imperial times, the state attempted to bring back the old order, but it proved impossible to turn the clock back. [150] However, the old idea persisted that the main aim of marriage and of sexual intercourse in marriage was to provide the state with boys who would become soldiers and girls who would bear soldier-sons. But the attempts to tie the man to the marriage bond proved an uphill struggle. [151] The sexual act was not perceived as an intimate and personal encounter of husband and wife; rather it expressed the dominating power of the male. The inevitable consequence was that the Romans did not have a high idea of sex; it was simply too impersonal. [152]

Pagan scholars, particularly the physicians, did not advocate celibacy, but did not tire from warning against the excesses of sex. They were obviously somewhat afraid of it. In principle, sexual activity was an expression of health and vigour, but it could also become the cause of physical weakness and even of all kinds of illnesses. One gets the impression that even a famous physician such as Galen found it better if people would have no sex at all. [153]

The atttitude of the authors of the Old and New Testaments with regard to sexuality was relaxed; the subject does not have pride of place in the Bible. Jesus obviously found sex less important and interesting and more matter-of-fact than modern people. [154] The Church of the first centuries had to steer her course between the looseness of pagan morals and the danger of 'over-spiritualising'. Christian authors, beginning with Paul, rated virginity higher than marriage, which does not necessarily mean that they considered marriage as inferior. [155] In the first two centuries of the Church, the Fathers did not devote much space to such subjects as body, sex, and marriage; Christianity had other preoccupations at that time. [156]

In later Christian authors, beginning with Tertullian, it is often possible to detect a tendency towards rigorism. Nowhere marriage is condemned as something that is bad in itself, and the same can be applied to sexual intercourse within marriage. Yet on the other hand the Fathers did not extol it either. [157] They preferred the celibate state, but took care to point out that marriage is a divine institution, and that begetting children was the fulfilling of God's mandate. [158] It would be wrong to portray the Fathers as sex-obsessed. What they had to say on the subjects of marriage and sexuality forms only a small part of their enormous output. [159]

7. The 'others'

It is a common trait of mankind in all ages to make a, sometimes sharp, distinction, between 'us' and 'them'. This distinction can assume a dualistic character, namely when, as is often the case, the others are seen as despicable, uncivilized, and inferior. In the most extreme cases the right to existence can be denied to them.

The sentiment of being superior to all others was strongly present in ancient China. According to Chinese philosophical ideology the earth was a square that was divided into smaller squares. In the middle square the Chinese Emperor was at home; from there he reigns. This central square is surrounded by four other squares where the vassals live who rule the Chinese population. These central squares are in their turn surrounded by concentric regions where the non-Chinese live; they are barbarians, although varying from almost civilized to utterly wild. These peoples did not share in the full humanity that was the part of the Chinese, and of them alone. They were less than human. [160]

The ancient Egyptians, who lived in a splendid isolation, considered themselves as 'the true men'. The consequence of this viewpoint was that non-Egyptians were seen as not so true, and even as less than human. The Egyptian texts and the iconography make it clear that the inhabitants of the country of the Nile had a definite feeling of superiority over all others. The non-Egyptian world seemed to them a world of chaos and darkness, even of non-existence. [161]

Ancient Israel lived in the conviction that God had concluded a Covenant with them, which made them his chosen people. The consequence was that non-Jews were not a party to this Covenant and were, therefore, not chosen. They were the *gentes*, the 'Gentiles', in Hebrew the *goyim*. This means a marked antagonism to non-Jewish peoples. This idea of election was a climatic element in Israel's mental make-up. On the ideological or ideal plane this attitude led to radical dualism, implying the wholesale destruction of the Canaanite tribes. However, in practice it never went so far; until late in biblical times many Canaanites lived among the Jewish population in Palestine. [162]

Unlike the Israelites, the Greeks did not pride themselves on their religion but on their, in their eyes, far superior civilization. To be civilized meant to speak Greek, to speak Greek as a native Greek speaker. Who could not do this was a barbarian, and to be a barbarian was to be inferior. [163]

The Romans constitute a special case. They felt themselves to be superior to all others, but felt uncomfortable in this respect with regard to the Greeks, for in the eyes of the Hellenes the Romans were barbarians themselves. [164] The evident sentiment of superiority the Romans had was not based on the idea they had of their own civilization but of power. They felt it to be their god-given task to subject as much as possible of the world to their rule.

8. Slavery

All ancient peoples held slaves. Even Israel was no exception to this. In the New Testament slavery was accepted as a matter of fact, although the Christian concept that all men are equal before God struck at the root of this institution.

According to Greek social ideology, the real distinction was not between free and unfree, but between human beings and objects. The Hellenes had a very low opinion of the human dignity of slaves who were no more than utensils to them. They had a deep contempt of manual labour; the task of the free man was to run the town, to cultivate art and science, to teach, to administer justice, and to wage war. Since slaves did none of these things but laboured, they were despised. [165]

Just as Greek society, the Romans could not do without slaves, without many slaves. Household slaves were usually better treated than the countless slaves who worked on the land or in the mines, the latter category being the worst off. But no matter where they worked or which tasks they had to perform, they were the lesser sort, not really a human being, but rather a thing, a possession. They were wholly and totally subjected to the power of their masters; they had no legal rights at all, were not entitled to have possessions of their own, and could be bought and sold at the master's will. [166]

PART VII IMPERIALISM

Reduced to its most simple meaning, the term 'imperialism' signifies the building of an empire. By 'empire' a state is meant in which more than one nation or several nations that formerly led an independent existence, are now united under one rule. Empires are 'universal', that is, they are all-embracing; all empires tend to become world-empires encompassing the whole world. Never, however, has there been an empire the frontiers of which were those of the world. The sense of unity and necessity in them is so strong that they believe themselves to be immortal. What is relevant to our main subject is that empires virtually deny the right of existence to other states; in fact, they consider these states as non-existent, which is the sheerest dualism. [167]

1. Imperialism in Mesopotomia and Asia Minor

Imperialism is almost as old as civilization itself. It is an intriguing question whether the urge to subject other nations to one common rule is something anthropological, something innate to human nature, or that it is a product of peculiar historical circumstances. The fact is that by no means all nations in history have developed imperialistic tendencies. The region stretching from Central Anatolia south-eastward to the Delta of the Euphrates and the Tigris, along an axis running from south-east to north-west, saw the birth of the first great empires.

The very first was Sumer, in the Mesopotamian river delta, where about 2435 B.C. a certain Luzalzagissi, the ruler of the city of Umma, began to conquer neighbouring city states. This man who was soon called 'King of the Lands', was the first of a long line of brutal and remorseless conquerors that stretches through the whole of history. His conquests formed together the first Empire, though compared with later empires it was rather small. [168]

This Empire was succeeded by that of Akkad into which it was, in fact, engulfed. Around 2430 B.C. the great conqueror Sargon began building up a new reign that was much larger than the old one of Sumer; it is called 'Sumer and Akkad' and comprised the whole of Mesopotamia with Assyria, and Elam, Kurdistan and Syria. Perhaps this realm must be seen as the first real Empire, rather than Sumer, since it contained many non-Akkadian nations. [169] The end of this Empire came around 2000 B.C.

Some centuries passed before a new irresistible conqueror presented himself. This time it was a Babylonian, the famous Hammurabi. In rapid campaigns he submitted the whole of Mesopotamia to his will around 1760 B.C. He had a divine sanction for his conquests; the supreme god of the Babylonian *pantheon* had ordered him 'to make justice appear in the land'; he was the beloved son of the sun-god of Babylon. This made his reign more than historical and political. [170]

Somewhat more to the west, a new imperialistic nation began to manifest itself, the Hittites. They lived in Anatolia, a region that proved as fertile for empire-builders as that between the great rivers. Here King Hattusilis made great conquests around 1625 B.C. His successor was even master of Babylon for some time. For a time Hittite power suffered an eclipse but around 1360 B.C. they came back in full strength, building up the New Hittite Empire. The greater part of Asia Minor and of Syria was then in Hittite hands. Hittite emperors styled themselves 'Great King', that is King of Kings, far more than an ordinary king. They too saw their rule as being divinely sanctioned. [171]

The road to the east was blocked by the Assyrians who began to rise to power and fame around 1780 B.C., but became really powerful only around 1300 B.C. Their rulers brought together an Empire of considerable extent, larger than any other so far. It comprised not only the whole of Mesopotamia with Babylonia but also Elam and western Iran, Armenia, Anatolia, Syria, Palestine, and even Egypt. Their kings assumed the title of 'King of the Universe'; they too were the special favourites of their gods. [172]

Shortly before 600 B.C. Babylonia came to the fore again. Assyria was beaten by the Babylonians in 612 B.C. In 605 Nebuchadnessar II became king; he is the real founder of the New Babylonian Empire. This Empire remained somewhat smaller than its Assyrian predecessor, since it did not comprise Egypt. But Jerusalem was captured. [173] Then all of a sudden a new conqueror appeared in the east who would sweep away all the ancient imperialistic pretensions.

2. The Persian Empire

The foundation of the enormous Persian Empire was the work of King Cyrus II; he started his career as a conqueror immediately after his ascension to the throne in 559. He began with subjecting Media whose king was his suzerain. Then followed Lydia, in western Asia Minor, the acquisition of which meant that the Aegean was reached and the first Greeks came under Persian rule. Eastward from Persia enormous territories were conquered until in the east almost the Indus was reached and more to the north the regions east and west of the Amudary'a, as far north as Lake Aral. Then the New Babylonian Empire fell into his hands. Later Syria and Palestine followed. It was left to his son Cambyses to occupy Egypt. [174]

It cannot have seemed difficult for the successors of Cyrus and Cambyses to submit the other half of the Greeks, in Hellas proper, to their rule. After all Greece was no more than a loose confederation of petty states. Part of the Balkans, with the Danube as the northern frontier, fell into Persian hands indeed. But when Xerxes I, who became Great King in 485, tried his hand against the Greeks themselves, he suffered a resounding defeat; after decades of warfare he had to leave them in peace. [175]

3. The Macedonian Empire

The next great blast of imperialism, the most powerful of all so far, came from the West. Suddenly the kings of an almost forgotten nation, despised by the Greeks as semi-barbarians, the Macedonians, entered world-history, not only as forceful rulers but above all as great conquerors. Their King Philip II subjected Greece in 338 B.C. He probably had plans to fight the Persians, but it was his son Alexander who executed them. [176] In 334 B.C. he entered Asia Minor and defeated the Persians several times in great battles; in 331 his opponent, the Great King Darius III, was murdered; Alexander was king of Persia now. He did not remain content with the downfall of the Persian Empire but pursued his victorious march eastward and, crossing the Indus, finally entered India. He then saw himself forced to return. During the march westward he died in Babylon in 323 B.C. The Macedonian Empire that he had founded was the largest the world had ever seen so far. It comprised all the Persian conquests, including Egypt, stretching even further in the east, and Greece and the Balkans with the Danube as the northern frontier. [177]

The successors of Alexander, the so-called *Diadochi*, proved unable to keep this enormous Empire together. Soon enough there were three successor kingdoms, one in Greece and Macedonia, one in Egypt, and the Seleucid Empire. The latter was the largest of the three; in its greatest extent it comprised all the territories between the Aegean and the Indus, with Syria and Palestine. The history of the successor kingdoms is one of incessant mutual warfare, which was mostly to the detriment of the Seleucid Empire. Its greatest losses were suffered east of the Tigris, where Persian imperialism powerfully reasserted itself. [178] Around 250 B.C. Parthia made itself independent; its rulers founded a Parthian Empire that bordered on the Euphrates in the west. [179]

4. The Roman Empire

The next great imperialistic push came from still farther west, from Rome, initially an insignificant hill village on the Tiber, but destined to become the greatest power centre of all Antiquity. Their inexorable drive led to centuries of warfare. The result of all that conquering was that the Roman Empire in its greatest extent, reached in the second century A.D., contained the southern half of Europe with the Rhine and the Danube as its frontiers, but also encompassed England, further the whole littoral of North Africa with Egypt, and Syria, Palestine and the whole of Asia Minor. In the west there were no ancient imperialistic states; those in the East, the Macedonian successor states, were all brought down by the Roman fist.

The Romans saw themselves entrusted with a god-given task; it was the will of the gods that they should go on and on conquering. No state, no nation, no tribe had the right to resist them. They had the choice between voluntarily submitting to Roman rule (which happened very rarely) or to be defeated. In the worst cases Rome did not shy away from genocide to get rid of a tough opponent. [180]

As I wrote above, no Empire ever succeeded in becoming a world-empire. Rome too had to acknowledge that there was an end to its conquering. In the west, all ideas of expansion were given up after it had proved impossible to conquer Germany. [181] In the East the Euphrates front never became really quiet. As the successors of the Seleucid Empire the Romans were forced to deal with the Parthian Empire, which proved a formidable opponent. More than once the Romans were heavily defeated. [182] After the demise of the Parthian Empire there was again a Persian renaissance : around A.D. 220 the Sasanian Empire was founded that in the west bordered on the Euphrates and in the East reached even farther than its Parthian predecessor, since the Indus was its frontier. Much as the Romans, and later the Byzantines, desired to be rid of the Sasanian menace, they never succeeded in gaining the ultimate triumph, while they themselves sometimes suffered heavy defeats. On the whole the Euphrates remained the 'frontier of Europe' with Mesopotamia as a often hotly contested glacis between the two Empires. [183]

CONCLUSION

I have restricted myself in this chapter to the really great dualistic themes of Antiquity. This meant that many others that found a place in the Volumes I-XIV were not mentioned at all. I am thinking here, for instance, of the relation between Jews and Samaritans, or of that between Upper and Lower Egypt, or of the civil wars of the first century B.C. in Rome. Such smaller dualisms were often very painful for those concerned, but they were not constitutive for the ancient world. With this 'constitutive' I mean that the five great dualistic themes that were treated in this chapter, *horror materiae*, two-worlds dualism, knowledge, two races of men, and imperialism, were present always and everywhere in the ancient world. They were fundamental parts of it.

We are now standing on the treshold of the Middle Ages. The question now confronting us is how the centuries between 500 and 1500 would cope with the kinds of dualism treated so far. Would one or other of them disappear from sight? Would this or that one remain forcefully present? Would there also be new ones? Already Chapter II demonstrates that the theme of imperialistic dualism was by no means dead.

NOTES TO CHAPTER I

1. Vol. VI, Preface 3.
2. Vol. VI, Preface 4.
3. Vol. XIII, Preface.
4. Laeuchli, *Mithraic Dualism* 61/62.
5. Vol. I, Ch. I. § 15.
6. Vol. I, Ch. IV, § 10.
7. Vol. I, Ch. II, §§ 6, 8, and 9.
8. Vol. III, Ch. III. §§ 20-22.
9. Vol. XIV, Ch. I, Part III.
10. Vol. XIV, Ch. I, Part IV.
11. Vol. XIV, Ch. I, Part V.
12. Vol. IV, Ch. IV, §§ 8 and 9.
13. Vol. V, Ch. II, § 22.
14. Vol. V, Ch. V, § 22.
15. Vol. V, Ch. III, § 25.
16. Vol. VI, Ch. III, § 2.
17. Vol. IV, Ch. IV, §§ 8 and 9.
18. Vol. IV, Ch. I, § 6a.
19. Vol. V, Ch. III, § 15e.

20. Vol. V, Ch. II, § 21.
21. Vol. V, Ch. II, § 22.
22. Vol. V. Ch. II, § 23.
23. Vol. III, Ch. III, § 19b.
24. Vol. VI, Ch. III, § 1c.
25. Vol. XIV, Ch. I, Part III, §§ 2-4.
26. Vol. XIV, Ch. I, Part III, § 5.
27. Vol. XIV, Ch. I, Part III, § 6.
28. Vol. XIV, Ch. I, Part IV, § 1.
29. Vol. XIV, Ch. I, Part IV, § 3d.
30. Vol. XIV, Ch. I, Part IV, § 5e-m.
31. Vol. XIV, Ch. I, Part IV, § 6.
32. Vol. XIV, Ch. I, Part V, § 1.
33. Vol. XIV, Ch. I, Part V, § 2.
34. Vol. XIV, Ch. I, Part V, § 3.
35. Vol. VIII, Ch. I, §§ 10-13.
36. Vol. VII, Ch. V, § 9h.
37. Vol. VIII. Ch. II, § 2.
38. Vol. VIII, Ch. II, § 7.
39. Vol. VIII, Ch. II, § 9b.
40. Vol. VIII, Ch. I, § 9j.
41. Vol. VIII, Ch. II, § 10e-f.
42. Vol. VII, Ch. III, § 4.
43. Vol. VII, Ch. III, § 5d-e.
44. Vol. VII, Ch. III, §6f-g.
45. Vol. VIII, Ch. IV, § 7.
46. Vol. VII, Ch. IV, § 8.
47. Vol. VII, Ch. IV, § 9.
48. Vol. VIII, Ch. IV, §§ 15-17.
49. Vol. VIII, Ch. V, § 17.
50. Vol. VIII. Ch. V, § 18b.
51. Vol. VIII. Ch. VI.

52. Vol. VIII, Ch. VII, § 4c and f.
53. Vol. VIII, Ch. VII, § 5.
54. Vol. VIII, Ch. VIII, §§ 5 and 9.
55. Vol. IX, Ch. II, §§ 7-9, 12-14, and 18a.
56. Vol. IX, Ch. III, §§ 7, 11, and 12.
57. Vol. IX, Ch. IV, §§ 10, 18, 24, and 28.
58. Vol. XIII, Ch. IV, § 2.
59. Vol. XIII, Ch. IV, § 4.
60. Vol. XIII. Ch. IV, § 5.
61. Vol. XIII, Ch. IV, § 7.
62. Vol. XIII, Ch. IV, § 9b.
63. Vol. XIII, Ch. IV, § 10.
64. Vol. XIII, Ch. IV, § 11.
65. Vol. XIII, Ch. V, Part I, § 1.
66. Vol. XIII. Ch. V, Part I, § 3.
67. Vol. XIII. Ch. V, Part I, § 4.
68. Vol. XIII, Ch. V, Part II, §§ 1-8.
69. Vol. XIII, Ch. V, Part III.
70. Vol. XIII, Ch. VI, Part I, § 3.
71. Vol. XIII, Ch. VI, Part I, §§ 4 and 5.
72. Vol. XIII, Ch. VI, Part I, §§ 6 and 8.
73. Vol. XIII, Ch. VI, Part II, § 4k.
74. Vol. XIII, Ch. VI, Part III, § 4.
75. Vol. XIII, Ch. VI, Part IV, § 1.
76. Vol. XIII, Ch. VI, Part VI, § 1.
77. Vol. XIII, Ch. VI, Part VII, § 8c.
78. Vol. XIII, Ch. VII, Part I, § 3.
79. Vol. XIII, Ch. VII, Part I, § 4.
80. Vol. XIII, Ch. VII, Part II, § 3, 4, and 6.
81. Vol. XIII, Ch. VII, Part III, §§ 4 and 5.
82. Vol. XIII, Ch. VII, Part III, § 12.
83. Vol. XIII, Ch. VII, Part IV, §§ 4 and 5.

84. Vol. XIII, Ch. VII, Part IV, § 10.
85. Vol. XIII, Epilogue.
86. Vol. IV, Ch. IV, §§ 8 and 9.
87. Vol. XIII, Ch. I, § 5.
88. Vol. I, Ch. II, § 4.
89. Vol. I, Ch. II, § 8.
90. Vol. I, Ch. III, § 7a.
91. Vol. VI, Ch. III, § 2.
92. Vol. VI, Ch. III, § 3.
93. Vol. XIV, Ch. I, Part I, § 2.
94. Vol. XIV, Ch. I, Part II, §§ 1-6.
95. Vol. XIV, Ch. I, Part II, §§ 7-9.
96. Vol. XIV, Ch. I, Part II, § 10.
97. Vol. XIV, Ch. I, Part II, § 11.
98. Vol. XIV, Ch. I, Part V, § 1.
99. Vol. XIV, Ch. I, Part V, § 4.
100. Vols. VII, VIII, and IX; I refer the interested reader to the charts at the end of Vol. VIII.
101. Vol. VII, Ch. II.
102. Boehm, *Kritik der Grundlagen des Zeitalters*, especially Kap. I.
103. Ar., *Metaphysica* 980a.
104. Ar., *Metaphysica* 981a.
105. Ar., *Metaphysica* 981b.
106. Ar., *Nicomachean Ethics* 1139b.
107. Ar., *Metaphysica* 982a.
108. Ar., *Metaphysica* 982a.
109. Ar., *Metaphysica* 981a-982b.
110. Ar., *Metaphysica* 982b.
111. Ar., *Metaphysica* 982b-983b.
112. Ar., *Metaphysica* 983a.
113. Ar., *Metaphysica* 982b.
114. Ar., *Nicomachean Ethics* 1179a13.

115. Ar., *Nicomachean Ethics* 1175a25-30.
116. Ar., *Nicomachean Ethics* 1176b5.
117. Ar., *Nicomachean Ethics* 1177a-b.
118. Ar., *Nicomachean Ethics* 1176b-1178a.
119. Boehm, *Kritik der Grundlagen des Zeitalters* 35.
120. Vol. I, Ch. I, § 5.
121. Vol. III, Ch. III, § 1a.
122. Vol. VI, Ch. III, § 4a.
123. Vol. IX, Ch. V, Part III, § 10.
124. Vol. IX, Ch. V, Part II.
125. Vol. VIII, Ch. IX, § 3.
126. Vol. XIII, Ch. Ch. III, § 7.
127. Vol. XIII, Ch. V, Part I, § 3e.
128. Vol. XIII, Ch. V, Part II and Part III.
129. Vol. XIII, Ch. V, Фart IV, § 3.
130. Vol. IV, Ch. II, § 12m.
131. Vol. V, Ch. II, § 14.
132. Vol. II, Ch. IV, § 4a-h.
133. Vol. I, Ch. III, § 7d.
134. Vol. V, Ch. II, § 14g.
135. Vol. VIII, Ch. I, § 18b.
136. Vol. VIII, Ch. II, § 9n.
137. Vol. VIII, Ch. IV, § 8.
138. Vol. VIII, Ch. IV, § 15.
139. Vol. VIII, Ch. V, § 23.
140. Vol. VIII, Ch. VI, § 81.
141. Vol. IX, Ch. I, § 2e.
142. Vol. IX, Ch. I, § 2h.
143. Vol. IX, Ch. I, § 4g.
144. Vol. IX, Ch. II, § 13.
145. Vol. IX, Ch. II, § 19.

146. Vol. IX, Ch. III, § 11e.
147. Vol. IX, Ch. IV, § 18b,c.
148. Vol. XIV, Ch. III, § 3.
149. Vol. XIV, Ch. III, Part II, § 5.
150. Vol. XIV, Ch. III, Part II, § 6.
151. Vol. XIV, Ch. III, Part II, § 7.
152. Vol. XIV, Ch. III, Part II, § 9.
153. Vol. XIV, CH. III, Part II, § 10.
154. Vol. XIV, Ch. III, Part III, § 2a.
155. Vol. XIV, Ch. III, Part III, § 3a.
156. Vol. XIV, Ch. III, Part III, § 5.
157. Vol. XIV, Ch. III, Part III, § 7.
158. Vol. XIV, Ch. III, Part III, § 9.
159. Vol. XIV, Ch. III, Part III, § 16.
160. Vol. V, Ch. III, § 15c.
161. Vol. IV, Ch. I, § 3.
162. Vol. IV, Ch. II, § 15.
163. Vol. II, Ch. III, § 3.
164. Vol. XI, Ch. VI.
165. Vol. II, Ch. IV, § 4i, j.
166. Vol. XI, Ch. IV, Part II, §§ 2, 3, and 6.
167. Vol. IV, Ch. III, § 1.
168. Vol. IV, Ch. III, § 2.
169. Vol. IV, Ch. III, §§ 3 and 4.
170. Vol. IV, Ch. III, § 5.
171. Vol. IV, Ch. III. § 6.
172. Vol. IV, Ch. III, § 7.
173. Vol. IV, Ch. III, § 8.
174. Vol. IV, Ch. IV, § 3.
175. Vol. II, Ch. I and Ch. II, § 4d.
176. Vol. II, Ch. II, § 5.
177. Vol. IV, Ch. IV, § 3e.

178. Vol. V, Ch. I, § 1.
179. Vol. V, Ch. I, § 2.
180. The whole styory in Vol. X.
181. Vol. X, Ch. VI, § 15.
182. Vol. V, Ch. I, § 2.
183. Vol. V, Ch. I, § 3, and Vol. XI, Ch. III. § 6.

CHAPTER II

UNIVERSALISM CONTRA PARTICULARISM :
THE BYZANTINE RECONQUEST OF THE WEST

PART I A NEW CAPITAL AS THE SEAT
OF A NEW IMPERIALISM

1. The new capital

The foundation of Constantinople is surrounded by legends. Philostorgius, the Church historian, tells us that in A.D. 324 the Emperor Constantine the Great outlined the boundaries of the plot where the new town would stand. He did this with his spear in his hand. His courtiers who politely walked behind him, were astonished by the enormous extent of the site. "How long will you go on?", they asked him. And the reply was : "I shall go on until he who walks ahead of me will stop." [1] Since nobody walked ahead of him, the Emperor could only have meant that a divine being preceded him, or rather, that he was divinely inspired in his planning of the new capital. [2] The construction of the new town began in 325; on May 11th, 330, it was dedicated with a forty days long festival. [3] If Rome had always celebrated its foundation date on April 21st, Constantinople could now boast its own birthday.

Although it was meant as and really became a new town, it was not a totally new foundation. On the promontory jutting out into the Sea of Marmora stood an already age-old town, the ancient colony Byzantium, founded by Megara in about 660 B.C. It had fared very badly at the hands of the Emperor Septimius Severus. This man had become the ruler of the West in 193 as the result of a military coup, but the forces of a usurper, Pescennius Niger, [4] held out against him in Byzantium. The town was submitted to a long and bloody siege lasting from November 193 to July 196. When it was at last captured, the whole garrison and all the notables were massacred. It was almost totally destroyed, but it was later rebuilt, for its situation on the passage from the Black Sea to the Aegean was too important to let it lie in ruins. [5] However, in A.D. 270 it was thoroughly sacked by the Goths. As a result it was in far from great shape in 324.

What were Constantine's reasons for building a new town, and not just an ordinary town, but one that would replace Rome as the capital of the Empire? One of these reasons, and perhaps not the least, will have been to found a new city bearing his own name, for he had no mean idea of himself. It was of course impossible to rebaptize Rome; so it had to be another town. Zosimus, another Church historian, recounts that the Emperor had no love for Rome, and that the *Senatus populusque romanus* did not love him either, because the ruler, although nominally not a Christian, had not taken part in a pagan ceremony. However this may be, Constantine left the capital in September 326, never to return.[6]

Hesychius offers an explanation that really struck root. It was he who coined the term 'the new Rome' for Constantinople. He states that at that time the affairs of the ancient Rome were steadily declining. [7] "And thus", he concludes his relation. "Constantinople was brought to greatness, because she received the title of 'queen' which she inherited [from Rome] which she wears until the present day." [8] Hesychius was writing in the sixth century, that is, two centuries after the city's foundation. So we cannot be sure that it was called 'the new Rome' right from the start. Yet one thing is certain : this tradition is very old. Another point is that there are evidently dualistic traits in it ; 'old' and 'new' and 'decline' and 'greatness' are contrasted.

2. Imperialistic claims

Although Constantine endowed the Empire with a new capital that would be Christian from the outset, he did not dream of founding a new Empire. What he intended to do was to reestablish and to reinvigorate the existing Roman Empire, thus giving it a new lease of life. [9] Correct as this viewpoint is, the fact that this reinvigoration had to come from the East should not be overlooked. The specific form of universalism that we call 'imperialism' originated in the East. [10] The first Empires were those of Sumer and Akkad, [11] later to be succeeded by the Assyrian [12] and Babylonian Empires, [13] and also by that of the Hittites. [14] Although the extent of these realms was not large, their rulers claimed universal dominance. These Empires were all swallowed up by that of the Persians which became a truly enormous one. [15] Had the centre of gravity lain in the East so far, it now shifted westward, since the successor to the Persian Empire became that of the Macedonians which was larger still. [16] Once again the centre of gravity shifted westward, to Rome, whose Empire was incomparably larger than all the Empires that had preceded it. [17]

We are, however, entitled to ask whether the westward trend was as determining as it seems. Viewed in terms of political power as well in those of civilization, Rome, the capital and imperial centre, stood somewhat on the edge of the ancient world. The Iberians, the Celts, and the Germanic tribes, did not count for much in these respects; the North Africans contributed somewhat more perhaps, but Egypt was the only country here with a really old and important culture. The bulk of the population, the venerable seats of learning, the best educated people, and the old centres of power were all to be found in the East, Egypt included. Thus, when Constantine transferred the capital to Byzantium, imperialism was, by way of speaking, returning home. It was there, on the Bosporus, that Europe and Asia met each other. Today Istanbul, the Islamic successor to Constantinople, is the only city in the world that is situated in two continents.

3. The extent of Zeno's Empire

Would it have been possible for the imperial rulers in the East to maintain or reestablish their grip on the western half of the Empire? Roman power had been crumbling away in the West until in 476 nothing was left of it. When the

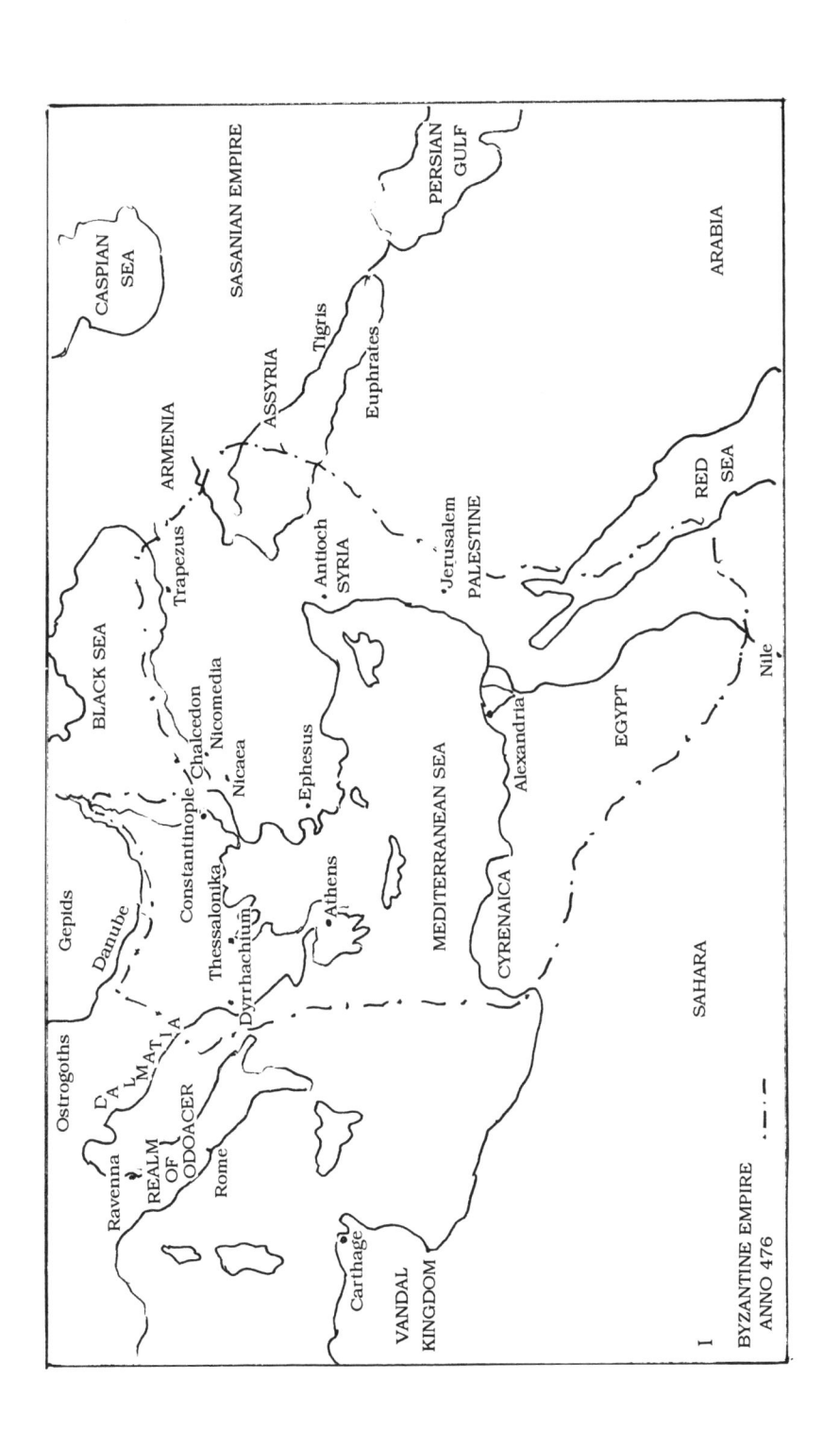

BYZANTINE EMPIRE
ANNO 476

last western Emperor was deposed in that year, Zeno was Emperor (474-491) of what we shall henceforward call 'the Byzantine Empire'; he was not a Greek but an Isaurian, a member of a mountain tribe in the Taurus range. How great was the Empire he ruled?

In the East, beyond the Euphrates, provinces that once belonged to the Roman Empire, had been lost to the Sasanian Empire long ago : Armenia, Assyria, and the south-eastern part of Mesopotamia with Nisibis [18]. The Byzantine-Sasanian frontier ran northward from a point on the upper Euphrates to the most easterly shores of the Black Sea, near Trapezus (Trabzond). That is, if we may speak of a real frontier, since the Roman possession of territories beyond the Euphrates had always been somewhat insecure; in 476 only north-west Mesopotamia was in Byzantine hands. For the time being and as long as it would last, all was quiet on the eastern front. In the East the Byzantine Empire encompassed all of Asia Minor as well as Syria and Palestine. In North Africa Egypt and Cyrenaica (Libya) belonged to it; Germanic tribes had not ventured so far.

The situation in the Balkans had long been far less stable. In 395 the Visigoths arrived. In the graphic words of Gibbon, "the barriers of the Danube were thrown open; the savage warriors of Scythia issued from their forests". [19] For fifteen long years the whole of the Balkans, up to the very walls of Constantinople, were harassed by these barbarians, until their king Alaric decided that Rome would be a better prey; they went thither and plundered the city in 410. [20] The heritage of this period was the presence of large numbers of Goths, who were Arians, in the Byzantine army. The next unwelcome visitors were the Mongolians who also raided the entire Balkan area and even showed up at the capital. But they too, led by the infamous Attila, turned westward, but could not conquer the West. They were defeated, Attila died, and the Hunnic Empire disappeared off the map.

It was not yet over. Towards the end of the fifth century, the Ostrogoths under their king Theodoric invaded the Balkans; for the third time in this century the capital was under threat. But Zeno, the Emperor, made a clever move. He promised Italy to Theodoric, 'whom he did not like', says Jordanes, [21] if only he could conquer it. Theodoric succeeded in doing this; he defeated

Odoacer, who was 'king of the Germans in Italy'. [22] That was in 491. Ravenna, not Rome, became the residence of Italy's new king. To the population of Italy Theodoric was not their lawful ruler but a usurper. He had been proclaimed king by his men "without waiting for directions from the new *princeps*" (Zeno's successor was Anastasius I, 491-518). [23] Realizing how the land lay, Theodoric asked Anastasius for the imperial insignia that Odoacer had sent to Constantinople in 476. After much bickering the Byzantine ruler acknowledged him as Italy's ruler. The Ostrogoth did not receive the insignia but, instead, became viceroy of the Emperor. Anastasius had rather have this Arian king in Italy than in the Balkans; he was prepared to pay a price for it.

Around 500 the situation in the Balkans had become relatively stable. The northern frontier followed the course of the Danube from the Black Sea to the confluence of the Sava and the Danube and from there turned sharply southward, in modern terms roughly between Croatia on the one (non-Byzantine) side and Bosnia and Serbia on the other (which means, in terms of Roman provinces, that Dalmatia had remained in Ostrogoth hands). The frontier reached the Adriatic north of Dyrrhachium (Dürres), that is, at the northern tip of the modern Albania. North of the Danube, Dacia (the modern Romania) had been lost long ago.

4. Theodora

That Anastasius had recognized Theodoric as the legal king of Italy did not necessarily mean that Constantinople had renounced its claim to rule the West as it did the East. In 468 an attempt had already been made to wrest Tunisia from the hands of the Vandals, but the naval expedition had failed dismally. Further attempts had to wait until the Empire was in stronger hands. These days came when Justinian I (527-565) succeeded to the throne. Like his predecessors, he was not a native Greek but an Illyrian or Albanian, a Romanized one, for his vernacular was Latin.

Justinian was a remarkable person, but perhaps his wife, Theodora, was more remarkable still. Most of what we know about her comes from the vitriolic pen of the historian Procopius who did not know whom he hated more fiercely, the Emperor or the Empress. We therefore have to take what he writes of her with more than just a grain of salt. He says himself that describing them meant an unpleasant and very difficult task that caused him to violently tremble [24]. Not the best guarantee for an objective treatment!

The tourist who stands admiringly before the marvellous sixth-century mosaic in the choir of San Vitale in Ravenna, which depicts Theodora, does not see the whole reality. What he sees is an Empress decked out in imperial glory. On her left stand her maids of honour, on her right two clerics. The group, posing as though for a photograph, is still in the forecourt of a church but on the point of entering it. Theodora wears a precious diadem with ropes of pearls hanging down from it. Around her head is a nimbus. She carries a golden chalice in her hands, which she is obviously bringing to the altar of the church. That an offering is meant is shown by an embroidering on the fringe of her stately robe depicting the Three Kings with their gifts. Theodora is portrayed as important, distinguished, wealthy, and above all pious. What the tourist does not see is the unedifying story behind this splendour.

For this tale we have to rely on Procopius' account who, as Browning states, "though inspired by bitter hostility and full of damaging imputations, is probably trustworthy in its main facts." [25] Posing as a puritanical moralist, he relates, with obvious relish, bawdy stories about Theodora's youthful misbehaviour. In order to discover her origin we have to descend to the lowest social layers of the society of the capital. Her father was a bear-keeper (bears performed on the streets and in shows). Given the names, the family was in all probability Greek. Her father died early, leaving his wife and her three daughters destitute behind. The eldest girl soon found work on the stage, taking her little sister Theodora with her as her servant. In those days the difference between actresses and prostitutes was not great, and although Theodora was too young [26] to have sexual intercourse, we soon find her in a brothel where she learned all the ins and outs of the trade, 'ready for all lascivious services'.

Once old enough, she too appeared on the stage. Witty and animated as she was, she possessed an evident *vis comica*, acting in vaudevilles which involved a fair amount of strip-tease. She was none too prude, of course. After the performances she was often picked up by young men from the *jeunesse dorée* of the capital with whom she then duly slept. Occasionally she got pregnant, but a child was never born; she was an all-rounder, really.

Clever and ambitious as she was, she slowly but certainly slept her way to the top. In due time she became the concubine of a high government official and accompanied him to North Africa when he became governor of a province there. But her tongue was too sharp for her protector's taste, and she had to go. Procopius says that she saw no other way for earning her livelihood than to act as an ordinary prostitute (which she had not been so far), first in Alexandria, then everywhere in the Near East, and finally back again in Constantinople. "Thus was born and raised that woman, spoken ill of by many whores and all people." [27]. However, in the meantime a great change had come over her.

According to an ancient anonymous source, Theodora, while still in the Orient, had a vision prophecying that she would become the wife of a great potentate. [28] She seems to have undergone some sort of religious conversion. Anyhow, back in the capital she began to lead a decent life. She now lived in a small private house and earned her income by spinning wool. She made the acquaintance of some clerics and probably under their influence began to lean towards Monophysitism. Gibbon says that she "assumed, like a skilful actress, a decent character", in other words, that her new behaviour was a sham. [29] Yet it is also conceivable that she was really fed up with her way of life and that her bad reputation worried her. Procopius relates that the better-off had shunned her as if she were contagious. [30]

It was then, around 520, that she met Justinian. The future Emperor, a nephew of the reigning monarch Justin I (518-527), was born in 482. Since Justin had no son, his nephew was destined for the throne. His uncle had made him a *patricius*, the highest possible rank for a subject. He had grown to be a rather cool man, friendly but unapproachable, a hard worker with a thorough knowledge of the files. When he met Theodora for the first time, he must have been about thirty-eight or forty years old. And he could trust his eyes, for she was exceedingly beautiful. Even the spiteful Procopius admits that she had a beautiful face and that she was charming. [31] No wonder then that the Crown Prince was immediately captivated by her beauty.

Theodora now became what the French would call the *maîtresse en titre* of Justinian. He even persuaded his uncle to bestow on her the title of Patrician. Yet he could not marry her, since he already had a wife, the Princess Euphemia. This insignificant lady had always complied with all the wishes of her husband, but she remained steadfast on one point only : no Theodora in the palace! However, she conveniently died in 524; a year later the Crown Prince married his paramour in the Aya Sofia. In 527 Justin made his nephew co-Emperor; he died soon after. Theodora was now Empress; the bear-keeper's daughter had risen as high as was humanly possible. Her husband doubtless knew of her scandalous reputation, but he did not err in his judgment. She remained faithful to him all her married life (she died in 548). She had a keen eye for politics and was made of a somewhat tougher fibre than her husband so that she became a real support for him in moments of crisis.

5. The grand design

Louis Bréhier entitles the first part of his book on the Byzantine Empire 'the universal Roman Empire'. [32] It was Justinian's great aim to restore the unity of the Roman Empire; was he not the successor of Caesar and Augustus and of all the great monarchs who had held sway over all the lands from the Euphrates to the Rhine and from the Sahara to the Danube and beyond? He saw the Germanic kings who now ruled the West as his vassals with no right to reign as sovereign princes. It was, again, an instance of the dualistic opposition of universalism and particularism.

The Emperor had yet another reason for reconquering the West. Almost all those Germanic usurper kings were Arians, heretics, that is. And it was the religious duty of the Christian Emperor to guarantee the unity of the faith. In the words of an ancient text, the united Roman Empire had once reached to the shores of two oceans, and the Romans [the westerners] had lost it through their carelessness. [33] It deserves attention that the direction of the conquest was now reversed : no longer was it from west to east but from east to west, which was the original direction.

PART II THE CONQUEST OF NORTH AFRICA

1. Mounting tension

Justinian's first target was the Vandal kingdom in North Africa. [34] Tension between Constantinople and Carthage had been mounting since Gelimer had become king of the Vandals (530-534) after deposing the Rome-friendly Hilderic (523-530). [35] Gelimer was a fanatical Arian who, in contrast to his mild predecessor, repressed the orthodox. Bishops and other refugees fled to the eastern capital and related how Gelimer was persecuting their co-religionists. Justinian sent two ambassadors to Carthage in order to remonstrate with Gelimer, but the king treated them in a dishonourable fashion and sent them back with empty hands. A second envoy visited but had to return with a letter in which the king unequivocally told the Emperor to mind his own business. And, says Procopius, "the Emperor, who was already angry with Gelimer, after the receipt of this letter decided to undertake a campaign of revenge against him." [36]

2. The decision to fight

The war was popular with the populace of the capital who, being exempt from military service, would not have to fight. [37] But the more responsible citizens were far from happy with the idea. They remembered only too well the disastrous outcome of the first campaign against the Vandals in 468. [38] Financial experts feared that the costs of the expedition would be unbearably high, while the soldiers, with several campaigns against the Persians behind them, did not relish the idea of having to fight in a country that was totally unknown to them. John the Cappadocian, the *praefectus praetorio*, voiced this discontent in a courageous speech to the Emperor. He pointed out that, in addition to conquering North Africa, it would be necessary to occupy Sicily and Italy too - which seems to have been exactly the Emperor's intention.

If we may believe Procopius, Justinian showed himself to be convinced by these arguments and was ready to renounce his plans. But then an oriental bishop told him that he had had a vision in a dream. God had ordered him to reproach the monarch that he was coming back on his promise to liberate the orthodox of North Africa. "I will", the Lord had said, "assist him in the war myself and make him master of Libya." On hearing this, Justinian hesitated no longer and decided to fight. [39]

3. The landing in North Africa and the chances of war

The Emperor entrusted the command of the campaign to count Belisarius, an experienced general, who had already fought against the Persians. On the 22nd July 533 an enormous armada left the capital. Ninety-two men-of-war escorted five hundred transport ships manned by twenty thousand sailors and carrying twenty thousand infantry and some five or six thousand cavalry. On board was also Procopius the historian; he frankly confessed that the undertaking struck fear into him. [40] After a difficult crossing lasting three months, Belisarius landed his troops mid September at Caput Vada, the modern Rass Kaboudia, a cape about a hundred and thirty miles south of Carthage. [41]

Did Belisarius' opponent stand a chance against him? Diehl describes Gelimer as being 'of an indecisive and weak nature, nervous and sentimental'. [42] The news that the Byzantines were coming had immediately led to revolts in the province of Tripolis and in Sardinia, and Gelimer had weakened his initial position by sending his best land and naval forces to Sardinia to suppress the rebellion there. Furthermore, the African Vandals were no longer the hardened warriors they had been when they arrived there a century earlier. According to Procopius, they were the most effeminate nation he knew; the greater part of them lived in sumptuous villas, "as real parasites passing their time in festivities and mightily enjoying the pleasures of love." [43] In addition to this they lived in the midst of a hostile population; in 533 their numbers cannot have been more than some two hundred thousand. [44]

Although Gelimer's strategic position was not brilliant, he had, thinks Diehl, a reasonable chance of effectively resisting the Byzantine onslaught. He could with his excellent light cavalry have harassed the enemy so much in guerila warfare that they might have preferred to depart. Instead, he did the one thing he should not have done : confront them in open battles. [45] On the 13th of September the Vandal king tried to stop the Byzantine march on his capital at Decimum, thirty miles to the south of it, but was defeated. [46] Two days later Belisarius' troops entered Carthage without encountering resistance; the remaining Vandals sought refuge in the churches, but the orthodox had illuminated the streets. Belisarius made straight for the royal palace and sat down on Gelimer's throne, [47] thus symbolically taking possession of the Vandal kingdom. Then he was brought a breakfast in the great dining hall of the palace. [48]

4. The end of the Vandal kingdom

However, the Vandals had lost a battle and their capital but not yet the war. Gelimer mustered as many men as he could and called back the expeditionary force from Sardinia that had just succeeded in quelling the rebellion there. [49] However, attempts to recover the capital failed dismally. [50] Belisarius then marched out and found Gelimer's army at Tricameron, about nineteen miles from Carthage. There the Vandals were defeated for a second time. [51] Among the booty were the cult objects that Titus had brought to Rome from the Temple of Jerusalem in A.D. 70 and which had fallen into Vandal hands when they plundered Rome in 455. According to Procopius, Justinian had them sent back to Jerusalem. [52]

Seeing his troops being routed, Gelimer fled southward on horseback, leaving his family and his treasures to the hands of the victors. Months later, in March 534, he surrendered to Belisarius and was sent to Constantinople. Procopius graphically describes how he had to march through the streets of the imperial city with the purple mantle on his shoulders. He did not shed a tear and let not even a sigh be heard. Yet when he arrived before the throne of Justinian in the hippodrome, he said repeatedly : "Vanity of vanities, and all is vanity". The mantle was taken from his shoulders and he had to prostrate himself before the throne. [53] The kingdom of the Vandals had come to an end.

5. The fighting goes on

The Emperor was triumphant. "God, in his mercy, gave us not only Africa and all her provinces but also returned our imperial insignia which had been taken away by the Vandals when they took Rome." [54] Yet Justinianus exulted too early. To cut a long story short, the war in North Africa lasted another fifteen years, until 548. It is true that the superior Byzantine navy succeeded in securing Corsica, Sardinia, and the Balearic islands, but the grip of the conquerors on the former Vandal kingdom was not particularly strong, especially not on Numidia. As soon as Belisarius' ships had weighed anchor, the Berbers of Numidia rose in revolt, subjecting the remaining Byzantine forces to heavy losses. Reinforcements had to be sent. [55]

"Those 'naked Maurusians [Berbers]', as Belisarius had contemptuously called them, [56] caused the Byzantines more trouble than all the forces of the Vandal kingdom together." [57] The heavily armed imperial troops proved no match for the rapid Berber cavalry, which resorted to hit-and-run raids. Yet from time to time almost regular battles took place. The author Corippus describes these battles in a long Latin poem in which it is hard to distinguish *Wahrheit und Dichtung*. At one moment the Berbers were on the point of recapturing Carthage; Belisarius arrived just in time to save it. [58]

Only five years after the beginning of the revolt, in 539, an able Byzantine general, the *patricius* Solomon, succeeded in pacifying Numidia. He boldly penetrated into the Aurès mountains, the heartland of the resistance, and forced the rebel chiefs to recognize the Emperor as their suzerain. [59] Once again a note of triumph was sounded. "Since then all the Libyans [North Africans], in as far as they were under Roman [Byzantine] dominion, enjoyed a stable peace and also [the benefits of] Solomon's clever and very moderate rule, so that they no longer thought of war and felt themselves to be the happiest of men." [60]

This euphoria, if it really existed, did not last for long. The Berbers were not to be trusted, as Procopius knew. "They are a thoroughly fickle nation and, therefore, full of mistrust against the whole world ... Since they are not even capable of remaining faithful to one another, they also have no confidence in whomsoever and will compulsorily view their fellow-beings with suspicion." [61]. This is the characteristic way of speaking of imperialists who simply cannot comprehend that a nation may want to preserve its independence, although it could have the blessings of being part of an Empire.

6. Byzantine misrule

In 541 African envoys arrived in the capital to pay homage to the Emperor telling him that the country had recovered its ancient prosperity under his benevolent rule. But "unfortunately appearances were more brilliant than the reality." [62] In 543 Justinian appointed a nephew, Sergius, as governor of the former kingdom of the Vandals. He could not have made a worse choice. Sergius was the prototype of the arrogant colonial administrator without any understanding for the people he had to govern. "It was he above all who was guilty of all the misfortunes that befell the Libyan [North African] nation." His own soldiers despised him because he looked down on them; they found him a coward and a degenerate. [63]

Soon chiefs of the most important tribe came to Sergius to complain of the rude behaviour of the Byzantine troops. Feeling that their commander was being threatened, his guards massacred the whole party after the interview, with the exception of one who escaped. It did not last long before all the tribes revolted. Again years of the greatest confusion followed. In 544 the experienced Solomon took command again but was defeated on the frontiers of Numidia. His army, behaving dishonourably, took to its heels, deserting him. The general was surrounded by enemy soldiers and perished together with his guards who themselves fought to the death. [64]

7. The final victory

For the time being the Berbers were lord and master of the whole country; they pillaged and burned everywhere, while the discouraged Byzantines were in no position to defend the population. Thinking back to the days of Belisarius, Procopius sighed that "now all had been lost in such a way that it made no difference then, if nothing at all would have happened [i.e. of the first Byzantine victories]." [65] However, in 546 Justinian made the right choice at last, for he made Johannes Troglita commander-in-chief in North Africa. Corippus, a North African himself, but not a Vandal - his full name was Flaccus Cresconius Corippus -, born ca. 500 as an inhabitant of the Vandal kingdom, almost stumbles over his words when it comes to praise the new commander. This is not surprising since he, a poor teacher in the countryside, wrote his *De bellis lybicis*, an epic of five thousand (mediocre) hexameters exactly to please this Johannes. [66] The poet compared his hero at length to that other hero, Aeneas. [67]

The new general arrived at the end of the year 546 with large reinforcements in North Africa. [68] He kept the often seditious Byzantine troops firmly under control and conducted the war with an iron hand. He was also a subtle diplomat who succeeded in winning over various indigenous chiefs. [69] In two years of often desperate fighting Johannes succeeded in quelling the rebellion. In the spring of 548 it was all over; North Africa had been pacified. Procopius was under no illusion about what this 'pacification' meant. Although he may have been exaggerating, after fifteen years of warfare the condition of what once was a prosperous kingdom was disastrous. The Vandal nation hardly existed anymore, while the Berbers also had suffered enormous losses. The cost in human life had been very great for the Byzantine troops too. Large parts of the country were almost entirely depopulated. [70]

PART III THE CONQUEST OF ITALY

1. Justinian's second target

Justinian was one of those imprudent rulers who are not content with having only one war on their hands. For a long time he engaged in war on two, and sometimes even on three fronts. The war in North Africa was not yet over when he ordered the invasion in Italy. And at the same time he had to fight the Persians in the East. It is true that much of the oriental problem was due to Persian aggressiveness, but it would have been a more sensible policy if the Byzantines had left Italy for what it was for the time being and had restricted themselves to solving the eastern problem, either *manu militari* or by means of diplomacy. Justinian, however, was not prepared to relinquish his great plans for recovering the West.

2. The Ostrogothic kingdom in Italy

Justinian's second target was the Ostrogothic kingdom in Italy. Basically the Emperor had every reason to be satisfied with the situation on the other side of the Adriatic. Its king, Theodoric the Great (493-526), although being illiterate himself, was the protector of the Roman civilization which he admired. In Rome the Senate was still in session as though nothing had changed. In his days celebrities such as Cassiodorus and Boethius were found at his court. He might have been a 'barbarian', but he was not a brute; he tried to be an honest and just ruler. His relations with the Byzantine Empire were, at least officially, excellent. His claim to Italy had been acknowledged by Constantinople; he was the Emperor's viceroy as well as a *patricius*.

Yet there was a hitch in the clock. Theodoric was an Arian, just as his Ostrogoths. Although this Arian king did not oppress the indigenous orthodox population as his Vandal colleagues in North Africa had done, this Christian population did not love him. An additional sore point was that Rome was the seat of the papacy. There were in fact two centres, two focuses of interest in Italy : Ravenna where the court resided, and Rome where the Pope and the

Senate were at home. Constantinople was naturally more in sympathy with Rome than with Ravenna; it also suspected Theodoric of having ambitions. [71] Procopius, who has much praise for him, says that he declined to call himself Emperor and contented himself with the title of *rex*, but that he ruled as if he was an emperor. [72]

3. Problems about the succession of Theodoric

When Theodoric died on the 30th of August 526, he was succeeded by his eight-year-old son Athalaric; his mother Amalasuntha (Amalaswintha) acted as his guardian and as regent. [73] This woman was as much of a Roman as was possible for an Ostrogoth; she gave her son a Roman education, which was not to the taste of the Gothic nobles. They told her that Theodoric had become king of such a great country without ever having heard of grammar. The young king went the wrong way under the influence of the Gothic youths who became his companions and became a profligate. He never really ruled, since he died in 534 when he was only sixteen years old. [74]

This made Amalasuntha's position now highly insecure. She therefore began secret negotiations with Justinian telling him that she was ready to secede Italy to him. The Emperor then sent Peter, a skilful diplomat, to Italy in order to come to an agreement with the Ostrogothic queen. [75] Peter found Italy in a state of confusion. Amalasuntha had changed her mind and now planned to marry a Gothic nobleman, Theodatus (Theodahad). This ambitious and unscrupulous man was her opponent and her enemy, but she hoped to win him over by making him her husband and, in consequence, King of Italy. The wedding took place indeed, but soon he placed his wife under arrest. The poor woman was interned on a small island in the middle of a lake where some thugs killed her, [76] whether or not at the instigation of her loving consort, but surely with his approval.

Ever ready to believe the worst of his arch-enemy Theodora, Procopius believed that she was behind it, out of jealousy, because she feared the Ostrogothic queen might come to the capital and there make an all too favourable impression on her husband whom she found fickle. [77] However, if we apply the old juridical rule of *cui bono*, who profits by it, the suspect is rather Theodatus who now became the sole ruler of Italy. Hearing of the queen's murder, Peter stated that this was tantamount to a declaration of war. [78] In this way the Ostrogoths provided Justinian with a motive to wage war on them. [79]

4. The successful phase of the Italian campaign

The war began in the autumn of 535 with the occupation by the Byzantines of the Ostrogothic territories in Dalmatia, roughly equivalent to the western part of modern Croatia; [80] the whole of the eastern coast of the Adriatic, from the peninsula of Istria southward, was now in Byzantine hands. In the same period Belisarius landed with imperial troops in Sicily and overran the Gothic garrisons there. On December 31st 535 he triumphantly entered Syracuse.

We see the shadow of the Franks already falling over Europe, since both the Ostrogoths and the Byzantines competed for their friendship; Justinian invited them to become his allies. In his letter to them he stated that Italy was his property, which the Goths had taken away from him. He saw the Franks as his natural allies since they too were orthodox, in contrast to the Ostrogoths who were Arians. He sent them money; in return they promised their help. [81] However, Theodatus also wanted to form an alliance with the Franks. Fearing that Belisarius would land in Italy, he sent them a large amount of money and promised them the territories that the Goths possessed in Gallia (the Provence and the French Riviera), if they would assist him. [82] The Franks pocketed the money from both sides and remained neutral for the time being.

Seeing his kingdom threatened in the north-east and in the south-west, Theodatus began to find his situation desperate. He was an incapable man, not the one his people needed in these dire straits. He was no longer young and was not fond of the idea of having to go to war. In no uncertain terms he declared that he understood nothing of war and warfare; he would rather be a peasant than have the troubles of a king. [83] It did not help him, neither in the eyes of his own nation nor in those of the indigenous Latin

II ----
THE BYZANTINE EMPIRE
IN 563

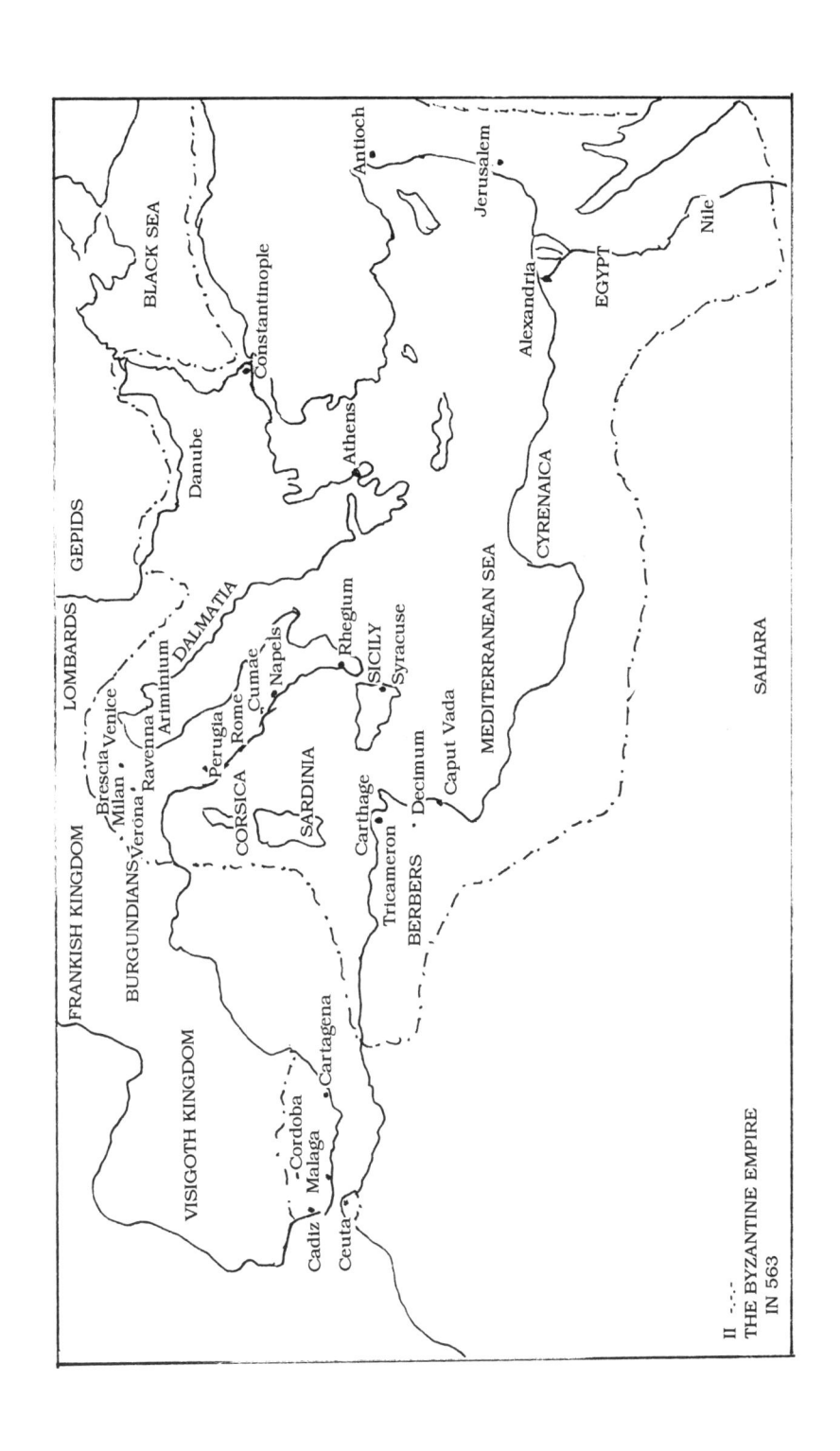

population, that he prided himself on his knowledge of Latin literature and Platonic philosophy. [84] He was a weakling whom the wily Peter made more afraid still; he imagined himself already walking in chains through the streets of Constantinople. [85] In his desperate need Theodatus made an wholly unexpected move : he sent Pope Agapitus I (535-536) to Constantinople to intercede for him with the Emperor. How curious that this Arian ruler implored the help of the orthodox Pontiff! Nothing came of it, for soon after his arrival in the capital early in 536 the Pope died there.

In the spring of that year Belisarius, coming from Messina, landed in Italy near Reggio di Calabria (Rhegium). It is remarkable that the conquerors followed exactly the same route as the Allies in 1943, when they attacked what Churchill called 'the soft underbelly of Europe' : first North Africa, then Sicily, then Italy. The indigenous population immediately chose the side of the invaders. Without meeting any resistance Belisarius reached Naples, the first town with a strong Gothic garrison. The native inhabitants sent an emissary to Belisarius asking him not to storm the city : it could easily go wrong. It was far more advisable to defeat Theodatus in the open field and capture Rome. Then Naples and all other cities would capitulate to him. But Belisarius haughtily answered that he needed no advice from the Neapolitans, from civilians, he meant. The still mainly Greek population, fearing the Gothic garrison more than the Byzantine besiegers, then decided to resist. Belisarius had the walls stormed more than once, but the assailants were repulsed every time with heavy losses. [86] When the besieged asked the Ostrogothic king for help, he did no more than consult the oracles.

Belisarius was already thinking of giving up and marching on Rome, when he was shown a dry tunnel of the waterworks leading underneath the walls into the town. [87] Covered by the darkness of the night, four hundred Byzantine soldiers passed through this tunnel; undetected they arrived under a garden in the town centre. The walls of the exit, however, were too steep for them to get out. However, then a soldier succeeded in climbing up the wall using his hands and feet. In the garden stood an olive tree to which he fastened a rope. Using this rope, all the men got out of the pit one by one. Then they captured two wall towers, cutting down the unsuspecting sentinels;

soon the Byzantines streamed into the town. There was much looting and massacring until this was stopped by Belisarius. [88]

The catastrophe of Naples backfired on Theodatus. In November 536 a Gothic army assembly deposed the king and chose a certain Wittigis as his successor. Hearing this, Theodatus fled northward to Ravenna, but was killed by an Ostrogoth before he got there. The brand new king was not really a good choice, being just as devoid of military and political capacities as his predecessor; it was not much of an asset that he had always been a good soldier. He began his reign with an irreparable blunder. He went to Rome but did not stay there to confront the Byzantines. Instead, he made Pope Silverius (536-537) and the senators swear that they would remain faithful to the Gothic nation. There was never much love lost between that nation - and the other Germanic tribes - and the indigenous population; they thoroughly distrusted another.

Leaving four thousand men behind for the defence of the city, Wittigis hastened to Ravenna, the Ostrogothic capital. His main reason to go there was that he wanted to marry Matasuntha, the daughter of Queen Amalasuntha. This union was intended to fortify his position, since he was a commoner and not a noble; it would connect him with the House of Theodoric. The wedding took place indeed, although the bride demurred; [89] as the chronicles express it, he became her partner 'through duress rather than affection'. [90] He bought off a possible intervention by Franks by now actually ceding the Provence to them. [91]

Meanwhile Belisarius marched on Rome. Its Latin population had not the slightest intention of keeping the oath sworn to Wittigis and was ready to open the gates for the Byzantines. The Ostrogothic garrison, judging the defence hopeless under these circumstances, left the city through the Porta Flaminia in the north, while the imperial troops marched in through the Porta Asinaria in the south. The date was the ninth of December 536; Belisarius sent the keys of the city to the Emperor. After sixty years, Procopius states solemnly, Rome was 'Roman' again. [92] Having achieved this easy success, the Byzantines pushed further north and occupied the whole of Tuscany. [93]

5. The Ostrogothic counter-offensive

Threatened with the loss of his whole kingdom, Wittigis awoke from his torpor and became, in the words, of Jordanes, 'a furious lion'. [94] With a large army, thrice as big as the force of five thousand men with which Belisarius guarded Rome, he marched southward. He attacked the Byzantine troops before the walls of Rome and beat them back into the city. If he had hoped to take it by surprise, he had missed his chance. It was now March 537. [95] The siege lasted a whole year. Both sides suffered badly from starvation and diseases, just as the Roman population itself. There was often heavy fighting. Time after time the Goths stormed the walls, but always in vain. Belisarius was everywhere, performing miracles of valour, endurance, and resourcefulness. At the same time he needed all his diplomatic skill to calm the civilian population down, for it had become restless during the long siege. "[They] felt the lack of their usual baths and the want of the most necessary things very bitterly; without sleep they had to guard the walls night and day." [96]

Although Belisarius had been greeted as a liberator, little was needed to stir up bad feeling between East and West. The following incident is an instance of this friction. The reigning bishop of Rome, Silverius, was accused of connivance with the Goths. Witnesses testified against him; he himself subscribed a confession to this effect. The background of this was probably that he had been Theodatus' candidate for the papacy. In the tense atmosphere of the beleaguered city, suspicion was soon rife. The hapless bishop was cited before the Byzantine commander. Yet it was not he but the general's imperious wife Antonina who indicted him. She was a close friend of the Empress Theodora and came from the same unsavoury background. [97] We may therefore safely suspect that Theodora had something to do with Silverius' fall; it is not unthinkable that she found him too orthodox to her taste.

However, this may be, the bishop was duly condemned, stripped of his pontifical robes, clad in a monk's habit, and shipped off to exile in the East. The obedient clergy then chose, as his successor, the imperial candidate, Vigilius, a deacon (537-555), who, it was said, had bribed his way to the papal throne.[98] It was a historical event in so far that never before had a Pope been deposed by the secular arm. The affair proved that Constantinople wanted to keep a firm hand on the Latin Church.

The tides of war were slowly turning against the besiegers. Their manpower was constantly being depleted by casualties and illnesses,[99] while reinforcements from the East could freely enter the city since the imperial navy commanded the seas.[100] In March 538 Belisarius succeeded in dispatching John, one of his generals, northward with a considerable contingent of troops; the nickname of that general was the 'Sanguinary', an epithet that, as Gibbon remarks, "might do honour to a tiger".[101] Without meeting much resistance John could take Ariminium (Rimini) on the Adriatic coast. Since this town was not far from Ravenna, the Ostrogothic beleaguering force began to withdraw from Rome. Belisarius, once again free in his movements, followed Wittigis to the north where he laid siege to Ariminium; strong Byzantine reinforcements arrived in June.[102] With these fresh troops Belisarius launched himself on the besiegers of Ariminium and forced them to withdraw.[103]

6. A Frankish intervention

However, the victorious Byzantines now suffered a serious setback. In the spring of 538 a Byzantine task force, dispatched by Belisarius from Rome, had landed on the coast of Liguria and captured Milan with the help of its Latin population. At that moment, the Franks, or rather their allies the Burgundians, entered the fray. An army of ten thousand soldiers of this Germanic tribe invaded Italy, which they could hardly have done without the consent of Theodebert I (533-548, he was a grandson of Clovis), king of the Austrasian Franks. In cooperation with the Ostrogoths they laid siege to Milan. The Franks were quickly becoming the new imperialist nation in the West. Procopius says they believed that they could appropriate the larger part of Italy without trouble, since both Goths and Byzantines were weakened by the war. "They found it intolerable that others would fight for so long for the possession of a country so near to their own, while they had only to look on quietly and keep out of the affair." [104]

Before the Byzantines had had time to react, Milan was taken and submitted to a horrible ordeal. The town was largely destroyed; all the men capable of carrying arms were massacred, and all the womanfolk were presented to the Burgundians out of gratitude for their assistance. Soon enough the whole of Liguria was again in the hands of the Ostrogoths; it was the spring of 539. [105] The Byzantine historiographer Agathias, who lived a generation later, writes that Theodebert felt deeply insulted, because Justinian posed as the sovereign of all the Germanic nations in the West; he even threatened to bring the war to the gates of Constantinople. Yet before he could execute this grand design, he was killed by a wild bull during a hunt. [106]

7. The reduction of the Ostrogothic kingdom

In spite of this setback in the valley of the Po, Belisarius methodically proceeded with the reduction of what remained of the Ostrogothic kingdom. At the end of 539 he invested Ravenna. Curiously enough, the outlook was far from rosy for either party. Wittigis realized that he was soon to lose his capital. And Belisarius feared a new invasion of the valley of the Po by the Franks. He knew that Justinian needed him on the eastern front. Since the Emperor found this front more important than the Italian one, he was prepared to conclude a peace treaty with Wittigis according to which this king would be allowed to keep Italy north of the Po. When the imperial envoys arrived in the army camp before Ravenna with the concept-treaty, Belisarius was furious, for he had not been notified of the Emperor's plans. He saw himself deprived of his hope to send the Ostrogothic king to Constantinople in chains. And he duly refused to sign the treaty.

The Ostrogoth commanders, who had enough of their incompetent king, now hatched a most curious plan. Fearing that the Ostrogothic nation would be deported to the Balkans in the event of a final defeat, they decided to offer Belisarius the imperial dignity. As far as I know, this is the first time that a Germanic nation thought it could dispose of the imperial crown. But the Byzantine commander remained steadfastly loyal to his sovereign and refused to become the ruler of a new Western Empire.

Was there a remarkable change beginning to stand out against the historical horizon? Two of the most powerful Germanic nations were toying with the idea of Empire. We do not know whether the Frankish kings were consciously thinking of it, but deeply in their minds it must have been already present. And now we see the Ostrogoths moving in the same direction, since they wanted to have an Emperor of their own, and perhaps even for the West. A change is also detectable in the character of the dualistic conflict. It was basically, as I explained above, a conflict between universalism (the Byzantine imperialism) and particularism (the existence of separate Germanic states in the West which was not to be tolerated by Constantinople). But now it was slowly becoming possible that it would be transformed into a conflict between two universalisms.

The wily, and none too honest, Byzantine general now entered, as Gibbon has it, "into a dark and crooked path, as it might lead to the voluntary submission of the Goths." [107] He let the Goths know that he would be happy to accept their offer; they had only to open the gates of Ravenna to him so that he could march in as the new Emperor. And so it happened! Procopius, who was an eye-witness to the triumphant entry of the Byzantines into the town, was so astonished by this totally unexpected event that he said it must be the work of a superhuman power. But for the Ostrogothic women it was rather the result of the cowardice of their own soldiers whom they spat contemptuously in the face. Belisarius then revealed to the duped Goths that he had not the slightest intention of becoming their Emperor. Ravenna, no longer the Ostrogothic capital now, acquired a strong Byzantine garrison. All this happened in May 540. [108] Shortly afterwards Belisarius returned to Constantinople taking Wittigis and the royal treasure with him. The war that by now had lasted five years seemed to have come to a successful end.

8. New hope for the Ostrogoths

However, the recall of Belisarius, who was needed on the oriental front, gave the Ostrogoths new hope; they still maintained considerable forces in the region between the Po and the Alps. This part of Italy, with the important city of Milan, was firmly in their hands. In the autumn of 541 an Ostrogothic army assembly chose a certain Totila as their king, a very able man.[109] The Byzantines soon got to feel that the Gothic command was in strong hands now, for they failed to take Verona.[110] Somewhat later King Totila started a powerful counter-offensive. His armies swept southward through the whole length of the boot, conquering Naples in the spring of 543.[111]

We may believe Procopius when he writes that these developments worried the Emperor greatly. To remedy the situation, Belisarius was recalled from the Persian front and sent to Italy for a second time.[112] He arrived in Ravenna in the summer of 544 to confront a not yet desperate but in any case very serious situation.[113] However, it soon appeared that the forces at his disposal were too weak to redress it. He implored Justinian to send him considerable reinforcements. In the meantime Totila went from strength to strength.[114] At the end of 545 fresh Byzantine troops began to arrive, but at the same time Totila appeared before Rome and began to invest it.[115] Pope Vigilius, who was in Sicily, sent a fleet with provisions in order to succour the starving population, but it sailed straight into the hands of the beleaguerers.[116]

Belisarius who, to add to the misfortune, had fallen ill, was unable to relieve the town. On December 17th 546 Totila triumphantly entered the city. The king went straight to the Saint Peter to pray; on his way there his soldiers killed everyone they found on their way, six hundred and eighty soldiers and civilians. Later, Totila forbade further killings but gave the town over to his soldiery to pillage it, which they did thoroughly.[117] Totila now believed himself to be in a position to successfully end the war. He proposed to Justinian that he should recognize him as King of Italy in exchange for which he was ready to recognize the Emperor as his suzerain. But Justinian refused.[118]

As a result Totila decided to combat the Byzantines in southern Italy. Having too few troops at his disposal to garrison Rome, he resolved to raze it to the ground and turn it it 'into a sheep-walk'. Hearing of this, Belisarius sent him a letter in which he presented him with a choice : either he would win the war, but then have destroyed his best possession, or he would lose it, but in that case he might not expect clemency from the victor. The king then decided to spare the town. [119] After he had departed with the bulk of his forces to the south in the spring of 547, Belisarius recaptured it, finding only an 'all but inhabitable wreck'. [120]

The fortunes of war waged to and fro now, but on the whole Belisarius was unable to dislodge the Goths from their strongholds. [121] And the Emperor did not send sufficient reinforcements for which Pope Vigilius, who was in Constantinople then, ardently implored him. [122] It must be admitted that Justinian was hard-pressed, not only on the eastern front, but also on the Danube frontier from where Gepids and Langobards raided the Balkans. [123]

Once again the unfortunate Belisarius fell into disfavour with his lord; in the beginning of 549 he was recalled, never to have another command. [124] Totila, however, went from strength to strength. He again invested Rome in the summer of 549 and took it through treason on January 16th 550. [125] His position had become stronger than ever. What was in Byzantine hands still was the island of Sicily, Ravenna, and a number of strongholds on the southern coast. In view of this, Totila, for the second time, proposed peace, but again the Emperor refused; he had too much invested in the Italian campaign, now in its sixteenth year, to abandon it. It would have meant a major defeat.

However, Totila was also not without problems. The Franks were strengthening their grip on northern Italy, even pressing as far as Venice. [126] And the Ostrogothic king had no forces to spare to stop them. He asked King Theodebert of the Franks for the hand of his daughter, but was flatly rebuffed. [127] Yet a complete reversal of fortunes was at hand. Even in 550 it did not look that way, for the Goths raided the Greek islands in the Adriatic and the western coasts of Greece with a fleet of three hundred ships. [128]

9. The final phase

Late in 550 Justinian appointed a successor to Belisarius, Narses, his Greek chamberlain. He was an eunuch and, just like Admiral Nelson, a man of a diminutive stature, but with as much as metal in him. He had little military experience but proved a natural talent. Nobody knew this, of course, and Procopius was himself surprised by the appointment. "Nobody understood why this was the will of the Emperor. For no man can look into his decisions without him allowing it." [129]

The new commander arrived in Italy with fresh troops in the autumn of 551 and won some initial successes which showed that great changes were at hand. He was ready for offensive action in the spring of 552. Gone were the days when the Byzantine army had to remain on the defensive. Narses marched southward with large forces while Totila came north with his men. The two armies met in Umbria near a village called Taginae. The disposition of the Byzantine troops showed what a mixed bag the Emperor's army was : Germanic regiments, namely Lombards and Heruli in the centre, Greeks on the flanks, while the cavalry for a large part consisted of Huns. The Goths, led by Totila, were the first to attack but suffered a crushing defeat at the cost of eight thousand lives. Among them was the king himself. Fleeing from the battle-field, he was overtaken by a Germanic warrior who ran his spear through him. His men hastily buried him in a secret place. The pursuing Byzantines found it, and not believing that their great opponent was really dead, dug up his corpse to ascertain that it was really his. [130] Narses had his blood-stained garments and his bejewelled hat sent to Constantinople where they were laid at the Emperor's feet. [131]

Not all Gothic resistance had ended yet. The army chose a new king, Teja, the last one. Narses began to reconquer Gothic strongholds like Spoleto and Perugia and also took Rome, a city which had changed hands five times during Justinian's reign. [132] Pushing southward, he laid siege to Cumae which was defended by Teja's brother Aligern. The new king came from the Po valley to relieve him with the last great Ostrogothic army. He pitched his camp close to the Vesuvius. Under the constant pressure of the Byzantines, the

Goths finally found a refuge on Mons Lactarius. Confronted by starvation, they decided to attack. Preceded by the king, they descended the slopes and hurled themselves on the Byzantines. Teja fought heroically until he was killed by an enemy spear. The battle raged on for a long time, until the remnants of the Gothic army at last capitulated. [133] Thus the Ostrogothic kingdom came to an end, for no new king was chosen.

Before Teja fell in battle, he had succeeded in creating a diversion; he had asked and acquired the help of the Austrasian Franks. But their invasion of Italy was to nobody's advantage. With seventy five thousand men, they marched southward, plundering through the whole length of the boot. When they returned northward, they were intercepted by Narses who, in the spring of 554, almost annihilated them near Capua. [134]

It cost Narses some more years to reduce the last pockets of Gothic resistance - the last Gothic garrisons, those of Brescia and Verona, capitulated only in 563 -, but at last, after twenty years of fighting, Italy with Sicily, Sardinia, and Corsica, had become a Byzantine possession, ruled by an exarch, residing in Ravenna. Henceforward, we speak of Italy as the 'Exarchate of Ravenna'.

10. The end of the grand design

In his grand design to recover the West in its entirety Justinian took only one step further. Profiting from internal troubles of the Visigoths, Byzantine troops were able to conquer the southernmost part of Spain, with the cities of Cartagena, Malaga, Cordoba, and Cadiz. And that was the end of the grand design.

Compared to the enormous cost in human lives and money, not only to the Byzantine forces but also to the populations of North Africa and Italy, the results were disappointing. The greater part of the Iberian peninsula and all of the West beyond the Alps had remained in the hands of Germanic kings. But at least the shores of the Mediterranean were in Byzantine hands now, with the exception of the stretch between Valencia and the Alps. For the time being the dualistic struggle between (Byzantine) universalism and (Germanic) particularism had not been decided in favour of universalism. It was a remarkable corollary of the long-drawn out struggle that it gave the imperialists of the future, the Franks, a welcome chance to test their strength.

PART III THE FRAGMENTATION OF ITALY

1. A sequel to the story of the Byzantine conquest

There is, however, a sequel to the story of the Byzantine conquest of Italy. Part of their hard won gains were lost again some fifteen years later. "The character of the medieval history of Italy was decided in the sixth century", states Bury categorically. The near future of that country was to be neither Byzantine nor Frankish. For the Langobards, or Lombards, came. Bury describes the significance of this event in the following terms. "These two events, the imperial conquest and the Lombard conquest, possessed a high importance not merely for Italy but for the whole western world. The first secured more frequent intercourse between East and West, the second promoted the rise of papal power." [135]

2. The Gepids

The story of the Lombard migrations must begin with mentioning the Gepids, yet another Germanic tribe, of the same ethnic stock as the Ostrogoths. In the course of the Germanic migrations they settled in what now is Romania and were subjugated there by their neighbours to the east, the Huns. However, in 454 they freed themselves and moved further westward. We then find them in the Hungarian *puszta*, east of the Danube, on both sides of the Tisza (Theiss). Justinian I did not want to have those Gepids so close to his northern frontier where they constantly threatened Sirmium, just south of the Danube. [136] It is at this point that the Lombards come into the picture.

3. Enmity between Lombards and Gepids

These Lombards had been moving southward from their original habitat on the Lower Elbe, until they had established themselves in the sixth century to the west of the Danube in western Hungary and in Austria. They too did not like having the Gepids as their neighbours; it was the same with the Avars, a Mongolian tribe, who after the fall of the Hunnic Empire had been moving westward and finally settled in Romania and the Ukraine so that they had become the neighbours of the Gepids. In Constantinople it was seen as being in Byzantium's interest to bring Lombards and Avars together and play them off against the Gepids, not foreseeing that, with the Avars, they were inviting a new and far more formidable enemy.

The little love lost between these two Germanic nations, the Gepids and the Lombards, is exemplified by a verbal tilt between Alboin, a future Lombard king, and Cunimund, the Gepid Crown Prince. "The Lombards resemble in figure and in smell the mares of our Sarmatian plains", this was the polite remark of the Gepid host to his Lombard guest. But Alboin retaliated. "Add another resemblance, you have felt how strongly they kick." For Alboin had killed a brother of Cunimund on the battlefield. Fighting between the Gepids and Alboin's party who were already drawing their swords was on the brink of breaking out, when King Turisund intervened and calmed down their passions. [137]

4. The Lombard-Avar alliance

Justinian was already dead when, over the heads of the Gepids, their two neighbours found each other in an alliance. The Avars would, apart from half of the booty, get all the Gepids' land. They were even promised that part of Hungary where the Lombards lived. For this nation would move on to invade Italy and settle there. This is a curious stipulation, indeed. For what about the Lombards' fate if they would not succeed in the conquest of Italy? They too would have been homeless then. Were they so sure of their cause? [138]

III ITALY AFTER THE LOMBARD INVASION

······· Lombard frontier in the north
–·–·–· Byzantine frontiers

The double attack took place in 567. Among the many fallen Gepids was Cunimund, who had succeeded his father Turisund to the throne. [139] His head was brought to the victorious Alboin, now king of the Lombards. It is related that he had a cup made out of the skull of his enemy. The historian Paulus Diaconus testifies that he saw this cup two centuries later in the hands of the Lombard Duke Ratchis. [140] It transformded Alboin into a man with an enormous reputation among all Germanic nations; he became the hero of songs sung all over western and central Europe. [141] This was the end of the Gepid nation; what remained of it became the slaves of the Avars and the Lombards. The Avars duly shifted westward, occupied Hungary, and from there harassed Byzantine territory with more ferocity than the Gepids ever had done. The reader will find more of this in Chapter II.

5. The Lombards invade Italy

The Lombards, in their turn, left the habitat where they had lived for over a century now, crossed the Alps, and invaded the Po valley in 568. They met with little resistance. Narses, the first exarch of Ravenna, had made himself, and Byzantine rule, increasingly impopular by his greed and avarice. A delegation from Rome told Justin II that the rule of the Ostrogoths had been more tolerable than that of the Byzantines. Narses was deposed and a certain Longinus replaced him. [142] It was too late to regain the hearts of the Latins. Milan fell without an arrow having actually been fired. Verona followed and many other cities. The newcomers made the indigenous Latin population so afraid that the inhabitants of the region of Aquileia fled to islands in the Adriatic, which became the origin of the water-logged city of Venice. However, the invaders were unable to take Genoa, which only fell into their hands in 650. Pavia (then Ticinum) put up a stout resistance but was captured in 571 and became the new Lombard capital. Alboin stopped in the north of Tuscany most of which remained Byzantine for the time being. But bands of his followers pushed on to the south and conquered the cities of Spoleto and Benevento in 571. Both, with their territories, became duchies that were at

104

first practically independent of the Lombard kingdom; however, the energetic King Authari (584-590) later brought them under central control.

6. What remained of the Exarchate of Ravenna

Not much of the Exarchate of Ravenna remained in Byzantine possession after Cremona too had fallen in the years after 590. Apart from Liguria, with Genoa, it comprised Ravenna itself with a strip of land along the Adriatic with the cities of Rimini and Ascona. Tuscany was slowly but surely being incorporated into the Lombard kingdom. From the Byzantine territory on the Adriatic coast a narrow band of land, precariously held, connected this, via Perugia, with the region of Rome which remained in Byzantine hands. South of this band of land and of Rome we find the Duchies of Spoleto and Benevento, which incessantly tried to enlarge their domains. Naples with its surroundings was a Byzantine enclave. In the far south what was still Byzantine was Calabria with Tarento in the heel and Reggio in the toe, and further the islands of Sicily, Corsica, and Sardinia.

7. Conclusion

The conquest of a large part of Italy by the Lombards meant a resounding defeat of Byzantine universalism against Germanic particularism. The Lombards gave their kingdom in the north their own name : Lombardy. [143] A far reaching consequence is that Italy became fragmented into a number of mutually independent and often inimical political entities. This situation persisted until the unification of Italy in 1870.

NOTES TO CHAPTER I

1. Philostorg., *Kirchengesch.* 2.9.
2. Vassiliev, *History* 59.
3. It is not wholly certain to whom exactly the city was dedicated. There are three different texts, but all of them of a later date than 330 : a. a pagan one 'To Constantine who shines like Helios', b. a Christian one

'To you, Christ God, I dedicate this town', c. another Christian one 'You are, o Christ, the king and master of this world; I dedicate to you this town, your servant, with the sceptre and all the might of Rome. Keep her and save her from all damage'. See Dragon, *Naissance 38/39*.

4. See Vol. XI, Ch. III, § 2c.
5. Dio Cassius 74.6-14.
6. Zosimus, *HE 2.29-30*.
7. Hesychius, *Patria 1*.
8. Hesychius, *Patria 42*.
9. Dragon, *Naissance 23/24*.
10. See Vol. IV, Ch. III, § 1.
11. See Vol. IV, Ch. III, §§ 2-4.
12. See Vol. IV, Ch. III, § 7.
13. See Vol. IV, Ch. III, §§ 5 and 8.
14. See Vol. IV, Ch. III, § 6.
15. See Vol. IV, Ch. IV, § 3a-d.
16. See Vol. IV, Ch. IV, § 3e.
17. Roman imperialism is the subject of Vol. X.
18. See Vol. XI, Ch. III, § 6.
19. Gibbon, *Decline*, Vol. II 91.
20. Vol. XI, Ch. III, § 7f,g.
21. Jordanes, *Romana* 348-349.
22. Vol. XI, Ch. III, § 7h.
23. Anonymus Valesianus 57, quoted by Vassiliev, *History* 111.
24. Proc., *Anekdota* 1.4.
25. Browning, *Justinian and Theodora* 65.
26. The exact date of her birth is not known, probably around 500, Diehl, *Théodora* 14.
27. Proc., *Anekdota* 9.
28. Quoted by Gibbon, *Decline* II, 482.
29. Gibbon, *Decline* II, 482.
30. Proc., *Anekdota* 9.
31. Proc., *Anekdota* 10.

32. Bréhier, *Vie et mort* I.
33. Quoted by Vassiliev, *History* 134; the source is *Novellae Justiniani* 30 (44).
34. The reader will find an extensive treatment of the African campaign in Rubin's opus postumum, *Zeitalter Justinians*. II, 1-58.
35. Hilderic was a grandson of the Roman Emperor Valentinianus III, whose daughter Eudocia was married to the Vandal king Huneric. Having lived for forty years in the eastern capital, he had become a personal friend of Justinian.
36. Proc., *Bello vandalico* 1.9.
37. Gibbon, *Decline* II, 530.
38. Proc., Bello vandalico 1.6.
39. Proc., *Bello vandalico* 1.10.
40. Proc., *Bello vandalico* 1.12.
41. Proc., *Bello vandalico* 1.15.
42. Diehl, *Justinien* I, 174.
43. Proc., *Bello vandalico* 2.6.
44. Diehl, *Afrique byzantine* I, 8/9.
45. Diehl, *Justinien* I, 174.
46. Proc. *Bello vandalico 1.19.*
47. Proc., Bello vandalico 1.20.
48. Proc., *Bello vandalico 1.21.*
49. Proc., *Bello vandalico* 1.25.
50. Proc., *Bello vandalico* 2.1.
51. Proc., *Bello vandalico* 2.3.
52. Proc., *Bello vandalico* 2.9.
53. Proc., *Bello vandalico* 2.10.
54. *Codex Justiniani 1.27.17, Corpus iuris civilis 2.*
55. Proc., *Bello vandalico* 2.8.
56. Proc., *Bello vandalico* 1.19.
57. Diehl, *Afrique byzantine* I, 42.
58. Proc., *Bello vandalico* 2.15.
59. Proc., *Bello vandalico* 2.20.

60. Proc., *Bello vandalico* 2.21.
61. Proc., *Bello vandalico* 2.26.
62. Diehl, *Afrique byzantine* II, 333/334.
63. Proc., *Bello vandalico* 2.22; *Anekdota* 5.5.
64. Proc., *Bello vandalico* 2.21.
65. Proc., *Bello vandalico* 2.27.
66. Corippus, *Johannidos* 1.1-22.
67. Corippus, *Johannidos* 1.197-207.
68. Corippus, *Johannidos* 1.125-365.
69. Diehl, *Afrique byzantine* I, 365.
70. Proc., *Anekdota* 18.
71. Barker, *Justinian* 146/147.
72. Proc., *Bello gotico* 1.1.
73. Jordanes, *Romana* 367.
74. Proc., *Bello gotico* 1.2.
75. Proc., *Bello gotico* 1.3.
76. Jordanes, *Romana* 367-368.
77. Proc., *Anekdota* 16.1-5.
78. Proc., *Bello gotico* 1.4.
79. The Italian campaign is described in great detail by Rubin, *Zeitalter Justinians*. II, 59-200.
80. Proc., *Bello gotico* 1.7.
81. Proc., *Bello gotico* 1.5.
82. Proc., *Bello gotico* 1.13.
83. Proc., *Bello gotico* 1.6.
84. Proc., *Bello gotico* 1.3.
85. Proc., *Bello gotico* 1.6.
86. Proc., *Bello gotico* 1.8.
87. Proc., *Bello gotico* 1.9.
88. Proc., *Bello gotico* 1.10.
89. Proc., *Bello gotico* 1.11.

90. *Chronicle of Marcellinus* anno 535/536; Jordanes, *Romana* 372-373, *Getica* 311.
91. Proc., *Bello gotico* 1.13.
92. Proc., *Bello gotico* 1.14.
93. Proc., *Bello gotico* 1.16.
94. Jordanes, *Getica* 138.
95. Proc., *Bello gotico* 1.18.
96. Proc., *Bello gotico* 1.20.
97. Proc., *Anekdota* 1.
98. Sources in Gibbon, *Decline and Fall*, II, 570 : Liberatus, *Breviarium* c. 22, and Anastasius, *De vita pontificum* p. 39.
99. Proc., *Bello gotico* 2.4.
100. Proc., *Bello gotico* 2.5.
101. Gibbon, *Decline and Fall*. II, 572, note 98.
102. Proc., *Bello gotico* 2.10.
103. Proc., *Bello gotico* 2.17.
104. Proc., *Bello gotico* 2.25.
105. Proc., *Bello gotico* 2.21.
106. Agathias, *Historiae* 1.4.
107. Gibbon, *Decline and Fall* II, 579.
108. Proc., *Bello gotico* 2.29.
109. Proc., *Bello gotico* 3.2.
110. Proc., *Bello gotico* 3.3-4.
111. Proc., *Bello gotico* 3.5-7.
112. Proc., *Bello gotico* 3.10.
113. Proc., *Bello gotico* 3.10-11.
114. Proc., *Bello gotico* 3.13.
115. Proc., *Bello gotico* 3.13.
116. Proc., *Bello gotico* 3.15.
117. Proc., *Bello gotico* 3.20.
118. Proc., *Bello gotico* 3.21.
119. Proc., *Bello gotico* 3.22.

120. Barker, *Justinian* 161.
121. Proc., *Bello gotico* 3.26.
122. Proc., *Bello gotico* 3.35.
123. Proc., *Bello gotico* 3.33-34.
124. Proc., *Bello gotico* 3.35.
125. Proc., *Bello gotico* 3.36.
126. Proc., *Bello gotico* 3.37.
127. Proc., *Bello gotico* 3.37.
128. Proc., *Bello gotico* 4.22.
129. Proc., *Bello gotico* 4.21.
130. Proc., *Bello gotico* 4.29-32.
131. Theophanes, *Chronographia* AM 6044, AD 551/552.
132. Proc., *Bello gotico* 4.33.
133. Proc., *Bello gotico* 4.34-35.
134. Agathias, *Historiae* 1.20-2.9.
135. Bury, *Later Roman Empire* II, 145.
136. Alexander P. Kazhan s.v. 'Gepids', *Oxf.Dict. of Byz.*, Vol 2, 844.
137. Paulus Diaconus, *De gestibus Langobardorum* 1.23-24.
138. Bury, *Later Roman Empire* II, 115/116.
139. Paulus Diaconus, *De gestibus Langobardorum* 1.27.
140. Paulus Diaconus, *De gestibus Langobardorum* 2.28.
141. Paulus Diaconus, *De gestibus Langobardorum* 1.27.
142. Paulus Diaconus, *De gestibus Langobardorum* 2.5. This historian accused the revengeful Narses of having invited the Lombards but this accusation is certainly groundless. The Lombards needed no invitation.
143. Curiously enough, their ethnic name lives on in the German verb *lombardieren* = pawning, and in the Dutch word *lommerd*. A *lommerd* is a pawnshop. In the later Middle Ages northern Italy was the first region in Europe to possess banks. When these capitalist institutions spread to Germany (Augsburg) and the Netherlands (Bruges), banks were called *lombards*. This remained popular in Dutch as *lommerd*. More popular still is the nickname 'Uncle John' (*Ome Jan*) for the municipal pawnshop in Amsterdam, a centuries old institution that still exists.

CHAPTER III

THE SLAV THREAT AND AVAR IMPERIALISM

PART I THE SLAV THREAT

1. War on many fronts

As I wrote in Chapter I, Justinian belonged to that imprudent breed of rulers who wage war on more than one front simultaneously. On how many fronts did he conduct wars? This depends on how we count them. One may say that there were two fronts at a time, the western reconquest and the Persian front in the East. But in the West there were really two synchronous campaigns, in North Africa and in Italy. That makes three. We may perhaps add a fourth, namely the Danube front. Here an endless succession of barbarian tribes attempted to penetrate Byzantine territory. Constantinople would have been far more able to cope with this threat if only it did not have to divide its non inexhaustible forces over so many fronts.

Before we turn to the struggle on the Euphrates front, we must devote a short chapter to the situation in the Balkans. Right from the outset of Justinian's reign hardly a year passed without some tribe trying (and succeeding in) crossing the Danube. The real or supposed riches of the Empire irresistibly attracted them. They were of different ethnic origin, Slavs, Huns, Bulgarians, Avars, and still more besides.

2. An old presence

The Slavs had been present in the eastern Empire for a long time. Bury states that "in the fifth century there was a considerable Slavonic element in the lands south of the Ister [Danube], holding the position of Roman *coloni*. They formed a layer of population which would give security and permanence to the future invaders of kindred race." This author further points out that the stay of the Ostrogoths and the Lombards (Langobards) in Italy and that of the Vandals in North Africa - to which we may add that of the Visigoths in Spain - was of relatively short duration, but that the Franks in western Europe and the Slavs in eastern Europe were there to stay. [1]

2. Opening the sluices

"The departure of the Ostrogoths was like the opening of a sluice;" writes Bury, "the Slavs and the Bulgarians whom their presence had held back, were let loose on the Empire and began periodical invasions." Some other nations came too; there were, for instance, Hun settlements in the Dobrudza. [2] Fearing for his capital, in 521 Anastasius built the Long Walls across the peninsula on which Constantinople stood in order to protect it against Slav attacks. [3] Among the tribes that are frequently mentioned are the Slovenes, the Bulgarians, and the Wends (also called Antai). [4] Bury thinks that the Bulgarians of the sixth century were soon subjected and assimilated by other Slav tribes. [5]

It serves no purpose to describe invasion after invasion since they were such a regularly occurring event. The overall picture is that the Emperors were incapable of defending the northern frontier. An interesting point is that the Byzantines, in order to ward off the Slavs, barbarians in their eyes, had to trust to the barbarians in their own armies. Marauding Slav bands, pillaging and massacring throughout the whole Balkan peninsula, penetrated deeply into Byzantine territory. In 551 they were in Thrace, not far from the capital; in 558 they appeared before the walls of Thessalonica. Justinian did what he could to protect the hapless citizens. Along the Danube numerous fortresses were built; cities were heavily fortified. The famous passage into Greece, the defile of Thermopylae, was provided with fortresses, walls and a permanent garrison of two thousand men. The whole country-side was dotted with forts and strongholds everywhere. In the course of time, the Slav incursions became less of a walk-over. [6]

One may assume that not all marauders returned to their original habitat. Quite a number stayed behind and settled somewhere in Byzantine territory; in due time they were christianized. There were Slav settlements even in Greece. These Slavs no longer presented a direct threat, but, as Bury remarks, with their great love of independence, "they introduced an element of dissolution [into the Empire]." [7] We may, therefore, see the relationship between the Byzantines and Slavs as dualistic, since the latter, not wishing to remain dependent on the Empire, finally destroyed part of it.

PART II AVAR IMPERIALISM

1. The coming of the Avars

In the last years of Justinian's reign a new cloud appeared on the northern horizon. The Avars began to make their presence felt. Avars were Tartars, Mongolians, that is, belonging to the same language group as the Huns. Originally they formed part of the Hunnic Empire, but in the end they broke free from their masters and turned westward. We must situate them in what now is Hungary. Justinian paid subsidies to keep them off Byzantine territory, but nonetheless we see them pillaging Thrace in 562. After Justinian's death in 565, his successor Justin II (565-578), a nephew of the deceased Emperor, was confronted by an aggressive Avar kingdom on his northern frontier. [8]

2. What the Avars wanted

The heathen Avars were by no means friendly disposed towards Byzantium. Their aim was to get hold of Sirmium, a (no longer existing) Byzantine town, just south of the Danube; it would be an excellent sally-basis for raids into

Byzantine country. Since it was too strong to be conquered, the Avars sent an embassy to Constantinople; the envoys were to claim Sirmium and more subsidies. Justin, just seven days Emperor then, went to great lengths to make an unforgettable impression on these uncouth barbarians. The long road the envoys had to follow to the throne hall was lined with armed guards, so that they had to run the gauntlet between them. Having reached the imperial presence, they at first saw nothing but a veil behind which the great ruler sat hidden. It was withdrawn, and behold!, there sat Justin in his imperial robes. Overwhelmed by all this splendour, the envoys fell to the ground. But when the negotiations began, with the help of interpreters, they firmly stood their ground. They told Justin how powerful their king, the Khagan, was, and they claimed the same advantages Justinian had always granted them.

The Emperor's response could not have been more haughty. His forces, he declared, were still strong enough to chastize such barbarians as those Avars were. "Retire from our presence!", he concluded. [9] The dualistic opposition between the realms of civilization and barbarity is fully apparent here. The envoys returned home; their reports impressed their king, whose name was Baian (Bagan), as much as Justin had wanted.

3. The capture of Sirmium

For a short while Baian turned his attention westward. However, in 577 a splendid opportunity presented itself. The bulk of the Byzantine army was needed on the eastern front where there was heavy fighting with the Persians. Simultaneously an avalanche of Slavs rolled over the peninsula, a hundred thousand of them, it is reported. Many of them were there to stay; "it is from this time that we must date the first intrusion of a Slavonic element on a considerable scale into the Balkan peninsula." [10] In his despair the Byzantine governor of the badly harassed province of Illyria asked for Baian's help. The king needed not be asked twice. With ships provided by the Byzantines he crossed the Danube, ravaged the lands occupied by the Slavs, but did not miss the opportunity to lay siege to Sirmium. [11] In 581 the town fell into his hands; Tiberius II, who was now Emperor (578-582), even consented to pay him a yearly tribute. Bury speaks here of 'a turning-point in the history of the peninsula', since with the fall of Sirmium the bolt on the gate to the Balkan had been removed. [12]

In the summer of 583 Baian captured a number of fortress towns along the Danube, among them Viminacium, thus making the northern frontier ever more porous. In 584 yet another treaty was signed; the next Emperor, Maurice (582-602), had to pay still more gold to the Avars. During the twenty years of his reign they remained a painful problem. Sometimes they seemed to roam freely over the peninsula without anyone holding them back. In 587 they appeared before Adrianople, in 597 before Thessalonika. They usually destroyed the towns they had captured (they themselves were nomads living in tents), but they spared the hot-water baths at Anchialus (now Pomorie on the Bulgarian Black Sea coast) so that the women of the Khagan's harem could wash themselves there. [13]

4. Avar insolence

The Khagan, paying the Byzantine Emperors back in kind, treated the envoys sent to him with the greatest insolence, swearing that he would destroy the Long Walls of Constantinople. [14] When a Byzantine ambassador rebuked him for his behaviour, "boiling blood whipped up great passion in the Khagan; his whole face grew crimson with anger, while his eyes gleamed golden-bright with the flame of wrath ... His eyebrows shot up and almost threatened to fly off his forehead." The Byzantines were dispatched back to the Emperor in dishonour. [15]

Once the Khagan heard that the Byzantines possessed 'creatures of remarkable size and physique', and he requested to see one of these beasts. The Emperor was weak enough to send him one. Or did he want to impress him? Yet when the animal arrived - it was an elephant, of course -, the Khagan had it sent back, whether "because of lack of interest or scorn of the marvel, I [Theophylactus] cannot say." Another time he asked the Emperor for

IV
AVARS AND SLAVS

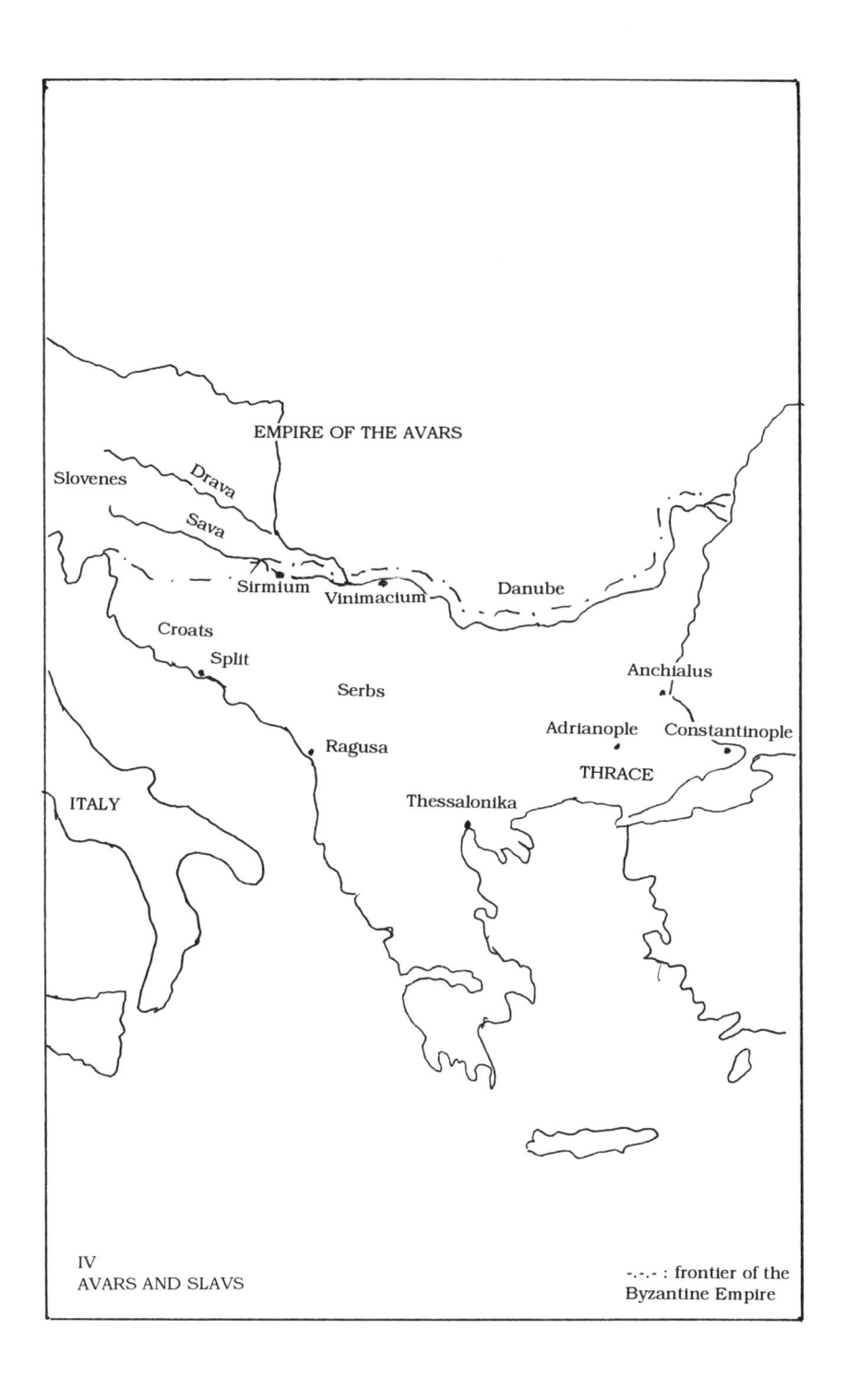

-.-.- : frontier of the Byzantine Empire

a golden couch, and, believe it or believe it not, got it. But the Khagan found it a stingy gift and returned it. [16]

5. An imperial counter-offensive

Great campaigns were mounted against the Avars which brought victories but no definitive success. In 591, when peace with the Persians had been concluded, Maurice had his hands free and took the field in person, to everybody's surprise, for since the days of Theodosius I the Great, two centuries ago, no Emperor had ever marched out in armour. His family implored him in vain to stay home. [17] Maurice did not give in and marched out. He did not get very far, only to Anchialus. The weather was awful and there was an almost total eclipse of the sun. When the Emperor heard that Persian ambassadors had arrived in the capital he returned home. [18]

Intermittent fighting continued throughout the rest of Maurice's reign, without the Byzantines being able to push the Avars and the Slavs back over the Danube. However, around 600 a capable Byzantine general, called Priscus, won great victories over the Avars, with the result that they recognized the Danube as the frontier between them and the Byzantines. [19]

6. An Avar embuscade

For a long time the Avars left the Byzantines in peace. This did not mean that they were sitting idle, for they now harassed the Lombards in Northern Italy instead. In 610 Heraclius I became Emperor; the reign of this powerful ruler lasted thirty-one years (610-641). The Avars did not even take advantage of the enormous problems Byzantium had with its Persian neighbours in Asia. In 619 the Khagan made peaceful overtures letting it be known that he wanted to conclude a treaty with the Emperor, whose greatest worry was not the Avars but the Persians.

Heraclius prepared to give the Avar envoys a splendid reception with all the pageantry the Empire could offer; his aim was to make them feel humble, of course. But his guests came with shock troops that were embuscaded in the woods opposite the Long Walls. Their commission was to catch the Emperor while he was receiving the Khagan in the open field. However, he escaped from their hands in the nick of time, leaving his royal dress behind; holding his imperial crown under his arm, he stormed into Constantinople, with the Avars at his heels. They advanced as far as the suburbs, closer than they had ever had been. Taking the imperial robes with them they departed, leading a considerable number of captives away. [20] But Heraclius, with the Persian War on his hands, turned a blind eye to the Khagan's treacherous conduct. He ransomed the captives and in 620 concluded a peace treaty with the Avars. [21]

7. A double attack on the capital

In June 626 the Avars appeared before the capital once again. There were Bulgarians and Slavs in their army of twenty thousand men. They came well-prepared, even provided with siege machines; small boats manned by Slavs swarmed in the Golden Horn. When the Khagan had arrived in person, an enormous attack was mounted, but it was repulsed, by the intervention of the Holy Virgin, as the Byzantines believed.

The threat to the capital became twofold when the Persians arrived on the Asiatic side of the Bosporus. There was a great risk that they and the Avars would join forces in a concerted attack. The magistrates of Constantinople sent deputies to the Khagan - he was the son of Baian who had lived to an extremely old age [22] - who were admitted to the presence together with Persian envoys. The Khagan made these sit and let the Byzantines stand, thus expressing his contempt for the latter. He told them : "You cannot escape the arms of the Avars and Persians, unless you soar into the air like birds or dive into the water like fishes." But these proved hollow words. The city was very ably defended; an attempt to ferry over Persian troops on rafts was prevented by a Byzantine sally. Finally the Avars found themselves in difficulties; the siege lasted too long, and starvation threatened their troops. In August they beat the retreat. [23] It seemed that, in spite of their haughty behaviour, the Avars had now learned a lesson. They retreated beyond the Danube and stayed there, while their grip on the neighbouring tribes became ever less secure. No longer they threatened the Byzantine Empire. [24] What remained of their power was finally broken by Charlemagne.

8. The arrival of ever more Slavs

The demise of the Avars gave the Slavs more freedom of movement. Many of them had earlier established themselves in the Balkans, as already related, and now ever more came, crossing the Danube in a constant stream. Slovenes settled in the land of the rivers Drava and Sava where they are still to be found; somewhat later Croats and Serbs arrived who occupied their present habitats, all of them in the western half of the peninsula. Later still, after 650, the Bulgarians erected a kingdom in the eastern part of the Balkans. The arrival of the western Slavs made the indigenous Christian population so afraid that many of them fled to islands in the Adriatic. Ragusa, for instance, is such a settlement, while others found a refuge around an old palace of Diocletian, thereby founding the town of Split (Spalato = *palatium*). In due time the Slovenes, the Croats, and the Serbians became Christians. Their princes at least nominally acknowledged the suzerainty of the Byzantine Emperor who saw these tribes as being in his service. After the withdrawal of the Avars the Danube was of old the northern frontier of the Empire. It is, however, a fact that its grip on the pensinsula had become much weaker.

9. Evaluation

How must we evaluate the struggle between the Avars and the Byzantines? Was it a dualistic conflict between universalism and particularism, such as I described the conquest of North Africa and Italy by Byzantium? Yet it does not appear that the Empire cherished imperial designs on the lands beyond the Danube, more in particular on the Avar country. It was rather the other way round. There doubtless existed something like an Avar imperialism that as late as the end of the eighth century made even Charlemagne nervous. The

Avar Khagans, especially the indomitable Baian, found themselves at least the equals of the Byzantine rulers, if not superior to them. This is evident by the tall language they used, such as breaking down the Long Walls, and also by their insolent behaviour towards imperial envoys.

The Avars were an illiterate nation that left no written sources behind. All that we know of them has been passed down by Byzantine authors. We cannot know whether they really wanted to replace the Byzantine Empire with an Avar one, at least in Europe, leaving its Asiatic part to the Persians. What would they have done if they had actually captured Constantinople? Only plunder it? Destroy it? Leave it in ruins? Or would they have established their own seat of power there? It is true that they were nomads not used to dwelling in towns. But the Vandals were also nomads who finally felt fully at ease in Carthage. Anyhow, I think we know enough to speak of a dualistic struggle between two imperialisms.

NOTES TO CHAPTER III

1. Bury, *Later Roman Empire* II, 17/18.
2. Bury, *Later Roman Empire* II, 20.
3. Bury, *Later Roman Empire* I, 295.
4. There is still a Wend population in eastern Germany, in the region east of Berlin. It is the subject of a fascinating novel by Werner Bergengrün, *Am Himmel wie auf Erden* (1940).
5. Bury, *Later Roman Empire* II, 21.
6. Bury, *Later Roman Empire* II, 21-24.
7. Bury, *Later Roman Empire II*, 114.
8. The most recent exposition of their coming is that by Avenarius, *Die Awaren*. Ch. 4 Pannonien in der ersten Hälfte des 6. Jh. und die Ankunft der Awaren. See also Szadeczky-Kardoss, *Avarica*. III Über die Wandlungen der Ostgrenzen der awarischen Machtssphäre.
9. I take this from Gibbon, *Decline and Fall* II, 730/731, who has taken it from Corippus.
10. Bury, *Later Roman Empire* II, 117/118.

11. Extensive treatment of this and of what followed in Avenarius, *Die Awaren*. Ch. 4 Die awarischen Eroberungszüge bis zum Jahre 626. A Die awarischen Excursionen in die byzantinischen Provinzen.
12. Bury, *Later Roman Empire* II, 118.
13. Theophylactus, *History* 1.4.4.
14. Theophylactus, *History* 1.4.8.
15. Theophylactus, *History* 1.6.1-3. Other instances of Baian's insolent behaviour are related by Menander, *Excerpta* 14 (113).
16. Theophylactus, *History* 1.3.8-12.
17. Theophylactus, *History* 5.16.1-4.
18. Theophylactus, *History* 5.16.1-6.
19. Theophylactus, *History* 7.15.4.
20. Theophanes, *Chronographia* AD 617/618; Nikephoros, *Short history* 10.
21. Theophanes, *Chronographia* AD 618/619.
22. Georg.Pis., *Bellum avaricum* 85-94.
23. Georg.Pis. presents a poetic description in his *Bellum avaricum*; Nikephoros, *Short history* 13; Theophanes, *Chronographia* AD 624/625 (315); *Chronicon paschale*, I, pp. 721/722.
24. Avenarius, *Die Awaren*. 6. Die Offensive gegen die Awaren, 123.

CHAPTER IV

TWO MIGHTY IMPERIALISMS IN CONFLICT:
THE STRUGGLE BETWEEN BYZANTIUM
AND PERSIA

1. Persian imperialism as an old problem

The eastern frontier of the Byzantine Empire was just as insecure as the Danube line. It was constantly threatened by the Persians. This was an old problem, since the threat to the West had already existed in the days of Cyrus and Xerxes. [1] Alexander the Great had done his best to put an end to the Persian Empire for good, [2] but Persian imperialism gained a powerful new impulse when King Mithridates I founded the Parthian Empire around 150 B.C. It tried to extend its territories and its influence westward but in due time was confronted with the Roman Empire. The Euphrates was to remain the boundary line between West and East for a very long time. [3]

The conflict between the Parthian, later the (Neo-)Persian Empires was of a dualistic nature. They bordered on each other with only the Euphrates, a river not hard to cross, between them. Both were Empires, which were heir to a great imperial tradition, and claimed the same regions of the ancient world. In the first and second centuries A.D. there was intermittent warfare that brought no definite success to either party. However, in the first decades of the third century an ambitious vassal of the Parthian king made himself master of the whole realm of his master, being crowned as king in 226. With him the Sasanian dynasty began; the Parthian Empire is henceforward called the (Neo-)Persian or Sasanian Empire. Since this new king, Ardashir I, styled himself 'King of kings', it was clear from which direction the wind was blowing. Soon enough the new aggressiveness became apparent when he began attacking the Roman border fortresses on the Euphrates. The mood prevailing in Iran became still more evident, when Shapur I ascended the throne in 241 and changed the royal title into the still more ambitious 'King of kings of Iran and of Non-Iran'.

It never became wholly clear in whose power Mesopotamia and Armenia were; both countries were a bone of contention between the two Empires, which led to much bloody fighting. But in 298 Diocletian succeeded in occupying these two regions; in the peace treaty the Persians had to acknowledge this. More than four decades later the Persians got restive again; there was so much raiding and counter-raiding in Mesopotamia that it became a no man's land. We know that the Emperor Julian the Apostate fell in 363 in an attempt to regulate the Persian problem once and for all. In 384 peace was concluded; Mesopotamia and Armenia remained divided between the two Empires. [4]

2. First clashes with the Byzantine Empire

This peaceful coexistence was interrupted only by a short war in 420-421, concluded by a peace treaty meant to last for a century. It only lasted eighty years, for in A.D. 502 hostilities broke out over Armenia, one of the bones of contention. This war lasted three years and went on the whole unfavourably for the Byzantines; three important fortress towns in Armenia were captured by the Persians. Nisibis in Mesopotamia was also lost but was later regained by the Byzantines. In 505 peace was concluded, now for a more modest period, namely seven years. It was a truce rather than a real peace, although the seven years finally became twenty-one. [5]

3. The cardinal error of Justinian I

Previté-Orton writes that "the cardinal error of Justinian [whose reign we have now reached] was to attempt wide western conquest and to reign and build with unexampled splendour, when the resources of the Eastern Empire required careful husbanding if they were to suffice for its mere defence." [6] There never was sufficient cash in hand to pay for both the wars in the West and the defence of the East, to say nothing of the building programme. If Justinian wanted to wage war on the Germanic states in the West, he should have been content with defensive measures in the East. It is true that he had no aggressive designs there, but on the other hand he should have been cautious enough not to provoke the Sasanians. And provoking was what he did.

Byzantine missionaries were busy converting the tribes that lived beyond Armenia in the Caucasus region, thus turning them into the natural allies of Byzantium. This made the Persians nervous and suspicious. For the Persians the last straw was that the Byzantines began to build a fortress town, called Dara, just north of Nisibis, shortly after the ascension to the throne of Justinian. It is conceivable that the first great victories in the West had turned his head a little. One of our sources says that "the whole earth cannot contain him; he is always scrutinizing the aether and the retreats beyond the ocean, if he may win some new world" - a fine statement of universalistic designs. [7]

Unfortunately his opponent was a man of the same ilk, King Chosroes I Nushirvan, who ruled Persia for forty-eight years (531-579). We should not think of him as of a wild firebrand, for he was a man with cultural interests. With typical western superciliousness Gibbon says that his studies were 'ostentatious and superficial', but that they had the result that "the light of science was dispersed over Persia ... Seven Greek philosophers who visited his court were invited and deceived by the strange assurance that a disciple of Plato was seated on the Persian throne. " It was too good to be true, obviously! Annals were written, theological disputes were held over which the king presided, Greek and Hindu writings were translated into Persian, an academy was founded. [8]

4. The 'eternal peace'

When Chosroes came to the throne, he inherited a war that had started in 527, when the Byzantines were attempting to establish themselves near Nisibis, in a Mesopotamian region that the Persians considered their own. Belisarius, the commander, won a great victory at Dara in 530. [9] Before the battle Perozen, the Persian commander, had sent a message to Belisarius, that he should prepare a bath for him in Dara (which was occupied by the Byzantines), since he wanted to take his bath there the next day. [10] Yet "for the first time since long the Persians suffered in this battle their first defeat." [11]

It did not suit Chosroes to have this war on his hands, when he became Great King. In 532 an 'eternal peace' was concluded between Byzantium and Persia on the basis of the *status quo ante*. This entailed that the Byzantines evacuated the Nisibis region. Chosroes did not remain sitting idle. He organized his realm very ably and extended his rule eastward to the river Oxus (the Amu'darya). The progress made by Justinian in the West made him feel uncomfortable. "He felt that this appetite of universal dominion would end one day with also menacing the Sasanian monarchy." [12] He had not only the reputation of being a great scholar, but also that of a mighty warrior and ruler. "Now he could no longer contain himself, but looked forward for pretenses to break the peace treaty [with the Byzantines]", writes Procopius. [13] It was an eternal peace, but "eternally is so long", says a medieval Dutch poem. Envoys came from both King Vitiges of the Ostrogoths and from the Armenians who felt oppressed by the Byzantines, to ask his help. If we believe Procopius, Chosroes was not unwilling to come to their assistance. [14]

5. Five years of warfare

A war began that would last five years (540-545) with bloody battles and large-scale devastations. The main war theatres were Syria, Mesopotamia, and Armenia. Belisarius was called back from the West but had insufficient forces at his disposal. Under the personal command of the Great King the Persians began the war by invading Syria, massacring and pillaging everywhere; countless people were led away as slaves. Then the Persians appeared before Antioch; this rich and populous city fell into their hands after a short siege. The inhabitants had to pay for the fact that they had scoffed at the Persians and their king from the walls, telling them that they were no true people but only clowns. When these clowns took the city, they slaughtered the population, killing young and old, man and woman. The survivors were led away in captivity. The churches were thoroughly plundered, and finally the town was set on fire. [15]

In 541 Chosroes extended his operations to the Caucasus region, to the Lazica and Iberian kingdoms at the south-eastern end of the Black Sea, which were dependent on Byzantium. The possession of Lazica (also called Colchis) would give Persia an outlet to the Black Sea. To secure this country the Byzantines had built a new fortress town there on the coast, called Petra; it served also to keep the indigenous population in check, for it did not love the Byzantines. It was no great problem for Chosroes to capture Petra. According to Procopius, the possession of the Lazica country and especially of Petra was of the greatest importance to Chosroes. "From here he could without difficulty attack the [Byzantine] towns along the [southern] Black Sea coast from both the land and the sea side, then subject the Cappadocians and their neighbours, the Galatians and the Bithynians, and finally even attack Constantinople by storm, without meeting any resistance at all." [16]

Warfare continued with a Persian invasion of northern Syria in 542, of Armenia in 543, and of the Byzantine part of Mesopotamia in 544. One of the few successes of the Byzantines in this war was that the Persians were unable to take Edessa (now Urfa); even women and children rushed to the walls to help the defenders. For most of the time the Byzantines seemed to be nowhere, but in 543 Belisarius retaliated at last, leading an army of thirty thousand men into Persarmenia; however, after some initial successes the offensive ran to seed. Soon afterwards Belisarius was recalled to Italy. [17]

In 543 a Persian ambassador, Isdiguce, called a 'barbarian' by Procopius, arrived in the Byzantine capital; his aim was obviously to impress the Byzantines. He came with his wife and daughters and with a retinue of two satraps, a number of eunuchs, five hundred horses and some camels. Procopius reproaches the Emperor for having been too permissive for this Isdiguce who walked freely about in the capital, whereas Byzantine envoys to the court of the Great King were treated with the greatest insolence. [18] Gibbon defined the relationship by stating that "the successor of Cyrus assumed the majesty of the Eastern sun and graciously permitted his younger brother Justinian to reign over the West with the pale and reflected splendour of the moon." [19] A temporary result of the diplomatic to and fro was that a truce was concluded to last for five years; this cost Justinian money, for he had to pay Chosroes.

6. War in the Caucasus region

It was not to be expected that this truce would hold. The inhabitants of the Colchis country, the Lazi, were restless under Persian rule, especially because the Magi were busy propagating the Zoroastrian faith among those Christians. [20] They sought the help of Justianian who, even before the truce ended, sent a force of nine thousand men; their task was the recapture of Petra. So in 549 the war began anew with the Caucasus region as its main theatre. Unable to take the fortress town, the Byzantines at last raised the siege.

Fighting continued in this difficult country with its heavily wooded mountain slopes cut by ravines and narrow passes. Its possession was important for the Byzantines, because it held the Sasanian Empire off from the Black Sea. Justinian pumped ever more troops into Colchis until at last he had fifteen thousand men there. Fierce struggles were fought for the few strongholds that dominated the country; in 551 the Byzantines gained a spectacular success by taking Petra. This town,that was situated on a steep rock, was valiantly defended by a garrison of more than three thousand Persians. The Byzantines, six thousand in number under the command of the seventy-year-old general Bessos, moved cleverly constructed siege machines against the walls, among them a new type of battering ram. The besieged maintained a heavy fire on the attackers, hurling pots at them containing a highly combustible stuff, which they called 'oil of Medea'.

When a breach was made, the infantry scaled the walls, led by their old and corpulent general. After desperate and most bloody fighting the Byzantines penetrated the fortress. Of the seven hundred and thirty Persians who were taken prisoner, only eighteen were not wounded, it is said. Five hundred defenders had fled into the citadel. All attempts to convince them that they had better surrender having failed, Bessos had the citadel set on fire, hoping that the sight of the flames would induce them to lay down their arms. But they did not come out, and all of them perished in the fire. [21]

On the whole the strategic situation was more favourable for the Byzantines than for their opponents. The Black Sea was a comfortable supply route for them, while the Persian lines ran through inhospitable country over great distances. In the end the ageing Chosroes had to admit that he could not dislodge the Byzantines from Colchis. In 555 a provisional treaty was signed, followed in 562 by an official peace treaty for a period of fifty years. In this document the Persian ruler styled himself in the most lofty manner : "The divine, good, pacific, ancient Chosroes, king of kings, fortunate, pious, beneficent, to whom the gods have given great fortune and great empire, the giant of giants, who is formed in the image of the gods, to Justinian Caesar, our brother."

Bury's comment is illustrative of the prevailing western attitude to 'the East'. "The style of this address, compared with the most imposing list of Justinian's titles, illustrates the difference between the oriental insanity of an Asiatic despot and the vanity of a Roman Emperor, which, even as it becomes intemperate, remains sane." [22] He was obviously not aware of the fact that he was creating a dualistic opposition, a very strong one at that, namely between 'insanity' and 'sane'.

The negotiations were conducted by the respective embassies at the Byzantine-Persian frontier with the help of twelve interpreters; the treaty was drafted in the Greek and Persian languages. It regulated the future relations of the two Empires in some detail, the most important clause being that the Persians would evacuate Colchis. This was a really great success for the Byzantines, for, as Bury expresses it, "the question was at stake whether the great-Asiatic power was to have access to the Euxine [the Black Sea], and these operations decided that on the waters of that sea the Romans [the Byzantines] were to remain without rivals." [23] The threat to the northern coasts of the Black Sea, and even that to Constantinople itself, had been removed. Of course, a price had to be paid : thirty thousand Byzantine *aurei* changed hands. The outcome of the war, although unfavourable for him, did not lessen Chosroes' contempt for the Byzantines. "Of the nations vanquished by his invincible arms, he esteemed the Romans as the least formidable." [24]

7. How long is half a century?

Half a century is a long time for a peace treaty to hold, especially when it concerns two mighty Empires poised against each other like two bulls with their horns interlocked. The situation of peace, unstable though it was, survived Justinian's lifetime, who died in November 565, but not that of Chosroes who reigned until 579. When Justin II was Emperor, a call for help came from Persarmenia; its Christian population, feeling uncomfortable under Persian rule, complained to the Emperor, declaring that they confessed the same religion as he did. Justin proved ready to help them. Chosroes protested, but the Byzantine ruler explained that he could not ignore the complaints of fellow-Christians. [25]

At the turn of the century a Turkish embassy presented itself at the court of Constantinople. This was a historic event, for it was the first appearance of Turks in Europe. The envoys had come from afar, since the Turkish power centre was to be found in Central Asia, near the Chinese border in the Altai region. Their realm, governed by a Khan, was a loose confederation of four tribal kingdoms; it stretched westward onto the northeastern frontier of the Persian Empire on the Oxus river. The Persians felt uncomfortable with having them so near and even refused to negotiate with them.

It is a curious detail that the Turkish ambassadors brought silk (the Turks commanded the silk route) to Chosroes, but this king had it burnt. Justin, however, was more interested in silk, because silk garments were a sign of distinction. [26] It was not only commerce that brought the Byzantines and the Turks together, not even in the first place. Their stratego-political situation was similar. To quote Bury, the Byzantine Empire was placed "between the Avars [former subjects of the Turks] and the Persians, just as the latter [the Persian Empire] was placed between the Turks [on their north frontier] and the Romans." [27] Having concluded an alliance with the Turks, Justin judged that he was in a good position now to reopen the hostilities. In 572 he refused to pay the tribute that was annually due to the Persians; it made the Empire economically dependent on that of the Sasanians.

8. War in Syria

The commander on the Byzantine side was Justinian, a grand-nephew of the Emperor of the same name. He was unable to prevent the Persians from capturing the important town of Dara in Mesopotamia, the fortress that served to keep the Persian garrison at Nisibis in check. Justin II was so upset by this bad news that he became mentally deranged and acquiesced in an armistice, which again cost the Byzantines a handsome sum of money. [28]

Before this armistice was concluded, a Persian invasion had taken place into northern Syria; they met with no resistance in the open field. They could not take Antioch, but Apamea went up in flames. [29] With this short foray a story is connected that I will not withhold from the reader, because it perfectly illustrates the tensions that existed in the relationships between Byzantines, Persians, and Turks, and also between Christians and pagans. The Persians are said to have made two hundred and ninety-two thousand Syrians captive who were deported to Persia. Chosroes saw a chance for winning over the Turks to his side. From the mass of prisoners he had two thousand beautiful girls selected, decked them out as brides, and sent them as a present to the Turkish Khan. The girls had no intention at all to marry heathen Turks or to become their concubines ; they were Christians and were resolved to remain true to the faith. With this in mind, they expressed the wish to take a bath in the frontier river; they asked the escorting soldiers to leave them alone for a while, and these were decent enough to do so. Then all the girls drowned themselves in the water. Bury says that this story

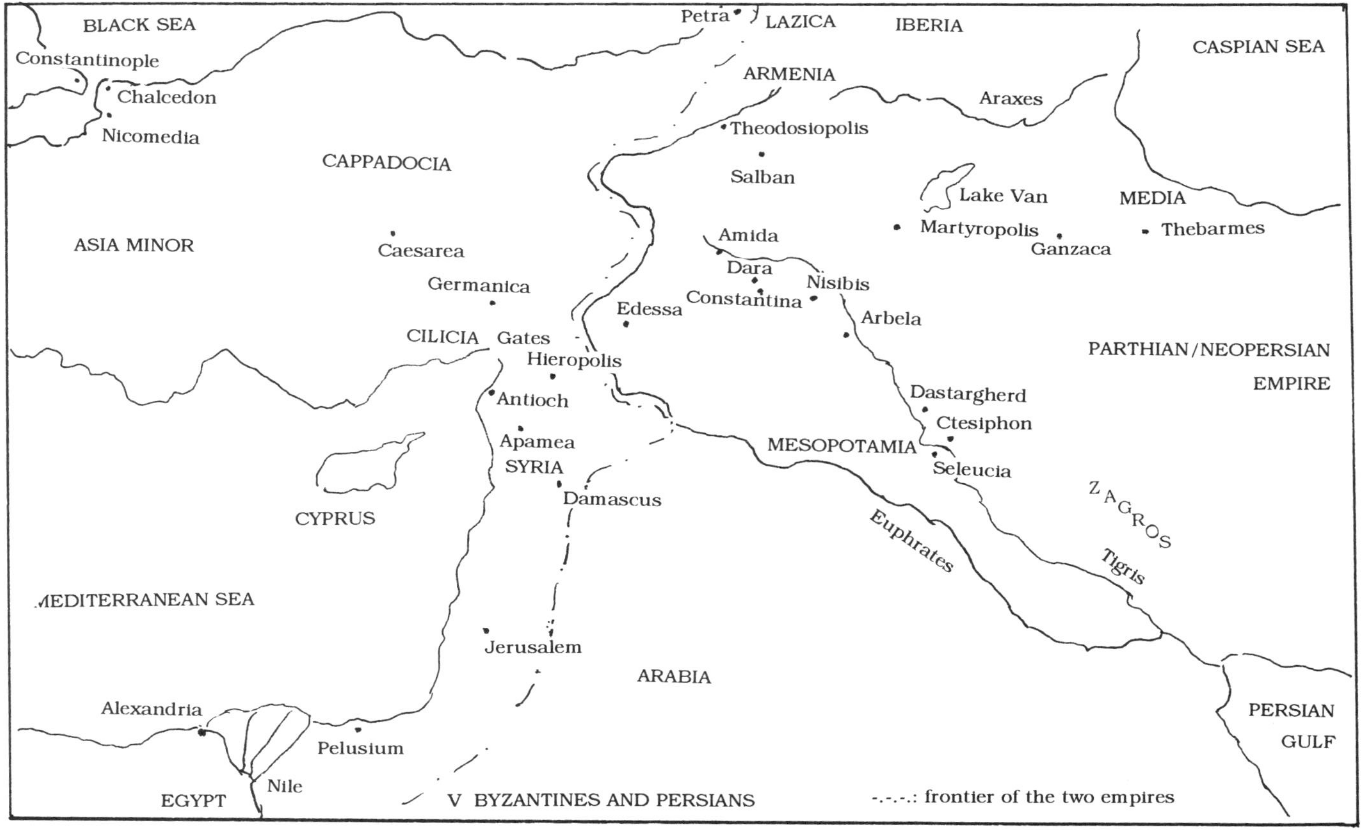
BLACK SEA
Constantinople
Chalcedon
Nicomedia
CAPPADOCIA
ASIA MINOR
Caesarea
Germanica
CILICIA
Gates
Hieropolis
Antioch
Apamea
SYRIA
Damascus
CYPRUS
MEDITERRANEAN SEA
Jerusalem
ARABIA
Alexandria
Pelusium
Nile
EGYPT
Petra
LAZICA
IBERIA
ARMENIA
CASPIAN SEA
Araxes
Theodosiopolis
Salban
Lake Van
MEDIA
Martyropolis
Ganzaca
Thebarmes
Amida
Dara
Nisibis
Constantina
Edessa
Arbela
PARTHIAN/NEOPERSIAN
EMPIRE
Dastargherd
Ctesiphon
MESOPOTAMIA
Seleucia
ZAGROS
Euphrates
Tigris
PERSIAN
GULF
V BYZANTINES AND PERSIANS
-.-.-.: frontier of the two empires

demonstrates "the overpowering dread of the Turkish Minotaur so many centuries before they set foot in Europe," [30], but this is perhaps antedating.

9. Fighting in Persarmenia

In 575 the expiring truce was converted in a formal peace treaty for three years; it did, howver, not apply to Persarmenia where the fighting continued relentlessly. It was there that the Byzantines scored their first important success against the Persians, who were commanded by Chosroes in person. They were routed by Justinian's army who spurred on his men in a remarkable speech in which he not only told them to be 'Spartans in combat' but also brought forward a religious argument. "We do not do obeisance to a god that turns to ashes, who is now ablaze but is soon not visible; smoke and fuel do not constitute religion, but their fading proves their falsehood" [31] - an evident allusion to the Zoroastrian religion with its fire-ritual. The defeated Chosroes fled, leaving his tent with all his valuables in the hands of the victors. Even his elephants were captured and sent to Constantinople. [32] Chosroes was so ashamed of this personal defeat that he made a law forbidding Persian kings to take part in wars henceforward. [33]

10. Successful operations

In 578 the peace treaty was not renewed; soon there was fighting along the whole eastern front. The Byzantines, under the command of Maurice, the future Emperor, were generally successful. With a strong and well-trained army they got as far as Lake Van. This opened the possibility that the Persians would give in, but in 579 Chosroes died and Hormisdas IV became the new Great King. The Byzantine historian Theophylactus has little good to say of him. [34] Shortly before Justin II had also died to be succeeded by Tiberius II (578-582). Hormisdas decided to continue the war.

A bold attempt was made by Maurice to march on the Persian capital Ctesiphon, but it misfired (580), probably because an Arabian chieftain who was thought to be an ally of the Byzantines, informed the Persians of the intended attack. [35] Nevertheless, in the next year Maurice gained a signal victory at Constantina (Constantia, now Tela d'Mazdalat), north of Nisibis (the modern Nusayban). [36] When Tiberius II died, Maurice succeeded him (582-602). The new Emperor conducted the war with great energy and not without success. He would have been even more successful, if he had not reduced the pay of his men which made them mutinous (588).

11. A disputed succession in Persia

Then the unexpected happened : the Persians fell out with one another. Hormisdas was a cruel tyrant who made many victims among his own people. Theophylactus, in his usual rhetorical style, states that "the river [Tigris] constituted an unclothed tomb for those consigned to death by the king." [37] In 590 a Persian general, Baram (Varahram) revolted against the king and thus unleashed a civil war, wich resulted in the death of Hormisdas and his becoming king in September. [38]

Although also defeated and humbled, Hormisdas' son Chosroes (II) did not abandon his claims to the throne; he told his opponent this in a letter the beginning of which perfectly demonstrates the universalistic idea that Persians Emperors had of themselves (since the days of Cyrus I!). "Chosroes, king of kings, master of dynasts, lord of nations, prince of peace, saviour for mankind, among the gods a righteous immortal man, a god most manifest among man, exceedingly glorious, victorious, who rises with the sun and bestows eyes on the night, distinguished in his ancestry, a king who hates war, bounteous, who employs the Asones [unidentified], and preserves the monarchy for Persians." [39] A Persian king believed himself to be more than human.

Yet for the time being the master of dynasts had to keep a very low profile. He fled to Byzantine territory and sent a message, written on tablets, to the Emperor Maurice, who was delighted with this news. [40] Perhaps this letter was, as Bury remarks, 'not due to the brain of Chosroes but to the pen of Theophylactus', but even in that case the arguments used in it are worth considering. First of all, addressing his Byzantine colleague Chosroes did not use the lofty titles he had employed in his letter to Baram. He continued to state that "God had effected that the whole world should be illuminated from the very beginning by two eyes, namely by the most powerful kingdom of the Romans and by the most prudent sceptre of the Persian state." This is the time-honoured idea of the division of the whole world into two power blocks, presented as an arrangement that forms part of the creational order. A few lines further Chosroes spoke of 'God's excellent dispositions'. We should, however, not forget that on an earlier occasion the King of kings had called himself the sun and the Byzantine Emperor the moon. The practical upshot of this letter was that Chosroes asked Maurice's help to bring him to the Persian throne. [41]

Maurice did not want the fugitive to come to his capital; he thought it more sensible for him to stay as close as possible to the Persian frontier. Persian ambassadors were dispatched to Constantinople then; what they said to Maurice is equally illuminating of the Byzantine-Persian relationship. Chosroes' envoys must have harboured the suspicion that the Byzantines would seize this opportunity to bring down the Persian Empire for good. For they stated that "it is impossible for a single monarchy to embrace the innumerable cares of the organization of the universe [sic], and with one mind's rudder to direct a creation as great as that over which the sun watches. For it is never possible for the earth to resemble the unity of the divine and primary rule, and to obtain a disposition corresponding to that of the upper order." This is a remarkable politico-philosophical statement. It points out that there is an essential difference between the upper (divine) and lower (human) orders, a difference that might even be called dualistic. For the upper order is primary and all-embracing, whereas the lower order is in the care of mankind, "whose nature is unstable and whose judgment most worthless because of its tendency towards evil."

Chosroes' spokesmen then descended to a more practical level. "Even though the Persians were to be deprived of power [i.e. by the Byzantines], their power would immediately transfer to other men [i.e. not to the Byzantines]." In the East imperialistic nations had always succeeded each other, the Medes and the Persians and the Parthians. The speaker then held Alexander's adventures before the Emperor's eyes. He called the Macedonian king a 'stripling' with an 'insane and unreasonbable ambition' who became 'an immature sport of fortune' since "he attempted to subjugate the universe to a single unitary power ... as far as the sky is spread and the sun's eye shines with sparkling rays." Coming to the end of his speech, the ambassador descended to a still lower level of practical politics : if Maurice was ready to help Chosroes to win the throne, Persia was prepared to restitute Dara and Martyropolis (situated to the east of the Tigris) to Byzantium. [42]

The veiled warnings of the envoys were superfluous, since it is highly improbable that Maurice really wanted to become the master of the whole Persian Empire. He would be content to put a monarch on the throne who would then be dependent on him. He therefore resolved to assist Chosroes in his undertaking. When Baram heard this, he too sent ambassadors to Maurice asking him to desist from his plans and offering him the strategic city of Nisibis and all of Mesopotamia in return. [43] In a short campaign Chosroes, helped by a Byzantine force, succeeded in routing his opponent's army and in becoming king of Persia as Chosroes II (591-628).

12. The fall of Maurice and of Narses

Maurice was succeeded by Phocas (602-610), a usurper who had won the throne through an army rebellion. When he heard that the populace of the capital had chosen the triumphant Phocas's side, Maurice took off his imperial robes and fled with his family in the middle of the night in a boat. He landed at Chalcedon, on the opposite shore of the Bosporus, but was arrested there by Phocas's soldiers and brought back to the capital. There his five children were slaughtered before his eyes after which he himself was killed. Their heads were displayed on stakes on the Campus of the Tribunal for several days, "and the inhabitants of the city would go forth and view them until the heads began to smell." [44]

Chosroes II had felt indebted to Maurice personally so that, as long as this Byzantine Emperor lived, that is, to 602, peace prevailed. However, when Phocas had become Emperor, the Persian ruler regained his freedom of action.

He coveted the rich Byzantine province of Syria. But this province was guarded by an army under the command of the old but still formidable general Narses with the help of whose name Persian mothers threatened their naughty children. [45] Another person who thought very ill of what had been done to Maurice was Narses. Phocas did not have the support of the imperial bureau and of many military commanders. The Byzantine historiographer Theophanes even suggests that Narses had invited Chosroes to declare war on the Byzantines. [46]

What is certain is that Phocas feared the famous old warrior. Suspecting that the Emperor would deprive him of his command, Narses revolted and occupied Edessa, on the far side of the Euphrates. A general who was loyal to Phocas laid siege to Edessa whereupon Narses escaped to Hieropolis; this move brought him back to northern Syria. There Domentziolos, a nephew of the new Emperor, came to him asking him to return to Constantinople and assuring him that he would suffer no harm at the hands of Phocas. Narses believed him and went back to the capital, only to be committed to the pile. [47]

13. Chosroes II attacks

With his most redoutable opponent out of the way and with far less able Byzantine generals now confronting him, Chosroes attacked. His first target was the fortress town of Dara - 'the key to the Empire' [48] - which he captured after a year long siege (604/605). After this success his armies streamed into Syria, Armenia, where the Byzantine frontier town Theodosiopolis (near the sources of the Euphrates) fell into their hands in 607, and Mesopotamia where the Byzantines lost the important cities of Amida (near the sources of the Tigris) and Edessa. Pushing relentlessly further, Persian troops came to beleaguer Caesarea in the heartland of Cappadocia, while reconnoitring elements even appeared in the vicinity of Chalcedon on the Bosporus. It seemed likely that all the Asiatic possessions of Byzantium would be lost. [49]

14. The fall of Phocas

This catastrophic situation, combined with the misrule of Phocas who raged far and wide against his opponents, among them the Monophysites, caused revolt after revolt. In Syria in 608 the Monophysites rose in rebellion against the imperial policy; they were even ready to welcome the Persians as their liberators. In 610 Antioch saw a Jewish rising. [50] Discontent reigned everywhere; the number of disaffected Byzantines was enormous. Then a strong leader stepped forward, Heraclius, the exarch of North Africa. He became the energetic leader of the opposition. In 608 he began by seizing Egypt, because he needed a considerable fleet. With this fleet his son, also called Heraclius, sailed into the harbour of the capital on October 10th 610. Never at a loss for a gripping image Gibbon writes that "Phocas beheld from the windows of his palace his approaching and inevitable fate." [51]

The arrival of the fleet caused widespread rioting against Phocas in the city. A personal enemy of the Emperor, a certain Photius, who hated him, it is said, because Phocas had seduced his wife, penetrated the palace. Hearing that Heraclius' men had come ashore, all Phocas's retinue took to their heels, so that Photius found his enemy abandoned by everyone. Helped by some soldiers, he arrested the Emperor, tore his imperial robes off him, bound his arms together behind his back, and brought him to the exarch Heraclius who was still on board. He greeted the fallen ruler with these words : "Is it thus, you wretch, that you have governed the state?", whereupon Phocas answered : "No doubt you will do it better." He then met the cruel fate of a cruel man. His right arm and his genitals were cut off, and what remained of him was dragged to the market-place of the Bull to be burnt in public. Heraclius now became Emperor as Heraclius I (610-641). [52]

15. No counter-offensive yet

The advent to the throne of Heraclius, energetic and powerful though he was and having the support (for the time being) of the population, did not of course spell a sudden reversal of fortune. We are not very well informed about what happened on the Asiatic front. Byzantine historiographers often followed the rule that is popular in autocratic states : no news is good news. Mishaps that are not mentioned did not happen. One Byzantine historiographer even candidly expresses this with these words that "it is fit to commit to silence the greater part of our distress." [53] Nevertheless, it could not be concealed that "the Emperor Heraclius found the affairs of the Roman [Byzantine] state undone, for the Avars had devastated Europe, while the Persians had destroyed all Asia and had captured the cities and annihilated in battle the Romans." [54]

For the moment the news remained desperately bad; tidings came that Antioch had fallen into the hands of the Persians. But Heraclius needed time to restore the structures of the state and to reorganize the army. The only thing he could do was to send "ambassadors to Chosroes urging him to cease shedding the blood of men, to appoint levies, and receive tribute. But the latter dismissed the ambassadors empty-handed, without having spoken to them, for he hoped to seize the Roman state in its entirety." [55]. The new Emperor was forced to look on when the Persian general Shahr Barz [56], nicknamed 'the Royal Boar' [57], invaded Syria with a large force with which he took Damascus in 613 or 614, pushed on to the Phoenician cities on the coast, and from there to Jerusalem which was captured in 614 or 615. The Holy Cross became Persian booty and was brought to their land. [58]

In 617 or 618 Heraclius sent a second embassy to Chosroes, not in his own name but in that of the Senate. The envoys carried with them a long letter in which it was argued that the Persian ruler should not impute the misdeeds of Phocas to the present Emperor; it was namely so that Chosroes posed as the avenger of Maurice, but had not ceased his aggression when Heraclius had ascended the throne. The ambassadors may well have wished that they had stayed at home, for Chosroes did not even receive them but, instead, imprisoned them. The message he sent to Heraclius was this. "I shall not spare you until you renounce the crucified one and worship the sun." [59] More than once it transpires that the Persian War was not only a political conflict, but that it had also a religious background. Judging his situation desperate, Heraclius thought of going to Libya. However, as Nikephoros tells us, Sergius, the patriarch of Constantinople, brought him to the Aya Sofia and made him swear that he would not leave the imperial city. [60]

The all too easy successes of the Persians can, at least partly, be explained by the grave dissensions, mainly of a religious nature, between the different population groups in the Empire. In Syria the strong Nestorian element felt inclined towards the Persians because they found these more tolerant than the Byzantine government. In Egypt there was bitter enmity between the orthodox and the Monophysites. And in Jerusalem it was the hatred between the Christians and the Jews that decided the fate of the city. [61]

There can be no doubt that the Jews of Jerusalem committed atrocities against the Christians, a sizeable number of whom were massacred. [62] There is no excuse for such crimes, of course, but there is a background. Both Maurice and Heraclius I followed a policy that was far from friendly towards the Jews. Especially the latter seems to have had a superstitious fear of Jews. There exists a story that an astrologer had told him that his Empire would be brought down by circumcized people. These people were not circumscribed, but he understood them as Jews. Who else? he will have thought. He probably feared that the Byzantine Jews were conspiring against the state - an old bogey this, that of the Jewish conspiracy and of conspiracies in general, whether Jewish, Marxist, capitalistic, clerical, Jesuit, freemason, you name it. Persons in power are often somewhat paranoiac, or very paranoiac, if we think of a man like Stalin. They always fear they will loose the power they have, through a disloyal opposition or a sinister conspiracy in which their best friends, even members of their family, may be involved. Did not Saddam Hussein also have his own son-in-law executed? Did Hitler not have his own brother-in-law, the SS-commander Fegelein, put against the wall? There is evidence that Heraclius staged a Europe-wide campaign against Jewry. He concluded a treaty with Sisibut, the Visigothic king of Spain, that he would force his Jewish subjects to let themselves be baptized. Later he tried to convince the Frankish king Dagobert that he should persecute his Jews; he urged him that they should be baptized. The same policy was followed with regard to his own Jewish subjects. [63] There is no excuse for such folly, but in 614 Heraclius must have felt that his Empire was teetering on the brink of the abyss.

16. The Persians march on

Palestinian refugees fled *en masse* to Alexandria in Egypt, but if they hoped to be safe from the Persians there, they were fatally wrong. Perhaps they counted on the circumstance that the country of the Nile had not seen an invader for centuries. Relentlessly continuing their triumphant march, the Persians invaded Egypt. In no time Pelusium, the heavily fortified frontier town, was in their hands. From there the Persian army spread rapidly over the almost defenseless country, which fell like a ripe apple into their hands. [64] It came almost to the frontiers of Ethiopia. Chosroes entered Alexandria in person. In Libya, which the Emperor considered his last refuge, the Great King pushed on to Tripoli, inflicting heavy losses on the Greek colonies in Cyrene. [65] This was a heavy blow for the Byzantines, for just as Egypt had always been the granary of the city of Rome, it now provided the population of Constantinople with grain. The immediate consequence of the fall of Egypt was famine in the capital, while the loss of the Holy Cross utterly demoralized the populace. It was as though God had forsaken his faithful. And if all this were not yet enough, a second large Persian army engulfed Asia Minor and appeared before the walls of Chalcedon, just opposite Constantinople. [66]

In a remarkable short time the Sasanian Empire had reached the extent the Persian Empire had had in the days of Cyrus II and Xerxes. It seemed to be in their power to launch the decisive attack on the European part of the Byzantine Empire, thus dealing it the death-blow. The only consolation Heraclius had was that Chalcedon held firm. It was in this seemingly hopeless situation that he received a letter from Chosroes. Styling himself 'the noblest of the gods, the king and master of the whole earth', he dubbed Heraclius 'his vile and insensate slave'; the dualistic opposition could not be expressed in stronger terms. "Are you ignorant that I have subdued land and sea to my laws? And could I not also destroy Constantinople?" Yet Chosroes was so magnanimous that he would not do this. "I will pardon all your faults [the master is speaking to his servant]. If you will come hither with your wife and children, I will give you lands, vines, and olive groves, which will supply you with the necessities of life. I will look upon you with a kindly glance." What Chosroes meant is that the Byzantine ruler should surrender the remainder of his Empire to him. Heraclius should not think that his God could save him. "Christ ... was not able to save himself from the Jews, who killed him by nailing him to the cross." [67]

It lasted a long time before Heraclius was ready to mount a counter-offensive, for he also had to ward off the Avars. In Chapter II it was related how he barely escaped their hands in 619. It took until 622 before he could set off. In the meantime the situation had deteriorated still more, because the Persians had captured Chalcedon in 617. [68] There is even one report, by the Armenian historiographer Sebeos, that the Persians actually attacked Constantinople itself, but that the Byzantine navy was still strong enough to destroy the invading army, which lost four thousand men. [69]

17. The great counter-offensive

a. Triumph in Cappadocia

Heraclius led the great counter-offensive in person. "In this year [622] ... the Emperor Heraclius, after celebrating the Easter feast, straightaway set out against Persia on Monday evening." The orator George of Pisidia wished him all the best in blood-soaked verse, telling the Emperor that he would dye his black buskins red in Persian blood. [70] If the Persians might have thought that Heraclius would sail up the Black Sea and land his troops in Armenia, a hot-spot in the East-West struggle, they had deceived themselves. Instead, the fleet travelled down the Aegean coast of Asia Minor in a southwardly direction and then turned east; the landing took place at the so-called Gates that lead from Cilicia to Syria. From there Heraclius could strike in any direction, protect the Syrian Christians, and recruit men for the army. In the coastal plain he subjected his men to regular and heavy training. [71] These preparations lasted half a year.

Winter was already approaching when he broke up at last and marched northward through the heartland of Asia Minor. High hopes were placed on the fact that he dispersed bands of guerilleros. [72] A far more important result was that the Persian troops that kept Chalcedon occupied, watching their chance to capture Constantinople, now were called back for fear that their line of communication would be cut.

The two armies came near each other somewhere in Cappadocia. The Persian general Shahr Barz, who commanded the returning contingents, tried to lure Heraclius away by feigning to move towards the Gates, but the Emperor did not follow him. Shahr Barz retraced his steps and both armies prepared their ranks for battle. There is no telling where exactly they stood. The pious George, always ready to tell us that Heraclius was conducting a crusade against a heathen and godless nation, describes in verse how Shahr Barz amused himself by having nude girls dance before him to the sound of cymbals and musical instruments; Heraclius sought peace of mind by listening to psalm singing, accompanied by divine music. Perhaps the poet was giving himself away somewhat by mentioning that here too there were girls around, but very decent ones, of course. [73]

We know the approximate date of the great clash between the two armies, since just before there had been a lunar eclipse on the 22nd of January 623 (and the winter is very severe on the Cappadocian plateau!). The sources we have at our disposal do not enable us to reconstruct the course of events, but one thing is certain : the Persians were routed. They had to fight with the low sun in their eyes - "those rays that they worshipped as a god", says George sarcastically. Many Persians, flying through the rugged mountain country, came to grief when they were overtaken by the Byzantines. It seemed like a hunt on mountain goats, they found. [74] George, the court poet, never at a loss for words of praise for Heraclius, found him already to be greater than Alexander. [75]

b. Persia invaded

The victorious Emperor led his army into winter quarters in Pontus and returned to the capital because of problems with the Avars. He set out again on March 15th and celebrated Easter at Nicomedia on March 27th. How high his star had risen is shown by the fact that he took his wife, the Empress Martina, with him. She was his second wife whom he had married after his first wife, Eudocia, had succumbed to an epileptic fit. Martina was his niece, and the marriage was, therefore, incestuous, a circumstance that was looked upon poorly by the inhabitants of Constantinople; she was called 'the accursed thing', and even George, the poet laureate, never mentions her name. Their union resembled that of Justinian and Theodora, for whereas Heraclius could be hesitant, Martina was a powerful woman who had a strong influence on her husband. [76]

Heraclius joined his troops in Pontus and marched eastward with them. It seems that Chosroes underrated his opponent - always a fatal thing in warfare -, because he had already sent Shahr Barz back to Chalcedon, but once again this general had to retrace his steps. The Byzantines invaded the Sasanian Empire from an unexpected side. From Asia Minor Heraclius led his troops through Armenia into Colchis (Lazica, the modern Georgia); after having continued his eastward march for some time, he turned sharply south. He was now definitely in Persian territory, in the northern part of Media, the present-day Azerbaijan, burning and slaughtering everywhere. Having crossed the wild river Araxes (the Araks), far to the south, he sent a message to Chosroes that he was ready for peace, if only the Great King would offer acceptable conditions. Did he really mean this and did he hope that the imminent threat to his territories would induce his opponent to conclude a really lasting peace? Or was it a diplomatic hoax intended to lay the burden of what was coming on the shoulders of Chosroes? Whatever the case, the Persians were not ready for peace but for battle.

Chosroes came marching north with a large army. He advanced as far as the town of Ganzaca (perhaps the modern Takht-i-Soleima). That the struggle between the two Empires had a religious background, is also demonstrated by a remark of Theophanes who says that Chosroes "forced the Christians [the orthodox, that is] to convert to the religion of Nestorius so as to wound the Emperor." [77] The Byzantines, in their turn, did not stay behind. When they took Ganzaca, they hoped to find the Holy Cross there, but it was elsewhere. Instead, they found a statue of Chosroes, which they called a 'blasphemy'; it represented the Great King in the temple of the Sun, venerating it in adoration. The indignant Byzantines destroyed it. When they had reached Thebarmes, where Zoroaster was said to have been born, they burned down its Temple of Fire, in revenge for what the Persians had done to Jerusalem.

c. In the winter quarters

The morale of the troops was so high that Heraclius might have pushed on as far as Ctesiphon, but winter was approaching, and he thought it prudent to look for winter quarters. It was obviously a difficult decision, for Heraclius had to have recourse to an unusual expedient, the so-called *sors evangelica*. He first made the army purify itself for three days. "He then opened the Holy Gospel and found a passage that directed him to winter in Albania." As a diligent Bible reader I should like to know on which passage the imperial eye fell. The Albania in question is not the Balkan country, but a Caucasian region, north of Armenia and bordering on the Caspian Sea. Plodding on through the snow he reached it with fifty thousand captives in his train. These he liberated, because he pitied them 'in his compassionate heart'. But it was also difficult to sustain them, of course; still more important, he hoped to wean the Persians away from their allegiance to Chosroes whom Theophanes calls 'the destroyer of the world'. [78]

d. Uneventful years

When the winter was over and the campaign of 624 could begin, the Persians took the initiative. They had now two armies in the field which combined their forces : that of Shahr Barz, and the other that of a newly appointed general,

Sarablangas, nicknamed 'the Panther of the Realm', an energetic man, says Theophanes, but 'filled with vanity'. Their aim was to prevent Heraclius from penetrating Persia. Making a detour, the Emperor tried to reach the Araxes and cross it, but he was intercepted by the two Persian armies. Heraclius attacked and won a victory, costing Sarablangas his life. Once again it became apparent that the Byzantines saw this as a deadly, a dualistic struggle between two religions, for the Emperor exhorted his troops with these words : "May we win the crown of martyrdom so that we may be praised in the future and receive our recompense from God." In spite of his great victory, Heraclius did not press his advantage, probably because the Caucasian allies he had recruited were none too trustworthy.

Thus the year 624 passed without anything decisive happening. There was a lot of manoeuvring and counter-manoeuvring, but the armies did not engage each other. Late in the year Heraclius moved to Persarmenia. The winter had already set in when he made a night attack with shock troops on the town of Salban where Shahr Barz had established his temporary headquarters. It became a catastrophe for the Persians. Shahr Barz fled in the cold winter night, 'naked and unshod as he was', leaving 'his golden belt, set with precious stones, and boots' behind. He was almost the only one to escape. When the Byzantine horses thundered through the streets, the Persian staff and body guards climbed upon the roofs of the houses. Then the Byzantines set these houses on fire so that many of them perished in the flames, while "others were bound in fetters." Heraclius' compassion obviously had its limits! The Byzantine army spent the rest of this winter in Persarmenia. [79]

On March 1st 625 Heraclius broke up his camp; once again avoiding invading Persia proper, he took his way southward, crossing the passes of the Taurus, still thick with snow, into Cilicia. From there marching eastward for seven days, he crossed the Tigris and recaptured Amida and Martyropolis (the modern Silvan); these towns had been Byzantine possessions. This news led to great rejoicing in Constantinople. There developed now a steeple chase between the Byzantine army and the forces of Shahr Barz who had a personal bone to pick with Heraclius. Crossing the Taurus for the second time, the

Emperor came to the town of Germanicia in Cilicia. We are now back in Byzantine territory; as of old the struggle was in fact a frontier war.

Near this town a battle was fought in which Heraclius, recognizable by his purple boots and receiving many blows, fought 'in a superhuman manner', to quote the admiring Theophanes. Even Shahr Barz flowed over with admiration. "Do you see ... how boldly the Caesar stands in battle, how he fights alone against such a multitude and wards off blows like an anvil?" It is not clear what happened further in this year, but it seems that Heraclius did not pursue the campaign energetically. He spent the winter north of the river Halys (the Kizil-Irmak) in Asia Minor. [80]

e. Chosroes' master stroke

The war was clearly now in an impasse. In three years of campaigning Heraclius I had achieved not much to boast of. But then Chosroes decided to deal the Byzantines a decisive blow. I am referring to the events of the year 626 of which I have already written in Chapter I. The Persian Emperor acted in collusion with the Avars who came to beleaguer Constantinople from the landside. They pitched their tents before the Long Walls, but the city was so ably defended that they were incapable of taking it. Finally, they withdrew, both exhausted and hungry.

Chosroes entrusted an army to his experienced general Shahr Barz who was to his Persian master what Belisarius had been to Justinian I. Hindered by nobody, he crossed the whole length of Asia Minor and appeared again in Chalcedon, opposite the capital. An attempt to ferry Persian troops over the Bosporus for a combined attack on the capital failed disastrously, because the Byzantine navy was in firm control of the sea routes. After the retreat of the Avars Shahr Barz stayed where he was and spent the winter in Chalcedon. [81]

We might expect that Heraclius would have hastened to come the help of his beleaguered imperial city - did the end of the Byzantine Empire not seem near? -, but he did nothing of the kind. He only sent one contingent back. A retreat would probably have been a dangerous thing, for Chosroes had selected a large army to watch him. Élite troops, the so-called 'Golden Spearmen', closely followed his movements; they were under the command of yet another capable general, called Sain (or Saes). Heraclius entrusted part of his troops to his brother Theodore with the task of opposing Sain.

These two armies confronted each other somewhere in Mesopotamia. Then something happened that Theophanes considered a miracle, 'by the mediation of the Theotokos [the Holy Virgin]'. When battle was in progress, there was suddenly a violent hailstorm that heavily battered the Persians, while the Byzantines enjoyed fair weather; the victory was theirs. The defeat of his élite troops made Chosroes very angry. He freely poured out the phials of his wrath on the unfortunate Sain. This made the poor man so depressive that he fell ill and died. On the orders of Chosroes the body was preserved in salt and sent to him. In an access of what Bury calls *Kaiserwahnsinn*, the king had the corpse flogged. Yet it is remarkable, says this same author, that "he never lost faith in Shahr Barz, numerous defeats and failures notwithstanding." [82] Theophanes and other Byzantine historiographers never failed to point out the difference between the civilized manners of Heraclius and the rude and brutal behaviour of Chosroes.

f. The Turkish allies

Heraclius had no reason to be bothered. Constantinople was now safe; the Avars were driven back across the Danube, and Shahr Barz was pinned down in Chalcedon; of course, there was a risk that he would return to swell the Persian ranks. With the forces that remained Heraclius took the same route as in 623, through Colchis into Azerbaijan. May we believe Theophanes, he got reinforcements, namely Turkish contingents. When marching through Colchis, Heraclius had invited them to join him. [83] And they came! Laying Persian country waste, they advanced as far as Tiflis (Tbilisi, now the capital of Georgia), where the conjunction of the two armies took place. Theophanes' relation is intended to show how deeply in awe of Byzantine power the Turks were at that time. Their commander did obeisance to Heraclius, kissing his neck. "And the entire army of the Turks [forty thousand men, according to

Theophanes] fell flat on the ground, reverencing the Emperor with an honour that is unknown among all nations." Their general "took as much pleasure in the Emperor's conversation as he was astonished by his appearance and wisdom." This reminds me of the encounter of the Queen of Sheba with King Solomo.

"Taking these men along, the Emperor advanced on Chosroes." [84] Byzantines and Turks fighting together, that was a spectacle that would seem improbable to the former in later days. [85] Theophanes says that Chosroes was distracted when he heard of all those Byzantines and Turks marching on him, but with regard to the Turks, who were not yet the disciplined and redoutable warriors of the later Middle Ages, he could soon feel relieved. It was already September, and winter was approaching. Not relishing the idea of a winter campaign, the Turks "started, little by little, to slip away until all of them had returned home." [86]

g. A battle on hallowed ground

It is difficult to ascertain what Heraclius did after the departure of his untrustworthy Turkish allies. We can only pin him down in the autumn of 627. On October 7th he was in a town north of Arbela (Arbil, in Iraq, east of Mosul) in Assyria. Chosroes must have become very irritated because none of his generals had been able to stop his formidable enemy who now stood well inside Persian territory. He nominated a new commander-in-chief, Razates, whom he sent on his way with this encouraging message : "If you cannot conquer, you can die." The terrified man followed Heraclius at some distance, 'trailing behind, like a hungry dog', says Theophanes contemptuously. The Byzantines marched southward with the Tigris to their right.

On Saturday December 12th 627 he joined battle with Razates near the place where Nineveh once stood. The story of this battle is full of Alexandrian reminiscences. The battlefield of Gaugamela, where Alexander the Great in 331 B.C. had won a decisive victory over the armies of Darius III, was not far off. In the eyes of his historiographers Heraclius behaved like a second Alexander, excelling in personal valour. Riding on his charger Dorkon, he was challenged by Razates, who had nothing to lose, except his head. The Persian general almost killed the Emperor : one of his arrows brushed his lips, another scraped his ankle. Then one of the bodyguards rode on and severely wounded Razates in the shoulder with his sword; the man fell off his horse and was killed by the Emperor who cut off his head. The battle ended at nightfall in a devastating Byzantine victory. Twenty-eight Persian standards fell into Byzantine hands; Heraclius' personal booty was the massive golden armour of Razates. [87]

h. After Chosroes

After this great victory Heraclius continued his southward march, always with the Tigris to his right. He first crossed the Great Zab (Zei Badinan) and on December 23^d the Lesser Zab (Zei Koya), both tributaries of the Tigris; the bridges on both Zabs had been seized by an advance party. On Christmas Eve he reached the park of Veklal, a possession of the royal treasurer. where he celebrated Christmas and the New Year. Such a park has a Persian name, *pairi-daeza*, which the Greeks rendered as *paradeisos*, our paradise. Hundreds of gazelles grazed there, wild asses and sheep, oxen, and pigs. The soldiers had no lack of meat for their Christmas dinner! "The whole army rested contentedly and gave glory to God." The Byzantines had an incredible piece of good luck, for they intercepted a Persian courier who was on his way to Chalcedon with a message from Chosroes to Shahr Barz that he should return with great speed. Another courier was expedited with the false news that the Persians had won a great victory over the Byzantines, so that Shahr Barz could stay where he was.

Chosroes was in his royal residence Dastargherd then, some twenty miles north of the Persian capital Ctesiphon. Hearing that the Byzantines were so near, he panicked; his money and his possessions were packed on a long train of elephants, camels, and mules. The Great King himself escaped with his family through a gap made in the city wall near the palace and fled south as fast as he could. He spent the night in a small farm-house. Ctesiphon had not seen the king within its walls for twenty-four years, for he had received an oracle that it would be his end if he ever came there. In spite of this warning he passed through the capital and then sped on eastward to the Persian heartland. But before he did this, he crossed the Tigris on the pontoon bridge that connected Ctesiphon with Seleucia and deposited his treasures in this town just opposite the capital.

Having destroyed the palaces they found on their way, the Byzantines entered Dastargherd in the first days of 627 and celebrated Epiphany there. The royal palaces in this town were all committed to the flames. "These priceless, wonderful and astonishing structures he [Heraclius] demolished to the ground so that Chosroes might learn how great a pain the Romans [the Byzantines] had suffered when their cities were laid waste and burnt by them," says Theophanes. [88] Does history not repeat itself? It does! We must think here of Alexander who set the palaces of Persepolis on fire as a retribution for what the Persians had one to Athens in 480 B.C.

At this juncture Heraclius made a peace offering to Chosroes. "Let us extinguish the fire before it consumes everything." This proves that it was not his intention to destroy the Sasanian Empire. To justify his presence on Persian soil he used a hypocritical argument. "It is not of my free will that I am burning Persia, but constrained by you." However, Chosroes, in his folly, turned down this proposal. [89] Its acceptance might have saved him, but its rejection was his undoing.

Heraclius marched on until he stood opposite Ctesiphon, on the bank of the Tigris. He made no attempt to capture the capital, although it was the great prize of the campaign. It was winter, he had still a river between his army and the city, and Ctesiphon was then one of the best defended frontier towns in the world. And perhaps he had information that something was brewing against Chosroes so that he could lean back and wait. In any case, he led his troops into their winter quarters north of the Zagros range, which he crossed just in time to avoid an exceptionally heavy snow-storm.

j. Chosroes' fall

Discontent with Chosroes was widespread among his subjects; he was cruel and despotic. The fact that the enemy was operating freely on Persian soil did not enhance his prestige. Ill with dysentery, he probably felt his end was near and expressed his intention to crown one of his sons. His candidate was, however, not his first-born, Siroes, the crown prince, who took this very badly and began to conspire against his father with a number of generals. Twenty-two satraps chose his side. Siroes was lavish with promises : the soldiers would get more pay, the Christians would have freedom of religion, and taxes would be reduced.

A party was sent to arrest Chosroes; he fled but was caught. Not one of his courtiers lifted a finger to help him. He was imprisoned in a castle or tower with the sinister name of 'House of Darkness' or 'Castle of Forgetfulness'. He arrived there 'in iron fetters, his elbows bound behind his back, and with iron weights hung on his feet and his neck'. In this dungeon his loving son submitted him to the most exquisite of cruelties. The satraps might come and insult him, even spit upon him. His favourite son, the intended Emperor, was killed before his eyes, together with his other sons (Siroes's half-brothers). His diet was water and bread. It is reported that a heap of gold, silver, and precious stones was put before him, and that he was told to "enjoy these things which you have loved so insanely and amassed." One chronicle says that he was starved to death, another that he was shot through with arrows, "and thus in slow pain he gave up his wicked soul." The new Emperor was called Siroes, who else. His Persian name was Kavad-Shiruya; he came to the throne in February 628. [90]

Heraclius remarked that Chosroes would have come to no harm if only he had himself given up to him, thus subtly pointing out the difference between a civilized Christian ruler and a pagan parricide. "It had never been his wish that a king - not even Chosroes - should lose his glory." He even went so far as to declare that "I would have hastened ..., were he to have survived, to restore him to his own kingship, complete though my victory over him might have been." Propaganda of a man who wanted to pose as an equitable ruler? Or does it, and let us pay attention to that 'complete victory', express his failed hope that he might have become the protector of the Sasanian Empire? Be this as it may, he also said that what was done to the murdered Emperor was 'a just punishment'. Heraclius condescendingly addressed Kavad as 'my dear son', not as 'my brother', as kings used to call one another. [91]

k. Peace concluded

Kavad immediately made peace with Heraclius, on April 3^d; the war was immensely impopular in his country, and he would have trouble to maintain himself. The *Chronicon paschale* has preserved for us the triumphant letters and manifestos the Emperor sent to the capital in which he also described the fate of Chosroes and how his campaign had progressed. [92] Now Heraclius could joyfully return to Constantinople, fulfilling what Theophanes calls a *theoria*, a 'mystical allegory'. "For God completed all of creation in six days and called the seventh day a day of rest. So the Emperor also, after undergoing many toils for six years, returned in the seventh to the City amid joy and rested there." Gibbon found this Sabbath metaphor 'used somewhat profanely'. [93] What Theophanes suggests is that Heraclius was an (almost divine) world ruler. He made his triumphal entry into the capital where the population received him 'dancing with joy'. [94] He brought four elephants with him which "he paraded at hippodrome contests to the delight of the citizens." [95]

An immediate result of the conclusion of the peace was that the Persians evacuated all the Byzantine provinces that they had conquered, even Egypt. The Holy Cross was restituted to the Byzantines. [96] One year later Heraclius brought the Cross back to Jerusalem and reinstated it there in its proper place. However, he spoilt this solemn occasion by banishing the Jews from the Holy City and ordering them not to come nearer to it than three miles. [97] It is interesting to note that Heraclius was accorded by law the surname of 'Scipio', an epithet that would fall to his successors too. In this manner the Byzantine present was linked to the Roman past. [98]

18. The final result

The future of the Byzantine Empire now looked rosy. The Sasanian Empire was defeated and made powerless by internal dissensions. The Avars were repulsed over the Danube. As of old this river and the Euphrates were the frontiers of the Empire. It should, however, not be forgotten that there was basically no change in the situation. The Persians might have been prevented from conquering the Asiatic part of the Empire, or perhaps all of it in collusion with the Avars, but the two Empires were still confronting each other on the Euphrates as they had already done for centuries.

The new situation which looked like a reinvigoration of the Byzantine Empire, was in fact only an Indian summer, lasting no more than five years. For both the Byzantines and the Persians a deadly danger arose in a quarter where they least of all expected it, in the Arabian desert. In 633 the Arabs began attacking Syria. What happened then and later must be the subject of a later chapter.

NOTES TO CHAPTER IV

1. See Vol. II, Ch. I.
2. See Vol. IV, Ch. IV, §§ 1-3.
3. See Vol. V, Ch. I, § 2.
4. See Vol. XI, Ch. III, § 6.
5. Proc., *Bello persico* 1.7-9.
6. Previté-Orton, *Medieval History I, 192.*
7. Quotation given by Bury, *Later Roman Empire* II, 418, without mentioning the source.
8. Gibbon, *Decline and Fall* II, 604/605.
9. Proc., *Bello persico* 1.14.
10. Proc., *Bello Persico* 1.13.
11. Proc. *Bello persico* 1.14.
12. Diehl, *Justinien* I, 513.

13. Proc., *Bello persico* 21.
14. Proc., *Bello persico* 2.2.3.
15. Proc., *Bello persico* 2.5-9.
16. Proc., *Bello gotico* 4.7, *Bello persico* 2.28.
17. Proc., *Bello persico* 2.19.
18. Proc., *Bello persico* 1.28.
19. Gibbon, *Decline and Fall* II, 622.
20. Proc., *Bello gotico* 4.8.
21. Proc., *Bello gotico* 4.11-12.
22. Bury, *Later Roman Empire* I, 467.
23. Bury, *Later Roman Empire* I, 466.
24. Quoted by Gibbon, *Decline and Fall* II, 623.
25. Evagrius, *HE* 5.7.
26. Menander, *Excerpta* 106-107.7.
27. Bury, *Later Roman Empire* II, 97.
28. Theophylactus, *Short history* 3.11.2-3.
29. Theophylactus, *Short history* 3.10.8-9.
30. Bury, *Later Roman Empire* II, 100; the source of this story is Ioh.Eph., *EH* 6.7.
31. Theophylactus, *Short history* 3.13.15.
32. It is possible that many details of the battle were invented by Theophylactus and also that it was he who put the words into the mouth of Justinian. In this context this does not matter, since it perfectly expresses what the Byzantines thought of the Persian religion. See also Ioh.Eph., *EH* 6.8-9.
33. Evagrius, *HE* 5.15.
34. Theophylactus, *Short History* 3.16.
35. Theophylactus, *Short History* 3.17.7; Ioh.Eph., *HE* 3.40 and 6.16-18; Evagrius, *HE* 5.20.
36. Joh., Eph., 6.26; in John the town is called Tella.
37. Theophylactus, *Short History* 3.16.9.
38. Theophylactus, *Short History* 4.7.1.
39. Theophylactus, *Short History* 4.8.5.
40. Theophylactus, *Short History* 4.10.4-10.

41. Theophylactus, *Short History* 4.11.
42. Theophylactus, *Short History* 4.13.4-24.
43. Theophylactus, *Short History* 4.14.8.
44. Theophanes, *Chronographia* AM 6094, AD 601/602 (288-290), and AM 6095, AD 602/603 (290-291); *Chronicon paschale* anno 602, I, 693.
45. Theophanes, *Chronographia* AM 6097, AD 605 (293).
46. Theophanes, *Chronographia* AM 6095, AD 602/603 (292).
47. Theophanes, *Chronographia* AM 6097, AD 604/605 (292-293).
48. Bréhier, *Monde byzantin* I, 47.
49. Theophanes, *Chronographia* AM 6100, AD 607/608 (296) and AM 6102, AD 609/610 (299).
50. Theophanes, *Chronographia* AM 6101, AD 608/609 (296).
51. Gibbon, *Decline and Fall* II, 782.
52. Nikephoros, *Short History* 1-2; *Chronicon paschale* I, 699-701.
53. Georg.Pis., *Bellum avaricum* 1.12. quoted by Bury, *Later Roman Empire* II, 214.
54. Theophanes, *Chronographia* AM 6103, AD 610/611 (299-300).
55. Theophanes, *Chronographia* AM 6105, AD 612/613 (300). The historicity of this report is sometimes doubted since no other historian has it, editor's note 1, pp.430/431.
56. The Greeks called him Sabazos.
57. His Persian name was Sahrvaraz.
58. Theophanes, *Chronographia* AM 6106, AD 613/614 (300-301); Nikephoros, *Short History* 12; *Chronicon paschale* anno 614, I, 704.
59. Theophanes, *Chronographia* AM 6109, AD 616/617 (301).
60. Nikephoros, *Short History* 8.
61. Gibbon, *Decline and Fall* II, 785, is guilty of an anti-Semitic remark in this context : "He [Chosroes] could enlist for this holy warfare an army of six-and-twenty thousand Jews, whose furious bigotry might compensate in some degree for their want of valour and discipline."
62. Gibbon, *Decline and Fall* II, 785, states that Jews [and Arabs] massacred ninety thousand Christians in the Holy City. Theophanes, *Chronographia* AM 6106, AD 613/614, says that "the Jews bought the Christians [i.e. from the Persians], each man to his means, and killed them," and he adds "*some* (my italics) say 90.000." Other historians present differing numbers of those killed, Theophanes, *Chronographia* 431, (editor's) note 1. The *Chronicon paschale*, anno 614, I, 704, says

that clerics, monks, and nuns were killed in their thousands, obviously by the Persians, but does not mention Jewish atrocities.
63. Fredegarius, *Chronicon* 4.65.
64. Theophanes, *Chronographia* AM 6107, AD 614/615 (301).
65. Theopahnes, *Chronographia*, AM 6107, AD 614/615.
66. *Chronicon paschale* anno 615, I, 706.
67. Quoted by Bury, *Later Roman Empire* II, 220.
68. Theophanes, *Chronographia* AM 6108, AD 615/616.
69. Quoted by Bury, *Later Roman Empire* II, 224.
70. Georg.Pis., *Fragm.A 20/21. PG 92, 1984 (reprint of ed. 1868)*.
71. Theophanes, *Chronographia* AM 6113, AD 620/621; Georg.Pis., *Expeditio persica* 3.118-121.
72. Georg.Pis., *Expeditio persica* 2.218/219.
73. Georg.Pis., *Expeditio persica* 2.239-241.
74. Theophanes, *Chronographia* AM 6113, AD 620/621 (304-306); Georg.Pis., *Expeditio persica* 3.1-40.
75. Georg.Pis., *Expeditio persica* 3.48.
76. Bury, *Later Roman Empire* II, 213 and 231.
77. Theophanes, *Chronographia* AM 6116, AD 623/624.
78. Theophanes, *Chronographia* AM 6114, AD 621/622 (307/308); Bury, *Later Roman Empire* II, 232.
79. Theophanes, *Chronographia* AM 6115, AD 622/623 (308-312).
80. Theophanes, *Chronographia* AM 6116, AD 623/624 (312-314).
81. Theophanes, *Chronographia* AM 6117, AD 624/625 (315-316).
82. Bury, *Later Roman Empire* II, 238/239; Theophanes, *Chronographia* AM 6117, AD 624/625.
83. Theophanes, *Chronographia* AM 6117, AD 624, 625 (315).
84. Theophanes, *Chronographia* AM 6117, AD 624/625 (315).
85. There was even a matrimonial alliance concluded. In a secret interview with the Turkish commander, who was called Ziebel, Heraclius showed him a portrait of his daughter Eudocia, the only child of his first wife, then fifteen years old, and promised to give her in wedlock to his Turkish ally. Later she was sent eastward indeed, but Ziebel died, and the poor girl could return home, Gibbon, *Decline and Fall* II, 798/799, and his note 103.

86. Theophanes, *Chronographia* AM 6117, AD 625/626 (317).
87. Nikephoros, *Short History* 14; Theophanes, *Chronographia* AM 6118, AD 625/626 (317-319).
88. Theophanes, *Chronographia* AM 6118, AD 625/626 (320-323).
89. Theophanes, *Chronographia* AM 6618, AD 625/626 (324).
90. Theophanes, *Chronographia* AM 6118, AD 625/626 (325-327); Nikephoros, *Short History* 15.
91. Nikephoros, *Short History* 15.
92. *Chronicon paschale*, anno 628, I 727-734.
93. Gibbon, *Decline and Fall* II, 804, note 114.
94. Theophanes, *Chronographia* AM 6119, AD 626/627 (327-328).
95. Nikephoros, *Short History* 18.
96. Nikephoros, *Short History* 17; Theophanes, *Chronographia* AM 6118, AD 625/626).
97. Theophanes, *Chronographia* AM 6129, AD 627/628.
98. Bury, *Later Roman Empire* II, 245.

CHAPTER V

BYZANTINE HOOLIGANISM

1. Popular amusement

In the ancient world of Rome and Byzantium, popular amusement was mainly provided by the circuses. We should, however, not understand by the concept of 'circus' as being what it is today, namely a tent or even a building where a performance is given by acrobats, tamed animals, and equestrian display, and clowns in the intervals. In Antiquity, a circus was what we today would call a stadium or a hippodrome. Here the gladiatior games took place; during the persecution of the Christians the public witnessed the martyrs being maimed and killed by wild animals. The main sport, however, was chariot racing.

In the Byzantine Empire there were circuses not only in Constantinople but also in many important centres such as Antioch, Damascus, Alexandria, and Thessalonika. Some of these circuses were exceedingly big; in the Roman world the biggest of them all must have been the Circus Maximus, which could seat up to two hundred thousand spectators, while the Hippodrome of Constantinople could seat a mere one hundred thousand persons.

2. A solemn occasion

Chariot races were to the ancient world what football matches (football in the sense of soccer) were to ours, namely the most beloved form of amusement. Perhaps 'amusement' is not the most appropriate denotation, because chariot racing was also a solemn occasion. The whole population of a town, I am thinking now of the capital, got 'high' at that event, even on the day before. Long before the gates were opened, a great multitude of spectators stood jostling each other before them. Then they all streamed in to take their seats under the purple veils of silk that protected them from the sun. On the front benches sat the most prominent members of the circus clubs, with sashes in their specific colours draped around them. On reserved seats sat the ambassadors of foreign nations. High above the ranks one saw the imperial box; somewhat lower stood the soldiers of the palace guard in order to protect the sovereign from assaults. The box was enclosed at the back side by heavy bronze doors; no steps led to this box from the lower ranks. Then the Emperor appeared with a crown on his head and the sceptre in his hand; as if he was a bishop, he made the sign of the cross over the spectators. The Empress and her retinue could also follow the races from the upper galleries of the church of Saint Stephen.

The races were followed by the spectators with incredible tension; there was applause, there were cries and menaces, some overheated spectators would even jump into the arena. The circus police had a hard job, wielding their batons, to keep the rival clubs apart. After the first rounds clowns and acrobats appeared, and pantomimes were presented. At the end of the morning the Emperor and his retinue withdrew to have their lunch at a neighbouring palace. The public in the meantime ate the provisions they had brought with them. Sometimes the imperial lunch lasted long, too long for the taste of the public. On one occasion, when the Emperor Phocas was slow in returning, the multitude began to sing : "Rise up, imperial sun, rise up, appear", half respectfully, half teasingly. But when the sun did not rise up, they became insulting : "You are enjoying the bottle again; once again you are seeing double!" [1] In the afternoon a spate of races again took place.

At the end of the long racing day, with its many sensations, feelings often ran high. Victories and defeats equally led to slanging-matches, to insults, to blows, which spilt over into the town itself where street battles would take place. The police interceded but were often powerless to stop the disturbances since all of the discontent and the frustrations of the non-privileged were invested in them. [2]

3. The charioteers

Just as the names of famous football players are today on everybody's lips - so that even analphabetes in these matters like me may know them -, so were the names of famous charioteers commonly known. Like the best known footballers, they were professionals. They already began their careers as teenagers and remained active for some thirty years. Some gained such a renown that statues of them were erected in the hippodrome. But just as that of our professional football players, their social status was low. Sometimes, however, a high-ranking person, in order to gain popularity with the populace or from sheer love of sport, climbed upon a chariot drawn by four horses and took part in a race; we may here think of the Emperor Nero in Rome and of the Emperors Theophilos (829-842) and Michael III (842-867) in Constantinople.

4. Fan clubs

In modern historiography on Byzantium the term 'circus factions' is much bandied about; it refers to the fan clubs of the charioteers, just as modern football clubs have their supporter clubs. However, Alan Cameron, a modern expert who studied the matter in depth, categorically states that "in every single text in which the word *factio* occurs, there can be no question but that it refers to the professional performers, not to their fan clubs. Furthermore, by the time the partisans had become at all prominent in the life of cities, the word factio had fallen out of use even to describe the professionals." [3] So it seems pointless to speak of 'circus factions'.

Yet this does not alter the fact that there were really fan clubs. Famous charioteers had their admirers and supporters; the terms 'Blues' and 'Greens' are well-known. One thing is very important : we should not think of them as political parties, just as the rivalries between the modern associations of supporters have no political implications. [4] The idea of naming the clubs after colours originated in Rome and from there spread to the East. It should be noted, first, that there were not only Blues and Greens, but also Reds and

Whites, and secondly, that these groups not only existed in Constantinople, but were also found in many other oriental cities, at least before 700.

It is often thought that the circus parties were closely connected with the *dêmoi*, the residential areas of a town. If this were true, the whole population of, for instance, Constantinople would belong to one of the parties which would make them something more than simply sporting associations 5. But Cameron and others combat this notion. There seems to be no difference between the terms Blue/Greens and the *dêmoi*; Byzantine authors, says Cameron, use them 'quite interchangeably'. The term *dêmoi* does not refer to residential areas, he argues. [5]

Another widespread idea is that the circus parties were related to the religious discord in the Empire, especially in the capital. In this perspective the Blues would be orthodox, and the Greens Monophysites. The converse was also thought to be correct, so that all monophysites were Greens. The indefatigable Cameron also demolishes this thesis; he contends that it is impossible for modern scholars to assume that circus riots could spring from something "as simple as the victory or defeat of this or that colour in the hippodrome". [6] Yet the street battles between the supporters of our football teams also have nothing to do with religious opinions - nor with politics. If their favourite club wins, they behave like madmen, and if it loses, they go even more berserk.

Perhaps there is more legitimacy to the supposition that the Blues and the Greens represented social classes, the former being more the party of the upper classes, for instance, of the landowning aristocracy and its clients, and the latter the party of the rest, not only of the poor but also of the world of business. When still a young prince, says Procopius, Justinian favoured the Blues, and many other young men of the *jeunesse dorée* did like him, for Procopius speaks of sons of men in high places. [7]

Cameron devotes a section to 'the differences between Blues and Greens'; [8] he clearly implies that there were differences, but he does not specify them at all. However, when all is said and done, some were Blues and others were Greens (who seem to have been the larger party). "The truth is, of course, that Blues hated Greens, not because they were lower-class or heretics - but simply because they were Greens." [9] And vice versa, I suppose. Let me compare this to the situation in my country, the Netherlands. Our two best-known football clubs are Ajax (Amsterdam) and Feyenoord (Rotterdam); both have their own supporter associations. There may be a touch of intercity rivalry between the two fan clubs, as there always has been between the two cities. Yet it is far from being a tale of two cities, for the respective adherents come from across the whole country, not just from the towns in question. There may have been an element of anti-Semitism in the Blue-Green rivalry, as one scholar or other thinks. There is also some sort of anti-Semitism in the Ajax-Feyenoord opposition, for Ajax is often thought to be a 'Jew club' - strange enough, because there is not a single Jew playing in the highest-placed teams. Nevertheless, the cry 'Jews! Jews!' is heard often enough, when these teams are in the field. But the determining factor is that both supporter groups thoroughly hate each other.

5. What united the two parties

What remains is that the Blue-Green rivalry was an important facet of Byzantine life, especially of that in the capital. Procopius says that "of old the people was split into two parties" [10] and elsewhere that "in every city the *dêmoi* are split into *Venetoi* (Blues) and *Prasinoi* (Greens)." [11] It was not so, of course, that every citizen in every town was an adherent of either the Blues or the Greens; what Procopius wants to convey is that their rivalry was a case of general interest.

I feel that it would be more illuminating and rewarding, not to define the differences between the Blues and Greens, but what united them. Both parties loved sport, especially chariot racing. But they also loved violence. With regard to modern supporter associations I sometimes ask myself if the love of violence is not greater than the love of sport, so that a match is often hardly more than an occasion for the hooliganism afterwards. Perhaps this was also true for Byzantine society. Procopius offers an illuminating passage here. "They ever fight battles with the opposing party, without knowing exactly why they are ready to incur such great risks ... Without any real reason there grows in them a hatred against their fellow-beings, and this sentiment lasts into all eternity and does not allow of relationships or consanguinity or the law of friendship, even when the partisans, who are divided from one another by their colours, are brothers or so. When it comes to the triumph of a colour, they do not trouble their head because of what is either human or divine. It does not concern them at all, when somebody commits a sacrilege or when the law and the constitution suffer violence by the way of acting of themselves or of their enemies; it does also not bother them when they perhaps go short of the necessities of life or even that in the darkest hour the fatherland will suffer damage." And this author concludes that he can see nothing in all this but a mental disease. [12]

6. A dualistic situation

I am not going to embark on a debate with Procopius on whether this kind of conduct is really the effect of a mental disorder, although I am quite ready to believe him when I see how modern football hooligans behave. What is really important is that he depicts a clearly dualistic situation. I am not thinking so much of the mutual enmity of the colours, but rather of their common opposition to the established order.

Every great city, whether past or present, whether ancient or modern, harbours a bottom layer of anarchism, disorderliness, lawlessness, and criminality. The litmus test of a political entity is how it copes with it (eradicating it is impossible). The social control that can keep unruly elements in check in small towns and villages is largely lacking in the anonymity of big cities to which misfits usually flock. Cities also attract people who do not have enough to do, the unemployed whether voluntarily or unvoluntarily, people who are living just at the subsistence level or even below it, in short many people who have no perspective in life, who bear a grudge against society at large, who look for revenge. And we should not forget those who are better off, but who are bored and looking for amusement, preferably of a sensational character. Many of them are young men, even scions of wealthy families, ready to shock their elders. Every great city contains an explosive mixture of discontent, frustration, and sensationalism. Even my hometown Amsterdam, which looks peaceful enough to the visiting tourist, has a long tradition, stretching from the Middle Ages to the present, of uproar and riots.

The Greek cities were no exception to this. In Vol. II, Ch. IV, § 2, I described how factional strife was endemic to the *poleis*. Factions (which were not equivalent to our modern political parties) tore each other to pieces and committed indescribable atrocities against each other. Ideally a Greek *polis* was a *microcosmos* that mirrored the order and beauty of the *macrocosmos*, a little world in which every citizen had his or her allotted place. In reality a *polis* was very often a hotbed of hatred where civil strife was the order of the day. Here we see the fierce opposition of the ideal order and the practice of anarchy and lawlessness. In my opinion, the factionalism of the Greens and the Blues fits perfectly into this time-honoured Greek tradition.

Contemporary Byzantine authors invariably found the Blue-Green rioting futile and inane, but true as this may be, these riots often had very serious consequences. Cameron very aptly says that "it may be the soccer hooliganism of today and the Blues and Greens of Byzantium can cast mutual illumination on each other." [13] This is certainly true; the one may help to understand the other. On a Sunday in January 1997 supporters of both Ajax and Feyenoord arranged to meet each other in a meadow near the town of Beverwijk in my country; this was obviously considered neutral terrain. The meeting was not called for friendly intercourse or an exchange of sportive insights. Quite the contrary! When the two parties had found each other, a formal battle ensued, fought with clubs, staves, claw-hammers, and even knives. There were many wounded, some of them severely hurt, one even fatally.

7. Rioting Blues and Greens

The same merciless spirit characterizes the rioting of the Blues and Greens. "Burn here, burn there! Not a Green anywhere." We are listening to a Blue chorus, of course. And the Greens respond in the same amiable mood : "Set alight, set alight! Not a Blue in sight." [14] The occasion that caused this versification to flourish was this. In November 561 there were races in the Hippodrome during which the Greens attacked the Blues. The Emperor, Justinian I, found this important enough to appear at the scene in person. Seeing the fighting, he sent riot police into the arena, but they proved incapable of separating the fighting bands. On both sides there were dead and wounded. The Greens had been the first to attack, but then the Blues attempted to chase them out of their seats. The rioting spread to the neighbouring quarters with the Greens stoning any Blues they encountered. Much property was stolen. On the orders of the Emperor, many ringleaders were arrested and tortured. Since Justinian was suspected of being favourable to the Blues rather than to the Greens, those who decked themselves out with the latter colour fell out with him. The wives and mothers of the Greens began to shout against him in the churches. Then the police came and drove them away beating them with sticks. [15]

This is only one example of what happened almost every year. It was not only the rivalry of the Blues and Greens that caused disturbances; the background was also the often deplorable economic situation or a famine. In 556 Justinian appeared in the circus but was insulted because there was no bread; he reacted harshly. [16] More than once did the popular fury direct itself against the magistrates; the year 559 bore witness to street fighting; several public buildings, such as the palace of the commander of the guard and the navy arsenal, went up in flames. [17] In 560 the rumour ran that the Emperor had died. "So the people suddenly seized the bread from the shops and the bakeries; at the third hour no bread could be found in the whole city." The rioting came to an end when the Senate "sent the prefect to have lights lit throughout the city to show that the Emperor was well. In this way the city was calmed after the disturbance." [18] (The illumination usually only occurred on festive occasions.) During occurences like these it is impossible to distinguish the Blues from the Greens; when the magistrates were the target, they obviously acted in unison.

8. The Nika revolt

Rioting was a fairly normal state of affairs in the capital; during the reign of Justinian I there were at least twelve rebellions. One of these, the so-called 'Nika revolt' laid a great part of the city in ruins. The origin of these troubles which almost cost the Emperor his throne, is to be found in the races of January 13th 532.

a. A shouting-match in the Hippodrome

There was a shouting-match between the official herald and the Greens at the circus in January, a record of which has been preserved in its entirety by Theophanes. [19] It was about a certain Kallopodios who had been a Green in former days, but had changed his allegiance to the Blues at the ascent of Justinian to the throne (this Emperor was thought to be a supporter of the Blues.) The Greens began to insult him in chorus and cried that he would share Judas' fate. The herald told them to stop; they had not come to the circus in order to be insulting. Yet they persisted, whereupon the angry herald screamed : "Silence, you Jews, Manichaeans, and Samaritans!"

Now it was the turn of the Greens to feel insulted; they shouted that they were baptized according to the rules. The herald retorted that he would have them beheaded if they did not keep quiet. They did not keep quiet, but, instead, shouted that everyone who was known to be a Green ran the risk of being publicly punished [in other words, they felt they were discriminated against]. Some of them, they said, had already been murdered. Here the Blues tuned in. "The only murderers in this stadium are you." "You yourselves are killers", the Greens gave back. Once again the exasperated herald attempted to silence them. "You God-hated blasphemers, will you never be silent?" And the Greens loudly concluded that justice existed no more. "Better a pagan than a Blue, God knows." The Greens then left the stadium.

b. A bungled hanging

Riots followed, and the prefect had seven trouble-makers arrested. They were condemned to be publicly hanged. Five of them were ordinarily executed, but two of them, one Green and one Blue, slipped out of the rope and fell to the ground, both still alive. The hangman must have been a clumsy fellow, for when he tried to hang them again, they found themselves on the ground for a second time. Now their adherents rushed to the scaffold, rescued them, and brought them to safety. Monks ferried them over the Golden Horn to the church of St. Lawrence that had the privilege of non-extradition. The prefect posted guards around the building so that they could not get out.

The fact that of the two escapees one was Blue and the other Green brought the parties together. January 13th was a racing-day; the Emperor was bold enough to appear in the Hippodrome. The situation was tense to the utmost; the public kept shouting all the time, clamouring for a pardon for the two men. Until the end Justinian remained obdurate. The usual cry 'Victory to our Emperor Justinian!' was not heard this time; instead, the ever angrier public began to shout : "Long may the Greens and the Blues live", united now in a plea for mercy. It was a historical moment, for the two parties had never been so close to each other. And then they began to shout in unison : 'Nika, Nika!' [triumph], not to the Emperor, but to themselves.

c. A hot night and a hot day

It became a very hot night. The insurgents rushed *en masse* to the *Praetorium*, where they demanded that the prefect free the two men in the asylum church. When he refused, the soldiers guarding the building were massacred; the rebels broke into it, freed the detainees they found there, and set the church on fire. During the hours of darkness there was much looting, while fires flared up here and there. The new day did not bring reflection. The rebels even rattled the gates of the heavily guarded imperial palace; they demanded the deposition of a number of hated high officials, among them the city prefect.

Justinian, who had by now become really frightened, ceded to their wishes. As so often in revolutions, the concessions only made things worse.

d. A show of force and its consequences

The Emperor felt that a solid show of force had become necessary. On the 15th he ordered Belisarius, the famous general, to quell the insurgence with the troops (barbarians!) that were stationed in the capital. Just at this unfortunate moment the priests of the Aya Sofia had arranged a procession with the holy relics with the intention of calming the overheated feelings. The priests were manhandled by the soldiers, which led to an unprecedented explosion of popular fury. All the populace's discontent with the way they had to live, mostly in poverty, and with the way they were governed - their deep dissatisfaction with the 'establishment' - now broke through.

The troops were bombarded from the roofs with stones and tiles, which made them quickly withdraw. Sensing victory, the people began to set buildings on fire. Soon an impressive number of these were ablaze. Soldiers and police who tried to stop them were killed. For three long days there was nothing but chaos and anarchy. Many private houses were looted. The fires spread continuously. Some buildings were deliberately set on fire, like the Senate House and a wing of the imperial palace; others caught fire because the flames, fanned by a strong wind, sprang from building to building. In this way, the Aya Sofia, the Zeuxippos Baths, the quarter of the silver smiths, the porticoes on the Forum, the Sampson hospital in which all the patients perished, and innumerable private houses went up in flames . The city looked as if it had been hit by the eruption of a volcano. The stench of burnt material was unbearable; in many quarters nothing was left standing.

e. A counter-Emperor

The terrorized Justinian was thinking of taking to his heels; with the Empress Theodora and a wagon of his treasures he hoped to escape to Thrace. No doubt, his situation was dangerous to the extreme. Part of his palace already lay in ruins; the guards who protected his palace were repeatedly attacked by the mob; the corpses of those who were killed were thrown into the sea. Many women were also killed. These were days of no mercy. When the rumour spread that the Emperor had indeed fled - this was not true, he did finally not depart at all -, the mob wanted to crown a new Emperor. Their candidate, found on the 16th, was Probus, a royal prince; their cry was : 'Another emperor for the city!'. But Probus was not at home; to punish him for his absence his palace was burnt to the ground.

On the 18th Justinian made a manful attempt to reverse the course of events. Taking his courage into his hands, he went to the Hippodrome where it all had begun. Holding the Gospel book before him, he addressed the public with the following words. "I swear by this holy book that I pardon all your offenses; I will not arrest any of you, if you will behave orderly. You are not responsible for what has happened. It is my sins what made me refuse what you requested in this Hippodrome [namely, that the two quasi-hanged would go scot-free]." Some of those present were won over, by servants of the Emperor distributing money, writes Theophanes; they intoned a chorus of praise for the ruler. But their song was drowned out by the voices of the majority who screamed : "You are lying, ass, your oath is a perjury." Insults were heaped upon the luckless Emperor.

That same day the crowd found another candidate for the throne, Hypation, another royal prince. In spite of the fact that he wanted to remain loyal to the Emperor, and although his wife protested, he was literally dragged to the Forum of Constantine, crowned (with a golden chain, for lack of a diadem), hoisted on a shield, and proclaimed Emperor. He was then brought to the Hippodrome and seated in the imperial lodge. Serious plans were made for an all-out assault on the imperial residence. Many senators had chosen the side of the rebellion; the end of the Empire seemed near. The despairing monarch thought everything was lost, but Theodora remained steadfast and rekindled the spirits of her husband. He was now firmly resolved to crush the rebellion.

f. The rebellion smothered in blood

Money was lavishly distributed among the rebels, particularly among the Blues who were of old more pro-Emperor than the Greens. Many of them detached themselves from the rebellion. Then Belisarius, with the shock-troops he had assembled, opened the attack on the Hippodrome, the heart of the insurrection. They forced their entry from both sides and began to shower the people in the circus with arrows. No mercy was shown, the carnage was immense. Running through the arena, the soldiers kept slaughtering for hours. The number of victims was at least thirty thousand; some sources even speak of fifty thousand. "On that day peace was restored", says Theophanes. The revolt was indeed over, but the 'peace' was that of a cemetery.

g. The revenge

Thus followed the revenge of the victors. The Emperor-of-one-day, Hypation, and his cousin Pompeius who had accompanied him, were brought before Justinian. Throwing themselves on their knees, they implored his pardon. Hypation pleaded that violence was done to him so that he was forced to play a role he did not want to play. Some say that Justinian was ready to spare him, but that Theodora was adamant. Both were executed; their corpses were thrown into the sea and their estates confiscated. Of the senators and other officials who had lent their support to the revolt some were executed and others exiled. Their possesions too were seized. For a long time after no chariot races were held. [20]

9. The aftermath

Fifteen years of relative quiet followed. However, from 547 onward there were new disturbances every year. The parties once again began fighting and insulting each other. Once again Justinian was insulted, and to his immense chagrin, for he had a Persian ambassador with him. [21] The Hippodrome and the capital saw the usual scenes : reciprocal speaking-choruses of insults, the hurling of objects, blows, and later street-fighting and even incendiarism. But now the government was alerted; repressions and arrests immediately followed; it no longer mattered whether a hooligan was a Blue or a Green. The days came, to quote Malalas, who was a contemporary witness, that "the city had returned to order; everyone henceforward enjoyed liberty, and all could without fear pursue their fears and their pleasures." [22]

10. The new Aya Sofia

Human existence is such that even from the most negative circumstances something positive may result. When the sun began to shine on the morning after the troops had smothered the Nika-revolt on its sixth day in blood, what one saw was an immense field of still smouldering ruins; the streets were strewn with corpses, while in the arena they lay about in piles. Among the victims was the old Aya Sofia, built by Constantine the Great and repaired by Theodosius II. In order to show that order had triumphed, Justinian decided to erect "a church such as since Adam had never been seen yet and the like of which would never be seen again." [23]

Like the destroyed one, the new church would be dedicated to the Holy Wisdom, the *Hagia Sophia*. This gigantic building that we now know by the name of Aya Sofia, was consecrated on December 27th 537. Standing before the ambo, the proud monarch stretched out his arms and exclaimed : "O, Solomo, I have triumphed over you." [24] This was evidently a point against Judaism, but I suppose that he also wanted to surpass Rome, where there was a Saint Peter, but not yet the grandiose Renaissance building we know. What Justinian could not foresee was that his splendid church would eventually be turned into a mosque, to which the four minarets on the corners testify.

11. The struggle of order and disorder

The struggle we have witnessed was one between order and disorder in Byzantine society; there was, especially in the capital, a *residuum* of anarchy and lawlessness. Its forces were often pitted against each other, but they could also join hands and then turn against the powers that were. It was a dualistic struggle with no quarter given on both sides. There were moments when the established order came near collapsing. That the forces of anarchy were deliberately aiming at this order is demonstrated by the fact that the favourite target of the mob were the public buildings, the stone representatives of that order; not even the imperial palace was spared.

NOTES TO CHAPTER IV

1. Theophanes, *Chronographia* AM 6101, AD 608/609 (296).
2. Diehl. *Justinien* II, 445-455.
3. Cameron, *Circus Factions* 14.
4. This is what my corrector Dr. Jo Swabe remarks at this point : "Not quite 100 % true, some British football fan clubs unfortunately have associations with fascist organizations."
5. Cameron, *Circus factions* 2.
6. Cameron, *Circus Factions* 126.
7. Procopius, *Anekdota* 7.23, 35, and 42.
8. Cameron, *Circus Factions* 95-101.
9. Cameron, *Circus Factions* 103.
10. Procopius, *Anekdota* 7.1.
11. Procopius, *Bello persico* 1.24.2.
12. Procopius, *Bello persico* 1.24.3-6.
13. Cameron, *Circus Factions* 271.
14. Theophanes, *Chronographia* AM 6054, AD 561/562 (236).
15. Theophanes, *Chronographia*. AM 6054, AD 561/562 (236)
16. Malalas, *Chronographia* 488.
17. Malalas, *Chronographia* 490-491.
18. Theophanes, *Chronographia* AM 6053, AD 560/561 (234-235).
19. Theophanes, *Chronographia* AM 6024, AD 531/532 (182).
20. Theophanes, *Chronographia* AM 6024, AD 531/532 (181-186); *Malalas*, Chronographia 473-477; *Chronicon paschale* anno 532. A detailed report in Diehl, *Justinien* II, 458-466.

21. Malalas, *Chronographia* 488.
22. Quoted from Diehl, *Justinien* II, 466.
23. Quoted by Diehl, *Justinien* II, 471.
24. Quoted by Diehl, *Justinien* II, 486.

CHAPTER VI

RELIGIOUS DISSENSIONS

PART I SAMARITANS AND JEWS

1. The overall situation of the Jews

Within the frontiers of the Byzantine Empire many Diaspora Jews lived. Although it is hard to say how many of them there were, there must have been considerable agglomerations of them in cities like Alexandria, Antioch, Thebes, Constantinople, and many others. Often they grouped together in Jewish quarters (not ghettoes!), for instance in the capital near the Golden Horn, where there was a *Hebraice Skala*, a Jewish Stairs. Their communities were autonomous; the Jews regulated their own social and religious affairs. The Jewish religion was a *religio licita*. The rabbis, everywhere important as religious leaders, teachers, and judges, needed to be officially recognized by the government.

The Jews, especially those living in Palestine, profited from the bitter divisions within the Christian Church caused by the Monophysite question (of which more will be said later). The bishops had already enough problems and did not want to create more. The ecclesiastical authorities of the Byzantine Church did not want to hear of forced conversions, as was advocated by some emperors, for instance Heraclius I; they found that a forced conversion was without value. They held that the Jews were entitled to practise their own religion. [1] The bishops maintained a strict control over the monks (as they had been instructed by the Council of Chalcedon of 451 to do), for fanatical elements among these had often made assaults on synagogues. Avi-Yonah concludes : "As a result of this particular constellation the Jews enjoyed a last period of peace before the end of Byzantine rule over Palestine. This relative quiet lasted for 76 years, from the Council of Chalcedon to the accession of Justinian (451-527)." [2]

2. Samaritan revolts

The Samaritans of Palestine whose main centre was Nablus, were worse off than the Jews. They were monotheists, recognizing only the God of Israel. Of the Old Testament they acknowledged no more than the *Pentateuch*, the five Books of Moses. They had their own High Priest and their own sanctuary on Mount Gerizim. There was not much love lost between them and the Jews. Neither was there between them and the Byzantine government. During the Later Roman Empire and the early Byzantine Empire they enjoyed the status of a *religio licita*, the same status that the Jews had. It must be admitted that their situation was precarious. Avi-Yonah calls their position 'ambivalent', "They were believers in the God of Israel and non-Jews at the same time." So they were neither Jews nor Gentiles and "in consequence suffered from the disadvantages of both estates." In the fifth and sixth centuries their situation deteriorated yet further. "They had suddenly become aware of the fact that because of the spread of Christianity in Palestine they had no future within the country; and yet they lacked an outside base, such as was provided by the Jewish Diaspora." [3]

Feeling oppressed by the Byzantine officials in Palestine, they frequently rebelled; revolts took place in 451 and 484, making the rulers distrustful of them. [4] In 529 things came to a head. The Samaritans felt extremely frustrated by the tax laws, the greed of the officials, and the inimical attitude of the Christian population towards them. Procopius says that Justinian wanted them to adopt the Christian faith; some in the cities did so, according to him, and assumed Christian names, but the agrarian population remained stubbornly attached to their own religion. They rose in revolt, choosing a certain Julianus, a 'robber king', says Malalas, as their emperor. Pagans and Manichaeans, who also felt oppressed, came to swell their ranks. The whole province was turned upside down; everywhere churches went up in flames, and many Christians were killed by the insurgents.

Imperial troops, helped by Arab bands from the desert, suppressed the revolt. With the memory of the Nika-revolt still fresh, Justianian did not feel inclined to mercy. Twenty thousand insurgents were killed by the soldiery; twenty thousand others were sold as slaves to Arab traders who in their turn sold them at Persian markets, a very profitable affair for them. Julianus was caught alive and beheaded with the crown still on his head; this crown was sent to the Emperor to show that it was all over. [5]

It was an unadulterated dualistic relationship; both sides were irreconcilable. In 530 rebellious Samaritans tried to get the help of the Persians. [6] Byzantine squads hunted the rebels throughout the mountains and, once caught, killed them. With great violence, attempts were made to force the Samaritans into conversion. Their synagogues were destroyed and could not be rebuilt. Almost all of their civic rights were taken away from them; for instance, they were no longer allowed to hold public functions. [7]

Later Justinian went back on his initial severity somewhat. In a *Novella* of 551 he declared : "Now, however, we see that they [the Samaritans] have returned to quiet; therefore, we do not deem it necessary to maintain our initial severe viewpoint, in particular because we have changed our mind moved by the intercession of bishop Sergius of Caesarea for them ... On account of this we have issued the present decree and stipulate that the Samaritans will have the competence to make wills and to dispose of their fortune." [8] Diehl writes that the practice was less rigorous than the letter of the law; Samaritans were converted indeed, at least for the sake of appearances, but later many of them returned to their old allegiance.

In 556 there was a renewed outburst. This time the Samaritans were helped by the Jews. "So the world could see the spectacle that the two deadly enemies of yore joined hands to fight a third opponent." [9] They massacred many Christians in Caesarea; when the city prefect came to their help, they killed him too. The *comes* for the Orient, Amantius, arrived with troops, arrested the ringleaders, and had them executed. [10] Justinian's successor, Justin II, judged that the Samaritans were beyond or below the law. "They have made themselves unworthy of the humanity of the law by their folly; it is only their own fault that they are deprived both of divine mercy and imperial liberality." [11]

3. The Jewish policy of Byzantium

Perhaps the reader will say : but the Samaritans were no Jews. This may be, in any case the Jews did not see them as their co-religionists. The Byzantine government, however, found the difference far too subtle to be of any practical use : Samaritans and Jews, they both were enemies of the Byzantine order. The fact that up to the age of Justinian I the Jews, not only in Palestine, but also in the rest of the Empire, enjoyed a period of quiet should not lead us to pull the wool over our eyes. None of the Emperors before Justinian was well disposed towards the Jews. When the Emperor Zeno heard that some Jews "had been burnt in the course of a riot at Antioch, he replied : 'What a pity that the living were not burnt also.'" [12]

a. Anti-Jewish measures of Justinian I

With the advent of Justinian, things changed radically. The rebellious behaviour of the Samaritans ricocheted on the Jews who were more severely treated than ever before. It is important to pay attention to the rationale of the new anti-Jewish policy. A decree was issued that enlarged the concept of 'heretic' considerably. Thus far it had referred to heterodox Christians, like the Monophysites, but now it came to mean 'anyone who is not orthodox', so it also applied to Jews. [13] The new legislation, issued during Justinian's reign and consisting of a number of unpleasant measures, did not seriously undermine the Jewish position at first. That they were forbidden to teach in the academies, for instance, did not really concern them, since we may assume that not many Jews held academic posts. It was more vexating that the authorities, not relishing the idea that the Jews had a liturgical language of their own, put pressure on them to exchange the original Hebrew Old Testament for the Greek translation, the Septuagint.

It was a far more severe blow, however, for Judaism to lose its status of *religio licita* and for the ecclesiastical canons to have force of law for Jews. This is all the more curious since the Emperors were adamantly against ecclesiastical claims that canonical laws should have the status of public law; they now acquiesced in this request in so far (and because) it concerned Jews. Procopius accused Justinian of forcing the Jews 'to neglect the divine service and to transgress their laws.' [14] Attempts were also made to convert them to the Christian faith by means of persuasion; there were even some forced conversions.

In the town of Borion in Cyrene a splendid synagogue was converted into a church; "all the Jews were forced to relinquish the religion of their forefathers and to become Christians." [15] It is also possible that many Jews changed their allegiance of their own accord 'for fear of the existing laws'. [16] More cases of forced conversions were reported during the reign of Mauricius. Here it was a bishop of Melitene who compelled the Jews of his diocese to have themselves baptized; it may explain something that this dignitary, called Domitian, was a brother of the Emperor, for forced baptism was not ecclesiastical policy. Anyhow, he seems not to have been very successful; a Christian historiographer remarks that the Jews in question "became only Christian hypocrites". [17]

Things went from bad to worse during the reign of Phocas (603-610) whose position, as the reader will remember, was none too secure. To fortify it, he too had the idea of forcing the Jews to become Christians. This man was a paragon of brutality and tactlessness. It was his policy to put an end to Judaism by compelling all the Jews under his jurisdiction to let themselves be baptized. He did not get very far with this, for he was soon enough killed. There were, however, nasty incidents.

The following story is told by the author of *The Didascalia of Jacob now baptized*, and related by Avi-Yonah. [18] This source gives the locality as Carthage, but another source speaks of Jerusalem. Be this as it may, it is reported that the local governor made the Jews appear before him and asked them : "Are you slaves of the Emperor?" to which they answered that they were the Emperor's slaves indeed. Well then, the consequence was that they should be baptized. At this communication the Jews were stricken dumb. Requested to answer, their spokesman said timidly : "We shall not do it because the time for baptism has not yet come." The governor consequently flew into a rage, hitting the man in the face with both hands, and crying : "If you are slaves, why do you not do as your lord wills?" This outburst terrorized the Jews. They were baptized against their wishes and were very sad about it.

The terrible thing is that there is an almost complete similarity between the situation the Jews were in and that of the Christians during the days of the still pagan Empire, when inimical local potentates interrogated them and forced them to sacrifice to the statue of the Emperor. "Baptism", concludes Avi-Yonah rightly, "had thus become a matter of politics, a sign of fidelity to the Emperor. The Jews could not object to it, unless they wished to appear as traitors to the state." [19] But as far as I can see, the Byzantine Church largely stayed out of this policy, for, with the exception of that bishop who was the Emperor's brother, it was executed by imperial officials and not by bishops. Nonetheless, in the course of the sixth and seventh centuries the Jewish policy of the Empire became evermore dualistic.

b. Heraclius I and his fear of Jews

Jews were never trusted, neither by the pagan and Christian Emperors of Rome nor by the Christian Emperors of Byzantium. In an earlier chapter we saw how distrustful Heraclius I was of Jews. Superstitious as he was, he believed in an oracle telling him that 'circumcized people' would make him lose his throne. To prevent this he took counter-measures; he even thought of forcing the Jews to convert (which would not undo their circumcision!), and he tried to win Germanic rulers of the West for his policy. An unambiguous sign of his unfriendly attitude to Judaism was that, when he had brought back the Holy Cross to Jerusalem, he banished the Jews from the city and forbade them to come within three miles of its walls. The Holy City that for a thousand years had been the home of the Temple and the hallowed centre of Judaism, would now be the city of the Cross. It was as if the Cross would be defiled if Jews came near it, although the one who died on it was a circumcized Jew.

c. Jewish reactions

However, just like the Samaritans, the Jews were not the meekest subjects of the Emperors. They sometimes paid back in kind. This happened, for instance, during the reign of Phocas. In Antioch, where they were numerous, his policy of forced conversions led to a violent outburst, for they were already exasperated by the Jew-unfriendly Jewish policy. In 610 they rose up in revolt and killed many Christians, especially landowners, "and burnt them." Among the victims was Anastasius, the Patriarch of Antioch. After having killed him and having stuffed his genitals into his mouth, a Jewish mob "dragged him along the main street." Troops were dispatched against them, but were "unable to stop the killing." Only when reinforcements had arrived, the rioting could be put to an end ; "now many Jews were killed and maimed and banished from the city." [20]

Earlier I related how abominably bad the relations were in Jerusalem, a city the possession of which Jews and Christians disputed with each other. Soon enough a third contestant, the Islam, would present itself. In 614 or 615 the Persians captured the Holy City. The Christians were exasperated by their removing the Holy Cross and by the deportation of Zacharias, the Patriarch of Jerusalem; the conquerors obviously meant to deal a devastating blow to the Christian position. Soon the main body of the Persian army retired; only a small garrison remained behind. Then the Christians rose and were stupid enough to massacre many of the garrison, and numerous Jews too. The Persians returned, and although the city was tenaciously defended, they took it after a three day siege. They delivered the Christians to the mercy of the Jews and stood idly by as Christians were slaughtered by Jews in their tens of thousands.

PART II INTERLUDE ON CAESAROPAPISM

1. Commingling of the secular and religious spheres in the pagan world

A word must now be said of the Caesaropapism of the age. This term contains two others, *Caesar* [Emperor] and *Papa* [Pope or pontiff]. It refers to the tendency of Christian Emperors to play the Pope, to act as super-bishop, to be 'a sort of imperial pontiff'.[21] These rulers followed in the wake of the pagan rulers of Antiquity. Everywhere in the ancient world, in the Near East and in the Greek, Hellenistic, and Roman worlds the secular and religious realms had been inextricably interwoven. In fact, there had never been a clear-cut distinction between both realms; they belonged together and supported each other, forming part of the same socio-political fabric.

It was impossible, even dangerous, to shirk the obligations of the public cult; a person who did this was not only an atheist but by the same token a traitor to the state. Socrates was condemned for having wanted to 'introduce foreign gods'. Nobody knew exactly who or what these 'foreign gods' might be, but it was taken to mean that he rejected the public cult on which the welfare of the state rested. Christians who refused to sacrifice to the statue of the Emperor became *ipso facto* traitors and were consequently condemned to death. In the Graeco-Roman world there were many people, mostly educated ones, who did not believe in the traditional gods, but even they continued to take part in the public cult, perhaps with a wry smile.

The only society of Antiquity where state and religion were not so closely bound up was that of Israel. The first duty of a Jew was not to the state but to Jahve; this also applied to the kings themselves. The ritual and sacrificial cult was the domain of the priesthood, not of public officials. The kings were not divinized; their statues were not to be found in the Temple, and they fulfilled no priestly functions. Not a few kings were in fact idolators; we hear the prophets thundering against them.

2. The anti-political stance

In foregoing volumes I have brought the anti-political attitude, an anti-state stance, to the attention of the reader. Brought on the shortest possible denominator, it said that all power is wrong. This is an idea that can be found nowhere else in the ancient world. The nearest people came to it was in the Gnostic sects (which were not pagan, of course, but not Christian either), that were absolutely indifferent to the political scene and never mentioned it. The beginnings of the anti-state attitude are already to be found in the prophets, but they come to full bloom in the Jewish apocalypses, in Daniel for instance, a late Bible book that dates from about 165 B.C. and that was a reaction to the persecution of the Jews by the Seleucid rulers of Syria. [22]

In a very pregnant form this attitude is present in the Christian apocalypse, the Revelation of John, in which the great enemy is the Roman Empire, the enemy not so much of the Christians but rather of God. [23] Early Christians often repudiated the Empire, a political entity of which they formed part, of course, but to which they did not really belong. Authors like Hippolytus and Origen saw in the Empire hardly anything but the work of the devil. [24] Christians were citizens of another world, an idea that was forcefully expressed by Saint Augustine in his doctrine of the two cities. [25] This became concretely apparent in the Christian attitude to military service and warfare. There was a widespread feeling that a Christian should not take up arms. Later, when there were Christian soldiers indeed, the idea was that they could fulfil garrison or police duties but should not become involved in actions. [26]

The Roman Empire and the Christian Church were two universalisms competing with each other and opposing each other. The Empire claimed body and soul, and if not the inner soul, then at least public allegiance. The Church claimed the souls but not really the bodies, that is, it had no political aspirations. This opposition, dualistic in character as it was, led to fierce clashes that made many victims among Christians. [27]

3. Christian universalism and the Christian Empire

In 313 Constantine the Great put an end to the persecutions; Christianity now became a *religio licita*, along with the pagan religion and Judaism. On February 27th, 385, the Emperor Theodosius issued a decree ordering all citizens of the Roman Empire to confess the common divinity of the Father, the Son, and the Holy Ghost who form in equal majesty the Holy Trinity. This was a declaration of intent rather than a political reality. What is true, however, is that it transformed Christianity into the privileged religion of the Empire. [28] Later, in 391, he deprived paganism of its status of *religio licita* and forbade the pagan cult; in 393 this also spelt the end of the Olympic Games, which were seen as a heathen manifestation. Did Theodosius' measures turn the Empire into a Christian one, as so often is assumed? One post-Constantinian Emperor had been a declared pagan, Julian the Apostate; others were Arians. When Gibbon writes that the Theodosian decrees meant the final destruction of paganism, [29] this is a gross exaggeration. For a long time there would be pagans in the East and above all in the West in great numbers. During the fourth century the majority of the population was still pagan; it was only during the fifth and sixth centuries that a great shift took place and the majority became Christian, at least in the East.

Yet this is not the real point. This is the question whether the two universalisms, the political and the ecclesiastical, now fused so there was one homogeneous politico-ecclesiastical entity. In principle such a fusion is an impossibility : the secular and spiritual spheres are basically so distinct that they never can become one. This does not, however, alter the fact that many rulers and some high ecclesiastical dignitaries did find it quite feasible - which was asking for difficulties. Emperors and kings, presidents and ministers, are politicians, which means that they are always thinking in political terms; even patting a child on the head or congratulating a winning sportsman is a political deed. When it comes to religion, they may be pious and God-fearing - but power corrupts -, but they always remain what they are : politicians, people wielding power.

181

Before the fall of Western Empire in 476 there was no take-over of the Church by the state. Sometimes ecclesiastics tried to influence a ruler; we see, for instance, how Saint Ambrose publicly rebuked Theodosius II. [30] But another influential churchman, Saint Augustine, was deeply distrustful of the state; as is well-known, his two *civitates*, the temporal and the spiritual, would remain ever distinct and opposed. Emperors on their side tried to play their part in ecclesiastical politics; it was the theological dissensions and conflicts which gave them their chance. The background of their policy was that they wanted a unified religion in a unified state. To realize this, they freely meddled in ecclesiastical affairs, calling councils, banishing bishops, and issuing statements. The only fatal victims among heretics were made by an Emperor, albeit a usurper; I am referring here to the execution of Priscillian and his companions by Maximus in 385. [31]

4. Differing developments in West and East

If there ever was a risk of the Latin Church becoming dominated by the state, this wholly disappeared during the course of the fifth century as a result of the steady weakening of imperial rule in the West. We need only think here of Pope Leo I, whose intervention with King Genseric spared Rome Vandal massacring and incendiarism in 455. [32] The Latin Church became ever more independent of the Emperor. This remained true after 476; Constantinople was too far distant from Rome for the Emperors to exercize any influence there. The fact that during Justinian's reign Italy and Rome were conquered by the Byzantines made no significant difference to this.

    Yet the reverse was also true. The Patriarchs of Constantinople in their turn lived too far away from Rome to be kept under papal control. To quote Bury, "the oriental and occidental Churches had a tendency to separate along the political systems to which they belonged; and consistent with this tendency was the desire of the Patriarch of Constantinople, which in the fourth century became the most important city in the world, to free himself from the jurisdiction of Rome. In order to do so he naturally leaned on the power of the Emperor whose ecclesiastical authority was further increased by the fact that his capital was the Emperor's residence."

This same author spells out the differences between East and West in ecclsiastical matters. "The result was that in the West the ecclesiastical hierarchy was independent in spiritual matters, and afterwards attained secular power, but in the East the Church and the *Imperium* were closely allied, the Church being dependent on the Emperor [regarded as having a semi-pontifical character]. This was a leading feature in the Byzantine world." The ceremonial expression of this was the coronation of the Emperor by the Patriarch; the first Emperor to be crowned by him was Leo I in 457. [33]

5. Caesaropapism

Two remarks should here be made. The first is that the ecclesiastical opposition between West and East would become a constant in European history; it would grow ever worse, leading to a formal separation in 1054, and assuming a dualistic nature with an enmity that persists until the present day, although in the East far more than in the West now. The second comment is that we have here the origin of that Caesaropapism which would equally become a permanent feature of European history.

Frend states that there is a striking contrast between West and East regarding the nature of the *Imperium* and the *Sacerdotium*. "The Emperors at Constantinople regarded their office as involving a 'common oversight' over their realm, in all matters and especially in the religion of their subjects." [34] Already at Chalcedon in 451 the eastern Emperor Marcian impressed this view on the Council Fathers. "It is our policy that the whole people will feel to be united in the true and holy doctrine [the orthodox creed], come to the same religion, and practice the true Catholic religion." [35] "Royal and priestly office were derived from the same divine source; their exercise was different but complementary, and involved the Emperors in the duty of leading their people spiritually and materially to victory and salvation." [36]

Justinian expressed this opinion in the following terms. "The priestly power and the royal power are not widely separated, and sacred property is not far removed from that which all mankind hold in common or from that which is hold by the state, because the churches are endowed with all their material resources by the munificence of the royal power." In this way the ecclesiastics were unambiguously told that they were materially entirely dependent on the state. This does not mean that the Church always and everywhere passed under the yoke. As Patriarch of Alexandria, Athanasius manfully opposed the pro-Arian policy of the Emperor Constantius II and was accordingly punished with fivefold banishment.

6. Justinian's caesaropapist policy

It was Justinian I who particularly inaugurated this caesaropapist policy. He was quite honestly convinced of his own good intentions. "The well-ordered Church is the support of the Empire ... One should choose, in conformity with the doctrine of the Apostles, irreproachable priests." But then he gave himself away as the politician he basically was. "It is they [the priests] who by their prayers attract God's benevolence to public affairs." [37]

The background of the religious policy of Justinian and his successors is that they wanted unity in their Empire, in every respect, politically, socially, ecclesiastically, even liturgically if possible. This was all the more urgent for them, because the cohesion of the Empire was rather fragile, as the foregoing chapters will have amply shown. Their religious policy was not fundamentally different from that of their pagan predecessors in Rome : preferably there should be only one religion, acknowledged and protected by the state. [38]

The rulers were practical enough to realize that this was a utopian idea; there were many other religions, but violent repression of these would have led to serious disturbances. Therefore, other religions were tolerated as long as they kept moving within certain well-defined limits. [39] The Byzantine Empire was constantly threatened from both the outside and inside; this made the authorities nervous and apprehensive of those who they suspected of being enemies of the established order.

PART III RELIGIOUS POLICY WITH REGARD TO PAGANS AND THE HETERODOX

1. Imperial policy regarding pagans

As soon as Justinian had ascended the throne, he issued two laws against the pagans. He instructed all the imperial authorities to supervise "all societies of the pagan religion according to the laws so that they, when happening, no longer go unpunished." Christians who would take part in pagan rituals were made liable to undergo the severest [i.e. capital] punishment. Those who were still pagans were to report, with their families and servants, to the churches in order to be instructed in the Christian faith. Those who refused to do this would no longer enjoy the support of the state in anything. Justinian stigmatized the pagans as 'people suffering from madness'. He forbade them to teach Christian pupils. Those who wheresoever would be detected bringing sacrifices in secret or adoring the idols would be punished in the severest fashion. Those who were ready to accept the Christian faith but would do so only on appearance, would be punished with the loss of their goods. [40]

All this was not entirely new. Since the days of Constantine I decrees with more or less the same tenor had been issued. There was, however, an important difference. Constantine and his successors would not permit the practice of the pagan religion, but did not force the pagans to accept the Christian faith. Another point is that their decrees had been executed only sloppily, probably a practical necessity because in the fourth century the great majority of the population was still pagan. However, Justinian not only insisted on the strict appliance of the law, but was also ready to force people to convert. Knecht, a Roman Catholic priest, states that "through these laws he [Justinian] had transgressed the competence of a Christian ruler. The principle of religious coercion enunciated at the beginning of his rule, became determining for his future religious and ecclesiastical policy." [41]

Justinian did not leave it at words. "In this time [around 529] a great persecution of pagans took place. Many were detected and deprived of their offices. Some of them were executed." [42] It was the very first time that pagans were executed; earlier Christian rulers had always left them in peace, while their anti-pagan measures had signified a warning rather than a real threat. John of Ephesus tells us that the Emperor instructed him to find out whether there was sympathy for paganism in the capital. He reported that there were still many secret adherents, even among educated people. A *patricius* who was detected committed suicide. It seems that the persons in question were not relapsed Christians, for they were brought to the churches for instruction. [43]

Justinian inaugurated a powerful campaign of conversion, sending missionaries into the farthest corners of the Empire. Pagan sanctuaries were closed, one of these being the Isis Temple on Philae Island; Philae got a Christian bishop then. Yet John, who obviously was the imperial inspector in these matters, had to admit that he had not been able to eradicate the old faith everywhere. He also campaigned against pagan philosophy. There was only one centre of it left, the Academy in Athens. In 529 the ruler wrote to Athens that henceforth no philosophy should be taught there. This spelled the end of this almost a millennium old, venerable institution. Its last professors, among them Damascius and Simplicius, emigrated to Persia, to the court of Chosroes I. They seemed to have fancied that this Persian Emperor was a sort of Platonic philosopher-king. They soon enough became disillusioned. In 533 they returned to Athens, but the Academy was not reopened. [44] It will be evident that Justinian's attitude towards paganism was thoroughly dualistic : it should simply not be there.

2. Imperial policy regarding the heterodox

a. The Manichaeans

During Justinian's reign Manichaeans were still numerous in his Empire. What he had against them was not only they were no Christians, but also that their religion was Persian of origin. He issued decree after decree against Manichaeism. Manichaean books should be burnt. To be a Manichaean was made a capital offense; they must be banished from Byzantine territory, probably to Persia. [45]

b. The Montanists

On the whole the Emperor was very poorly disposed towards dissidents; among them were the Montanists, a heterodox sect in Asia Minor, about whom I extensively wrote in Volume XIII. [46] Imperial policy treated them with extreme viciousness. Justinian ordered them and other deviant sects to alter their religious allegiance and to return to the orthodox creed. In case of refusal the punishment would be that they may no longer bequeath their properties to their relatives (with the implication that they would fall to the state). In the heartland of Montanism, Phrygia, its adherents refused to give in; fleeing into their churches, they set them ablaze over their heads and perished in the flames. Other heretics were excecuted or committed suicide; many fled to the Persian Empire where they hoped to meet more tolerance.

The Arians fared somewhat better, but since many of them were very wealthy, they had to suffer from confiscations.

c. The Donatists

After the conquest of North Africa it was the turn of the Donatists who were still numerous there. [47] They were robbed of their whole ecclesiastical infrastructure : churches, buildings, cult objects, and estates, under the motto that they had taken all this from the orthodox. They were excluded from the public service; even if they converted, they were not allowed to become magistrates. Justianian stated expressly that "it was just enough for them to live." [48] In other words, they should be glad that their bare lives would be spared.

PART IV RELIGIOUS POLICY REGARDING THE MONOPHYSITES

1. What is Monophysitism?

As we have already seen, Justinian and other Emperors were confronted with many deviant opinions, when they wished to unite all their subjects in a common creed ; we have not yet spoken of the most important of these, namely Monophysitism. I wrote about the Monophysite movement extensively in Volume XI, [49] but feel that I ought to recapitulate this here for the benefit of the reader.

'Monophysitism' is a theological term that is a combination of two Greek words, namely *monê* and *phusis* = one nature. However, the term 'Monophysite' was not yet used during the period under discussion. It dates from the seventh century; the first to employ it was Anastasius Sinaitis between 686 and 689. The nature or natures of Christ formed an important theme in the Christological discussions of the first centuries during which Arianism was another big theme. All these discussions centred on the person of Jesus Christ : whether he was essentially divine, possessing a body only in appearance, or that he was fundamentally human, although divinely elected, as Arius taught. There is no need to go into this again; the reader will find ample information on these and related questions in Volume XIII.

Let us, with regard to Monophysitism, use the definition presented by Pauline Allen. "The concept of 'Monophysite' has become, in the history of Christology, the characteristic of those who, after the Council of Chalcedon, stuck to the Cyrillian [of Cyrillus of Jerusalem] formula that Jesus is one in one nature and who opposed the conciliar definition according to which Christ is one in two natures." In many respects, says this same scholar, it is an uncomfortable term since it depends on what is meant by *phusis*.

Western theologians distinguish real and verbal Monophysitism. The real Monophysites held that, although there were indeed two natures in Christ, the divine and the human, these natures were so closely intertwined that, as a result, something new came into being, a third nature so to speak, that is neither truly God nor truly man. The originator of this concept is thought to be Eutyches, but the problem with this man is that he was a muddle-head and none too clear in his expressions. Verbal Monophysites were those theologians who accepted the two-natures doctrine, with the proviso that there were two natures only before the Incarnation. They would not speak of there being two distinct natures in the historical Jesus; there was only one nature in him, they taught.

Arguing in an abstractly theological way, they acknowledged two modes of being in Jesus, but concretely there was only one nature. If we are using the number two, this does not refer to two natures in one person, but to a person with one nature who sometimes operates in a divine way and at another time humanly. It is possible to conclude from the external acts of Jesus that there were both divine and human aspects in him, but this ought not to lead to the idea that there were two natures in him. It will not astonish the perhaps slightly confused reader that the Chalcedonians threw all their opponents in a single pile without bothering themselves over such subtle distinctions. Part of the problem was that the theologians of these days could not yet sufficiently distinguish between 'nature' = the way a person essentially is, and *hypostasis* = his concrete being or presentation. It would be left to the medieval Schoolmen to solve this problem. Seen from this perspective, it is possible to state that the distance between the orthodox (the Chalcedonians) and the Monophysites was not so great as was thought at the time. [50]

2. The theology of Nestorius [51]

In 428 Theodosius II had appointed Nestorius, a Syrian, Patriarch of Constantinople. When he took up his post, he knew, or came to know soon enough, of discussions regarding the theological status of Mary, the mother of Jesus. Anastasius, a presbyter, declared in a sermon that one should prefetably not call Mary *theotokos* = God-bearer, because this would make herr somewhat divine and lead to 'Mariolatry'. Of course, the position of Mary cannot be discussed without bringing that of Jesus into the debate. What did

Anastasius mean? That, if Mary was not divine, Jesus was not divine either? Some thought that he meant exactly this.

Then the new Patriarch joined in the debate. He too would prefer not to speak of the *theotokos* but rather use the seemingly neutral term *Christotokos*. This did not ally the confusion. For, although Nestorius did not deny that Christ was divine, he pulled his divinity and his humanity apart by giving them a separate origin : his humanity came from Mary and his divinity came from God. His statements, although not directly heretical, were in any case unfortunate. He too was suspected of denying Jesus' divinity. Some accused him of holding that there were two Christs and two sons, namely a human person and the *Logos*. Probably these accusations were false, but Nestorius was certainly skating on thin ice.

The Patriarch was subjected to a heavy barrage from another Patriarch, Cyril of Alexandria, the guardian of Alexandrian, Athanasian Christology. Cyril had convinced himself that, in Nestorius' view, the divinity of Jesus was not an organical part of his person, but was superimposed on him. In Rome the ecclesiastical authorities began to sense that doctrinally Nestorius was on the wrong track. Since he refused to make a retractation that was satisfying to Rome, he was condemned by the Council of Ephesus in 431 and resigned his office some months later. Since the turmoil had not yet wholly subsided, a Council was convened at Chalcedon in 451; it defined Christ as having two natures 'inviolably united without confusion, division, separation, or change', so that there is only one organic person.

3. The Nestorian Church

In the West Nestorianism soon disappeared, but this was not so in the East. Nestorius had many adherents there, especially among Christians living under Sasanian rule beyond the Euphrates. In 410 the Apostolic Church of the East was founded with the Metropolitan of Ctesiphon as its *Katholikos*; in 424 it severed all links with Rome and with the oriental Patriarchs. This Church, the still existing Nestorian Church, was more 'Nestorian' that Nestorius himself. It adopted the two-natures doctrine, according to which Christ had two natures indeed, just as in orthodox doctrine, but these two natures remained so distinct from each other that it is almost impossible to speak of a real personal union. It is difficult to maintain, in the light of this doctrine, that Jesus is one person. It rather looked as though the presence of two sharply distinct natures implied the necessity of there also being two persons.

4. The road to Monophysitism

It was necessary to recall this dispute to mind since all the theological disputes raging in the East were interwoven and influenced each other. Without mentioning Nestorianism it is also impossible to satisfactorily explain the origins of Monophysitism. The Chalcedonian definition of Christ having two natures in one person continued to raise suspicion, as if it suggested that after all Jesus was not really one person. This led to the road to Monophysitism.

We must first of all hark back to Apollinaris (*fils*) who was bishop of Laodicea around 360, [52] and who was an inveterate enemy of Arianism. His fierce opposition to it left him dissatisfied with the definitions of the Council of Nicaea in 325, stating that there were two complete natures in Christ, so that he was just as much divine as he was human. Apollinaris did not think it possible for a person to have two natures; the humanity must necessarily impinge on the divinity. And to Apollinaris the divinity should have pride of place at any cost, even to the detriment of his humanity. If to Arius Jesus was far more human than divine, it was just the reverse to Apollinaris. In his vision Jesus' human part was not congruent with the divine element; it was inferior and forced the pneumatic element to remain at a safe distance from it. Apollinaris later broke away from the Church and went his own way; his doctrine was condemned several times, lastly by the Council of Constantinople in 381. Nevertheless, Apollinarians remained numerous in the East. There is a hint of Monophysitism in Apollonarism, to say it as prudently as possible.

5. Eutyches [53]

Eutyches was the archimandrite (abbot) of a big monastery in the capital. He was, in all probability, the first to openly state that there were not two natures in Christ. He was not known for his erudition and tact. In 448 a local synod condemned him, deposed him as archimandrite, and deprived him of his sacerdotal dignity. But Eutyches, although over seventy years old, fought back with such vigour, mobilizing support even in the highest circles, that a Council of Ephesus, the so-called 'Robbers' Council', reinstated him in his dignities in 449.

When Pope Leo protested against this decision to Theodosius II a year later, the Emperor did not even answer but let it be known that he (Theodosius) had never deviated from the religion of his ancestors; there was nothing wrong with the Council of Ephesus. The haughty ruler died shortly after; his successor was Marcian (450-457) who immediately acknowledged the supreme authority of Leo I over the whole Church. This averted the danger of an East-West breach in the Church which was by no means inconceivable already then. The new Emperor convened a new Council, at Chalcedon in 451; this duly deposed and condemned Eutyches once again, and also his most powerful supporter, Dioscurus, the Patriarch of Alexandria. In doctrinal respect, as related above, it condemned every form of Monophysitism; it declared Christ to be one person with two natures, 'truly God and at the same time truly man'.

6. Continuing opposition

Was the Monophysite controversy now over? The orthodox Emperor Marcian made it unequivocally clear that he thought that he had put a definite end to it. "All therefore shall be bound to hold the decision of the sacred Council of Chalcedon and indulge no further doubts. Take heed therefore to this edict of our serenity; abstain from profane words and cease all further discussion of religion." [54] Yet if he had imagined that he could lay the quarrels with a simple authoritative statement, he was wrong. Some grumbled at the doctrinal decision. Bishop Eustathius of Berytus declared that he had signed 'under duress and without agreement'. [55]

The Monophysite Movement was by no means dead; in many parts of the Eastern Empire it retained much support among the population and especially in Syrian and Egyptian monasteries. Two Patriarchs of Alexandria, Cyril and Dioscurus, had shown strong leanings towards Monophysitism; it may be guessed that loyalty towards the head of the Egyptian Church played a role for the monks of the country of the Nile. Since another Patriarch, Athanasius, had been the greatest protagonist of the doctrinal decrees of Nicaea, they accepted these wholeheartedly, at least in principle. But in following Cyril and Dioscurus, they began to deviate from the two-natures doctrine and to lean towards a one-nature Christology. Here too the need to combat Nestorianism forced many anti-Nestorians into the opposite error. When the Egyptian bishops, present at Chalcedon, cried : "Throw out the Nestorians. Christ is God!" [56], could they have thought *in foro interno* that he was far more divine than human?

Alexander Kahzdan supposes that there was possibly an influence of the old Osiris-religion, the idea of a god who dies and is revived, so that Jesus might be thought to be a new Osiris. A credal statement popular in Egypt, namely "We believe in a God who died for us", may point in this direction. [57] Finally, there was the old patriotism of the Egyptians telling them that they, with their venerable ancient civilization, need not accept dictates by either Rome or Byzantium.

In Syria the situation was, *mutatis mutandis*, identical. In both countries there was resentment against oppression by overbearing authorities and their indifference to the needs of the mainly agrarian population.

7. The influence of the monks

Because of their ascetiscism and their rectilinear devotion to religion, the monks were very popular with the local Christians and were venerated by them. They were what many faithful wanted to be, but in which they failed : perfect Christians. Yet the intellectuals loathed them, finding them fanatical and uneducated. while the authorities, the secular as well as the ecclesiastical, feared them for their unruliness and their grip on the Christian multitude.

'Chalcedon' had attempted to check the influence of the monks. It had made it perfectly clear that all authority rested with the bishops, not in the monasteries. The monks were told that they had to obey their bishops and should not occupy themselves with political activities. New monasteries might only be built with the local bishop's consent. It is evident that the oriental episcopate tried to impress on the monks who was boss. It all sounded authoritative enough, but the position of the monasteries was so strong that much of it remained, as Frend writes. 'a dead letter' [58], with the consequence that the monasteries radiated Monophysitism.

8. The overall situation in the middle of the fifth century

The result was that Egypt became almost exclusively monophysite and Syria to a large extent also. In between lay Palestine where the situation was different insofar that the position of orthodoxy was stronger there. But here there were also anti-Chalcedonian pockets. The man who was bishop of Jerusalem in the middle of the fifth century, Juvenal, was a strong supporter of Dioscurus. An interesting person whom we find living near Jerusalem from 443 was Eudocia, the widow of Theodosius II; she was an erudite woman and used her talents as a writer to propagate the ideas of Cyril. Another curious person was Peter the Iberian (ca. 409-488); he came from the Caucasus region and seems to have been of royal descent. He was a creature of Juvenal who made him bishop of Maiuma in 452. Maiuma was the harbour-town of Gaza, in the south of Palestine; being within easy reach of Egypt, Monophysite ideas could leak into Palestine along this way. His monastery near Maiuma was a hot-bed of Monophysitism. Yet in spite of these pressures, Palestine as a whole remained true to orthodoxy; in the end Peter had to retire to Egypt where he may well have felt more at home.

9. Vehemence in Egypt

Volume XIII will have demonstrated to the reader how vehement the *furor theologicus* could become. The Monophysite controversy was no exception to this. The Egyptian bishops who had signed the decrees of Chalcedon to a man, trembled at the thought of what their faithful might do to them. "We shall all be killed if we subscribe to [Pope] Leo's epistle [the famous Tomus in which the two-natures doctrine was expounded]. Every district in Egypt will rise against us." This is what these anguished men told their fellow-bishops at Chalcedon. [59]

Proterius, an arch-priest in Alexandria, was consecrated bishop of this city. Although this man had been a staunch supporter of his predecessor Dioscurus, he also wished to remain true to the Emperor and the Pope. This was his undoing. It did not interest the mob at all that he was a Monophysite at heart; what counted against him was that he was seen as a stooge of both Rome and Constantinople (political and theological considerations often went hand in hand in this matter). In March 457 the always rebellious populace of Alexandria rose in revolt against him. Several magistrates were killed; Proterius himself was lynched. The soldiers who attempted to restore order were driven back into the Serapeum; this was burned down, making many victims among them. The arrival of two thousand troops straight from Constantinople set things right again. [60] The whole east became divided over the Monophysite issue, so that we may speak of a quasi-schism. Sources relate that former friends no longer greeted one another in the street, and that many families were torn asunder by this question.

10. The Emperor Leo I manoeuvring

In 457 the Emperor Leo I succeeded to the throne of the East. Just as his predecessor Marcian, he was a Chalcedonian, that is orthodox, but, as the historiographer Zacharias Rhetor said, 'simple in his faith'. [61] Personally pious as he may have been, what bothered him were the religious dissensions in his realm, and he feared mob rule. Less than Marcian, however, he felt inclined to follow the papal guidance. Pope Leo I died on November 10th 461. According to Frend, this was a milestone in the history of ecclesiastical East-West relations, for from now on, "no Roman bishop, however vigorous and dedicated, could govern the Church in the East ... The Emperor and his Patriarch were to govern the Church there, restricted only by the distant power of veto in the hands of the Pope." [62]

The Emperor manoeuvred carefully, but removed some conspicuous Monophysite troublemakers from their positions. Antioch, for instance, rivalled with Alexandria for the position of the main centre of Monophysitism. In 469 Peter the Fuller, a quarrelsome monk, was consecrated Patriarch of Antioch, in a somewhat irregular manner, so it seems. However, the Emperor did not love this ambitious monk, deposed him, and ordered him to come to the capital where he was interned in a monastery in 471. [63]

Leo also deposed yet another Patriarch, Timothy, nicknamed *Felurus*, the Cat, bishop of Alexandria. [64] His election too had not been perfectly canonical; Theophanes even says that he had used 'magic' in order to be elected. He told the monks on nightly visits to their cells that he was an angel and had been sent "to tell everyone to refrain from communion with the part of Proterius and the party of Chalcedon, and to appoint Timothy the Cat bishop of Alexandria." [65] Theophanes has it that he was not even ordained which did not prevent him from consecrating bishops himself; it was rumoured that it was he who had hatched the plot against Proterius. [66] The Emperor Leo soon had enough of him, the more so because he was denounced as a murderer and a heritic by eminent Egyptian clerics, one of these being Symeon the Stylite. The Cat was deposed and sent into exile to Gangra (the modern Çankiri) in Paphlagonia. Nevertheless, Timothy stirred up troubled wherever he went. When he began holding assemblies in his town of exile, Leo banished him to the inhospitable Crimea. [67]

11. A caesaropapist intervention

After the death of Leo I his son Zeno (474-491) became Emperor. There was a break of two years in his reign, because an army coup, supported by the

Empress-Dowager Verina, brought Zeno's uncle Basiliscus to the throne. His short reign of only twenty months is memorable because of an enormous conflagration in the capital, that laid part of the inner city in ashes. The destruction of the Basilikê Library with its one hundred and twenty thousand books an irreparable loss to civilization; one of the texts lost was a forty meters long scroll on which the whole of the Iliad and the Odyssey were written in golden letters. Another catastrophe was the loss of the Lausus palace with many works of art, among them the Aphrodite of Cnidus. [68]

The usurper himself was highly unpopular because of his rapacity, so that the exasperated Senate restored Zeno to the throne in 477. Knowing himself lost, Basiliscus placed his crown on the altar of a church (the Aya Sofia?) and sought refuge in the baptistery. He was arrested and Zeno gave him his word that he would not be beheaded. Remaining true to his promise, the ruler had him locked up with his wife and children in a tower in Koukosor (perhaps the modern Gogsyn) in Cappadocia where they were starved to death. [69]

The short reign of Basiliscus saw the most powerful caesaropapist intervention in doctrinal affairs so far. The usurper lent his wholehearted support to the Monophysites. It is a puzzling why he did so; he was certainly not knowledgeable in theological matters nor was he conspicuous for personal piety. Perhaps his wife Zenonis had influenced him. In any case, Peter the Fuller, who languished behind the walls of a monastery, was allowed to come out into the open again, and Timothy the Cat was recalled from the Crimea. Surrounded by adherents, all Alexandrians, he rode triumphantly on a donkey to the Aya Sofia; the resemblance to Jesus' entry into Jerusalem is evident, but one source says that he fell off his ass, injuring his foot. Basiliscus came to the church in person to pay him homage. The Cat returned to Alexandria where he resumed his office among general rejoicing. Peter the Fuller did the same in Antioch. In this way the Monophysite party firmly established itself in Syria and Egypt.

As though he was a super-bishop, Basiliscus issued an encyclical, dated April 9th 475. He began with stating that what the Empire needed was unity in religion as its strong foundation. The fundament of this unity was to be and to remain the doctrinal canons of the Council of Nicaea, which had been confirmed by the Councils of Constantinople in 381 and Ephesus in 431 and 449 (the latter being the Robbers' Council). The imperial encyclical rejected the Tomus of Leo and all the canons of Chalcedon in 451, which were stigmatized as innovations on Nicaea. [70] All the bishops of the Empire were invited to sign; those not ready to do so would be banished.

The Tomus of Pope Leo I (449) was in fact a long letter written to Flavian, the then Patriarch of Constantinople. In this authoritative statement the Pontiff had declared that "two natures were united in Christ, without change, without division, and without confusion." [71] This doctrinal standpoint triumphed in Chalcedon in 451. Consequently, Basiliscus' encyclical was an unequivocally anti-Chalcedonian, Monophysite declaration. And taken into account the threat of banishment. it was also a declaration of war.

Alexandria and Antioch were the two great anti-Chalcedonian centres, vying with each other to be the most fanatical. Yet in his own capital Basiliscus was not so successful. Its Patriach, Acacius, refused to sign the declaration. To him it was an occasion for mourning; "clad in black, [he] draped the throne and the altar in black." [72] It is possible that, as Frend supposes, Acacius was at heart a Monophysite but did not want to be overruled by the Emperor. [73] Timothy who, when in the capital, saw its churches blocked to him on the orders of Acacius, retired to Ephesus, where he convoked a synod of his own with allegedly six hundred participants; this synod rejected Chalcedon, stating that it had "turned the world upside down." [74]

12. 'A doctrinal aberration'

Soon two great anti-Chalcedonians disappeared from the scene. Basiliscus was deposed and killed in the summer of 476, while Timothy the Cat died in Alexandria on July 31th 477 (he is still a saint in the calendar of the Coptic Church). The reinstated Zeno abolished all the acts of Basiliscus, including his encyclical, of course. Timothy escaped a second banishment by his timely death. The position of the Patriarch of Constantinople was formidably fortified; his see was declared the 'mother of our piety and of all Christians of the orthodox religion'. [75]

However, in Egypt and in Syria the Monophysite Movement was still strong. The majority of the faithful there favoured it, with the monks in the forefront. The new Patriarch of Antioch, Martyrius, issued an encyclical in which he claimed to adhere to the creed of the Councils of Nicaea and Constantinople and of the First Council of Ephesus (he was prudent enough not to mention the Robbers' Council), but he anathematized the canons of Chalcedon. In the words of Frend, "Chalcedon was reduced to the status of a doctrinal aberration." [76]

13. The *Henotikon*

Faced with this serious situation, Zeno made a manful attempt to restore unity. On July 28th 482 he issued the *Henotikon*, the 'instrument of unity'; although addressed to the clergy and faithful of Egypt, it was intended as a statement of general religious policy. Acacius, the Patriarch, who was hand in glove with the Emperor, had been his main adviser in this matter. Zeno's aim was a political one : to establish peace and harmony in his Empire, on the basis of a generally accepted creed. To achieve this end the schools of Constantinople (Chalcedonian) and of Alexandria and Antioch (anti-Chalcedonian) had to be reconciled.

The first part was not difficult : it referred to the canons of the Council of Nicaea which all parties accepted. The text spoke of "the only right and true faith pronounced through divine intervention only by the three hundred and eighteen Fathers assembled in Nicaea;" politician as he was, Zeno called this "the source and constitution of our power and the invincible shield of our Empire." In the same breath, the Councils of Constantinople and Ephesus I were confirmed; of course, Ephesus II was not mentioned, but neither was Chalcedon, at least not its doctrinal pronouncements. Nestorius was anathematized once again. The thorny question of whether there were one or two natures in Christ was simply side-stepped. The word 'nature' does not even figure in the *Henotikon*. It stated, however, that Jesus was both God and man (which was orthodox as well as Chalcedonian). There was not a word in this declaration to suggest that Rome might have a say in these matters; for the *Henotikon* Pope Leo's *Tomus* did not exist. At the end, all the faithful were invited to be one again and in agreement with one another. [77]

Judged from a political point of view, the *Henotikon* was too clever by half. Nobody was really satisfied. Staunch anti-Chalcedonians of whom there were many, missed an explicit condemnation of that Council. Some leading Monophysites accepted the *Henotikon only under pressure*. But there were also Chalcedonians in the East who protested against the failure not to mention Chalcedon's doctrinal canons. And as may be expected, Rome was not pleased at all. It appeared that the see of Constantinople considered itself to be the most prominent in the Church, and its Patriarch, as 'conspicuously the pontifex of the imperial state', as Pope Gelasius expressed it. [78] But as Bury writes, the Latin Church of the West "was no longer dependent on the Greeks for its theology; it had now its translation of the Bible, the *Vulgata* of Jerome, and an elaborate theology, presented by Augustine." [79]

At this moment circumstances were favouring Constantinople. Pope Simplicius was incapacitated by illness for months. He died in March 483 and was succeeded by Felix III. When the *Henotikon* was published, Patriarch Acacius had not deemed it necessary to inform Rome; Simplicius had already complained that "he [Acacius] was more partial to the Emperor than to the Pope." [80] At last the Vatican was prepared to answer the eastern pretensions; Felix unambiguously told Acacius that he should not consider himself 'the head of the whole Church'. When Acacius did not reply, Felix dispatched a delegation to the eastern capital. Its wily Patriarch lured its episcopal members into taking part in a communion service with him. Theophanes says that this was contrary to their instructions, and that Zeno himself, by means of bribery, had enticed them, not without having maltreated the legates. When they told Felix of this after their return to Rome, he was furious.

On July 28th 484 a synod was held in Rome deposing Acacius as a 'hypocrite and for having insulted the papal legates.' Some monks of an orthodox monastery in Constantinople made this judgment known to Acacius during a Sunday service; one source says that it was pinned to his pallium, while he stood at the altar. Some of these monks were killed by Acacius' supporters because of this. The Patriarch retaliated by ordering that Felix's name should no longer be mentioned. [81] This signified that there was now a situation of schism between the two ecclesiastical capitals, lasting until 519.

14. An anti-Chalcedonian backlash

Although Antioch was a Monophysite bulwark, it became the scene of a vehement anti-Chalcedonian backlash. It must be said that it was not only zeal for the true creed that spurred the actors on, for there were also strong political motives. The main actor was a general, Illus, a 'king-maker', since he had been instrumental in bringing Zeno back to the throne. But his *protégé* suspected him of plotting against him. This was probably true, for in 484 Illus actually rebelled, with the support of the Empress-Dowager Verina; he even went so far as to proclaim a certain Leontius Emperor. One of the elements in his opposition was that the *Henotikon* should be done away with.

The rebellion failed dismally; popular support for it was minimal. Illus and Leontius were driven back by imperial troops to a fortress in Isauria. in the southern part of Asia Minor, where they held out for four years. Finally they were overpowered and captured. "They were beheaded and their heads were sent to Zeno and brought into the Hippodrome fixed on poles. [They were taken] across to Sykai and exposed to the public view." [82] It was a triumph both for Zeno and the anti-Chalcedonians.

15. The star of Chalcedon rising again

Everywhere in the East ecclesiastical leaders emerged "to whom rejection of Chalcedon was a matter of creed", as Frend expresses it. [83] There were important anti-Chalcedonian strongholds, like Amida in Mesopotamia or the monastery of Madin on the Byzantine-Persian frontier, while in Syria, to quote Frend again, "there developed a distinctly Syriac-speaking Monophysitism. [84] However, although the Patriarchs of Antioch and Alexandria favoured

Monophysitism, we see also a pro-Chalcedonian reaction developing, led by erudite theologians. Even in the capital the star of Chalcedon began to rise again. Acacius died in 489, his equally schismatic successor in March 490, the Emperor Zeno in April 491, followed by Felix III in February 492 in Rome.

The *vox populi* in the capital was clearly pro-orthodox; the people asked of Ariadne, Zeno's widow, to give them 'an orthodox Emperor'. [85] Frend concludes that there was now real 'Roman' and 'Chalcedonian' patriotism in the capital. [86] In view of this, the choice of Ariadne, acting in agreement with the Senate, may surprise. They made a civil servant, called Anastasius, Emperor (491-518) (Zeno had no son). He was widely known as a pious Christian of exemplary behaviour, but he could hardly be considered orthodox. According to Theophanes, his mother had been a Manichaean and one of his uncles an Arian. [87] In the West they thought he was a Eutychian (= a Monophysite). [88] The new Emperor was decidely unorthodox, with an urge to preach. Even before he became a ruler, he had had his own chair in a church (probably the Aya Sofia) from where he spread his heterodox opinions. Euphemius, Patriarch of Constantinople and a convinced Chalcedonian, was far from pleased with this, especially when riots occurred as a consequence of this preaching. He had the chair overthrown. He threatened Anastasius that, if he would continue to play the priest, he would have him 'tonsure his head and parade him in a mockery among the crowd'. [89] Once Anastasius had been elected Emperor, Euphemius declared him 'as unworthy of the Christians and of the Empire'. He simply refused to take part in the coronation ceremony. When the Empress-Dowager and the Senate put pressure on him, he demanded that the new Emperor sign a pro-Chalcedonian declaration of faith, which he did. Anastasius was then crowned and married Ariadne, although he was already sixty and had never been married before. [90]

16. The Rome-Byzantium schism

One would think that, with the Emperor at least officially behind Chalcedon and with the Patriarch solidly in support of it, it would not have been difficult to heal the breach with Rome. However, in order to achieve this the *Henotikon* would have to be revoked and Patriach Acacius disavowed. [91] This did not seem probable. Felix's successor, Pope Gelasius (492-496), was not a man of a conciliatory disposition. This Pope put Anastasius and all his predecessors squarely in their places by authoritatively stating this. "There are in fact two [powers], Emperor Augustus, by which this world is sovereignly governed : the consecrated power of the bishops and the royal power. Of these, the responsiblity of the bishops is more weighty, since even for the rulers of the people they will have to give an account at the judgment seat of God." [92] Gelasius distrusted the Byzantines; to him the East was a region that abounded with heresies. The pro-Chalcedonian party in Constantinople suffered a severe setback, when a synod deposed Euphemius in 496, to the immense satisfaction of the Emperor Anastasius.

17. The action of Severus

For about a decade nothing much happened in the Monophysite controversy, but in 508 it flared up yet again. At that time a man came to the fore whose influence in favour of Monophysitism was almost decisive. This man, named Severus, came from a wealthy family of land-owners and was born around 465 in the town of Sozopolis in Pisidia, a province of Asia Minor. Although his family was Christian - his grandfather had even been a bishop -, he himself was not baptized until he had reached adulthood. Severus was certainly a pious man with an ascetic way of life. Nonetheless Frend states that "he saw Christianity as a rational creed and a higher philosophy based on the Bible and the teachings of the Fathers;" the road to it led through the schools of philosophy. [93]

His original idea was to follow a legal career, which was the normal road to the higher administrative positions. He studied grammar in Alexandria and later jurisprudence in Berytus. Then, around 486-488, a great change came over him. He was baptized, gave up the study of law, and became a monk. In the controversy under discussion one should always ask which side a Christian may choose. In the case of Severus there can be no doubt since he spoke of 'the evil Chalcedonian impiety'. Later he became a presbyter and founded a monastery near Maiuma, one of the strongholds of Monophysitism of which he became one of the great protagonists. He really came into his own in 508, when he visited Constantinople in the company of three hundred Palestinian monks; they came to complain that they were persecuted by the Chalcedonian Patriarch of Jerusalem, Elias.

Well-trained in rhetorics, backed by his study of philosophy, and thoroughly grounded in Patristic writings, Severus began a literary career that would last for thirty years. He left no great work, but fought endless controversies with Chalcedonian opponents, preached a great number of sermons, and conducted an endless correspondence. In these activities he was supported by Anastasius I. Thus he became the most outstanding Monophysite in the East. It appears that he could not care less what the West thought of all this, for he never refers to Latin opinion or authors.

Severus was at one with the Chalcedonians in stating that there was only one person in Jesus. He equally agreed that there was both divinity and humanity in him. But how did these combine? The Chalcedonian doctrine was that Christ was wholly consubstantial with the Father and wholly consubstantial with man; the Council had declared that he was 'in two natures without separation, that is to say, in two substances.' This meant that it employed the terms 'nature' and 'substance' as interchangeable. The Greek term for 'nature' is *phusis* and for 'substance' *ousia*, which can also be rendered as 'essence'. On the ground of his philosophical training Severus felt unable to accept that 'substance' and 'nature' meant the same thing; in his opinion only the divine persons could have ousia. The consequence was that there could be no two substances in Christ, and if substance and nature were the same thing, then there were also not two natures. He once went so far as to state that the two-natures doctrine was 'a Jewish turpitude'. [94]

As was usual in this kind of controversy, Severus got into problems when it came to explaining how Jesus' divinity fitted into his human person. There was, in his opinion, only one person with one nature and one *hypostasis*, which may be translated with 'existence'. Severus, however, dodged the question by declaring that, although Christ certainly was a composite (sunthetos) person, it must remain a divine mystery how this composition came about and how it looked exactly. It was Severus' disadvantage that his theological formulas were far less precise than those of Chalcedon.

The interesting question is why Severus did not accept the Chalcedonian formulas, for we see him hovering on the brink of it. It was impossible for him to accept the total consubstantiality of the Son with the Father. One could say indeed that he was consubstantial with the Father but then only with respect to his divine properties, not with respect to his humanity. Severus' great bogey was Pope Leo I with his much vilified *Tomus* that was qualified as 'Jewish'. Which Christ, he asked, died on the cross, the divine or the human one? In his opinion Leo was 'the common pillar of the heterodox', even a 'blasphemer'. [95]

There is surely an anti-Roman point in these polemics. It was not directed against the papal primacy, but Severus found the Latins bad theologians who did not understand the nature of the Trinity. I feel that there is here more than a shade of that *horror materiae* that appeared so often in the theological discussions of these centuries. Certainly, the godhead was merciful and wanted to redeem mankind. And certainly, the *Logos* appeared among us and took up his abode in the person of Jesus of Nazareth. But that the divine *Logos* could unite himself wholly and wholeheartedly with the humanity of this same person, that is where Severus stopped. It is as though he would not allow the godhead to become too intimate with humanity.

Severus, states Frend, "endowed the Monophysite movement with its philosophy and characteristic terminology." At the same time, "he was a cosmopolitan, as much at home in the capital or in Alexandria as in Antioch ... His letters betray a profound deference to the Emperor and loyalty to the Empire." [96] It is not wholly inconceivable that there was a tinge of nationalism in Monophysitism, in the sense that this theology was thought to be better suited to the Greek way of thinking; the two-natures theology might fit the Latin temperament better - and their clumsy and inexpert handling of philosophical and theological questions, Severus may have added *in foro interno*.

He received his remuneration for his deference to ruler and realm, when he was appointed bishop of Antioch in 512. His new flock was squarely behind him; they greeted him with cries of "Anathematize the Council of Chalcedon. Anathematize the Council that has turned the universe upside down ... Cursed be the Council, cursed be the Tome of Leo. Deliver the city from heresy." [97]

18. On the brink of victory?

It might now seem that Monophysitism was on the brink of a final victory. There was a formal breach with Rome, the court supported the Monophysites, their leading clerics held important offices in the oriental Church. However, the sniping went on all the time. Severus invariably called his opponents 'Diophysites' and heretics in need of conversion; the other side called the Monophysites 'Manichees' (since nothing could be worse than a Manichee) and dissenters fit for punishment. Not everybody in the Byzantine Empire was a Monophysite. Its European provinces were overwhelmingly Chalcedonian, and also the population of the capital.

At the end of 514 Anastasius remembered that there was a Pope in Rome. He wrote to the present incumbent of the Roman see, Hormisdas (514-523), asking for a meeting. But Rome was not in a conciliatory mood, and in July 517 Anastasius cut the slender cord with the words : "You may insult and thwart me, but you may not command me." In the night of July 8th 518 the eighty-eight-year-old Emperor died.

19. The new Emperor

He was succeeded by Justin I (518-527). His biographer Vasiliev describes the first part of his life as 'from swineherd to Emperor', [98] the Byzantine equivalent of 'from news-boy to millionaire'. His father was a poor peasant, and he himself is reported to have herded cows and swine. Most sources say that he was an Illyrian from a village near Skupic, the modern Skopje in Serbia; Procopius gives us the name of Justin's birthplace, namely Bederiana [99] that has been identified as the still existing village of Bader. [100] His year of birth is 451 or 452.

Thoroughly fed up with his extremely poor and boring way of life, the twenty-year-old Justin, along with two of his comrades, packed up their things (which were not many) and provided with some bread for food, set out for the capital on foot. On their arrival the three sturdy young men could immediately become members of Leo I's palace guard. [101] Justin cut a good figure as a soldier, attending faithfully to his duties, and thus made a rapid career. He fought on several fronts, for instance against the Persians, where he distinguished himself. Under Anastasius he became commander of the palace guard and even a senator. [102]

His great chance came when Anastasius died, for the old man had no sons and had never designated a successor. The throne was up for the man who would grab it. The commander of the palace guard was in a good position, the more so because he had a great military reputation. On the day of the election of the new Emperor by the Senate, confusion reigned; there were several candidates, one of them being Justinian. But the unanimous senatorial choice feel on Justin; this choice was not contested, because the army was behind it.

With a bleeding lip - an opponent had hit him in the face - Justin was brought to the imperial box in the Hippodrome; while the guards protected him from the gaze of the public with their shields, he changed into the imperial robes. Then the Patriarch crowned him. The event astonished many observers; it was 'beyond any expectation', as Evagrius wrote. [103], for Justin, although a courageous general, had no administrative qualifications at all. He did not exactly possess a reputation for erudition; John Lydus calls him 'a good, easy, quiet man who had no knowledge whatever except of military matters.' [104] If we may believe Procopius - who, as we know, loved slander, - he could not even write, [105] but this seems improbable.

20. Uproar in the Aya Sofia

Soon enough the wind of change began to blow strongly; it was by no means favourable to the Monophysites. What now began may be characterized as a Chalcedonian backlash. A new religious policy was conceived, but Vasiliev does not think that Justin was its architect. The new Emperor was sixty-five or sixty-six years old, he says, and he was not a well-educated man. In all probability it was his nephew Justinian (the later Emperor) who was behind the new policy. [106]

Six days after Justin's elevation, on July 15th 518, the usual solemn Sunday service took place in the Aya Sofia. The population found this an apt opportunity to express its views on the religious state of affairs. The large church was thronged with people. When the Patriarch with his retinue of priests strided through the church on his way to the altar, the congregation began to shout. "Long live the Patriarch! Long live the Emperor! ... Throw out Severus the Manichaean. Whoever does not say this is a Manichaean himself. Now proclaim the holy synod [= Chalcedon] ... Justin reigns; of whom are you [the Patriarch] afraid? ... Throw out Severus, throw out the new Judas!" This must make us somewhat reticent in speaking of an East-West split in the Church. For there was also a split between the European and Asiatic parts of the Empire. Monophysitism had no strongholds either in the West or in the European Byzantine provinces; its main bulwark was Egypt, especially Alexandria. Other regions that were more or less affected by it were Syria, with Antioch, and Armenia, but not so much Palestine and Asia Minor.

Wanting to conduct the service in a dignified way, the Patriarch asked the crowd to calm down. "First we shall worship at the holy altar and after that I will give answer you." But since the faithful remained clamouring and desired of him that he anathematize Severus, he ascended the pulpit to declare that "he was devoted to the orthodox faith till death. There is no need of confusion or tumult. No one dares to anathematize the holy synod [Chalcedon]." In spite of the fact that he unambiguously distanced himself from Severus, the clamouring continued, for the crowd loudly demanded that he should anathematize Severus. "Unless I get an answer, I shall stay here till late", somebody screamed.

The harassed Patriarch then said that he would entrust the decision to the Emperor. But no, the crowd wanted to have a service commemorating Chalcedon, obviously meant as an affirmation of it. A deacon announced that they would have it on the next day. Nothing, however, would pacify the congregation but the condemnation of Severus. Or else they would repudiate their Patriarch. Finally the wearied Patriarch and the bishops who were with him gave in. A declaration was read from the pulpit stating that "Severus had separated himself from this Holy Church. Therefore, we ... regard him as alien and ... anathematize him as one who has been condemned on account of his blasphemy." It was only after having listened to this statement that the crowd began to disperse. [107]

The commemoration service on Monday July 16th went along just as noisily. The crowd loudly protested its aversion to anti-Chalcedonians. Curiously enough, they demanded that the name of the bishop of Rome should again be inserted into the liturgical prayers, in other words, that there should be an end to the schism. John the Patriarch preached, praising the faithful for their zeal. He reaffirmed his faith in the canons of Nicaea, Constantinople, Ephesus I, and Chalcedon. Yet even after this the shouting continued; it appeared as though the congregation did not really trust their Patriarch. In order to satisfy them, the Patriarch promised to report their exclamations to His Majesty. But the people blocked the doors so that nobody could leave the church. It was only when the Patriarch had promised to insert the names of the four ecumenical Councils and the name of the bishop of Rome into the liturgical prayers that quiet returned. The rest of the service was held in good order. [108]

21. The popular demands ratified

If we look at the events in the Aya Sofia from the official side, we must call them non-events. For a congregation could not anathematize somebody, not even in collusion with the Patriarch of Constantinople. However, as Vasiliev writes, these events possessed 'a high degree of general interest'; [109] they certainly influenced the decisions of the authorities. Four days later, on July 20th, a synod convened in the capital in order to consider the demands of the people and the monks; it consisted of forty-three or forty-four bishops, but the Patriarch himself was absent. The synod canonically confirmed the popular demands. It reconfirmed the doctrinal decisions of the four great Councils, with Chalcedon included; the name of Pope Leo I should be mentioned during the liturgy (which meant that his *Tomus* was accepted). Patriarch Severus of Antioch was anathematized and deposed; he was called 'a wolf instead of a shepherd' and was accused of embezzling church property. [110] Somewhat later Patriarch John of Constantinople ratified the synodal decisions. [111] Later Patriarch John of Jerusalem also adhered to the decrees.

In Tyre, where Epiphanius was bishop (not to be confused with bishop Epiphanius of Salamis in Cyprus, the famous combater of heresies), the faithful convened in the main church on September 16th 518. The decrees of the Constantinopolitan synod were read, with the announcement that Severus had been deposed. This communciation was greeted with long exclamations of approval. Several bishops mounted the pulpit to pronounce their own excommunication of Severus. Somebody who was present made extensive notes of the proceedings that have been preserved. [112]

22. The schism healed

As might be expected, normal relations between Constantinople and Rome, where Hormisdas was Pope, were restored; the schism was as good as over. Both Justin and John sent personal letters to the Pope. There is also a remarkable letter from Justinian, the Crown Prince, asking Hormisdas to visit Constantinople 'for final settlement of the union'. [113] Hormisdas did not go himself but sent instead a delegation with instructions to officially end the schism. The legates crossed the Adriatic from Brindisi and then proceeded along the Via Egnatia to the capital. Everywhere they were heartily welcomed; special services were held in their honour. On Monday March 25th 519 they entered Constantinople, escorted by a crowd with lighted candles. The next day they were received by the Emperor.

On Thursday 28th, which happened to be Maundy Thursday, the schism was officially ended; the ceremony took place at the imperial palace, with the Senate present. The Patriarch signed the document, but he was not in great spirits; he may have felt his position somewhat diminished by the Hormisdas' triumph. However, the Pope would not have acquired this result without the active support of Justin. It was the Emperor who really wanted the schism to end, for, as Frend puts it, he "regarded the Empire as incomplete without the unity of old and new Rome". [114] Nevertheless, if Hormisdas now expected to be able to play a decisive role in the religious policy of Byzantium, he was completely mistaken. [115], for Justin "was an autocrat who was in no way willing to give up any of his prerogatives either in favor of the Pope or in favor of the Patriarch." [116]

The papal delegation remained in the capital until July 10th 520 in order to oversee the process of reconciliation. Soon enough difficulties arose; several oriental provinces stuck to their own theological interpretation. [117] Dorotheus, the bishop of Thessalonica, finally decided not to sign the document of reunification. Popular feeling ran high there; it even happened that the populace killed one of the papal delegates who had gone there to negotiate with Dorotheus. When Hormisdas asked the Emperor to send the refractory bishop to Rome 'for suitable prosecution', Justin flatly refused. [118]

23. Action against the anti-Chalcedonians

In the Patriarchate of Antioch[119] fifty-five Monophysite bishops or more were deposed during Justin's reign, the most important of these being Severus of Antioch. Severe action was taken against anti-Chalcedonian monasteries; the monks were given the choice of either signing the document of reunification (which implied the acceptance of Chalcedon) or else retiring into the desert, which many of them did indeed. [120]

The deposed Patriarch against whom a warrant to appear had been issued by Justin, managed to escape from Antioch under the cover of darkness, and sailed to Alexandria where he was welcomed by the Monophysite Patriarch Timothy IV. From Egypt he kept up a campaign of letters to support the anti-Chalcedonian resistance and even sent secret instructions to his clergy in Antioch. [121]

24. A Pope visits Constantinople

The papal delegation was still in Constantinople, when the Patriarch, John II, died in February 520; he was succeeded by the presbyter Epiphanius (not identical with his namesake, the bishop of Tyre). More than four months later he saw fit to notify Hormisdas of his election, adding that he had accepted the four Councils. [122] The Pope answered coolly. [123] Relations were not as cordial as they should have been.

Hormisdas having died on August 6th 523, he was succeeded by John I (523-526). The short reign of this pontiff is above all notable for the visit he paid to Constantinople, the first bishop of Rome ever to go there. He was greeted by the Emperor in person, who bowed to the ground before him and solemnly escorted him through the city. On Easter Sunday, April 19th 526, the Pope celebrated a Latin service in the Aya Sofia. Curiously enough, Justin asked him to crown him, although he already been crowned by the Patriacrh of Constantinople. It was a truly historical event, for Justin was the first Emperor ever to be crowned by a Pope. [124] The visit of John I to the eastern capital certainly strengthened the position of the Chalcedonians; he met and spoke with many oriental bishops. But Timothy IV of Alexandria did not come. On the return journey the Pope died in Ravenna on May 18th 526.

25. All heretics condemned

From that moment Justin also had not long to live. On the whole he executed a strict anti-Monophysite policy, but as the astute politician he was, he proceeded cautiously. Egypt, the great stronghold of Monophysitism, stayed out of harm's way under the guidance of Timothy IV. The reason is not hard to guess : Egypt, still a very rich country, good for a great part of the income of the state, and also the main provider of grain for the capital, should not be driven into a tight corner. [125]

In the last months of Justin's reign, when Justinian was already co-Emperor, a decree against all heretics was issued. [126] Who was a heretic? Anyone who was not orthodox, that is, a Chalcedonian. Thus the term 'heretic' included Monophysites, Montanists, Nestorians, Manichaeans and other Gnostics, Samaritans, Jews, and pagans. They were not allowed to hold any public office or legal profession or to teach.

Vasiliev divides the religious policy of Justin I into three periods. The first years, 518-520, were a time of severe persecution of and harsh measures against Monophysites; the man behind this was Vitalian, a *patricius* who was a powerful supporter of Chalcedon. With him out of the way - he was murdered in 520 - milder times dawned which lasted until 527. But if Justin and his Crown Prince Justinian had hoped that their lenient policy would bring the heterodox on other thoughts, they had finally to admit that they were wrong. Thus it came to that severe edict of 527. It was, of course, impossible to execute it in all its severity. The Gothic soldiers who served in the imperial armies, were exempted from it by the stipulations of the decree itself. Another point is that the see of Alexandria was in the hands of an outspoken Monophysite, the afore mentioned Timothy IV; he kept his office until 535 or 536.

26. Justinian's position

When Justinian I ascended to the imperial throne in 527, he found himself in an unenviable position. There can be no doubt that he himself was staunchly orthodox and always remained so. However, his powerful and influential wife Theodora was sympathetic towards the Monophysites, and he had to reckon with her. Furthermore, he did not want to have more *rumor in casa* than there already was; as a good politician, intent on the unity of his realm, he hoped that some sort of compromise would be possible. Was there no theological formula conceivable in which ecclesiastics like Severus and Timothy IV could also find themselves? They always had some influential supporters of their cause at the court.

Justinian had to reckon with a considerable measure of support for Monophysitism in the East, not only in Egypt, but also in Syria. In spite of the repression, the contours of an anti-Chalcedonian hierarchy became visible. There was a Monophysite Patriarch, Timothy IV of Alexandria; although in exile, Severus considered himself the legitimate incumbent of the patriarchal see of Antioch. Monophysite priests were being ordained, but many candidates had to be rejected because of their illiteracy. Naturally, Justinian was informed of these developments, which made him retrace his steps somewhat. In 530 or 531 he allowed the banished monks to return to their monasteries (but not the bishops to their sees).

27. A period of quiet

Once back in their old habitats, the monks drew up a memorandum that they sent to the Emperor. They attested their unwavering loyalty to his person and declared that they had nothing to do with Mani, Eutyches, or Nestorius. Yet they also gave their opinion that the Fathers of Chalcedon had taken the wrong course. [127] After the receipt of this memorandum a series of conferences were held in the capital between Chalcedonians and Monophysites (mainly Syrians). Although these did not amount to much, the parties were on speaking terms again. One of the discussions even took place in the presence of Justinian. On March 15th 533 the Emperor published a declaration of faith. [128] It was impeccably orthodox but begged the question of the two natures and did not mention any Council nor the *Tomus* of Leo I; although he anathematized Eutyches, Nestorius, and Apollinaris, he did not condemn Timothy or Severus. He knew very well that he was treading where angels fear to tread.

A period of quiet followed. Although the Emperor had passed over the teaching of Leo I in silence, Pope John II (533-535) declared that the imperial confession was in accordance with apostolic teaching (March 25th 534).

Severus was even invited to the capital by the Emperor himself. Monopysitism was making headway, even in Constantinople. For when Epiphanius, its Patriarch died, he was succeeded by Anthimus, the ascetic bishop of Trebizond, who was secretly devoted to the Monophysite cause. Severus had a great influence on him, and soon enough Anthimus came out into the open with an unambigously Monophysite statement. So there were three now Monophysite Patriarchs, those of Constantinople and Jerusalem, and Theodosius, the successor of Timothy in Alexandria. The Monophysites often acted as if there were no laws against them.

28. A second papal visit

In the beginning of March 536 Pope Agapitus I (535-536) arrived in Constantinople, bringing a message from the Ostrogothic King Theodahad that implored Justinian to cease his operations in Sicily and Dalmatia. However, this energetic ecclesiastic found that he could be more than a diplomatic messenger. He soon was on excellent terms with the Emperor; they conversed in Latin, a language that the ruler spoke much better than Greek. Anthimus was deposed and succeeded by the orthodox Menas. A synod condemned Anthimus as a heretic and anthematized Severus once again. The fact that Agapitus died suddenly in the capital on April 22nd 536 did not influence the force of the counter-attack, for on August 6th 536 Justinian sent Anthimus, Severus (who had arrived in the capital indeed), and their supporters into exile. Severus' writings were to be burned; nobody was allowed to posses them. He died on February 8th 538 in Alexandria, while nothing more was heard of Anthimus.

29. Justinian tackles the Egyptian problem

Justinian now felt strong enough to tackle the Egyptian problem (Antioch had already an orthodox Patriarch). Theodosius was summoned to Constantinople and deposed; his successor was orthodox. Frend categorically states that "there was never again any real hope of the Monophysites ruling the Church of the Empire." [129] Once again, oriental monks were hounded out of their monasteries; Monophysite faithful were arrested and tortured, sometimes even executed. Ephraim, the orthodox Patriarch of Antioch, was even given the nickname of 'the executioner of the faithful'.

Yet how unfavourably things might go for them, the Monophysites had a powerful protectress in the person of the Empress Theodora. They also had an unofficial head, namely Theodosius. After his deposition Justinian wanted to lock him up in a fortress, but his wife, acting as so often on her own initiative, lodged him in a palace in the capital. From there he continued to support, lead, and steer the Monophysites, until his death in 566.

30. The structuring of the Monophysite Church

The slow structuring of the Monophysite Church continued. An intrepid monk, James Bar'Addai, clandestinely consecrated bishop, travelled through the whole Orient, everywhere preaching and instructing; he ordained priests and nominated bishops. In the far-distant Byzantine provinces along the Persian frontier the Monophysite position became reasonably secure. James, the indefatigable missionary, remained active until 578; he is said to have consecrated twenty-seven bishops and ordained a hundred thousand priests. Justinian might rage as much as he could, it was finally of no use. When he died in 565, the Monophysite Church was a solid presence in the Asiatic half of the Empire. It was especially strong in Egypt, Syria, and in the eastern provinces of Asia Minor.

31. Monophysite kingdoms

In Chapter 8 of his book on the Monophysite movement Frend describes the Monophysite kingdoms that existed beyond the frontiers of the Byzantine Empire. South of the Egyptian border lay three Nubian kingdoms along the Nile in what is now Sudan. Later these kingdoms merged into one. Their populations became Monophysite almost to a man. Still farther south, in Ethiopia, Monophysitism was imported by Syrian and Egyptian missionaries.

Here too the indigenous population as a whole converted to Monophysitism. Armenia also, where the sense of independence has always been strong, chose Monophysitism.

32. Under Justinian's successors

Justinian's nephew and successor Justin II was personally orthodox; his wife Sophia had been a Monophysite, but found it better, once an Empress, to be orthodox. The new Emperor immediately made his position clear by issuing a manifest to all orthodox believers; in this he declared that anyone who acknowledged only one nature was not orthodox. [130] Up to about 571 he did not persecute the unorthodox. Then he began to harass the Monophysites. From 574 Justin was a burnt-out case; he became stark mad and was unable to govern. Sophia could not cope with the situation, and a certain Tiberius, a high official, was created co-Emperor. His own independent rule lasted only four years (578-582) and was a period of quiet for the Monophysites.

His successor, Maurice (582-602), was an able general who had won great renown in the war against the Persians. He was an unflincheable Chalcedonian; the quiet days for the Monophysites were now past. Many of them, even high-placed persons, were harassed and imprisoned. In spite of all this, the Monophysite movement steadily made progress. In Syria the orthodox were confined to pockets in the great cities, whereas the countryside was exclusively Monophysite.

Bad days dawned for the orthodox when Maurice was murdered and Phocas became Emperor (602-610). Not that Phocas was really interested in theological questions, but the Persian Emperor, as related in an earlier chapter, seized the opportunity to conquer the greater part of Byzantium's eastern possessions. While the Monophysites experienced no problems under Persian rule, orthodoxy was almost wiped out as an organized unity. In Chosroes' view Monophysitism was the religion of the majority.

Then came the enormous counter-offensive of Heraclius I that led to the restoration of Byzantine rule in the East within two years (627-628).

Although Monophysites and orthodox hated one another, fresh attempts were made under the guidance of the Emperor to find a doctrinal compromise. However, as Frend, whom I am following here, writes : "The further Heraclius went in his attempts to meet the Monophysites, the more certain he was to encounter opposition from the Chalcedonians, and in particular from the West." [131] The situation was truly dualistic : there were no intermediate terms, and the distance was unbridgeable. The circle was not squared yet, when the great Moslim onslaught began in 534 and the strongest Monophysite bulwarks, Syria and later also Egypt, all fell into Arab hands.

NOTES TO CHAPTER VI

1. Stephen B. Bowman s.v. 'Jews', *Oxf.Dict.Byz.* 2, 1041.
2. Avi-Yonah, *The Jews* 240.
3. Avi-Yonah, *The Jews* 241/242.
4. Stephen S. Bowman s.v. 'Samaritans', *Oxf.Dict.Byz.* 3, 1835.
5. Malalas, *Chronographia* 445-447; Proc., *Anekdota* 11.
6. Malalas, *Chronographia* 455.
7. Diehl, *Justinien* II, 328.
8. *Novella* 129 of Justinian, quoted by Knecht, *Religions-Politik* 51/52.
9. Knecht, *Religions-Politik* 52.
10. Malalas, *Chronographia* 487.
11. Quoted by Diehl, *Justinien* II, 329. This is an unequivocally dualistic statement.
12. The source is Malalas, *Chronographia* 389, quoted by Avi-Yonah, Jews 246.
13. Avi-Yonah, *The Jews* 247.
14. Proc., *Anekdota* 28.
15. Proc., *De aedificiis* 6.2, quoted by Avi-Yonah, *The Jews* 250.
16. Quotation by Avi-Yonah, *The Jews* 251, from the Byzantine poet Romanos.
17. Quoted by Avi-Yonah, *The Jews* 254.
18. Avi-Yonah, *The Jews* 254/255.

19. Avi-Yonah, *The Jews* 255.
20. Theophanes, *Chronographia* AM 6101, AD 608/609.
21. Bury, *Later Roman Empire* II, 1.
22. See Vol. IV, Ch. II, § 7.
23. See Vol. XII, Ch. I, § 2c.
24. See Vol. XII, Ch. I, § 3.
25. See Vol. XII, Ch. I, § 6.
26. See Vol. XIV, Ch. IV, § 4.
27. Vol. XII, Ch. I is entirely devoted to this theme.
28. It seems an anachronism to me to say that it now became the official religion of the state, as so many scholars do.
29. Gibbon, *Decline and Fall* II, 46.
30. See Vol. XII, Ch. II, Part III, § 5b.
31. See Vol. XIII, Ch. V, § 35.
32. See Vol. XI, Ch. III, § 7h.
33. Bury, *Later Roman Empire* I, 186/187.
34. Frend, *Monophysite Movement* 51 and note 4.
35. Mansi 7.129/130.
36. Frend, *Monophysite Movement* 51.
37. Corpus iuris civilis 1.3.43; 1.3.41 and 47, quoted by Diehl, *Justinien* II, 319.
38. Knecht, *Religions-Politik* 53 : "Justinian is not only a Christian, he is also an Emperor ... We are of the opinion that with Justinian the political motives were stronger than the religious."
39. On Justinian's Jewish legislation the reader will be amply informed by the detailed work of Rabello, *Giustiniano* (see Bibliography).
40. Complete text in Knecht, *Religions-Politik* 25-28.
41. Knecht, *Religions-Politik* 31.
42. Malalas, *Chronographia* 449.
43. Ion.Eph., *HE* 133-135.
44. Agathias 4.31.
45. Knecht, *Religions-Politik* 38-40.
46. Vol. XIII, Ch. V, Part II.

47. See Vol. XIII, Ch. V, Part III.
48. Quoted by Diehl, *Justinien* II, 230.
49. Vol. XIII, Ch. VIII, Part IV.
50. Pauline Allen s.v. 'Monophysitism', *TRE* 23 (1994), 219/220; A. Grillmeier s.v. 'Monophysitismus', *Lex.f.Theol.u.Kirche* 7 (1962), 563/564.
51. Vol. XIII, Ch. VII, Part III.
52. Vol. XIII, Ch. VII, Part I.
53. Vol. XIII, Ch. VII, Part IV.
54. *Acta Conciliorum Oecumenicorum* 2.II.3, quoted by Frend, *Monophysite Movement* 143.
55. Zacharias Rhetor, *Historia ecclesiastica* 3.1, quoted by Frend, *Monophysite Movement* 143.
56. *Acta Conciliorum Oecumenicorum* 2.I.2, § 124, quoted by Frend, Monophysite Movement 137.
57. Alexander P. Kahzdan s.v. 'Monophysitism', *The Oxford Dict. of Byzant.*, 2, 1399 (1991).
58. Frend, *Monophysite Movement* 144.
59. Mansi 7.51.
60. Frend, *Monophysite Movement* 149, following Zacharias, *Historia ecclesiastica* 3.2.
61. Zacharias Rhetor, *Historia ecclesiastica* by Frend, *Monophysite Movement* 157, note 2.
62. Frend, *Monophysite Movement* 164.
63. Frend, *Monophysite Movement* 167/168.
64. He owed this nickname either to his diminutive stature or to his lith way of moving.
65. Theophanes, *Chronographia* AM 5949, AD 456/457 (109/110). Timothy has published a collection of texts 'against those who say that there are two natures', texts found in the Fathers denying that there are two natures.
66. Theophanes, *Chronographia* AM 5959, AD 457/458 (110).
67. Theophanes, *Chronographia* AM 5952, AD 459/460 (111/112).
68. Bury, *Later Roman Empire* I, 252.
69. Theophanes, *Chronographia* AM 5969, AD 476/477 (124).
70. Text in Evagrius, *Historia ecclesiastica* 3.4.

71. Leo, *Epistola 38*.
72. Theophanes, *Chronographia* AM 5967, AD 474/475.
73. Frend, *Monophysite Movement* 170.
74. Evagrius, *Historia ecclesiastica* 3.5' Frend, *Monophysite Movement* 171.
75. Codex Justiniani 1.2,16, quoted by Frend, *Monophysite Movement* 174.
76. Frend, *Monophysite Movement* 174/175.
77. Evagrius, *Historia ecclesiastica* 3.12-22.
78. Gelasius, *Epistola ad episcopus Dardaniae* 35.1. CSEL 35.
79. Bury, *Later Roman Empire* I, 192.
80. Evagrius, *Historia ecclesiastica* 3.21.
81. Theophanes, *Chronographia* AM 5979, AD 487/488 (132); Frend, *Monophysite Movement* 181-183.
82. Theophanes, *Chronographia*, AM 5973, AD 480/481 and 486/487 (128-132); Bury, *Later Roman Empire* I, 256-258.
83. Frend, *Monophysite Movement* 185.
84. Frend, *Monophysite Movement* 185.
85. Frend, *Monophysite Movement* 190.
86. Frend, *Monophysite Movement* 190.
87. Theophanes, *Chronographia* AM 5983, AD 490/491 (136); Evagrius, *Historia ecclesiastica* 3.22.
88. Paulus Diaconus, *Historia Romanorum* 16.2.
89. Theophanes, *Chronographia* AM 5982, AD 489/490 (134).
90. Theophanes, *Chronographia* AM 5983, AD 490/491 (136)' Evagrius, *Historia ecclesiastica* 3.32.
91. Frend, *Monophysite Movement* 193.
92. Gelasius, *Epistola* 12.2-3, the so-called *Tomus Gelasii*, quoted by Frend, *Monophysite Movement* 195.
93. Frend, *Monophysite Movement* 202/203.
94. Severus, Homily 56.9, quoted by Frend, *Monophysite Movement* 211, note 3.
95. Quoted by Frend, *Monophysite Movement* 213 and note 2.
96. Frend, *Monophysite Movement* 213.

97. Quoted by Frend, *Monophysite Movement* 221 from the *Vita Severi* by Johannes of Beith-Aphthonia.
98. Vasiliev, *Justin the First*, Ch. II.
99. Procopius, *Anekdota* 6.2.
100. Vasiliev, *Justin the First* 56.
101. Procopius, *Anekdota* 6.3.
102. Procopius, *Ankekdota* 6.11.
103. Evagrius, *Historia ecclesiastica* 4.1.
104. Quoted by Vasiliev, *Justin the First* 83.
105. Procopius, *Anekdota* 6.11-16.
106. Vasiliev, *Justin the First* 135.
107. Obviously stenographic reports were made of this curious meeting, which found their way into Mansi 8, 1037-1136.
108. Mansi 8.1061-1066.
109. Vasiliev, *Justin the First* 144.
110. Text of the synodal decrees in Mansi 8.1037-1064.
111. Mansi 8.1065-1068.
112. Mansi 8.1081-1092.
113. Mansi 8.438.
114. Frend, *Monophysite Movement* 238.
115. Frend, *Monophysite Movement* 180.
116. Frend, *Monophysite Movement* 184.
117. Mansi 8.487-488.
118. Mansi 8.489-490.
119. A map on pp. 250/1 shows the episcopal sees that were in the hands of supporters of Severus.
120. Frend, *Monophysite Movement* 247/248.
121. Vasiliev, *Justin the First* 226/227; Frend, *Monophysite Movement* 252.
122. Mansi 8.502-503.
123. Mansi 8.500-501.
124. Vasiliev, *Justin the First* 216.
125. Vasiliev, *Justin the First* 224.
126. *Codex Justiniani* 1.1.5.

127. Text in Frend, *Monophysite Movement* 264/265.
128. Frend, *Monophysite Movement* 266/267.
129. Frend, *Monophysite Movement* 275.
130. Evagrius, *Historia ecclesiastica* 5.4.
131. Frend, *Monophysite Movement* 347.

CHAPTER VII

ARABIA BEFORE ISLAM

1. The land

The Arabian peninsula - or rather the *Gazirat al-'Arab*, the 'island of the Arabs', as the inhabitants themselves call it - was never occupied by Alexander the Great and his Diadochi nor by the Romans or the Byzantines. Not even the greatest conquerors of Antiquity felt the urge to penetrate into this vast, arid, and extremely hot expanse of land, with its length of 2200 km and a width of 1200 km. [1] On its western and southern rims the peninsula is bordered by mountain ridges the highest peaks of which rise to four thousand meters or more in what is now the Yemen. [2]

A coastal plain of about thirty miles wide stretches along the litoral of the Red Sea; here the old cities of Mecca and Medina are situated. The heartland of the peninsula is formed by a central plateau, called the Najd; it is a desert that stretches onto the Persian Gulf in the east, with a surface of 500.000 km², its area is a quarter of that of Europe. Its south-eastern part consists solely of sand which is why it is called the *Rub' al Khali*, the 'Empty Quarter'. It had to wait until 1931 before the first European travellers dared cross it.

Water is a very rare commodity in these regions; there are only a few *wadis*, valleys that, when there is rainfall, are filled with water, sometimes with even too much water. Agriculture is possible only in the south where the *monsoon* causes more rain to fall. [3] This is especially so in the Yemen, "the most fertile region of the whole Arabian peninsula. The richness and variety of its products, and the mildness of its climate, in vivid contrast to the baking hinterland, won for it in ancient times its name of *Arabia Felix*, that is, 'Arabia the Fortunate'". [4]

2. The inhabitants

We are accustomed to thinking of Arabs as nomads. In our mind's eye we see long rows of camels plodding slowly through the desert sand; bearded Bedouins walk in front of them in footlong *burnous*, while the women and the children sit on the animals among and on top of enormous sacks. They do not trek all the time; at regular intervals they set up camp in some place where there is water and fodder for their camels and their herds of sheep and goats. There they live in low black tents.

This picture is certainly not incorrect. Of old many Arabs were nomads indeed; even today not a few of them continue to trek, although they are much hindered by the oil pipelines that are difficult to cross. Yet there has always been also a sedentary population, in the oases and in the towns and villages along the southern and western coasts of the peninsula, and further in the north in the regions bordering on Palestine and Syria where there are many small towns. Such towns were often commercial centres because the caravans passed through them. The Yemen, in the south, had harbours; its sailors navigated the Red Sea and perhaps even the Indian Ocean. [5]

The inhabitants of the Arab peninsula are Semites, which means that they speak a language that is akin to Babylonian, Assyrian, Aramaic, Syrian, Hebrew, and Punic. This Arab language has, as every other language, its dialects; those of the north are different from those of the south, whereas the Yemen has a dialect of its own, written with a special script, the *musnad*. [6] Traditionally there is an antagonism between the north and south. [7]

3. Pre-Islamic Arab history

History [8] has been witness to some Arab kingdoms. Classical authors mention quite a number of them, all situated in the south-west; [9] 'Saba' is the

VI MOHAMMED'S ARABIA

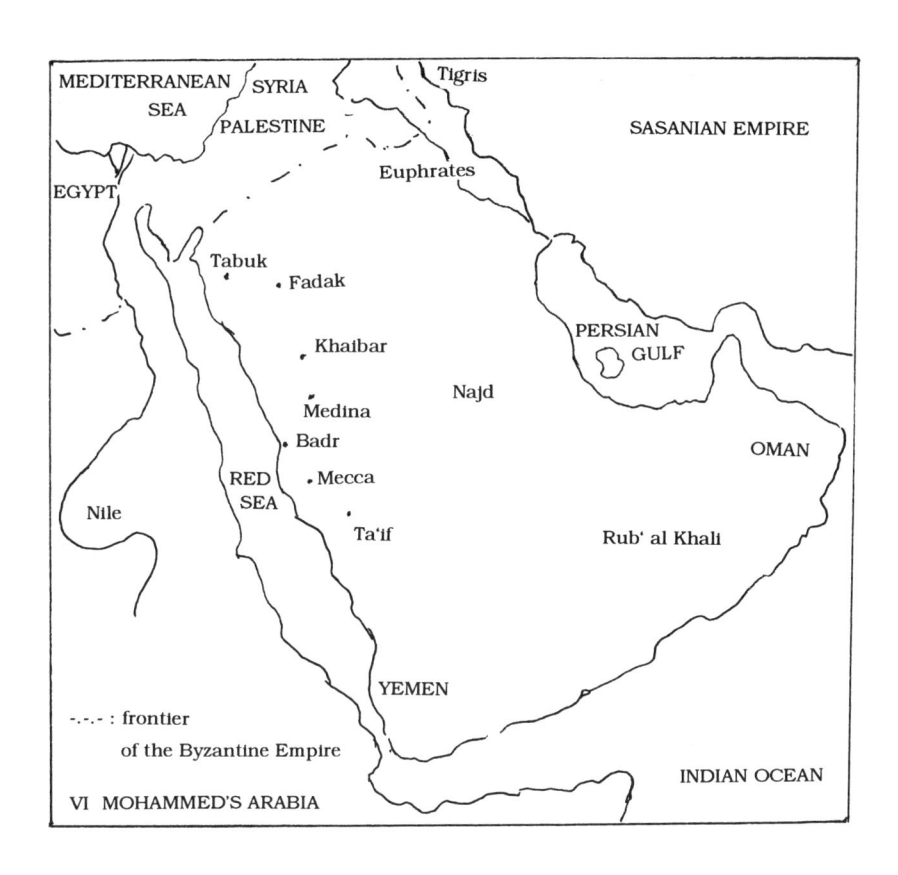

best-known because of the visit its (anonymous) queen paid to King Solomo. [10] The ruins of their cities can still be visited. [11] There was a Nabataean kingdom between the Dead Sea and the northern coast of the Arabian Gulf; its capital was Petra, today a favourite destination for tourists. The Nabataeans enjoyed an independent existence until the Emperor Trajan incorporated their state into the Roman Empire as the *Provincia Arabia* in A.D. 106. Another Arabian state, of a much later date, was the Kingdom of Palmyra, in north-west Syria; its most famous ruler was the legendary Queen Zenobia. The Emperor Aurelian put an end of her state in A.D. 273. For a long time the unfortunate queen lived on in Arabian legend as 'Queen Zabba'. [12]

In the ancient times we are speaking of there was no big, all-comprising Arabian state. The townships and the tribes looked after themselves and regulated their own affairs in an independent way. Individuals did the same, for Arabs are described as convinced individuals; they consider themselves free men at nobody's beck and call. In the tribes, which were mostly only small, all members enjoyed equal rights. Naturally there were leaders; their functions could even be hereditary. Yet they were not rulers in the true sense of the word. Their prestige was the result of personal abilities; I am speaking here of prestige, not power. They were listened to with respect during the deliberations, but did not possess the legal power to push through their will. The necessary decisions were taken and the conflicts were solved by the assemblies after, often endless, talking. There was no criminal law; cases of murder could lead to blood feud that could go on for generations. Although the Arabs were proud of their freedom, they kept slaves. It seems, however, that their existence was not particularly onerous; often they were set free. [13]

4. Social relations

The Arab population was not homogeneous socially. There was a dividing line between the town-dwellers and the nomads. Among the sedentary Arabs there were those who lived in cities, merchants, for instance, and those who inhabited the oases where they occupied themselves with agriculture. The nomads were differentiated into those who herded goats and sheep and those who possessed herds of camels and were wealthy. [14]

The position of Arab women was much better than that of their Greek and Roman sisters - at least as long as they were pagans, for under Islam this changed. The common rule was that people found their marriage partners within their own tribe, in endogamy, but exogamic unions were also possible. In such cases the woman usually followed her husband to his tribe, but it also occurred that each continued to live within his or her own tribe, in what one may call a 'living apart together' relationship; in that case the children remained with the mother. It is sometimes thought that this is a relic of an ancient matriarchate [15] in which descent was matrilinear. However this may be, women enjoyed a fair measure of independence. [16]

As is well-known, matriarchate does not mean at all that women were boss. Nowhere in the world has this been the case. In Arabia husband and wives, brothers and sisters lived separate lives; in this respect it must be taken into account that marriages were often polygamous. From an early age, men were trained to be warriors, not to say bandits and robbers. They went out to fight other tribes, to steal their cattle, and to violate their women. Certain masculine qualities of the pagan Arabs may already lead our thoughts to the time of the great conquests, for "the seeking out of danger and the striving for glorious deeds which are so characteristic of the Arab ... are bound up with his longing for distant regions and with the raids and other enterprises which take up a great part of his life." [17] There was also the frequent necessity of continuing a vendetta. When they were *chez soi*, they did not do a stroke of work, but they sat talking with their comrades for hours on end, drinking coffee or wine; the story-teller was greatly honoured.

The work was done by the women, all the work, although the men probably would not have called it so. They looked after the children, did all the household chores, tended the cattle, and tilled the small plots where the foodstuffs grew; they weaved, milled, and baked. There were, in consequence, two separate, albeit not necessarily antagonistic, spheres : a brotherhood of men and a sisterhood of women. [18]

5. Pagan Arab religion

With typical western superciliousness Carl Brockelmann states that "the religion of the Arabs, as well as their political life, were on a thoroughly primitive level." They were people of 'low culture'. [19] Their passion for beautiful story-telling and poetry, however, is not the effect of a low culture. [20] Primitive or not, these ancient Arabs were thoroughly religious; everything in their lives had something to do with extra-human powers. Magic played a very important role. This was necessary, because the whole world was seen as peopled with *dzjinns*, invisible spirits who were omnipresent. By means of magic they could be made harmless or forced to serve human beings.

A second important element were the sacred stones; each tribe probably had its own sacred stone. It could be carried into battle on the back of a camel. There still is such a stone in existence, the Black Stone, which is encased in a corner of the Ka'aba in Mecca; it is said that it was originally white, but that the sins of mankind made it black. [21] At a later stage *dzjinns* and stones were transformed into gods who had their shrines and their priests. [22] Pilgrimages were made to the most important sanctuaries, to Mecca, for instance, to mention only one of them. [23]

With the haughtiness he already displayed in an earlier passage, Brockelmann tells us that the pagan Arabs, 'like many other primitive peoples', believed 'in a God who was the creator of the world'; if this is primitive, I am primitive also. This God is named 'Allah', in whose name the old Semitic god-word *el* is found. It is not a personal name but a generic one, for it comes from *'al-'ilah* = the god. [24] It should be noted that the belief in Allah is pre-Islamitic. [25] His veneration and his cult grew steadily in importance, even before Mohammed's days. The ancient religion was polytheistic; there were many gods. The Arabic *pantheon*'s appearance varied from period to period and from region to region. A number of divinities, however, enjoyed, by manner of speaking, a national rank. In ancient times there were astral godheads, a god or a goddess of the sun, a god of the moon, and one of the stars. [26] Later the principal ones were three in number, al-

Manat, the goddess of fate, Allat, sometimes called 'the Lady', the equivalent of the Great Mother, and al-'Uzza, the mightiest.

Of old, Mecca was a great cult centre. Important assemblies were held there. Sacrifices were brought on the square where the Ka'aba stood, mostly of sheep. People danced rhytmically around the shrine and touched it. One was not allowed to go there straight from the street, so to speak; ablutions were required, a special dress should be worn, fasting was obligatory, as well as abstinence from sexual intercourse. [27]

Extraneous influences had their effect on this ancient religion. In the Yemen and in the north-western oases Judaism was a force; we know of Yemenitic rulers who converted to it. Elsewhere also there were small Jewish communities; a fairly large one was established in Medina. In the north where Arabs came into contact with Syrians and Palestinians, Christianity exercized a certain influence. In the south-west monotheistic inscriptions were found, dating from the fifth and sixth centuries A.D.; they are the work of Christian and Jewish rulers. They do not contain the names of pagan gods, but speak simply of 'God'. [28]

6. 'Fatalism'

A word must be said on a concept that is commonly considered as typically Arabian or Islamic, the concept of fatalism. The term 'fatalism' is derived from the Latin substantive *fatum*, fate; it denotes, as the Oxford Dictionary states, 'the doctrine that all things are determined or arbitrarily decreed by fate'. However, pious Muslims do not think that things are determined by fate but by Allah, by God; this denotes 'the conviction that God has predetermined the course of events in general'. [29]

Yet, if we stick to the subject under discussion in this chapter, that of pre-Islamic Arabia, we see that Allah does not yet have the absolute preponderance he would later have in Islam. Our source for this period is pre-Islamic poetry, and in this genre fate is a very important thing. The Swedish scholar Ringgren, who studied the subject in depth, basing himself on the available sources, says that in that early period "the religious attitude to man's destiny must have been comparatively weak [30] ... Pre-Islamic poetry is in principle irreligious ... God is mostly ruled out by the non-religious fatalism prevalent there." [31]

Several words are used for fate by these poets, terms like 'destiny, decree, allotment, lot'; they all denote a course of events that is inexorably determined and that cannot be changed or avoided by man. If the name of Allah is used in this context, it is often another word for 'fate'. Perhaps there was no great difference between him and Time. Anyhow, his activity is quite arbitrary. "He does what he likes to do, his will being immutable, and his decision attaining its goal." [32]

A very important manifestation of fate is death. All men are destined to die; nobody can escape it. Yet another agent is Time, irreversibly flowing onwards. We say that time cures all woes, but for the ancient Arabian poets this was not so. Time confuses and destroys : people die, friendships end, crops fail, realms fall. [33] Such sentiments are constantly expressed in the poetry : 'the conviction of the futility of life, of the fruitlessness of every outcry against overwhelming misery and of the vain expectation of better conditions tomorrow'. Arabic elegy is utterly pessimistic. [34] The question is whether this fatalistic pessimism was shared by the population at large; Ringgren thinks that, at least to a certain extent, it was. [35] In foregoing volumes I have more than once argued that pessimism is one of the gateways to dualism. There is certainly dualism in the idea of overpowering fate and the submissiveness and helplessness of man.

This was the world into which the prophet Mohammed was born.

NOTES TO CHAPTER VII

1. See K.A. Kitchen, *Documentation for Ancient Arabia. Part I Chronological framework and historical sources.* The World of Ancient Arabia Series. Liverpool University Press, 1994. I was unable to lay my hands on a recent book by Bruno Chiesa, *L'Arabie avant l'Islam.* Aix-en-Provence, 1994.

2. Moscati, *Ancient Semitic Civilizations* 13-15 : "The whole coastline of the Arabian peninsula is marked by its mountains, which rear themselves up, never far from the sea, to descend towards the interior upon a plateau sloping gently down towards Mesopotamia and the Persian Gulf; the outskirts of this plateau bear scarce and stunted vegetation; its interior is occupied by the vast and barren sand-wastes of the Arabian desert."

3. Brockelmann, *History of the Islamic Peoples* 1/2.

4. Moscati, *Ancient Semitic Civilizations* 15.

5. Gaudefroy-Demombynes/Platonov, *Le monde musulman et byzantin* 43-46.

6. Gaudefroy-Demombynes/Platonov, *Le monde musulman et byzantin* 44.

7. Gaudefroy-Demombynes/Platonov, *Le monde musulman et byzantin* 45.

8. Grohmann, *Arabien* 21 : "Die ältere Geschichte Arabiens und der Araber ... ist noch immer im Dunkel gehüllt ... Ins volle Licht treten die Araber dann 854 v.Chr."

9. See Robin, *Cités, royaumes et empires de l'Arabie avant l'Islam (see Bibliography)*.

10. 1Kings10.

11. Höfner, *Die vorislamischen Religionen Arabiens* 237.

12. Brockelmann, *History of the Islamic peoples* 6/7.

13. Gaudefroy-Demombynes/Platonov, *Monde musulman et byzantin,*, 52-54; Brockelmann, *History of the Islamic Peoples* 4/5.

14. Gaudefroy-Demombynes/Platonov, *Le monde musulman et byzantin* 51.

15. See Avanzini, *Remarques sur le 'matriarcat' en Arabie du Sud*.

16. See Bravmann, *Spiritual Background*, Ch. 12 Equality of birth of husband and wife (kafd'ah), and early Arab principle (see Bibliography).

17. Bravmann, *Spiritual Background* 66.

18. Gaudefroy-Demombynes/Platonov, *Le monde musulman* 59.

19. Brockelmann, *History of the Islamic Peoples* 8.

20. Moscati, *Ancient Semitic Civilizations* 13-15 : "The Arabs have been at all times *connoisseurs* of language; elegance of diction and pithiness of speech have always reckoned by them among the highest virtues."

21. Höfner, *Vorislamischen Religionen* 359 : "... dem bekannten schwarzen Stein, dem wohl ursprünglichsten und ältesten idol."

22. Höfner, *Vorislamischen Religionen* 358 : "... jene Geisterwesen, die Ginn heißen, werden hin und wieder den Rang von Göttern erlangt haben."

23. Höfner, *Vorislamischen Religionen* 360 : "Die von Mekka scheint allerdings schon in vorislamischer Zeit eine besondere Bedeutung gehabt zu haben."

24. Höfner, *Vorislamischen Religionen* 362.

25. Höfner, *Vorislamischen Religionen* 358 : "Mohammed brauchte also bei der Verkündigung seiner monotheistischen Lehre keinen neuen Gott einzuführen; er had lediglich Allah zum einzigen Gott gemacht, was durch das hohe Ansehen, das Allah schon vorher genoß, sehr erleichtert wurde."

26. The reader will find these divinities and their cults extensively treated in Höfner, *Vorislamischen Religionen*. A II Die Götterwelt.

27. Gaudefroy-Demombynes/Platonov, *Le monde musulman* 61-65.

28. Höfner, *Vorislamischen Religionen* 280; Robin, *Du paganisme au monothéisme. 3 La diffusion des religions monothéistes en Arabie du Sud avant l'Islam* (see Bibliography).

29. Ringgren, *Studies in Arabian fatalism* 3.

30. Ringgren, *Studies in Arabian fatalism* 199.

31. Ringgren, *Studies in Arabian fatalism* 14.

32. Ringgren, *Studies in Arabian fatalism* 46.

33. Ringgren, *Studies in Arabian fatalism* 30.

34. Ringgren, *Studies in Arabian fatalism* 57.

35. Ringgren, *Studies in Arabian fatalism* 57-60.

CHAPTER VIII

MOHAMMED

1. History and legend

The prophet Mohammed [1], the founder of one of the world-religions, has been and still is deeply venerated by hundreds of millions of Muslims all over the world as 'the Messenger of God'. No wonder that biographies about this imposing man abound in innumerable languages, not all of them sympathetic to his person, since he was long regarded the deadly enemy of Christianity. [2]

Any attempt to describe Mohammed's life, even as briefly as I intend to do here, presents the prospective biographer with considerable difficulties. All great historical persons appeal to the imagination of their contemporaries as well as of those who came later, which gives rise to legends. This is all the more so in the case of Mohammed because his Arabian compatriots love to sing the praise of their heroes, without strictly committing themselves to historical truth. [3] As Annemarie Schimmel remarks : "the numerous songs and stories told and retold among the people seem to establish a personal relationship with the Prophet, and this very warm feeling few outsiders realise. The Prophet appears like the venerable elder of the family who should be obeyed and imitated." [4]

There are two views of Mohammed, wrote the Danish scholar Frants Buhl long ago, "one as the ideal person, the exemplar for Islamic orthodoxy and praxis, and the other as the historical person, who first appears as a somewhat shadowy figure whose early life is little known, who then gradually emerges into the light of history." Buhl adds that these two views are not necessarily incompatible. [5]

2. Mohammed' early years

a. His descent, parents, and family

This is where our problem begins : with the Prophet's early years. The year of his birth cannot be ascertained with sufficient certainty; it is usually given as 'around A.D. 570', probably rather after that date than before it. Tradition has it that he was born in the 'Year of the Elephant', but there is no telling exactly which date this is; so it cannot be pinpointed on the time-line. However, we do know where he saw the light : in Mecca [6]. An Arabian tradition traces Mohammed's descent to Adam, in a direct line via Abraham (Ibrahim), 'the friend of the Compassionate [God]'. [7] The name 'Muhammad' was not uncommon among the Arabs. Some think that it is an epitheton attached to his birth-name which is supposed to have been 'Amin' = the faithful, but others deny this. Nonetheless, innumerable Muslim boys are given the name of the Prophet, because of the tradition that "everyone by the name of Muhammad will be called to enter Paradise." [8]

The Prophet was of modest descent; his family did not belong to the most important in Mecca. Almost nothing is known of his father. The name of this man is given as 'Abdullah' = Abd Allah = servant of Allah; the fact that the divine name occurs in it leads some scholars to think that this name is a reworking of one with a polytheistic ring. [9] We know little more of his mother Amina. Somewhat more light falls on Mohammed's four uncles, none of whom were favourably disposed towards their nephew's ideals originally. Abu Talib stuck to the forefatherly religion. Al-'Abbas (half-brother of Mohammed's father) [10] for a time even fought the Muslims, but although he later joined his nephew, he never became a fervent believer. Hamza too began by opposing the new religion, but later enthusiastically embraced it. [11] With the fourth uncle, Abu Lahab, it was the other way round; at first he protected his nephew. Yet when he was told by somebody that Mohammed had said that his ancestors were destined for hell, he became an enemy and henceforward considered his nephew as a deceiver. [12]

b. The young orphan

What we know of Mohammed's early life is that his father died when the son was still young. The child was then cared for by his mother Amina, which may have meant that he lived for some time with Amina's family. She died when he was six during a journey from Medina to Mecca. [13] The blank that surrounds the Prophet's childhood is filled in by many legends, not all of them necessarily false. The orphaned boy was entrusted to the care of his paternal grandfather, 'Abd al-Muttalib, who took him into his own house at Mecca. Mohammed seems to have been an exceptionally gifted child. It is reported that it was said of him : "By Allah, he will become something great." [14]; it need not be judged impossible that something of this kind was really said. Two years later his grandfather also died, and the young Mohammed was put in the care of his uncle Abu Talib who, although never becoming a Muslim, always remained his protector.

c. The legend of the opening of Mohammed's breast

Legend states that Abu Talib took the boy with him on caravan journeys into Syria, but some scholars think that these stories only serve as a backdrop for the prophecies of his future greatness.[15] Several times Christian Syrian monks, so it is said, predicted that he would become a great prophet. [16] The most intriguing of these legends is that of 'the opening of Mohammed's breast', a legend of which several versions exist. The probably oldest version situates this legend in the time that Mohammed was still with his mother. It goes as follows. "He and his brother were with our lambs behind the tents when his brother came running and said to us, 'Two men clothed in white have seized that ... brother of mine and thrown him down and opened his belly and are stirring it up.' We ran towards him and found him standing up with a livid face. We took hold of him and asked him what was the matter. He said, 'Two men in white raiment came and threw me down and opened my belly and searched therein for I know not what.' So we took him back to our tent." [17]

There is a later version of this legend that is put in the mouth of the Prophet himself. "Two men came to me with a basin full of snow. Then they seized me and opened up my belly, extracted my heart and split it; then they extracted a black drop from it and threw it away; then they washed my heart and my belly with that snow until they had thoroughly cleansed them." [18] What has been added to the earlier version is the purification rite. The Norwegian scholar Birkeland assumes that "the clot of blood most probably signifies impurity inherent in Muhammad as a member of a pagan society." The monotheistic Prophet had to be cleansed of his pagan polytheistic descent. [19] This same scholar thinks that the legend is connected with *Sura* 94.1 that reads thus. "The Prophet's heart and mind had indeed been expanded and purified; the burden which pressed on his soul had been removed." [20] If this is correct, then the burden that was removed is Mohammed's innate paganism. The legend demonstrates the dualistic aversion that Islam had of paganism.

3. His marriage with Khadija

It is possible that young Mohammed tended herds for some time. Somehow he built up a reputation for sobriety, honesty, and earnestness; we may believe him when he said later in his life that he had had no sexual relations before he married Khadija. This lady was an enterprising business woman whose caravans travelled to Syria. She was at the same time a divorcee and a widow, for she had divorced her first husband, while her second husband had died. She already had two sons and a daughter. She was older than Mohammed, but how much older is a matter of dispute.

"When she heard about the prophet's trustfulness, trustworthiness, and honorable character, she sent for him and proposed that he should take her goods to Syria and trade, while she would pay him more than she paid others ... The apostle of God accepted the proposal." [21] This meant that

Mohammed became Khadija's commercial agent and her caravan leader. He was then about twenty-five years old.

Mohammed's employer was more than satisfied with his commercial performance; soon she began to see him as something more than just an agent. Arabian chroniclers report that she often sent for him under the pretext of having to discuss her affairs with him, not neglecting to offer him the fruit of the season. Her employee always entered with downcast eyes, they add. [22] That he was shy is no wonder, for Khadija was "at that time ... the best-born woman in Quraysh [the clan to which they both belonged], of the greatest dignity and, too, the richest." [23] And she was also beautiful. Most chroniclers have it that she was forty when she married Mohammed, but this can hardly be true since she had five children with him. Perhaps Ibn Habib was nearer the mark, when he wrote that she was twenty-eight. [24]

That Khadija was attracted to Mohammad is equally no matter of surprise. It is true that he was poor and had had little education, but he was energetic and had proved to be a highly capable agent with an instinct for commerce. What is perhaps more telling is that he was a comely young man. The chroniclers sketch a very enticing portrait of him. He had big black eyes, and his eye-sight was as sharp as that of an eagle. His complexion was fair; his teeth resembled pearls. His voice was soft and clear; he spoke slowly. His hair was long, but well groomed; he grew an attractive beard. His legs were rather short but the upper part of his body was long so that, when he was seated, he seemed taller than all the others. He always walked very quickly. [25]

It was not Mohammed who proposed, but Khadija. Perhaps she was in need of a male protector, for Ishaq writes that "all her people were eager to get possession of her wealth, if it were possible." [26] The proposal was not made directly, but by means of an intermediary, for the family had to consent. The consent was obtained and the wedding took place; Mohammed subsequently moved into the house of his wife. All witnesses agree that it was a truly happy union. Seven children were born from it, four daughters and three sons, none of whom became older than forty. In all probability Khadija died in 619, that is, before her husband fled to Medina.

4. Mohammed as a visionary

a. On the way to monotheism

For fifteen years after his marriage Mohammed's life was outwardly uneventful. He seems to have been trading for his own account, and with success, without touching his wife's money. [27] Yet inwardly something must have stirred. We know almost nothing of his religious development; at first he would probably have shared the polytheistic beliefs of his people. Nevertheless, he was a religious man in the proper sense of the word, that is, a person for whom religion is more important than anything else. He had a meditative disposition and loved to ponder on spiritual matters.

Dissatisfied with Arab polytheism, he came to conceive of Allah, the supreme godhead, as the only god, one who would not tolerate other divinities beside him. There were others in Mecca who began to reason in the same way; there were also some Christians, slaves for instance. It is reported that he once heard a preacher proclaim monotheism at the fair of Ukaz, a sermon that he never forgot. [28] It is entirely conceivable that he came into contact with Jews and Christians of whose beliefs he may have learned of during his trips to Syria. Possibly the Judaeo-Christians in particular formed the channel along which notions of the Old and New Testaments reached Mohammed. [29]

b. The revelation

Every year Mohammed spent the month of Ramadan (that was not yet the month of general fasting) in a cave not far from Mecca. This cave is called Hira, on the summit of Mount Nur. [30] He lived ascetically then and meditated; his wife brought him the meagre food he needed. Mohammed's Arab biographers tell us that he had singular dreams and that he sometimes heard voices coming from the rocks or from trees; it happened that he was called by his name. Sometimes he heard a voice say very clearly : "Peace be upon you, o Messenger of God."

And then, in the night of the 27th day of Ramadan, the decisive revelation came to him. In one of the biographies, that of 'al-Tabari, the Prophet relates what happened in his own words. He saw a luminous being enter the cave who made himself known as the angel Gabriel. The apparition ordered Mohammed to read. He replied that he could not read. This command was given three times, each time the same response. [31]

Although this story of the apparition of an angel has become very popular, some marginal notes must be made. It seems somewhat strange that Mohammed, after fifteen years as a business man, would still have been illiterate. [32] The threefold repetition of the command to read may have something to do with the origination of the Koran; the Arabian word for 'to read', is *qara'*, in this context 'to recite', the root of which we find in the word *Qur'an* [Koran].

The second point is that the Koran itself does not make any mention of an apparition. [33] Ishaq's biography also does not refer to an angel; he only quotes the Koran where it speaks "of the month of *Ramadan* in which the *Qu'ran* was brought down as a guidance to men, and proofs of guidance and a decisive criterion." [34] 'A'isha, Mohammed's third wife, also did not know of an apparition. She relates that "unexpectedly the Truth came to him and said that he was the Messenger of God; then followed the thrice repeated command to read." [35] The text of the message as presented by the Koran is rather sober. "Read in the name of the Lord who created, who created man of blood coagulated. Read! Thy Lord is the most beneficent, who taught by the pen, who taught what they knew not to men." [36]

c. What did Mohammed really experience?

What Mohammed really experienced in the cave of Hira has, of course, always been a subject of discussion. A popular idea has ever been that he experienced nothing at all, because he was an impostor. Yet the testimony of Mohammed himself and the terms of the earliest sources are just a bit too explicit to allow for such a cheap solution. Pious souls have felt that the revelations were a trick of Satan to keep the Arabs away from Christianity.

Others, more psychologically disposed, have guessed that Mohammed was an epileptic and the vision was brought about by a fit - as if epileptic attacks were particularly conducive to religious revelations (to say nothing of the fact that none of the usual symptoms are mentioned in the sources.) [37] Or Mohammed was a hysteric, that is, a phantast and a liar.

I, for one, believe that the phenomenon was genuine, that is, that Mohammed indeed had a very uncommon experience of a religious nature. The question whether something from outside really came to him, or that it was the result of some intense inner feeling must remain unanswered. [38] I was not there, and neither were you, o sceptical reader. [39]

d. Later visions

It is almost impossible to record what happened after this first revelation in good chronological order. It is certain that more events of this kind occurred. It is an indubitable fact that Mohammed was a visionary. Such persons are known in other religions too; the annals of Judaism and Christianity also mention them. But Mohammed did not want to be associated with the would-be, self-made prophets and seers that every religion harbours, the great majority of whom are impostors, self-seekers, and mentally deranged persons. Criticisms of this kind were already made in Mohammed's own time. "Your Companion [Mohammed] is neither astray nor being misled, nor does he say [aught] of [his own] Desire ... The [Prophet's] [mind and heart] in no way falsified what he saw ... For truly did he see, of the signs of the Lord, the Greatest." [40] Mohammed knew that he was a singular person with a singular mission.

The Hira experience was by no means the only one he had during his life. More followed. Witnesses relate how he first heard a voice announcing something and then fell into a state of rapture. It is said that he became very heavy then, which perhaps meant that he became completely rigid. Some bystanders said that they heard something themselves, like the buzzing of bees. When he returned to his normal state, he dictated what he had heard. [41]

Experiences of this kind weighed heavily on him; tradition has it that he did not greatly like them. Sometimes he feared that he was going mad.

Once, it must have been in the beginning, he came home very shaken. Khadija poured water on his head and wrapped him in a blanket or mantle to calm him. She then went to her cousin Waraqa ibn Nofal, who was a Christian, well versed in the Bible, and told him what had happened to her husband. "If all you have said be true," he gave as his opinion, "the spirit has appeared to him, as he appeared long ago to Moses. Tell him to be of good heart, for he is to be the Prophet of his people." [42] And Khadija returned to reassure her husband with this message. This reads as if to show Mohammed as a prophet with the seal both of Judaism and Christianity.

5. 'The years of ridicule'

a. The first converts

Now followed what Glubb calls 'the years of ridicule'. What exactly was the message that Mohammed had to proclaim as the Messenger of God? The earliest texts do not state this explicitly, but it cannot have been anything else than the proclamation that there is only one God. This implied that Arab polytheism, with its many divinities, was a false religion. As might be expected, Mohammed did not make himself popular with this message. However, he made some converts. The very first was his own wife. She believed in him and his message and stood steadfastly by him until the end of her life, that is, exactly during the most trying period Mohammed had. He always spoke with respect and affection for her. [43]

A second convert was also one of the family, a young slave, Zaid ibn Harithad, whom his master had adopted as a son. Then a third, Ali ibn Abu Talib, a son of his uncle Abu Talib; this young man had also been adopted by his uncle. [44] We must take note of him, for he later married Mohammed's daughter Fatima. Abu Talib himself, although invited to embrace the new faith, declared that he was too old to forsake his forefatherly religion. Somewhat coarsely, he added that he did not want to lift his backside above his head, referring in this way to the manner of prostration that Muslims practise. This remark points to the resistance Mohammed would meet in his native town, a resistance in which ridicule played an important part.

An important convert was a friend of Mohammed, Abu Bekr, a well-to-do merchant, who was popular in Mecca; he was to become the first caliph. Although the Prophet himself wanted to keep his new insights strictly to himself for the time being, Abu Bekr was more talkative. There were some more converts, mostly poor people and slaves. [45] The circle was only small. What they came to believe in was that there is only one God, not more, since Islam had not yet attained its definite shape.

b. Public preaching

It was only after some years that Mohammed resolved to publicly preach his religion. The following Koran verses refer to this decision. "So call not on any god with God, or thou wilt be among those under the penalty. And admonish thy nearest kinsmen." [46] This time it is made clear what the message was: there is only one God. With the 'nearest kinsmen', the members of the Quraysh, Mohammed's clan, are meant.

The Arabian chronicler Baladhuri relates that Mohammed obeyed this call by placing himself on the Safa hill just opposite the Ka'aba; he then began to address the Meccan townsfolk. Commercially minded people as they were, what they had heard of Mohammed's theological opinions had not greatly interested them so far. "What have you?", they asked him. "What would you think," answered the Prophet, "if I told you that an enemy was to arrive this morning or tonight? Would you not take heed? - Certainly! - Well then! I warn you that you are in for a terrible chastisement!" But his uncle Abu Lahab retorted : "Go to the devil! Is it for this that you are convoking us?" [47]

The audience vaguely but correctly sensed that this chastisement would come because of their polytheistic beliefs. They did not like this, for the prosperity of Mecca resulted for a large part from the pilgrimages to the Ka'aba. They did and, indeed, could not realize that Mecca's greatest ascendancy would come from the injunction to Muslims to visit the Ka'aba at least once in their lives, if possible. They could not believe that one of them had a special message. "What kept men back from belief when Guidance came to them, was nothing but this : 'Has God sent a man [like us] to be [His] Apostle?'" [48] Although Mohammad complained that "the greater part of men refused to receive it [his message], except with ingratitude," [49], he became still more convinced of himself and his mission, even in the face of hardening opposition. "If the whole of mankind and of jinns were to gather to produce the like of this Koran, they could not produce the like thereof." [50]

c. The public enemy

"When he did that [namely, speak disparagingly of their gods], they took great offence and resolved unanimously to treat him as an enemy." [51] His own uncle Abu Lahab took the lead of those who began to harass him. He and others threw stones at the Prophet's house and heaped filth on his doorstep; when the uncle was caught *in flagrante delictu*, he hired agents to perform the same noble task. [52] Lahab's wife also insulted the Prophet. No wonder then that he called down a curse upon them. "Perish the house of the Father of Flame! [53] Perish he! No profit to him for all his wealth and all his gains! Burnt he will be soon in a Fire of blazing Flame! His wife shall carry the [crackling] wood as fuel, a twisted rope of palmleaf fibre around her [own] neck!" [54] This leaves no room for misunderstanding.

In spite of such opposition, Mohammed ever more clearly expounded the kernel of his message. "Turn away from those who join false gods with God. For sufficient are we [God] onto those who scoff, those who adopt, with God, another God. But soon will they come to know." [55] Slowly more converts began to come in, to be counted in tens rather than in hundreds. The most notable of them was Mohammed's uncle Hamza. Many of them were maltreated by their own relatives; some were put in chains, others beaten. Of Abu Bekr it is told that they dragged him along by his beard. [56] Many who had embraced the new religion were so abominably treated that a number of them decided to seek a refuge in Abyssinia. Baladhuri presents a list of their names. They were one hundred and nine persons, seventy-five Meccan men, nine Meccan women, and twenty-five non-Arab clients. [57]

On the whole, the Prophet's preaching to the Meccans had very little success. It was evidently not God's will that they would believe him. "If it had been your Lord's will, they would all have believed, all who are on earth! Will you then compel mankind against their will to believe?" [58] In 619 Khadija and Abu Talib, Mohammed's uncle and guardian, died shortly after one another, leaving him behind rather lonely. Very soon after Khadija's death the Prophet, now forty-nine years old, married Sauda bint Zamara, a fat, middle-aged widow. Glubb supposes that she was 'little more than a housekeeper'; she was still with Mohammed at the time of his death. [59]

6. No more success in Ta'if

Judging his situation in his home-town hopeless, Mohammed decided to try his luck in Ta'if, a town about eighty kilometers to the south-east; its climate was much milder than that of Mecca with its scorching heat. Yet the soil of this town with its rich orchards proved just as barren as the sands of Mecca. Having arrived at Ta'if on foot, alone or with his adoptive son Zaid, he did not take the risk of addressing the townsfolk directly. He first sought contact with three local chiefs who were relatives of his. Far from giving him permission to preach, they told him to disappear as quickly as possible. One of them asked: "If God needed a messenger, could he not have found someone better than you?" He asked them not to divulge why he had come, but they made it known so that street-boys ran after him throwing stones.

Mentally and physically wounded, he returned to Mecca, only to hear that his uncle Abu Lahab had had him outlawed, with the consequence that he could not reenter the city. With great difficulty he found a chief who was prepared to take him under his protection so that he could finally go home. [60]

7. Converts from Yathrib

a. Interested pilgrims from Yathrib

Having given up all hope of winning more converts among his fellow-townsmen, Mohammed restricted his efforts to non-Meccans who came to the fairs or who made the pilgrimage. Around three hundred and twenty-five kilometers north of Mecca lies Yathrib. A world separated the two towns. In Mecca water was a scarce commodity; hardly a blade of grass grew there. Yathrib was situated in a rich oasis with water in abundance; the inhabitants were mainly farmers who grew wheat and vegetables. Shade could be found under the countless date-palms. Many Jews, most of them artisans, lived there. The people of Yathrib were in close contact with those of Mecca since they used to travel to Mecca in order to sell their produce. In 620 seven or eight men who had come from Yathrib sat listening attentively to Mohammed. Although they seemed impressed, they returned homeward without having made a pledge.

b. The 'first 'Aqaba'

A year later seven of them returned, bringing five others with them. Obviously not daring to display missionary activities in Mecca itself, Mohammed met them in a valley outside the town. This time they allowed themselves to be convinced and so the first non-Meccans became Muslims. It should be noted that Mohammed told these converts that "God had prepared the way for Islam in that they lived side by side with the Jews, who were people of the scriptures and knowledge, while they themselves were polytheists and idolators." [61]

At this occasion they gave the Prophet the so-called 'first 'Aqaba' [62], or, also, 'the pledge of women', since no promise to fight for Islam was involved. This pledge obliged them 'to associate nothing with God [to venerate no idols], to commit no fornication, not to kill their offspring [unwanted female babies], not slander other people, not disobey the Prophet." If they fulfilled this pledge, paradise would be theirs. Mohammed sent a trusted Muslim with them back to Yathrib to instruct them further. [63] One may view this event as the institutional beginning of Islam. Glubb states, "these pledges are of interest, as they were presumably typical of what Muhammad asked of all converts at the time." [64]

c. The 'second 'Aqaba'

A year later a considerable number of pilgrims from Yathrib came to Mecca; the twelve of 'Aqaba were among them. They clearly had made converts, for in the night seventy-three men and two women gathered in the 'Aqaba valley. Then Mohammed appeared, accompanied by his uncle Abbas, who was still a pagan at the time. Abbas told those present that the Prophet wanted to go back with them to Yathrib. "If you think you can be faithful to what you have promised him and protect him from his opponents, then assume the burden you have undertaken." Then Mohammed himself spoke, saying: "I invite your allegiance on the basis that you protect me as you would your women and children." The leader of the group now took Mohammed's hand and said solemnly : "By Him who sent you with the truth we will protect as we will protect our women. We give our allegiance and we are men of war possessing arms which have passed from father to son."

The Prophet then made them appoint twelve leaders. Asked what they would have in return for their loyalty, he promised them Paradise. Finally they all filed along him pressing his hand. [65] This ceremony is called 'the second pledge of 'Aqaba'. [66] The new Muslims joined the caravan, which headed back to Yathrib the next day.

8. A change of heart

Thus far we have come to know the Prophet as a somewhat shy and peaceful man, but the insults and humiliations to which he had been subjected in the course of many years must have hardened his character. Now he had also a community that he had to protect. Ishaq relates this change of heart in the following words. "The apostle had not been given permission to fight or allowed to shed blood before the second 'Aqaba. He had simply been ordered to call men to God and to endure insults and to forgive the ignorant ... When Quraysh became insolent towards God and rejected his gracious purpose, accused his prophet of lying, and ill treated and exiled those who served him and proclaimed his unity [i.e. that there is only one God], believed in his prophet, and held fast to his religion, he [Allah] gave permission to his apostle to fight and to protect himself against those who wronged them and treated them badly." [67]

The Koran states expressly: "To those against whom war is made, permission is given [to fight], because they are wronged. And verily, God is Most Powerful for their aid. [They are] those who have been expelled from their homes in defiance of right, [for no cause] except that they say. 'our Lord is God'". [68] I relate this in full, because it opens a new chapter in world-history, that of war conducted in the name of Islam. For the time being, this had a defensive ring, but this would not remain so.

9. The *Hidjra*

a. The Muslims leave Mecca

Seeing that his followers had no future in Mecca, Mohammed "commanded his companions ... to emigrate to Yathrib and to link up with their brethern [there] ... So they went out in companies." [69] During the month of May 622 the Meccan Muslims left their town in small groups. Some of them were detained for a time by their relatives, but in the end no Muslim remained in Mecca except Mohammed and Abu Bekr with their families and those who were dependent on him. [70] "The Apostle stayed in Mecca waiting the Lord's permission to leave Mecca and to migrate to Yathrib." [71]

b. An attack on Mohammed planned

The ancient sources narrate that the pagan Meccans, feeling uncomfortable with the presence of the Prophet, and fearing an attack from the side of those of Yathrib, convoked an assembly of the elders of the town. All those who were present agreed that they should get rid of him. Should they put him under lock and key? This might elicit an attempt by his followers to liberate him. Then simply banish him - if only he were out of sight. Yet he might win adherents elsewhere and come back to destroy them. Finally they agreed upon the most simple solution: killing him. Mohammed, however, got wind of their plans and hid himself in Abu Bekr's house. World-history would have taken quite another course if his enemies had really assassinated him!

c. The migration to Yathrib

When the Prophet entered his friend's house, he said : "God has given me permission to depart and migrate." "Together?", asked Abu Bekr. "Together!", was the answer. Two camels were kept ready. The two men escaped in the night through a window at the back of the house. They did not go north on the road to Yathrib but south to Mount Thaur, so as to mislead their pursuers. They found a refuge in a cave where Abu Bekr's daughter brought them food. Back home, there was of course consternation and bewilderment, but no party was sent out to find them. They were probably glad that their enemy had disappeared. [72]

After three days in hiding the two men in the cave felt safe enough to depart. They rode on two camels and took with them a freedman of Abu Bekr on pillion behind him, and a guide, Abdullah ibn Arqat, a pagan Bedouin. They went on their way the 18th or 19th of June 622. They did not follow the main road northward, but chose circuitous roads so as not to be discovered. [73] "How little", ponders Glubb, "did Caesar [the Byzantine Emperor Heraclius I] or Chosroes [the Persian Emperor Chosroes II], surrounded by their great armies and engaged in a long and bitter war for world supremacy (as they thought), realise that four ragged Arabs riding silently through the bare mountains of the Hejaz were about to inaugurate a movement which would put an end to both their great imperial dominions." [74] Yes, indeed, there was world-history in the making!

The Muslims of Yathrib, having heard that the Prophet had left Mecca, went every morning to a point overlooking the road along which he would come. As soon as the midday sun became too hot, they returned home. After ten days of journeying the little party reached Qoba, the most southernly village of the oasis. Nobody was there to welcome them, because it was already the afternoon. A Jew who was outside saw them coming and called out to the Muslims. They came running and found four men sitting in the shadow of a palm-tree.[75] Mohammed was invited to be the guest of Qulthoom ibn Hidm where he rested for three days. His adopted son Ali joined him there; with him the last Muslim had left Mecca.

Three days later the Prophet mounted his camel again and went to the centre of the oasis.[76] Legend has it that the camel knelt down there and refused to go further. Mohammed accepted the offer of Khalid ibn Zaid, one of those who had taken the second 'Aqaba pledge, to be his guest.[77] For the rest of his life Yathrib was to be the home of the Prophet, and for this reason it came to be known as 'Medinat al-Nabi', or in short 'Medina', 'House of the Prophet'. We shall use this name in the sequel.

10. A new era

Let us, like the camel, stop for a moment. I have related these events in full colour, for they are of a world-historical nature, in more than just one respect. The journey of Mohammed from Mecca to Medina has been given the name of *Hidjra* (*Hegira, Hedzjra*), usually translated as 'flight'. The term does, however, not mean 'flight', but rather 'separation, breaking off'. It refers to the breach with his relatives in Mecca, in particular with his uncle Abu Lahab. To the Muslims the *Hidjra* signifies the beginning of a new era, different from those of the Jews and the Christians.[78] In our reckoning the year is 622, and its first date July 16th. This is not the date on which Mohammed arrived at Medina but the first day of the lunar year in which the *Hidjra* took place. The Muslims do not use the solar year but, instead, the lunar year so that their chronology does not tally with ours. In Latin, a Muslim year is referred to as

'AH' = *Anno Hegirae*. [79] With the *Hidjra* a totally new era had been ushered in.

This new era is, of course, that of a new religion that would become a world-religion, with Judaism and Christianity one of the three monotheistic creeds. However, the event also marks a profound change in Mohammed's character. From now on he would be a statesman and a general, one who would not only preach but fight. This change from a man who had been unable to get a footing in his home-town to the warrior who would go on from conquest to conquest is hard to explain. [80] Past experiences may have led him to this. And it is also true that those of Medina welcomed him, not so much out of enthusiasm for his religious ideas, but rather because they needed an inspired leader in their constant quarrels with other clans and tribes. The concept of 'Holy War' was thus born. We shall have to return to this.

11. Mohammed makes himself at home in Medina

The day on which the Prophet arrived in Medina was a Friday; that same evening he joined in the prayers. Friday prayers were to become a regular feature of the Muslim religion. [81] There was as yet only a shed available for the cult, but Mohammed ordered a prayer-house to be built. He took a hand in the construction himself, although he was not an artisan. It took a year for the building to be completed. [82] It was the very first mosque in the world. But not the last! Who drives from Amsterdam northward will, after having passed the Coen-tunnel, see a large mosque in the flat meadows; its slender minarets are clearly delineated against the sky above the city of Zaandam.

Next to the mosque living quarters were built for the Prophet and his family. There he housed his wife and daughters who had also safely escaped from Mecca. Shortly after his arrival at Medina he took yet another wife, 'A'isha, a daughter of Abu Bekr. [83] From a purely human view it was a curious union, the girl being only nine or ten years old. When she came to live in Mohammed's house, she brought her toys with her and sat playing with them on the floor; her husband, who was fifty-three then, sometimes joined her in her games. The marriage was not immediately consumed; Mohammed did so when the girl was thirteen years old (and he fifty-seven). 'A'isha always remained the Prophet's favourite wife, beautiful as she was. However, the question is whether she was simply chosen for her beauty. After all, she was a daughter of Abu Bekr, the most powerful and influential man in the Muslim community after Mohammed. This connection made the bound between the two men still closer. [84]

12. The foundation of a Muslim state

a. The Medinan Muslim community

In Medina, Mohammed was faced with several problems. There were seventy refugees from Mecca there, together with their families; they were called the 'Emigrants'. The Medinan Muslim community was much larger; they were called the 'Helpers'. As will be understood, there was often friction between the two groups, since the Emigrants had to be housed and fed. A specific problem was that every Arab needed the protection of his tribe, but as refugees the Emigrants were now tribeless. This problem was solved by Mohammed's making the Medinans 'adopt' the Meccans. In this way the Prophet became the acknowledged chief of the whole Muslim community. It was the only Muslim community in the world as yet. [85]

The Muslim community was only a minority in the Medina oasis, which was mainly populated by polytheists and the considerable Jewish community. Conceiving of life in the palm groves as peaceful would be entirely wrong. There were two rival clans there, the Aus and the Khazraj, who had been warring endlessly; just before the arrival of Mohammed there had been a bloody battle between them. The oasis was dotted with towers and strongholds where the women and children sought protection during the combats. One Khazraj chief, however, 'Abd Allah bin Ubayy, was attempting to put an end to this internecine warfare. At last he succeeded in this, which made him the accepted chief of the oasis, a sort of uncrowned king.

But in Mohammed, the newcomer, whose community was steadily growing, he had a competitor. The relationship between the two men always remained problematic. 'Abd Allah became a Muslim, but was said to be only halfheartedly so and to have often intrigued against the Prophet whom he had rather see depart from Medina. He died in 631. [86]

b. The Medinan Jews

Mohammed's relation with the Jews of Medina was equally fraught with difficulties. [87] The Jewish community was numerous, numbering some eight or ten thousand persons, probably forming the majority of the inhabitants of the oasis; they had a synagogue and a Torah school. They spoke the Arab language as their mother tongue.[88] On the whole they were wealthier and better educated than the pagans. Mohammed sincerely wished to come to an agreement with them. In his view the new religion was authentic Judaism; both the Muslims and the Jews were monotheists (the number of Christians in the oasis must have been exceedingly small.) What will have irritated the Jews was Mohammed's idea that the Jewish faith of his time, as the Jews practised it, was not the original pure one of Abraham's days. Nevertheless, it came to a 'Covenant between the Muslims and the Medinans and with the Jews'. [89] It inaugurated the Prophet's work as a statesman.

c. A totally new community

"A believer shall not slay a believer for the sake of an unbeliever, nor shall he aid an unbeliever against a believer ... Believers are friends onto the other to the exclusion of outsiders ... The peace of the believers is undivisible ... The believers must avenge the blood of one another in the way of God ... Whenever you differ about a matter it must be referred to God and to Muhammad." These articles were constitutive of the creation of a totally new community. Arabs had always been first and foremost members of their clans and tribes; their loyalty was to the tribe. Tribe members had always to help one another and to assist their tribe-fellows against other clans and tribes. However, the articles mentioned cut right across the sacrosanct boundaries of the tribe. Now believers, no matter of which clan or tribe, had to help one another, even against members of their own clan or tribe. Their essential loyalty had to be directed to the Islamic community. There is also dualism in this, expressed in the terms 'to the exclusion of others' and 'avenge the blood of one another'.

"To the Jew who follows us belong help and equality. He shall not be wronged nor shall his enemies be aided ... [They] are one community with the believers ... Each must help the other against anyone who attacks the people of this document [i.e. the Muslims and the Jews]." This did not imply that Jews had to convert to Islam; they were not required to do so, for "the Jews have their religion and the Muslims have theirs." At that moment Mohammed must have thought that a fruitful cohabitation of Jews and Muslims would be possible, but he proved to be too optimistic in this.

d. The breach with the Jews

The new creed was making headway among the polytheists of Medina; the Muslim community grew to perhaps fifteen hundred persons. Even, as I wrote already, 'Abd Allah bin Ubayy became a convert. Yet he and others of the same ilk were seen as Muslims of the second degree; they are contemptuously referred to as *munafiqin*, meaning something like 'hypocrites' or 'false Muslims'. [90]

"About this time the Jewish rabbis showed hostility to the apostle in envy, hatred, and malice ... [They] used to annoy the apostle with questions and introduce confusion, so as to confound the truth with falsity ... [They were] the rancorous opponents of the apostle and his companions, the men who asked questions and stirred up trouble against Islam to try to extinguish it." [91] The Prophet soon realized that an alliance with the Jews was impossible, let alone that they would convert to Islam. Two measures, both constitutive for Islam, exemplify this. Thus far Muslims used to pray turned to Jerusalem, but they were now told to pray in the direction of Mecca. The other measure was to adopt the Friday, and not the Saturday, the Sabbath, as the holy day of Islam.

e. The Medinan city-state

Not many months after the arrival of Mohammed at Medina he had become the most authoritative person in the oasis. The population living there, consisting of Muslims, Jews, and pagans, lacked, as of old, any form of cohesion. The Prophet wanted to make the whole population into a real community, with a leadership and laws, in short, into a city-state. He discussed this plan with the Muslims and the others and was obviously influential enough to make them all accept it. The result of their deliberations was the constitution of the city-state of Medina. Hamidullah states that this was the first written constitution in world-history. [92]

Its division into articles, forty-seven according to its first translator, Wellhausen, fifty-two according to Hamidullah, is not original. [93] The first half concerns the Muslims and the second the Jews. The second article states that the believers and the others form one and the same *ummah* (community), 'separated from the rest of mankind'. A sharp dividing line is drawn between the Muslims and their clientele on the one hand and the rest of the world on the other. The same is stated in article no. 15 where it is said that the believers are *maulas* (brothers) of each other, 'separated from all other people'.

A very important article is no. 13, for it entrusts the exercize of justice to the community, no longer leaving it to individuals. In consequence, art. 14 forbids the vendetta, at least among Muslims. The consequence of art. 18 is that it introduces compulsory military service. Hamidullah concludes that in this constitution the spiritual and temporal elements are mixed. The Prophet taught people how 'to balance these two sides of human life and to create a synthesis in which both the spiritual and the temporal are united'. [94] What came into being was a theocracy. [95]

13. A plethora of world-historical events

The year A.D. 622 - *anno Hegirae 1*, or *H 1* - had witnessed four or five world-historical events. The first is the introduction of a new era, the second the establishment of the first Muslim community, the third the erection of the first mosque, the fourth Mohammed's becoming a political leader and warlord, and the fifth the foundation of the first Muslim state. There have been years that were less rich in historical events!

14. Mohammed's last years

a. His later career

After this eventful year - a true *annus mirabilis* - the Prophet still had another ten years to live, for he died in June 632. During these ten years he was mainly ocupied with military expeditions and diplomatic obligations; the most important event, for Mohammed personally as well for the future of Islam, was the occupation of Mecca in January 630. The Prophet continued to live at Medina, perhaps because he felt safer there. To the Medinans, who feared that he might return to his native soil, he said : "May Allah preserve me from this! I shall live where you live and die where you die." [96] He made two pilgrimages to Mecca, however, in 631 and 632. This subject will be more extensively treated in Ch. 5.

b. His wives

Mohammed began his married life as a strictly monogamous person. After the death of Khadija he married Sauda, but ended his monogamous life by also marrying the young 'A'isha. His marital relations with Sauda cannot have amounted to much, but he was really enamoured of 'A'isha. She was eighteen when he died and never married again. Wilful and domineering as she was, she continued to play a role. [97]

In Medina the Prophet formed a harem; it is said that he had nine wives at the same time, some of whom were widows. [98] Sensuality will have had its part in this, but Mohammed also used these connections to strengthen his relations with persons and groups in his entourage. [99]

c. His children

Although Mohammed had many wives, he did not have many children. His marriage with Khadija was the most fruitful, since seven children resulted from it. Two sons died at a very early age; the third did not survive him. A solid tradition speaks of four daughters. They all played a certain role in Muslim society. The youngest and best-known was Fatima, a timid woman who was not interested in playing a political role. However, she did so by proxy because she was married to Ali, the adopted son of the Prophet, who for a short time was *caliph*. The marriage does not seem to have been very happy. She died shortly after the death of her father whom she had loved very much. The couple had four or five children. The later dynasty of the Fatimids claimed to have descended from them, but this is by no means certain.

d. His death and burial

After his return from Mecca in March 632 the sixty-three-year-old Prophet did not yet expect to die. In May he made preparations for a military expedition to Syria. But on a day in June he began to suffer of violent headaches; he had to take to his bed, because he also became feverish. His many wives busied themselves around his sickbed but to no avail. He died on the tenth day of his illness. Abu Bekr announced his death to the faithful of Medina. "O men, if anyone worships Muhammad, let him now know that Muhammad is dead. But if anyone worships God, let him know that God is alive and immortal forever." [100] The Prophet was buried in his own house. [101]

It is now time to study the religion he founded.

NOTES TO CHAPTER VIII

1. Spellings of his name vary considerably : Mohammed, Muhammed, Mohammad, Muhammad, Mahomet, to say nothing of (deliberate) misspellings like the medieval-Dutch Mahoen. The only correct spelling of his name, or rather the only correct rendering of his name in Arabic script is : Muhammad, in which the h is pronounced with a sound somewhere between a hard ch as in the Dutch and German

'lachen' and that in the English 'kitchen'. Throughout this volume I shall stick to the spelling 'Mohammed' which is fairly common and the most familiar to me. The name 'Mohammed' signifies 'the praised one'.

2. A mass of initial information is given by F. Buhl, *Muhammad, the prophet of Islam* (revised by A.T. Welch), *Enc. of Islam* VII, 361-376.

3. A critical study of the available sources is to be found in Blachère, *Le problème de Mahomet*. Ch. I *Les sources et les données complémentaires. Le problème chronologique.* See also Cook, *Muhammad*. Ch. 7 *The sources.* This author says, p. 61, that there are two types of source-material : the Koran and tradition. "The Koran is a scripture with a fixed content and - within certain limits - an invariant text. Tradition is more amorphous."

4. Annemarie Schimmel, *The Prophet in popular Muslim piety. Enc. of Islam* VII, 377. Also, more extensively, this same scholar's *Die Verehrung des Propheten in der islamischen Frömmigkeit.* (See Bibliography).

5. F. Buhl, *Muhammad, the Prophet of Islam. Enc. of Islam* VII, 360.

6. An account of what the Koran has to tell about Mohammed's Mecca and his Meccan years is to be found in Watt, *Muhammad's Mecca.* (See Bibliography).

7. Ishaq, *Life of Muhammad* 3. Ibn Ishaq wrote his work in the eighth century, one and a half century later. Critical remarks on Ishaq's book are made by Guillaume, *New Light of the Life of Muhammad* (see Bibliography). A genealogical tree of the clan of Quraysh (Mohammed's clan) is presented by Glubb, *The Life and Times of Muhammad* 63.

8. Annemarie Schimmel, *The Prophet in popular Muslim piety. Enc. of Islam* VII, 377.

9. F. Buhl, *The historical Muhammad. Enc. of Islam* VII, 362.

10. Of whom the Abassid *khalifs* derive their name.

11. G.M. Meredith-Owens s.v. 'Hamza b. 'Abd al-Muttalib'. Enc. of Islam *III, 152.*

12. W. Montgomery Watt s.v. Abu Lahab'. *Enc. of Islam* I, 136/137. On Abu Talib also Watt, *op.cit.* 152/153, and on Abu Lahab *op.cit.* 136/137. Further Lings, *Muhammad* 50.

13. W. Montgomery Watt s.v. 'Amina', *Enc. of Islam* I. The Koran 93.6 tells us that the Prophet grew up as an orphan.

14. Ishaq, *Life of Muhammad.* Ed. Guillaume 21.

15. F. Buhl, *The historical Muhammad. Enc. of Islam* VII, 362.

16. Ishaq, *Life of Muhammad.* Ed. Guillaume 22-25.

17. Ishaq, *Life of Muhammad* 105, ed. Guillaume 71/72.
18. Ishaq, *Life of Muhammad* 106, ed. Guillaume 72.
19. Birkeland, *The Legend of the Opening of Muhammad's Breast* 10.
20. Birkeland, *The Legend of the Opening of Muhammad's Breast* 44.
21. Ishaq, *Life of Muhammad* 119, ed. Guillaume 82.
22. Hamidullah, *Le prophète de l'Islam* I, 55.
23. Ishaq, *Life of Muhammad* 120, ed. Guillaume 82.
24. Hamidullah, *Le prophète de l'Islam, I* 54.
25. Hamidullah, *Le prophète de l'Islam*, I 54/55.
26. Ishaq, *Life of Muhammad* 120, ed. Guillaume 82.
27. Peters, *Muhammad and the Origins of Islam* 141 : "He was, like most Meccans, engaged in the local regional commerce in skins and raisins."
28. Hamidullah, *Le prophète de l'Islam* I, 63.
29. Gaudefroy-Demombynes, *Mahomed* 67.
30. Hamidullah, *Le prophète de l'Islam* describes this cave..
31. Hamidullah, *Le prophète de l'Islam* 65. The Arabic traditions with respect to this revelation are treated by Watt, *Muhammad at Mecca*, Ch. II, § 4 The call to be a prophet.
32. It is a moot point whether Mohammed was illiterate or not. Peters, *Muhammad and the Origins of Islam* 141: "The later Muslim tradition insisted that Muhammad could not read or write. The insistence appears apologetic - an illiterate Prophet could not 'steal' the writings of the Jews and Christians - nor does the word in question, *ummi*, bear quite that burden of meaning [of illiteracy] ... If Muhammad was engaged in commerce, it is likely that he possessed some literary skills, however modest; it is even more certain that he never literally 'read', nor was likely capable of reading, the Sacred Books of the Jews and Christians." Translations of the Old and New Testaments were not available in Arabic at that time; we may take it for granted that Mohammed did not know Hebrew, Greek, or Latin.
33. Peters, *Muhammad and the Origins of Islam* 142/143: "There is abundant evidence that Muhammad ... did not identify Gabriel as the agent of revelation until his Medina days ... Who was seen is less clear, and if Muhammad's being referred to as his 'servant' in verse 10 [of *Sura* 53] suggests that it is God himself, the Muslim tradition preferred to understand that it was Gabriel in all the other instances, chiefly because later in his own carrer Muhammad ... had unmistakably come to the same conclusion. But there is no other

	mention to Gabriel in the Meccan *Suras*, and it appears far more likely that God Himself first appeared to Muhammad."
34.	*Sura* 2.185; Ishaq, *Life of Muhammad* 155, ed. Guillaume 111.
35.	Glubb, *The Life and Times of Muhammad* 84. *Sura* 53.4-9 says: "It is no less than an inspiration sent down to him [Mohammed]. He was taught by one mighty in Power, endued with Wisdom, for he appeared in stately form, while he was in the highest part of the horizon. Then he approached and came closer, and was at a distance of but two bow-lengths or (even) nearer." The commentary by Abdullah Yusuf Ali in Vol. II, note 5087, says: "This is referred by the commentators to the angel Gabriel, through whom the inspiration came." However, note 5089 states that there are also commentators who refer this to God himself who conveyed the message to Mohammed in person.
36.	*Sura* 96.1-5.
37.	The idea that Mohammed's revelations were not genuine but the result of epileptic fits is very old. The ninth-century Byzantine author Theophanes already wrote : "He had an epileptic seizure." He continued with the statement that the Prophet mendaciously told his wife that he had seen the angel Gabriel. See Almond, *Heretic and hero*. Ch. 6 Muhammad as an epileptic. This idea was still cherished in the nineteenth century. (P. 25) "The idea of Muhammad as a deceived epileptic was common in much general literature."
38.	Goldziher, *Vorlesungen über den Islam. I Muhammad und der Islam* § 4: "Wovon er so in seinem tiefsten Innern angeregt wurde, fühlte er in ehrlicher, durch äußere Eindrücke unterstüzte Eingebung als göttliche Offenbarung, deren Werkzeug zu sein er aufrichtig überzeugt war."
39.	For an intriguing assessment of Mohammed as a prophet see Kellerhals, *Der Islam*. 5 Kap. § 4 *Wer war Mohammed?* This author considers Mohammed a false prophet according to biblical criteria, not because he would have proclaimed another God than the biblical one - which he did not -, but because he did not accept, and later Muslim theologians still less, the totality of the biblical self-revelation of God. In his *12. Kap., § 2a Die Frage der Offenbarung* he nuances this somewhat by stating that Mohammed's first revelations, whether with an interior or an exterior origin were doubless genuine, because, in the face of Arab polytheism, he proclaimed the one true God, but later he adulterated his message by contending that both Judaism and Christianity had distorted God's revelations.
40.	*Sura* 2-3, 11-12, 18.
41.	Hamidullah, *Le prophète de l'Islam* 66.
42.	Gaudefroy-Demombynes, *Mahomet* 70; Glubb, *Life and Times of Muhammad* 85/86.

43. Ishaq, *Life of Muhammad* 155. ed. Guillaume 111.
44. Ishaq, *Life of Muhammad* 158-159, ed. Guillaume 114.
45. Lists of these early followers are to be found in Ishaq, *Life of Muhammad* 162-165, ed. Guillaume 115-117.
46. Sura 26.213-214.
47. Gaudefroy-Demombynes, *Mahomet* 77.
48. Sura 17.94.
49. Sura 17.89.
50. Sura 17.88.
51. Ishaq, *Life of Muhammad* 167, ed. Guillaume 118.
52. Tabari, quoted by Hamidullah, *Prophète de l'Islam* 73.
53. Nick-name of Abu Lahab, because of his fiery temperament.
54. Sura 111.1-5.
55. Sura 15.95-96.
56. Ishaq, *Life of Muhammad* 184, ed. Guillaume 131.
57. Quoted by Hamidullah, *Prophète de l'Islam* 77. Many Muslim authors reject this story as a late invention (but Hamidullah, for one, does not), whereas most European historians accept it as historical. Watt, *Muhammad at Mecca* devotes several pages (109-117) to 'the Abyssinian affair'. He takes it for granted the emigration really happened; however, he does not ascribe to the persecution but rather to discord within the incipient Islamic community at Mecca. (117) "It is in accordance with Mohammed's character that he should have become quickly aware of the incipient schism and taking steps to heal it by suggesting the journey to Abyssinia." Soon enough many immigrants returned which "at least suggests that there was never a complete break between them and Muhammad. Certainly they came in the end to accept Muhammad's leadership." Did the discord amount to much then? A dissident voice is that of F. Buhl, *The historical Muhammad, Enc. of Islam* VII, 365, who says that this story "cannot be accepted as historical." But even he "does not rule out the possibility of some historical kernel behind the story. Nice examples these of the favourite custom of scholars to say 'yes, but...' or 'no, although ...'.
58. Sura 10.99.
59. Glubb, *Life and Times of Muhammad* 137. See for Sauda, Morsy, *Femmes du Prophète*. Ch. 5 Sawda, la deuxième épouse mecquoise.

60. Chronicles of Ibn Hisham and Baladhuri, quoted by Hamidullah, *Vie du Prophète* 97; Ishaq, *Life of Muhammad* 279, ed. Guillaume 192/193.

61. Ishaq, *Life of Muhammad* 286-289, ed. Guillaume 197/198.

62. 'Aqaba was the name of the valley where they met.

63. Ishaq, *Life of Muhammad* 289, ed. Guillaume 199.

64. Glubb, *Life and Times of Muhammad* 143. Goldziher, *Vorlesungen über den Islam. I Muhammed und der Islam* 4: "Die Offenbarungen die Muhammed auf mekkanischen Boden verkündete, hatten noch keine neue Religion bedeutet. Es wurden nur in kleinem Kreise religiöse Stimmungen hervorgerufen und eine von fester Umgrenzung noch weit entfernte gottergebene Weltbetrachtung genährt, aus denen Lehren und Formen noch nichts mit größerer Bestimmtheit hervortrat."

65. Ishaq, *Life of Muhammad* 293-299, ed. Guillaume 203-205.

66. The names of those present are given by Ishaq, *Life of Muhammad* 305-313, ed. Guillaume 208-212.

67. Ishaq, *Life of Muhammad* 313, ed. Guillaume 212.

68. *Sura* 22.39-40.

69. Ishaq, *Life of Muhammad* 314, ed. Guillaume 213.

70. Ishaq, *Life of Muhammad* 314-323, ed. Guillaume 213-218, relates who emigrated to Yathrib and how they were lodged there.

71. Ishaq, *Life of Muhammad* 313, ed. Guillaume 213.

72. Ishaq, *Life of Muhammad* 323-333, ed. Guillaume 221-227.

73. On p. 157 of Glubb, *Life and Times of Muhammad*, one will find a map of the probable route of Mohammed's escape to Yathrib.

74. Glubb, *Life and Times of Muhammad* 155.

75. Ishaq, *Life of Muhammad* 333-334, ed. Guillaume 227.

76. A map of Medina (Yathrib) can be found in Haykal, *Life of Muhammad*, between pp. 172 and 173.

77. Ishaq, *Life of Muhammad* 335-336, ed. Guillaume 228.

78. For the concordance of the Muslim and Christian chronologies with regard to the last ten years of Mohammed's life, see Gabrieli, *Mahomet* 105.

79. Watt s.v. 'Hidjra', *Enc. of Islam* III, 366/367.

80. The change from the shy and unsuccessful prophet of Mecca to the triumphant war-leader of Medina has always posed problems to the western mind, probably because it is used to the image of the peaceful

Jesus who rejected any idea of armed fighting for his cause. Almond, *Heretic and Hero* 28 : "Gibbon suggested that the Muhammad of the Medina period was an ambitious politician for whom fraud, perfidy, and injustice served to propagate the faith and who secretly smiled at the enthusiasm of his youth and the credulity of his proselytes." The Prophet had his defenders, but (29) "there were many who, like Gibbon, were of the opinion that, although Muhammad had begun with a sincere belief in his mission, he had lapsed into fraud and deception." However, in the view of the Muslims there is no problem at all, there being "no conflict between Muhammad the prophet and Muhammad the statesman. Indeed, his joint role is the proof of his unique status as the Messenger of God." In this context it is worthwile quoting Napoleon's opinion: "La religion du Christ est trop subtile pour des orientaux, il leur fallait des opinions plus politiques. A leurs yeux, Mahomet est supérieur à Christ, on le voit agir," quoted by Gabrieli, *Mahomet* 353, from Gaspar Gourgaud, *Saint-Hélène. Journal inédit de 1815 à 1818*. Paris (1899). The question of Mohammed's moral stature is extensively treated by Watt, *Muhammad. Prophet and Statesman* (see Bibliography). This book is an abridged combination of Watt's two books *Muhammad at Mecca* and *Muhammad at Medina*.

81. Ishaq, *Life of Muhammad* 335, ed. Guillaume 228.

82. Ishaq, *Life of Muhammad* 336-338, ed. Guillaume 228/229.

83. For 'A'isha see Abbott, *Aisha, the Beloved of Mohammed* (see Bibliography). This is, as far as I know, the only full-scale biography of 'A'isha. The author divides her life into three parts : 1. the Beloved of Mohammed; 2. Mother of the believers (she survived the prophet with half a century); 3. Saint and Sage in Islam. Also Morsy, *Les femmes du Prophète*. Ch. 3 Aïcha, la femme-enfant, contrasts this child-bride to Khadija: 'la femme-enfant symbolisée ici par Aïcha' (p. 53), and Khadija 'l'épouse maternelle'.

84. W. Montgomery Watt s.v. "A'isha bint Abi Bakr', *Enc. of Islam* I, 307/308. 'A'isha died in 678.

85. Ishaq, *Life of Muhammad* 344-346, ed. Guillaume 234/235.

86. W. Montgomery Watt s.v. "Abd Allah b. Ubayy', *Enc. of Islam* I, 53.

87. See for this subject Watt, *Muhammad at Medina*, Ch. II, § 2 Muhammad and the Jews. Mohammed's relations with the Medinan Jews are extensivley treated by A.J. Wensinck, *Mohammed en de Joden te Medina*. Leiden, 1928².

88. According to the Enc.Jud., Vol. 11, p. 1211, s.v. 'Medina', the Jewish tribes in Medina were 'either of Judean-Palestinian, mixed Judeo-Arabic, or Arab proselyte origin.'

89. Ishaq, *Life of Muhammad* 341-344, ed. Guillaume 231-233.

90. Ishaq, *Life of Muhammad* 351, ed. Guillaume 239.

91. Ishaq, *Life of Muhammad* 351-352, ed. Guillaume 239/240.
92. Hamidullah, *Prophète de l'Islam* 124.
93. The integral text is printed by Hamidullah, *Prophète de l'Islam* 133-137.
94. Hamidullah, *Prophète de l'Islam* 132.
95. Rodinson, *Mahomet* 216: "Médine formait, désormais, ... un État. Un État d'un type spécial, mais indubitablement un État. C'était un État théocratique, c'est-à-dire que le pouvoir suprême était devolu à Allah lui-même." See for this subject and for Mohammed's position in the Medinan state Watt, *Muhammad at Medina*. Ch. II The character of the Medinan state.
96. Gaudefroy-Demombynes, *Mahomet* 189.
97. Morsy, Les femmes du Prophète, Ch. 4, describes her as *la veuve politique*.
98. Short biographies of them in Morsy, *Les femmes du Prophète*. Ch. 5, §§ 6-11, and in Gaudefroy-Demombynes, *Mahomet*, 242-253 Les femmes du Prophète.
99. An attractive portrait of the Prophet's personality and character is painted by a Pakistani Muslim author, Ahmad, *The Life of Muhammad* (see Bibliography), 175-224. Mention is made of his wives, but it is not said how many there were nor why he married them. It appears that 'A'isha was somewhat jealous of Khadija; "he [the Prophet] often praised Khadija to his other wives and stressed her virtues and the sacrifices she had made in the cause of Islam. On one such occasion 'A'isha was piqued and said: 'O Messenger of Allah, why go on talking of the old lady? God has bestowed better and more attractive wives upon you.'"
In the biography of Sliman bin Ibrahim, *Het leven van Mohammed* (see Bibliography), 293, mention is even made of twenty-three wives, although the Prophet had intercourse with only [sic] twelve of them. Ibrahim states that the reason why he had so many wives was that he wanted to bind as many clans as possible to his cause.
One need not have a very deep insight into human nature to guess that life in Mohammed's harem was not always peaceful. If the Prophet's predilection was for some time focused on one or other of his wives, the others became easily incensed; especially 'A'isha readily wagged her sharp tongue. It even happened that the neglected wives rebelled and plotted against their common husband. See for this subject Haykal, *The Life of Muhammad*.
100. Ishaq, *Life of Muhammad* 1012-1013, ed. Guillaume 682/683.
101. Ishaq, *Life of Muhammad* 1019-1020, ed. Guillaume 688/689.

CHAPTER IX

ISLAM AS A RELIGION

1. Credal formulas

We find in the Koran a very brief summary of the Muslim creed. "O ye who have believed, believe in Allah and his Messenger and the Book which he has sent down to his Messenger and the Book which he has sent before; whoever disbelieves Allah and his angels and his Books and his Messenger and the Last Day, has strayed into error far." [1] A yet shorter credal formula is the *Shahada*, the words of which are well-known to Muslims and non-Muslims alike : "There is no God but Allah, and Muhammad is his Messenger," in Arabic *"La ilaha illa llah wa-Muhammadun rasulu llah."* The *Shahada* as such is not to be found in the Koran, but both halves of it are. [2] In the Islamic creed everything begins with 'Allah'; as I wrote in Chapter I, a great god called Allah was known in pre-Islamic Arabia. His name is probably a contraction of *'al-Ilah'*, which is not a personal name but a generic one, signifying 'the god'.

2. Islamic monotheism

Islam agrees with both Judaism and Christianity that there is only one God; it is one of the three monotheistic religions. This meant that Mohammed rejected the traditional Arabian divinities without compromise. "Have you considered al-Lat and al-'Uzzah, and the third, Manat, the other [goddess]? ... They are nothing but names which you [the Arabians] and your fathers have used; Allah did not give his authorization for them. They [i.e. those who believe in them] only follow opinion and their own liking." [3]

There is no worse sin for Islam than polytheism, the main characteristic of all paganism; this sin is the only unforgivable one. "Allah will not forgive the association of anything [any other god] with himself, though he forgives anything short of that [any other sin] to whom he wills; he who associated anything with Allah [has another god next to him] has devised a mighty deed of guilt." [4]

3. The nature of Allah

a. God not the Father

However, Allah is no Father and he has no Son. "He did not bring forth nor was he brought forth himself; he is alone from all eternity." A Muslim does not call God 'Father', 'our Father', as the most used Christian prayer says. That this element is absent from Islamic theology must have its consequences for the Muslim concept of God and the relationship with God; it means that the distance between God and man is greater in Islam than in Christianity.

b. The unitarian concept

The Islamic concept of God has no room for a Trinity; Allah is absolutely unitarian. The Christian trinitarian theology is wholly alien to Islam, so much so that Muslims often misunderstand the Trinity in this way that it would mean that there are three gods; the Christian trinitarian dogma is blasphemous in Muslim opinion. In Muslim eyes therefore Christians are idolators. In Volume XIII I made it abundantly clear that unitarian concepts of God, although not necessarily dualistic, open the road to dualism. There is always a risk that such concepts put God and world, God and mankind, so far apart that the distance between them becomes unbridgeable. Pious Muslims, however, do not experience this distance as unbridgeable.

c. The old problem of the One and the Many

God's absolute Oneness causes a problem with regard to creation, because the world is not one but multiple. The Christian idea that multiplicity is already present in the trinitarian God is wholly foreign, even abhorrent to the Muslim mind. In Christian theology the created world has a lower ontological status than God himself, but God saw that "it is good." [5] There are passages in the Koran that seem to deny this. "This present existence does seem beautiful only to those who do not believe." [6] "Know that this existence is only play and jest; only the unbeliever lets himself seduce by it, for this existence is nothing but seduction." [7] Worse, it is deceitfulness. [8] It is at this point that dualism begins to seep in. There are more elements that perhaps suggest a certain aversion to existence, for instance, the prohibition of alcoholic beverages and the severe fasting rules.

d. The attributes of God

Does this mean that God is not interested in the world? In other words, are we heading towards dualism? All the hundred and fourteen *Suras* of the Koran bear the inscription : 'In the name of Allah, the Merciful, the Compassionate', which signifies that he is concerned with the world. God is the Creator of all that is. "To him belongs whatever is in the heavens and whatever is in the earth." [9] Allah is not a Gnostic supreme divinity who leaves the creational work to a lower being, a Demiurge.

He is described by Muslim piety and invoked by the faithful with an endless variety of names. "To Allah belong the most beautiful names; so call upon him by them, and pay no attention to those who make covert hints in regard to his names [i.e. who do not take them seriously]; they will be recompensed for what they have been doing." [10] There are traditionally ninety-nine of such names. They can be divided into three categories : the names for goodness, the names for power, and the names for knowledge. [11] God is all-knowing. "He knows what is before them and what is behind them [he knows the past and the future of men]. [12] ... He knows what is hidden and what is publicly revealed." [13]

What the Koran constantly emphasizes is that God is a *tremendum*, somebody to be feared, to stand in awe of. Allah's tremendous qualities are endlessly repeated. Allah is 'the King, the Holy One, the Perfect, the Faithful, the Protector, the Sublime, the Overruling, the Majestic'. [14] What can people do other than submit themselves to him entirely? This is precisely what the word *Islam* means, namely 'submitting'. *Muslim* is the adjective of this word, one who submits him- or herself to Allah. [15] A Muslim is an *Abdallah*, an *abd Allah*, a servant or even slave of Allah. "The human being is first and foremost a slave of God." [16] The word 'slave' does not appeal to the western mind, but it should not be ignored that in the words Islam and Muslim the combination slm occurs, which suggests the word *salaam* = peace : a Muslim is a person who finds peace by submitting himself to Allah. [17] However, when all is said and done, the relations of the Muslims with God differ considerably from those of Jews and Christians.

4. Allah and love

a. Allah's concern for mankind

Is the Allah of the Koran also a loving God? He is certainly not indifferent to mankind. "We have created man, and we know what his soul whispers within him, for we are nearer to him than his jugular vein [18] ... Have you considered - if Allah makes the night continuous for you till the day of resurrection, who is a god other than Allah to bring you light? Will you not hear? ... Who is god other than Allah to bring you night in which to rest? Will you not then clearly see? But of his mercy he has appointed for you the night and the day that you may rest therein and seek his bounty; maybe, you will be thankful." [19] What these words convey is, once again, the idea of God's uniqueness and further that of his omnipotence and of his concern for mankind. Yet do they express love? I feel that they are somewhat to stern for this.

Reading the Koran, one gets the impression that Allah loves only conditionally. "Allah loves those who do well. [20] Allah loves those who continually do penance and loves those who keep themselves pure. [21] Allah loves those who act fairly." [22]. And "Allah loves those who fight for him [the Muslim soldiers in the Holy War], who fight in his way drawn up in ranks." [23]

b. The distant God

Just as God is not the Father of a divine Son, he is also not the Father of mankind; 'Father' is a word that is not used for God in the Koran. The Koran's God is not the one who lets it rain over the good and the bad, over the just and the unjust, over believers and disbelievers. The very great stress laid on God's majesty puts him at a greater distance from man than the Christian God. I know that in Islam Allah is the Merciful, the Compassionate. But rather than a father who opens his loving heart, he is a wise but stern king who pardons the transgressor from the height of his majesty.

c. Love of the neighbour

This idea that Muslims have of God must have consequences for their interpersonal relations. 'Love' is a word that only rarely occurs in the Koran. We will not find anything comparable to Jesus' great command to love 'the Lord your God with all your heart and your neighbour like yourself'. Even the love of Allah is not often mentioned. "There are people who, apart from Allah, make similar beings [idols] which they love with the same love as they have for Allah; but they who believe are still stronger in their love for Allah." [24] There is hardly more than this.

The love of one's neighbour is not mentioned at all. Naturally, there is the injunction to give alms, the *zakat*, one of the five 'pillars' of Islam; giving alms is the hallmark of the true believer, [25] just as not being generous is characteristic of the unbeliever. [26] Giving alms, however, is not the expression of an unconditional and all-comprising love; it is a sort of social welfare, since the gifts are destined for the poor and needy, for slaves and debtors. [27] This is important enough, but it is no substitute for loving your neighbour like yourself.

d. Whom Allah does not love

Allah is without mercy for disbelief and idolatry. He "is the patron of those who have believed [in Islam]; [he] brings them out of darkness [of paganism] into the light. But of those who have disbelieved, the patrons are the idols, the *at-tagut*, who bring them out of the light into the darkness; they are the inmates of Fire, therein to abide [the hell]." [28] Here we have a dualistic, almost Gnostic subdivision of mankind into two parts, both with their own 'patron', and both with their own ultimate destiny.

There is no mercy for those who persist in their disbelief. "The retribution for those who combat Allah and his Messenger and who exert themselves to bring perdition to the country [it seems that this passage refers to Jews] is that they will be executed or crucified, or that their hands and feet will be chopped off on both sides, or that they will be banished from the land. This will be a humiliation for them in this life, and in the afterlife there will be an enormous punishment for them ... They will want to escape from the Fire, but will not be able to come away from it. And for them there is lasting punishment." [29]

e. Disbelief

It is on this point, that of the relation between Allah and disbelievers and between Muslims and disbelievers, that Islam becomes truly dualistic. Disbelievers are guilty of *shirk*; this Arabic word signifies 'association', the fundamental sin, the greatest sin of all, of associating something with God, of putting idols beside him or even of putting idols in his place. God is the absolute reality; nothing can be added to him. He is certainly merciful and forgiving, but he will not pardon *shirk*. If he did so, he would admit that he is not the absolute reality. Atheism is also *shirk*, for this puts nothing else in the place of God. Those who commit such unforgivable sins are pagans, the *mushrikun* or 'associators'.

Disbelief is wide-spread in the western world; there is nothing reprehensible in the term. There are people who believe and those who do not. To believe or not is left to each person's own discretion. But *al-kufr*, disbelief, has horrible connotations for a Muslim; it is synonymous with blasphemy and infidelity. The person who practises *kufr*, is a *kafir*, plural *kafirun*, an atheist, and the most damnable of men, for he consciously rejects God and his mercy. Disbelievers are the worst of all creatures. [30] They are bad animals, blind, deaf and mute as they are. [31]; they are like people who crawl on their faces. [32] A veil is spread over their hearts so that they can comprehend nothing; [33] they lend their ear to the satans. [34] They are the worst of all beings, whereas believers are the best; the first will go to hell, the latter to heaven. [35] Enough to show that we have here a dualistic division of mankind into two opposed races.

5. Articles of the Muslim creed

a. Angels and devils

Islam shares with Judaism and Christianity a belief in angels and devils; both are creatures of God, but some of them rebelled against him and became devils, *shaitans*. They do what they can to obstruct the work of salvation and to mislead the faithful. In contrast, the angels, as messengers of God, assist people in every respect.

b. The prophets

A very important part of the Muslim creed is a belief in prophets. Many of them are known from the Bible, figures such as Adam, Noach, Abraham, and above all Jesus, who is called *Isa* in the Koran. Finally comes Mohammed, who is considered to be the 'seal' of the prophets. No more prophecies are needed after him. All the prophets have proclaimed the same teachings, although in a less perfect and definite form than Mohammed did. There is only one God, this is the main tenet that they all have in common. For this reason the Old and New Testaments are considered valuable books, although they must be explained, clarified, and completed by the Koran. The Thora and the Gospels are to be seen as inspired writings.

However, Mohammed, the last and greatest prophet, was not a divine being; he did not work miracles. He was sinful, like all other people, and in need of forgiveness. Yet he was Allah's elected Messenger and his words and teachings are considered authoritative and decisive. Following the precepts of the Koran will help the faithful to lead a life that pleases Allah. This does not mean that being a believer guarantees a Muslim a place in heaven. One should lead a life that is as blameless as possible.

c. The hell

"For those who have counted our signs false and been too proud to receive them, the gates of heaven will not be opened." [36] Those who were sinful, above all the idolators, will go to hell. Hell is a pool of fire; every conceivable horror will be the part of the doomed. They have the satans as their patrons. [37] It is even the case that Allah has led a group of people [the Muslims] along the straight road and that another group [the idolators] is justly destined to err. "It is they who have chosen the satans as their allies." [38] Once again we find that subdivision of mankind into two opposed parts, a subdivision that is basic.

d. The joys of heaven

Those who lived as good and pious Muslims will go to heaven. The joys of heaven are depicted in the most glowing terms. The saved will live in beautiful gardens through which clear streams run; the trees growing there offer their abundant fresh fruit. People recline under the trees on soft carpets with green cushions (green being the colour of Islam). Beautiful girls, untouched virgins all, with wide eyes - the *huris* - keep them company. [39]

6. The duties of the Muslim

a. The five pillars of Islam

Now that there are so many Muslims living in the countries of the West, we have become acquainted with the duties of a devote Muslim, especially the month of fasting. There are five of these duties, the so-called 'five pillars of Islam', the *arkan*. They are, of course, to be found in the Koran, but not as a group of five; this number is a product of Islamic tradition. It should be understood that the Islamic creed has two sources, the Koran and tradition.

b. Confessing and praying

The first and most important obligation is that of frequently repeating that there is no God but God and that Mohammed is his Messenger. It is this confession that makes one a true Muslim, far more than circumcision (Muslim boys, like Jewish ones, are circumcized in their earliest infancy. The difference is that Jewish boys are circumcized eight days after their birth, whereas Muslim boys undergo this operation between their first and third years.)

The second duty is the *salat*, the obligation to pray. Since very early times, probably even since Mohammed's own lifetime, the number of daily prayer times has been determined at five. Those who pray follow a fixed ritual of prayers and bows; they bend very deeply in the direction of Mecca, with their foreheads touching the ground. Some people have done this so often and so fervently that they have developed a callous spot on their foreheads, the so-called *zibiba*, the 'raisin'. Before praying, a Muslim has to cleanse himself with water, and if this not available, with sand. Prayers may be said anywhere, but the most preferable is to pray together in the *masgid*, in the mosque, that is, under the guidance of a prayer leader, the *imam*. The most appropriate time for communal prayer is the Friday afternoon, Friday being the liturgical day of Islam.

c. Giving alms and fasting

The third obligation, as already mentioned, is that of giving alms, the *zakat*. Then comes fasting. The Islamic fast is concentrated in the month of Ramadan; westerners are therefore used to call it 'the Ramadan'. The fact that the Islamic year is a lunar year has two important consequences, firstly, each month counts twenty-eight days, not thirty or thirty-one, and secondly, it moves regularly through the solar year. The fasting rule stipulates that no food or drink, even water, may be used as long as it is daylight. The most strict do not smoke and do not even swallow their own spittle.

This is a highly exacting obligation. In a country like the Netherlands the length of the fasting-day varies from eighteen hours in June to eight in December. Imagine what it means to drink no water in a hot climate! Absolved from this duty are children, those who are ill, pregnant women, and travellers. If possible, they should make up for it at a later time.

d. The pilgrimage to Mecca

The fifth and last obligation is the so-called *hajj*, the pilgrimage to Mecca. As mentioned before, going on pilgrimage to Mecca was already a well-known custom in pagan Arabia. The idea is that the custom of visiting the Ka'aba was established by Abraham. [40] Mohammed made it a religious duty for every Muslim to visit it at least once in his life, that is, if one has the necessary means and the opportunity, which means that many never undertake the journey. Those who have fulfilled this duty may wear the green turban and are called *hajji*; it is a title that may be attached to the name. Muslims who go to Mecca must keep themselves pure, that is, not only wash themselves ritually, but abstain from their usual occupations and even from sexual intercourse.

The traditional ceremonies are precisely prescribed : walking seven times around the Ka'aba and touching the Black Stone, the journey to Mount Arafat on the second day, and the sacrificing of camels and sheep in Mina. The seclusive and exclusive character of Islam is stressed by the fact that it is strictly forbidden for non-Muslims to take part in the ceremonies and to visit the holy places.

7. Islamic law

a. The *shari'ah*

A word must be said about the *shari'ah*. This is often supposed to be the Islamic law, but our western, modern term 'law' does not cover the real meaning of *shari'ah*. This is a complex of prescriptions ordained by Allah making it possible for the faithful to live as good Muslims. The one who does not obey these prescripts is a bad Muslim. The *shari'ah* enables the believers to have the right relations with Allah and with their fellow-men. It expresses the will of God regarding human behaviour; it has to be accepted and obeyed as it is. It is not for humans to change it.

The fact that there is a *shari'ah* creates a very sharp distinction between those who live according to it and those who do not - a distinction so sharp that it must be considered dualistic. In a number of Islamic states the *shari'ah* functions as public law, so that all citizens are bound by it. However, in modern Turkey, a secularized state, this is not the case. This causes considerable friction between the army that considers itself the guardian of the heritage of Kemal Ataturk, the founder of the present republic, and fundamentalistic groups and political parties, like the Welfare Party, that want to introduce the *shari'ah*.

b. The ban on alcohol

One of the best known injunctions is the prohibition on drinking alcoholic beverages. Warnings against the use of wine already date from Mohammed's onw lifetime. Originally the Prophet seems to have been not wholly averse to it; he saw it as a gift from Allah, 'a sign for people who are sensible'. [41] However, in wine and in gambling "there is great guilt, but also uses for the people, but their guilt is greater than their usefulness." [42] The total prohibition was perhaps occasioned by the fact that Mohammed saw drunken people bowing down for the *salat*. "Do not come to the Prayer when you are intoxicated, until you know what you are saying." [43] Finally, gambling and drinking were definitely forbidden as the works of Satan. [44] This prohibition has been extended by the lawschools to all alcoholic beverages. This is a clear case of puritanism; it fences off Islam from all other people, including Jews and Christians, who do not object to a moderate use of alcohol.

c. Women

Nowhere in the Koran it is explicitly stated that women are the lesser kind, "though the men have a rank above them." [45] All the same, they are ranked among 'the goods of this present life', together with 'children, hoards of gold and silver, and excellent horses, cattle, and land'. [46] A certain fear of impurity is expressed, for instance with regard to menstruation. "It is harmful; so withdraw from women in menstruation, and come not near them until they have purified themselves." [47] And the *salat* should not be performed by those who have slept with a woman before they have purified themselves. [48]

A way in which Islam is decidedly different from Judaism and Christianity is that the Koran permits husbands to have more than one wife, two, three, or even four. [49] Even to these wives marital fidelity may not necessarily be exclusive, since a man may also take his female slaves as his concubines, if only one pays them well. [50] It is possible to repudiate a wife and send her away; a divorced woman may marry another man. [51] Does it need any further argument that such stipulations are far from enhancing the status of women?

8. Islamic 'fatalism'

Something has already been said about Islamic 'fatalism'. It is, I argued, incorrect to speak of 'fatalism', since Muslims are not subject to fate, but to the will of Allah. We should, therefore, rather speak of 'determinism'. But this determinism sometimes looks like downright fatalism. "Those to Paradise and

I do not care, and those to Hell, and I do not care." [52] Annemarie Schimmel comments that this "expresses a strange, irrational relation between the human 'slave' and the Lord ... This statement translates well the Muslim's understanding of God's omnipotence and the absolute Lordly power." [53] This stressing of God's absolute power makes man stand before him as an *abd*, a slave rather than as a free human being. A Muslim, however, would never think in this way, for another *hadith* says : "Think about the creation but do not think about God." Muslim theologians feel that one should not speculate about God, but many Muslim philosophers freely do so.

The concept of free will does not exist in Islam. [54] "You cannot will, except it be that Allah wills it, for Allah is knowing and wise." [55] This does not mean that Muslims do not hold themselves responsible for their deeds. They do. Everybody is responsible for his own actions. [56] All the same, this strong accent on the will of Allah is one of the points in which the distance between God and man becomes manifest.

9. Determining the place of Islam

We can determine the place of Islam among the religions of this world, if we make use of two parameters, that of natural religion and that of the analogy of being.

a. Natural religion

By 'natural religion' I do not understand what David Hume meant by it; for him 'natural' was a synonym of 'rational'. Natural is a religion in which the basic elements of earthly and human existence play an essential part, elements that determine its character. Such elements are temple and priest, altar and sacrifice, bread and wine, fire and water, purifications and ablutions, prayer and prophecy, fasting and penance.

Some of these elements are clearly present in Islam : the concept of purity and the need to ritually cleanse oneself, the element of prophecy, concentrated in Mohammed, the Seal of the Prophets, the *salat*, the frequently repeated prayers, the need of repentance and the fasting of *Ramadan*. The picture becomes different if we broach the subject of sacrifices. It is well-known that Islam embraces sacrificial feasts, especially at the conclusion of the pilgrimage to Mecca. However, the Koran is remarkably silent on sacrifices, certainly if we compare this to the prominent place they have in the Old Testament. "Allah has appointed the Ka'aba, the Sacred House, as a standing institution for the people, likewise the sacred month [the Ramadan], and the offering [57] ... Do the *salat* for the Lord and bring sacrifices." [58] This is practically all there is. It is as though Allah himself is not greatly interested in sacrifices, but it is good for the faithful to bring them. Motivation, so abundantly present in the Old Testament, is conspicuously absent.

The words that the Muslims use for sacrifice signify 'to slaughter an animal' rather than 'offering', the victims in question being camels, cows, sheep, and goats. What takes place is ritual killing rather than bringing a real sacrifice. The Muslim practice is very similar to the Jewish *kosher* slaughter. Before the animal is killed, the name of God is pronounced over it : 'bismi-Llah; Allahu akbar', 'in the name of Allah; Allah is the most great.' The jugular vein is then cut and all the blood is let out. The meat is used for food; there is no indication of burnt-offerings.

Islam does not have temples. Mosques are prayer-houses; people go there to perform the *salat*, especially on Friday afternoons, to listen to sermons explaining the Koran, and to study the holy book. Yet there are no altars, nor is any liturgy performed around an altar. When the triumphant Muslim warriors who had conquered Constantinople in 1453, penetrated into the Aya Sofia, they saw a priest who was celebrating Mass. They killed him at the altar. As Muslims they needed neither altars nor priests. The difference between Islam and Christianity is tellingly sketched by the legend that once, when the Aya Sofia will be a Christian church again, this priest will return and continue celebrating his Mass.

Islam does not have priests either. An *imam* is a prayer-leader and a preacher but not an ordained priest, and certainly not a sacrificial priest. Being an *imam* is neither a profession nor a rank. There are no seminaries for *imams* nor the equivalent of rabbinical schools. Every male Muslim who is well versed in the *salat* may act as an *imam*. In practice, however, it is mostly a paid function for a man who has had some sort of theological training. The office is temporary; who longer leads the *salat* stops being an *imam*.

With the Shi'ite Muslims the function of *imam*, the imamate, is far more important. Here the *Imam* is thought to be a descendant of Ali; ordinarily there is only one *Imam*. This means that his function is not that of a prayer-leader, but much more. He possesses a very great authority, in spiritual as well as in civil affairs, which makes him resemble the Prophet himself; he is seen as the intermediary between God and man.

The wine that plays such a crucial role in Christian liturgy is forbidden in Islam. Water is used for ablutions only, but there is no holy water nor the all-important baptismal water.

The Islam does not possess many of the elements of natural religion. The most important of them in particular are absent : true sacrifice, the priest, the temple, the altar. For this reason it cannot be considered a truly natural religion. It is a religion of a book, of the Holy Book, the Koran; it is far more a religion of the book than Judaism and Christianity, although these religions have a holy book also.

b. The analogy of being

My second frame of reference is that of the analogy of being, the *analogia entis*. This concept comes from the Schoolmen, in particular from Thomas of Aquinas. One will not find it in the Bible or in the writings of the Church Fathers nor is it a specific tenet of the orthodox creed or an ecclesiastical dogma. It must rather be seen as an epitome, expressed in theological terms, of an essential part of Christian teaching, namely that of the relation between God and the creation. What it says is that there is likeness and agreement (but not identity) between the Creator and the created. [59] This implies that we can conclude the existence of God as Creator through the existents.

The elements of the natural religion that I mentioned in the foregoing paragraph are all practical expressions of the analogy of being. When my pious mother, who had never heard of this term, began to cut a bread for breakfast or lunch, she made a cross over its back with the knife. In this way she expressed that bread is not only matter but a gift from God.

The Roman Catholic and orthodox liturgies and their religious customs as well as the Jewish cult are all based on this analogy of being. Its elements are meant to connect people to God. Theologically, the idea is also expressed by the concept of God's immanence, of his being present in the world, of Immanuel, God with us. The Dutch guilder - I am writing in pre-euro days - bears on its rim the inscription 'God be with us'. In practice this serves to prevent dishonest people from clipping the coin, but for this purpose any other maxim might have done. It is not strange to find this pious wish on a piece of money, although money is the 'filthy lucre' and 'the root of all evil'. Yet even this humble and so often misused instrument of exchange is part of God's creation, and what we buy with it are the gifts of God.

Since Islam is, as I argued above, not a truly natural religion, it is also not one in which the analogy of being is a constitutive element. God's transcendency, together with his unicity, are so heavily stressed that little room is left for his immanence. God must be kept "free from all human comparisons [while] not admitting the slightest possibility of an 'analogia entis'." [60].

10. Is Islam dualistic?

a. A declaration of intent

The climatic question the answer to which must form the conclusion of this chapter, in both senses of the word, is whether or not Islam is a dualistic religion. I racked my brains for days on end over this issue, but I still find it very hard to answer. Perhaps what I am going to write and what I have written already in this chapter may give the impression that I am out to propagate the Christian religion, to the detriment of Islam. I do not have the slightest intention to denigrate or belittle the Muslim religion or to insult pious Muslims. However, just as I have in this whole series one overall theme, that of dualism, I have it in this chapter too. I have scrutinized the Jewish religion

[61], the New Testament, [62], and the Christian theology of the first centuries [63] for dualistic elements and tendencies, and there is no reason why I should not do the same for Islam. We should keep in mind what I stated several times in earlier volumes, that there exists no human constellation of whichever kind that is entirely free from dualism. But I also defend the thesis - for which I refer the reader to earlier volumes - that the Jewish and Roman Catholic religions are essentially perfectly undualistic. It is for this reason that I can use them as the frame of reference against which I may compare other religions to find out whether or not they are dualistic and what may be the dualistic elements in them.

b. Utterly opposed poles or not?

Let us start from my own definition of dualism. Are there two utterly opposed poles in Islam - God and mankind in this case - with absolutely no intermediate term or connecting links between them? If we judge from a theological viewpoint there is no dualism in Islam. God is the creator of all that is and he is concerned with mankind. Calling his exalted Name brings the believer into contact with him. There is no unbridgeable chasm between God and the Muslim nor between God the Creator and the creation.

So far so good. Yet when all is said and done, the distance between God and man proves to be much greater than in Judaism and Christianity. In theory, that is, in theologicis, there may be no dualism, but the picture might change when it comes to practice, that is, to the appreciation of Islamic religious sentiment. This is a difficult subject for an author who is not a Muslim himself, although he is, as a believer, somewhat better equipped than someone who is totally alien to any form of religion. We can, however, make headway, not erring too far, if we only follow the lead of the Koran. When the Koran speaks of Allah, it always does so to magnify him; we find this expressed in the famous Verse of the Throne in the second *sura*, but also in many other *suras*, often in glowing verses of great beauty. The written name of Allah is usually accompanied by a formula that expresses his greatness, for instance the words 'great' or 'majestic' or 'Great is his Majesty'. He is the overmighty ruler rather than the loving companion.

There is a marked and telling difference between the most usual prayer attitudes of Christians and Muslims. Prostration is the expression of the most total subjection to God. In western Christianity it has become very rare. In the ordination ceremony the candidates for the Roman Catholic priesthood throw themselves down in their full length before the altar, while the officiating priests do the same for a few moments at the beginning of the Good Friday liturgy. Yet one will not see an ordinary Christian, whether priest or layperson, choose the prostration as a posture for prayer. It is less rare in the Russian Orthodox Church. [64] Far more usual, at least in western Christianity, is kneeling, either on one or on both knees; in the liturgy of the oriental Churches one does not see kneeling but bowing. Genuflection is, just as prostration, but in a somewhat less radical form, an act of submission and also of penance and furthermore of deep respect. [65]

However, the typical liturgical prayer posture is to stand. Probably this is a Jewish heritage, because the posture Jews preferred for praying and still prefer is the standing one. Priests officiating at the altar are, apart from some genuflections, always standing. [66] The standing position expresses first and foremost that a human being is essentially different from the animals and approaches God from person to person. It also denotes self-consciousness, freedom and dignity, in short, the presentation of one who is created 'in the image of God'. As Ohm writes, "we stand before God because we are familiar with him and consider ourselves his children and behave as such." [67] (In the churches of the East standing is far more usual than in those of the West, where the faithful often kneel or sit during the liturgy.)

That church-goers relate to God as to their Father becomes apparent when during Mass the Our Father is recited. The whole congregation stands up then, probably according to a word of Jesus himself who once said : "When you stand praying ...", referring to the usual Jewish attitude. [68] The priest at the altar assumes the so-called *orante* posture, lifting both arms beside the head with the palms of the hands turned forward; many Mass attendants do the same.

In early Islam, the *orante* posture was fiercely combated by the lawgivers; it was supposed to be something magical, and it was also rejected as Christian. It was only later that it came to be accepted. [69] Other, very common prayer postures, like kneeling and standing, are by means unknown in Islam. "Guard strictly your [habit of] prayers ... and stand before God in a devout [frame of] mind." [70] Yet the most typical prayer posture is the *sagda* or prostration. Praying Muslims begin standing, then go down on their knees and bow deeply forward in the direction of Mecca until their foreheads touch the ground. The *sagda* is, in fact, the *proskunêsis*, the prostration of one who approached a Persian emperor.

The *sagda* is the bench mark of the true Muslim. It is an impressive sight to see large numbers of Muslims in a big mosque, all with their foreheads to the ground, and still more when they are doing the same in their thousands at Mecca during the hajj. It is, of course, an attitude of the most humble submission. "You will see them bow and prostrate themselves seeking grace from God and [his] good pleasure. On their faces are their marks [probably the dust from the ground], [being] the traces of their prostration [71] ... Not one of the beings in heaven and on earth but must come to [God] most gracious as a slave." [72] The word actually used here for praying Muslims is *abd*, slave, although this word should not be understood in its social sense. It has rather a religious meaning, more or less when a westerner, writing to somebody who is several rungs higher on the social ladder, signs his letter with 'your humble servant'.

There is an etymological connection here with the word 'mosque', *masgid*, which is either derived from the Arabic *sagada*, to throw oneself down, or from the Aramaean *masgeda*, the place where one throws oneself down. One scholar, J. Oestrup, says that "the clever Muhammed knew what he did when he forced his unbelieving Muslims to touch the floor with their foreheads when praying; the Islamic prayer ritual became the best drill for the passionate and ill-disciplined sons of the desert : it forced the individual to see himself as a member of a community and at the same time imprinted on him the notion of his own insignificance." [73]

If 'body language' means anything, then what the Muslim expresses is that he is in the presence of an all-powerful ruler who expects his humble obeisance.

In spite of the enormous preponderance of the need to adore God and to acknowledge his unicity and his majesty, or perhaps rather just because of this, Islam does not give the impression of being a devotional and an affectionate religion; it is rather an 'intellectual' or 'theological' religion, because of the great stress laid on its central dogma.

When speaking of God's activity in the world, Christian theology distinguishes between the primary cause and secondary causes. God is, of course, the first cause of all that is, of the world, of existence, of life, of me. When a pious Christian falls ill, he will not attribute this to God but to some virus. Islam does not know of secondary causes. Allah is the only cause who encapsulates and works everything. Annemarie Schimmel quotes to this effect an Arab sage who says that Allah is "the highest all-embracing Ego in which the smaller egos of the created universe live like pearls in the ocean." This leaves little room for a truly immanent God but also for the individuality of the human person.

c. Conclusion

Let me, in conclusion, quote the Swiss scholar Kellerhals at some length. The Islamic concept of God is, "in any case as it is conceived by Muslim theology, not identical with the monotheistic doctrine of God in the Bible, even where it uses the same terms. The more one elaborates conceptually the idea of God's unity and unicity, the more one, in order to exclude all entities and powers existing and working outside God as unworthy of veneration, and concentrates every existence and all causality on him, the more one denies all real being and effective power of realization to all that exists outside him, this image of God removes itself ever more from our imaginative faculty. This One, this only One, next to whom nothing else should be, becomes ever more pale, colourless, and inconceivable. In other words : the more this monotheism becomes white-hot, the more it consumes in this overheating all that is personal, warm with life, and intimately human in this image of God. Nothing

283

remains but the conceptual idea of a supreme being of whom one can only say what it is not but not what it is." [74] Elsewhere this same scholar calls ordinary Muslim believers 'deists', which would mean that they conceive of God as an abstraction or a concept rather than as a person. We are very close to dualism here or even teetering on the brink of the dualistic abyss.

NOTES TO CHAPTER IX

1. *Sura* 4.136.
2. Anton Schall s.v. 'Islam I', *TRE* 16,328.
3. *Sura* 53.19-23.
4. *Sura* 4.48.
5. Gen. 1.
6. *Sura* 2.212.
7. *Sura* 57.20.
8. *Sura* 3.185.
9. *Sura* 2.255
10. *Sura* 7.180.
11. Anton Schall s.v. 'Islam I', *TRE* 16.329.
12. *Sura* 2.255.
13. *Sura* 59.22.
14. *Sura* 59.23.
15. Muslims should not be called 'Mohammetans'; they do not think of themselves as followers of Mohammed, in the way Christians see themselves as followers of Jesus Christ.
16. Schimmel, *Deciphering the Signs of God* 179.
17. Lüling, *Die Wiederentdeckung des Propheten Muhammad* 241, says that the Arab concept of 'Islam' has a definite significance for the understanding of Islam as a religion. There are three word groups, namely *'aslama, muslim, and 'islam*, which have the root slm in common. This means 'to be whole, perfect, unimpaired'. P. 243 The original non-Islamic meaning of *muslim/islam* is 'leaving behind, giving up'. The religious meaning of *muslim/islam*, namely 'to submit oneself completely to God' does not tally, says this scholar (p. 242), with the original non-religious meaning. He points out (p. 244) that the terms *'aslama/muslim/'islam* occur relatively rarely in the Koran, namely sixty-

two times in all, whereas the terms *'amana/mu'min/'iman* = to believe, to be a believer, occur eight hundred and twelve times. The faithful (p. 245) are adressed as 'o you believers (*mu'min*)', never as 'o you muslims', while the title of caliphs is *emir* of the faithful, never *emir* of the Muslims. Does Lüling mean to say that the use of the terms 'Muslim' and 'Islam' is a fancy of the West rather than the expression of the self-understanding of the servants of Allah?

18. *Sura* 50.16.
19. *Sura* 78.71-72.
20. *Sura* 2.195; 3.141.
21. *Sura* 2.222.
22. *Sura* 49.9.
23. *Sura* 61.4.
24. *Sura* 2.165.
25. *Sura* 70.23-25.
26. *Sura* 75.31.
27. *Sura* 9.60.
28. *Sura* 2.258-259.
29. *Sura* 5.33 and 37.
30. *Sura* 98.6.
31. *Sura* 8.22 and 55.
32. *Sura* 67.22.
33. *Sura* 5.25.
34. *Sura* 6.112.
35. *Sura* 98.6,7.
36. *Sura* 7.40.
37. *Sura* 7.27.
38. *Sura* 7.30.
39. *Sura* 55.46-78. The word *huri* may leads to misunderstandings because it sounds like the English whore, the Dutch *hoer*, and the German *Hure*. The text, however, does not suggest any sexuality.
40. *Sura* 2.27-29.
41. *Sura* 16.67.
42. *Sura* 2.216.

43. *Sura* 4.43.
44. *Sura* 5.90.
45. *Sura* 2.228.
46. *Sura* 3.14.
47. *Sura* 2.222.
48. *Sura* 4.43.
49. *Sura* 4.3.
50. *Sura* 4.24-25.
51. *Sura* 2.227 and 232.
52. This quotation is from the *hadith qudsi*; a *hadith* is a sacred saying that is not be found in the Koran, but that is supposed to come directly or indirectly from the Prophet himself.
53. Schimmel, *Deciphering the Signs of God* 220/221.
54. There are, however, Muslim groups that defend free will.
55. *Suras* 76.30 and 81.29.
56. *Sura* 6.70.
57. *Sura* 5.97.
58. *Sura* 108.2.
59. The following example graphically exemplifies what precisely the analogy of being is. Once I saw on tv an international swimming contest. An Italian girl stood ready for the start. Suddenly she knelt down, bowed deeply forward, dipped her hand into the water, and made the sign of the cross. Then she stood ready again, waiting for the starting shot. The background of this moving gesture is this. When the Son of God descended into the waters of the Jordan for his baptism, all the waters of this world - thus the Christian tradition has it - became sanctified. Consequently, all waters may be used for sacral purposes, above all for baptism. Even a non-Roman Catholic, for instance a doctor, may, in case of emergency, baptize a baby with ordinary water.
60. Schimmel, *Deciphering the Signs of God* 225.
61. Vol. IV, Ch. II.
62. Vol. VII, Ch. IV.
63. Vol. XIII.
64. Ohm, *Die Gebetsgebärden* 365/366.
65. Ohm, *Die Gebetsgebärden* 344/345 and 350-355.

66. It is even so that an invalid priest who can say Mass only when remaining seated, needs a special permission for this.
67. Ohm, *Die Gebetsgeb*ärden 327.
68. Mc. 11:25.
69. Ohm, *Die Gebetsgebärden* 255.
70. *Sura* 2.239.
71. *Sura* 48.29.
72. *Sura* 19.94.
73. Ohm, *Die Gebetsgebärden* 363, who quotes from J. Oestrup, *Orientalische Höflichkeit. Formen und Formeln im Islam. Eine kulturgeschichtliche Studie.* (Aus dem Dänischen übersetzt von K. Wulff. Leipzig, 1929. p. 31.
74. Kellerhals, *Der Islam* 147/148.

CHAPTER X

MUSLIMS, JEWS, AND CHRISTIANS

1. Schoeps' opinion

There cannot be the slightest doubt that Jewish and Christian sources, in particular the Old and the New Testaments, influenced the teachings of the Prophet Mohammed and the development of the Koran text. But were Jewish and Christian teachings and traditions so dominant in the Prophet's religious thinking that they became an integral part of Islam? Or was their influence only marginal so that without them Islam would have become almost exactly the same religion that it actually is?

We should keep in mind Schoeps' opinion here, brought forward, both as a kind of conclusion and as a reference to the future, at the end of his book on Judaeo-Christianity (which, in his view, was the original form of Christianity). "We have here a fact of really world-historical impact, namely, that, although Judaeo-Christianity went down in the Christian Church, it was preserved in Islam, and in some of its more powerful impulses lived on until in our own days." [1] According to Schoeps' description, Judaeo-Christianity - *Judenchristentum* - was an attempt to unite the most essential features of both religions into one harmonious whole. In the end, neither Jews nor Christians accepted this idea. Must we adhere to this author's opinion that the real inheritor of the Judaeo-Christian concept was Islam? We shall have to return to this. Schoeps's opinion could give rise to the idea that we must think of Islam as an epiphenomenon of Judaism and Christianity, but this was certainly not in his mind.

We know that in Mohammed's days Jews were numerous in South Arabia and in the Yemen; there were Jews in Mecca, and quite a number of them also lived in Medina where they formed an organized religious community. If translations of parts of the Bible existed in Arabic, they are not mentioned in early Islamic sources nor have they been handed to us. We do not know whether the Prophet was personally acquainted with Jews in his Meccan days. However, since Jews and Christians regularly came to Mecca for commercial purposes, it is by no means inconceivable, and even highly probable, that Mohammed, who was very much interested in religion, had heard what these people taught. Whatever the case, his opponents saw reason enough to accuse him of not being at all original and of having found all that he wanted in the two older religions, so that he was only an epigone. He himself, however, claimed that he was not dependent on them but, instead, had renewed and thus superseded them so that his religion was something entirely new.

In the Koran his opponents found allusions to the Bible in such abundance that they might have thought that their accusations of theological plagiarism were justified. But to pious Muslims this is sheer blasphemy. The Koran comes directly from God and not from any other source. They explain the unmistakable similarities by pointing out that God also inspired the Bible. [2]

2. Mohammed's irritation with the Medinan Jews

In Chapter II I related that Mohammed, once in Medina, after his initial attempts to reach an agreement with the Jewish community in that city, gave up all hopes of winning those Jews over to his cause. He had very little success with them. "We made a covenant with the Children of Israel [to this effect] : Worship none but God [etc.]. Then you turned back, except a few among you, and those backslided." [3] He soon began to develop a negative opinion of Jews in general. Nonetheless, they were numerous and important enough in Arabia to take their presence into account. What must have been a real problem for him was that he was a newcomer, a novice in religious matters, as compared with the age-old Jewish religion. The Medinan Jews took advantage of this, as I wrote in Chapter II, by pestering the Prophet with questions. It irritated him that he was often the worst off in these word-battles.

3. The first blows

It seems that it came to blows already very early. There is a story that Mohammed invited one of the leading Medinan Jews to convert to Islam and to give God 'a fine loan' (the *zakat* is meant). But one of the Jews, a certain Pinechas, answered : "God must be really poor, when he needs a loan." Then the angry Abu Bekr boxed his ears and said : "Had there not been a covenant between us, I would have broken your neck," and he brought him bound before Mohammed, where the Jew denied having said this. [4]

Mohammed was evidently afraid of contact with Jews. "When you see men engaged in vain discourse [obviously discussions with or among Jews are meant] about our signs, turn away from them unless they turn to a difficult theme. If Satan ever makes you forget [this], then do not sit [again] in the company of those who do wrong." [5]

4. The growing distance

The following story, related by the Arabian author Beidawi, perfectly illustrates the ideological distance between Muslims and Jews, exemplified by the opposition between the archangels Gabriel and Michael. Umar, one of the earliest converts and later the second caliph of Islam as Umar I, once asked some Jews about Gabriel. They said : he is our enemy, for he revealed our secrets to Mohammed; he is also the executer of every reprisal and punishment. Michael, on the other hand, is the author of all plenty and welfare. Then Umar asked how their respective relations to God were. His Jewish spokesman said : Gabriel is standing to his right and Michael to his left, but between them there is enmity. [6] Since it was Gabriel who brought the message to the Prophet, this meant enmity between Muslims and Jews.

The Jews were depicted as hypocrites, speaking with two tongues. "When they [the Jews] met the men of Faith [the Muslims], they say : 'we believe', but when they meet each other in private, they say : 'shall you tell them [the Muslims] what God has revealed to you [the Jews], that they may engage them in argument before your Lord?'. Do you [Muslim] not understand their aim?," [7] this aim being to confound the Muslims.

5. Mohammed takes action against the Banu Qaynuqa'

Soon enough Muslim-Jewish relations in Medina were nearing the breaking-point. In March 624 a battle took place near Badr between an armed force from Mecca and a much smaller contingent of Medinan Muslims. The Muslims were victorious, thus enhancing Mohammed's prestige. It seems that he was now no longer prepared to tolerate Jewish recrimination. He went in person to the market square of one of the three Jewish tribes living in Medina, the Banu Qaynuga' and ordered them peremptorily to convert. "O assembly of Jews! Fear God so that will not happen to you what has hit [those of Mecca] and espouse Islam, for you know quite well that I am the Prophet who is sent." There was a barely hidden threat of military action in these words. The Jews retorted that Mohammed had defeated the Meccans only by accident. If it came to an armed conflict with them, he would see that they were men. [8]

As might be expected, the spark fell into the powder keg. The explosion that followed was caused by a nasty incident, a monument of utter tactlessness. A Muslim woman visited the shop of a Jewish goldsmith, a member of the Bany Qaynuga' tribe. She was veiled. Some young Jews began to provoke her to take her veil off, which she refused. Then the goldsmith, without her noticing it, fastened her dress to a table leg or the like. When she walked off, her dress remained behind so that she suddenly stood there half-naked. She cried out for shame and anger. A passing Muslim stormed in and, furious with rage, cut off the goldsmith's head. Other Jews came running and beat up the Muslim. Soon the fighting became general. The Jewish quarter remained encircled by armed Muslims for two weeks after which seven hundred combatants surrendered. [9]

Then the Prophet went to the Jewish quarter and thrice asked the Jews to convert to Islam, "and you will be safe." But they were not ready to do this. The third time he said : "Know that the earth belongs to Allah and his Messenger. I am going to expel you from this region. Whoever among you who possesses anything, let him sell it." [10] Their arms were confiscated. This is a purely dualistic statement : there is no room for disbelievers on this earth. It seems that Mohammed would at first have them all massacred, but the influential Medinan whom I mentioned earlier, Abd Allah ibn Ubayy, came to plead for them, because they were his clients who had protected them on more than one occasion. The Prophet would not listen. Then Ubayy took him by his collar and went on pleading; Mohammed became so angry that he became blue in the face. But finally he gave in : "You can have them." [11] The Banu Qaynuqa' were banished from Medina, but the two other tribes were left alone for the time being. [12]

6. The murder of the Jewish poet Ka'b

The next episode does not throw an all too favourable light on Mohammed's character. There lived in Medina a man called Ka'b al-Ashraf; he was of mixed descent, his father being a pagan Arab and his mother a Jewess; he saw himself as belonging to his mother's tribe, the an-Nadir. He bombarded Mohammed and the Muslims with satirical verses, which were widely and avidly read. Five men hatched a plot to kill the poet; it seems that the Prophet was party to this plot, one source even having it that he would have said : "Who wants to kill Ka'b, the enemy of Allah?", and another that Gabriel revealed to Mohammed that he wanted Ka'b to be killed. [13] And killed he was, at a lonely spot in the middle of the night. [14] This happened in 625.

7. The fate of the an-Nadir Jews

The Jewish tribe of the an-Nadir lived in the western part of the Medina oasis; most of their members were very wealthy. Mohammed seems to have been afraid of them; he feared becoming the victim of an attack. Whether or not a

Jewish attack on his life really took place is not certain; in any event, he laid siege to their quarter. Soon enough they capitulated. After the customary summons to convert to Islam (they refused), they were banished from Medina. They loaded all that camels could carry on the animals' backs, until the lintels of their houses, and departed with a train of six hundred camels. [15]

The an-Nadir Jews retreated to Khaybar, a town sixty miles due north of Medina. Since they were understandably very ill disposed towards Mohammed, they were ready to assist any attempts to bring him down. When the Meccans and others planned to lay siege to Medina, the an-Nadir readily became a party to it. The Muslims tried to put an end to their inimical activities by murdering two of their leaders. The first was an old man who was killed by assassins in his own house. The murder of the other, Usayr, was a treacherous affair. A Muslim delegation, allegedly sent by Mohammed himself, came to Khaybar and and invited Usayr to pay a visit to Medina. Despite warnings he went, accompanied by thirty of his friends. Somewhere between Khaybar and Medina the Jews were murdered; only one of them managed to escape. This happened probably early in 628. [16]

8. The ordeal of the Qurayza Jews

The Jews of the last tribe still at Medina, the Qurayza, kept a low profile, but this did not save them, since Mohammed had by now become deeply distrustful of all Jews. The Qurayza hoped to be able to remain neutral, but, as Watt states, "the rising Islamic state was not prepared to tolerate such sitting on the fence." [17] Their ordeal came soon after another battle with the enemies of Islam just outside the gates of Medina. When the victorious Prophet returned home, so Ibn Ishaq relates, "the angel Gabriel came to the apostle wearing an embroidered turban and riding a mule with a saddle covered with a piece of brocade." The angel said to him : "God commands you, Muhammad, to go to Banu Qurayza. I am about to go to them to shake their stronghold."

Under the command of the Prophet himself, the Muslims laid siege to the Jewish positions. After almost four weeks of siege the Jews were at the end of their tether. One of their chiefs, Ka'b ibn Assad, an 'enemy of God', says Ibn Ishaq, spelled out to the Jews the possibilities they still had. Firstly, they might convert to Islam, "and then your lives, your properties, your women and children will be saved." They said : "we will never abandon the law of *Torah* and never change it for another." Secondly, they might kill their wives and children and then engage the Muslims in a last desperate fight in which they would have nothing to lose. "If we conquer, we can acquire other wives and children." But they said : "Shall we kill those poor creatures? What will be the good of life, when they were dead?" The third possibility was that, because it was Sabbath eve, they could fall upon the Muslims unawares, since the enemy would not expect them. But they refused to profane the Sabbath in this way.

Letting it be known that they wished to surrender, they asked for conditions, but were told that these would not be granted. Then, at their request, Abu Lubaba, an old friend of the Jews, was sent to their headquarters. Asked if he thought that they should submit to Mohammed's judgment, he said "yes, and pointed with his hand to his throat signifying slaughter." Obviously at a loss what to do with the Qurayza Jews, Mohammed asked the opinion of an influential Muslim, Sa'd ibn Mu'adh, who had been wounded in the last battle. "When the apostle appointed him umpire in the matter of B. Qurayza, his people mounted him on a donkey on which they had put a leather cushion, for he was a corpulent man."

Sa'd asked the Prophet : "Do you covenant by Allah that you accept the judgment I pronounce on them?" The answer being in the affirmative, he decreed : "Then I give judgment that the men should be killed, the property divided, and the women and children taken as captives." Mohammed then had trenches dug on the market square; the Jews had to descend into those trenches where they were all beheaded. Their numbers are given as varying from six to nine hundred; there was one woman among them. The women, the children, and the booty were divided among the victors; Mohammed chose one of the women for himself. [18]

Watt, one of the great experts on early Islam, takes exception to 'some European writers [who] have criticized this sentence for what they call its savage and inhuman character," [19] and he goes out of his way to condone it, adducing there had been collusion between the Qurayza and the outside enemy who came to beleaguer Medina; the ordeal of the Jews was justified by the fact that they had broken their agreement with Mohammed. [20] This may have justified the military action against them, although the real reason was, in my opinion, that Mohammed simply would not tolerate any Jews in Medina. But did it also justify the killing of so many defenseless prisoners-of-war? I must admit that Mohammed's behaviour sometimes makes me feel uncomfortable : that he had at least twelve wives and concubines, that he married a nine-year-old girl whom he took to his bed when she was thirteen and he fifty-seven, his intention to massacre the Qaynuga' Jews, the murder of the Jewish poet Ka'b, and that he had all the male Jews of the Qurayza killed.

There was now no longer an organized Jewish community left in Medina, although there were still some Jews to be found in the oasis. Watt combats the view that Mohammed had a premeditated plan of clearing all Jews out of Medina. He adds, however, that "when circumstances were favourable ... and an occasion of hostilities presented itself of the type familar to Arabs, then Muhammad acted." Premeditated or not, the result was the same : Medina was virtually cleansed of Jews. And the reason for this is given as follows by Watt. "In Muhammad's first two years at Medina the Jews were the most dangerous critics of his claim to be a prophet, and the religious fervour of his followers, on which so much depended, was liable to be greatly reduced unless Jewish criticisms could be silenced and rendered impotent." [21] And silenced they were, in the most effective way!

9. The liquidation of Khaybar

Seen from his perspective, Mohammed could not yet feel entirely at ease, since there was still an active and inimical Jewish community at Khaybar. He therefore marched northward with an army and captured the forts of Khaybar one by one. Ibn Ishaq coolly states that "the women of Khaybar were distributed among the Muslims." Once again Mohammed added a Jewish woman to his harem. The men who survived the conquest of the oasis were allowed to stay, but their situation was insecure since Mohammed told them: "If we wish to expel you, we will expel you." They remained there only on sufferance. [22] This happened in 628. Other Jewish positions around Khaybar were subsequently captured. After the death of the Prophet in 632 caliph Umar I expelled the Jews from Khaybar.

10. The *dhimma*

When Mohammed had captured Mecca in 630, he permitted its local Jews to stay. Whereas the pagan Meccans were forced to embrace Islam, Jews (and Christians) might remain true to their own religion. However, this was not an act of tolerance in the western sense of the word. It was a concession and a concession requires a compensation. Jews and Christians had to pay the *jizya*, the poll-tax, later to be levied on all non-Muslims in Islamic countries. In principle, the *jizya*, like the *zakat*, had to be used for pensions, salaries, and charities, but under this pretext it was often paid into the prince's *khass*, his 'private' treasury. [23]

Henceforward Jews (and Christians) fell under the protection of the Islamic state. This is based on a lapidary phrase in the Koran : "[Do not] acknowledge the religion of ... the People of the Book, until they pay the *jizya*." [24] These 'People of the Book' are all those non-Muslims who possess written revelations, namely Jews, Christians, and later also Zoroastrians in Iraq and Iran. This system of protection is called *dhimma* = contract; its beneficiaries are called *ahl al-dhimma*, the people of the contract, or *dhimmi*. Its definitive regulation dates from the time of caliph Umar II (717-720). The *dhimmi* were second-rank people, of course, but as long as they duly paid the *jizya*, they were accorded a status that guaranteed them a reasonably quiet life, together with being able to exercize their religion (but this was often more theoretically true than in practice). In the first centuries of their conquests the Muslims were everywhere only a tiny minority in an ocean of non-Muslims; common sense dictated a policy of flexibility. [25]

11. Muslim objections against Judaism

Many persons, known from the Old Testament, found, in some form or other, their way into the Koran : Adam, Noach, Abraham, Moses, and still others. Especially Abraham - Ibrahim - played a great role. [26] "Abraham was neither a Jew nor a Christian, but he was true in the faith and bowed his will to God's, and he joined not gods with God." [27] In other words, he was a true Muslim and as such the ancestor of all Muslims. "Without doubt, among men, the nearest of kin to Abraham are those who follow him [the Muslims, not the Jews], as are also this Apostle [Mohammed] and those who believe." [28] As Watt formulates it, "Abraham had two great advantages : he was in a physical sense the father of the Arabs [namely through his son Ismaël] as well as of the Jews, and he lived before the *Torah* had been revealed to Moses and the Gospel to Jesus." [29]

In spite of the resemblances between the two religions, or even perhaps because of them, the attitude of Mohammed and Islam with regard to Judaism remained one of utter rejection. The process of bounding began already at a very early date, when, as related in Chapter II, Mohammed changed the direction of the praying from Jerusalem to Mecca and substituted the Friday for the Sabbath as the liturgical day. Abraham was appropriated for the new religion, when he was made into the founder of the Ka'aba, which he did with the assistance of his son Ismaël. [30] He even foretold the coming of the ultimate prophet in a prayer in which he said : "Lord, send among them an apostle of their own who shall rehearse your signs to them and instruct them in scripture and wisdom and sanctify them." [31]

The main Muslim objection to Judaism is that, whereas Abraham was a true prophet and an authentic Muslim, later Jewish sages distorted his message and steered it in a wrong direction; in consequence, Judaism no longer was a true religion. Jews disobey God's commands and do not understand that Abraham pointed to Mohammed; the Torah is said to have originally contained references to the Prophet, but that these had been deleted from it. "[Children of Israel,] cover not truth with falsehood, nor conceal the Truth when you know [what it is]." [32] They are roundly accused here of deliberate falsification. "The transgressors among them changed the word from that which had been given to them." [33]

The Jews could have known and should have known that the coming of Mohammed, "whom they found mentioned in their own [scriptures]" [34], was prophesied already by the *Torah*. This refers to Deut. 18:15, which verse says that "the Lord God will raise up for you a prophet among your midst, one of your brethrern, similar to me [Moses]." Jews and Christians interpret this as referring to the Messiah, but in the Koran it is thought to point to Mohammed. It is very wrong of Jews and Christians not to understand this. "So we [God] sent unto them a plague from heaven because they repeatedly transgressed." [35]

That the Jews are an obstinate people is also proved, says the Koran, by the fact that they have always disbelieved the prophets whom God sent to them. "If they [the Jews] reject you [Mohammed], so they rejected the apostles before you, who came with clear signs, books of dark prophecies and books of enlightenment [perhaps the biblical code of ethical behaviour is meant]." [36] It is base instincts that make the Jews oppose the Muslims. "Quite a number of the People of the Book [the Jews] wish they could turn you back to infidelity after you have believed, from selfish envy, after the Truth has become manifest to them [namely that Mohammed is the true prophet]." [37]

Enough to demonstrate what Mohammed felt about Judaism and Jews, but, as Watt remarks, "perhaps the trumpcard was that Jews and Christians denied one another's exclusive claims. The two claims were similar and therefore could not both be true." The Muslim standpoint was that "both went beyond what their revealed scriptures justified." [38]

12. Dualism?

Initially, the relations between Mohammed and the Medinan Jews were out-and-out dualistic, but later, after the Prophet's death, the relationship between the Muslims and the Jewish population became more relaxed. The Muslims had to accept the fact that not many Jews embraced Islam. One of the problems was that there were so many resemblances between the two religions; this forced the Muslims to draw a sharp distinction between them (the same problem that Christianity faced in its first centuries). God the Creator, heaven and hell, prophets and prayer, the weekly day of prayer, fasting and penance, the afterlife, and most of all, the idea of divine revelation, all these were elements common to both religions.

Was the attitude of early Islam towards Judaism and Jews dualistic? In my opinion it undoubtedly was. Mohammed accepted Judaism only as something *idealtypisch*, as something that did not really exist. He distinguished between an authentic message that had been given Abraham and Moses, and Judaism as a going concern; the Jewish religion as it stood was utterly wrong, he found. This implied, of course, that early Islam did not foster tender thoughts of Jewry. Mohammed deliberately destroyed the organized Jewish communities in and around Mecca and Medina, not without much bloodshed. His successors judged that they had better leave the Jews in peace; there were too many of them, they were hopeless cases, and when all was said and done, they paid handsome amounts of money through the poll-tax. However, this does not mean that they by any measure formed an integral part of the *umma*, the Islamic community.

13. Schoeps' opinion reconsidered

We are now in a position enabling us to clarify the point made by Schoeps, namely, that Islam preserved important impulses of Judaeo-Christianity. [39] What I am going to say applies to Judaism and Christianity alike. Both firmly, even vehemently, reject the proposition that Islam would be the true and only inheritor of their theological inheritance. Still less are they willing to hear that they are the unfaithful guardians of the message of Abraham, Moses, and Jesus. But things look very differently when we view them from a Muslim angle. It would be true what Abraham Katsh wrote, namely that "Muhammad never intended to establish Islam as a true religion. He considered himself the rightful custodian of the Book sent by Allah to 'confirm' the Scriptures. It is for this reason that in the beginning he saw no difference between Judaism and Christianity and believed that both Jews and Christians would welcome him."

If this is correct - as it doubtless is -, then we are justified in viewing early Islam as some sort of revitalized and renewed Judaeo-Christianity. Katsh adds that it was only later that Mohammed "realized that he could never gain support from either of them;" he then "presented Islam as a new faith." [40] I doubt, however, whether Mohammed ever saw his creed as a totally new faith. Not without good reason is he called 'the Seal of the Prophets', as the one in whom all the earlier prophecies, from Adam to Moses, are embodied. What he did was to reject Judaism and Christianity in so far as they had deviated from the original message, but to present, more faithfully than they were doing, their authenticity.

Schoeps also spoke of some of the more powerful impulses that Islam carried over into our own days. This must refer precisely to those elements that are common to both religions. These are, and they are constitutive of Islam indeed, monotheism, God the Creator, prophecy and prophets, fasting and penance, prayer and adoration, revelation and the Holy Book.

14. Mohammed and the Christians of Mecca and Medina

With Christians Mohammed himself did not experience the problems he had with Jews, this for the simple reason that there were so few Christians in Mecca, mainly persons of a low status, slaves for instance. There was no organized Christian community in that town. More Christians lived in Medina than in Mecca; this forced the Prophet to clarify his position regarding them. Mohammed was not unacquainted with the main tenets of the Christian creed, but he interpreted them in his own way.

15. Mohammed and Jesus

In Mohammed's view Jesus - Isa in the Koran - was an authentic prophet. His authenticity was apparent from the fact that he would have foretold the coming of Mohammed. "Jesus, the son of Mary, said : 'O Children of Israel! I am the apostle of God [sent] to you, confirming the Law [which came] before me [the *Torah*], and giving glad tidings of an apostle come after me whose name shall be Ahmad.' [41] Abraham and Jesus agree in this that they announced the coming of the Prophet. For with this Ahmad Mohammed is meant. However, it is unquestionable that Jesus never said something of this kind.

But Mohammed was also convinced that early Christianity had horribly distorted and falsified the original Jesus message. [42] Since Allah is absolutely one, he can have no son. Not being God's son, Jesus cannot be divine. In consequence there is also no Trinity. The Christian trinitarian dogma is blasphemous in Muslim opinion. Equally repellent to Muslims is the idea that Allah might have a *paredra*, as is the case in many pagan religions. "Christ Jesus, the son of Mary was [no more than] an apostle of God ... Say not 'three' (meaning the Trinity). Desist! It will be better for you [not to believe] in the Trinity, for God is One God. Glory be to him! Far exalted is he above having a son." [43] It is evident that the idea of God having a son diminishes him in Muslim eyes. [44]

This does not mean that Muslims would not respect and honour Isa-Jesus; they certainly do. In the Koran he is mentioned many times, with the result that all Muslims know of him. His name itself occurs twenty-five times, but when we also count his titles, there are some thirty-five mentions. [45] He is often called *Ibn Maryam*, son of Mary, while many titles are attached to his name : *Al-Masih* = Messiah (seven times), Servant, Prophet, Messenger, Word, Spirit, and others. [46] The title Messiah does not have the same weight as in Judaism and Christianity. "The Messiah, son of Mary, is nothing but a messenger." [47] As Parrinder states, "the negative side of this is a defence of the unity and transcendence of God. On the positive side it places the Messiah in the succession of messengers and prophets of the past, in fact as succeeding to Old Testament prophecy." [48] As 'prophet', *nabi*, Jesus is, with only one exception, always mentioned together with other prophets. [49]

16. Mohammed and Mary

It is remarkable that of the women mentioned in the Koran the only one who is given a name is Mary, the mother of Jesus. Parrinder says that her name is more often used in the Koran than in the New Testament, thirty-four times against nineteen. It should be added, however, that Mary's name is used twenty-three times in the combination 'Jesus, son of Mary'. She is never called 'the Virgin Mary'. [50]

We find the story of the Annunciation in the Koran, but not in the form it has in Luke. The name of the town where Mary lived, Nazareth, is not mentioned nor that of the divine being that appeared to her, in Luke Gabriel. He is said to have had 'the form of a human being, shapely', who said to Mary that she would become the mother of a boy (Luke spoke only 'what is born from you'). Mary objected that no man had ever touched her. The apparition replied that it was easy for the Lord, or, as in another *sura* : "God creates what he wills; when he decided upon a thing, he simply says 'Be", and it is." And the apparition went on to say : "O Mary, be obedient to the Lord, prostrate yourself, and bow with those who bow." [51] This means that she is told to behave as a Muslim woman.

Does the Koran teach the dogma of the virgin birth? This has always been a matter of dispute among Muslim exegetes. It is true that it is said in two places that "Mary guarded the chastity." [52], but this is also interpreted in the sense that she always remained faithful to her husband. Many modern Muslim scholars do not think that the virgin birth is taught by the Koran. But even if there would have been a virgin birth, this would not give Jesus a precedence over other prophets. In that case he would have had no earthly father, but Adam had neither an earthly father nor an earthly mother. Ibn Ishaq reports as a very early Muslim opinion that "if they [the Christians] say, Jesus was created without a man [intervening], I [God] created Adam from earth by that same power without a male or a female. And he was as Jesus was : flesh and blood and hair and skin. The creation of Jesus without a male is no more than this [53] ... Jesus in God's eyes is in the same position as

Adam." [54] Obviously precautions are taken that Jesus would not be more than Mohammed.

17. Jesus' life in the Koran

The story of Jesus' birth contains elements that are borrowed from apocryphal texts rather than from the canonical Gospels. Mary gave birth to her son not in a cave near Bethlehem but under a palm-tree in the desert. [55] The Koran possibly prefers this version because it transforms Jesus into a 'son of the desert', like the Arabs. The book gives him his full due as a miracle-worker, especially as a faith-healer of the sick and as somebody who restored the dead to life. Yet no mention is made of the nature miracles. "I shall heal the blind and the leprous and bring the dead to life." But here too some stories are plainly apocryphal. "I shall create for you from clay the form of a bird and I shall breath into it and it shall become a bird by the permission of God." [56]

Many important events and occurrences of Jesus' public life are not mentioned at all, in particular not the Last Supper. However, the crucifixion is referred to, although the relevant verses give rise to different interpretations. "Peace upon me [Jesus] the day of my birth, and the day of my death, and the day of my being raised up alive." [57] This text does not speak of a death on the cross, but does it speak of the resurrection? Maybe, but these words could also refer to the general resurrection at the end of time.

18. The Koran and the death of Jesus

The following is a very difficult Koran text. "So far their [the Jews'] violating their compact, and for their unbelief in the signs of God, their killing the prophets without justification, and their speaking against Mary a mighty slander, and for their saying : 'We killed the Messiah, Jesus, son of Mary, the messenger of God', though they did not kill him and did not crucify him, but he was counterfeited for them ... They did not certainly kill him." [58] This text has a definite anti-Judaistic colouring. Slander of Mary is mentioned nowhere in the New Testament, while the Jews would never have said 'we killed the Messiah', since they did not believe that Jesus was the Messiah.

The great problem is that, although the Jews claimed to have executed Jesus, they had not done so actually. "He was counterfeited." There are translations that make this somewhat less of a riddle, for instance : 'they did not cause his death on the cross', or 'only a likeness of that was shown to them'. [59] Parrinder states that "traditional Muslim interpretation has been that the Jews tried to kill Jesus but were unable to do so. "Perhaps somebody else died in his place." [60]

This reminds us of the Docetist position, which equally said that Jesus did not suffer death on the cross; they found the idea of the Son of God being crucified repellent. But who died in Jesus' place? Early Muslim authors suggest several substitutes, Judas, some other disciple, or Pilate, of all persons. [61] The Koran itself does not answer the question. There are also modern interpretations that say that not a substitute but Jesus himself died on the cross. It is brought forward that it was not the Jews who killed Jesus but the Romans. Jesus is viewed as the true 'abd, as the servant who was entirely obedient to God. [62]

The Koran nowhere says in as many words that Jesus rose from the grave and that he ascended to heaven. There is also nothing of his return at the end of times. He is clearly not an eschatological figure. It is important to note that, contrary to orthodox Christian opinion, Jesus' death on the cross is not given a redeeming value. It needs no argument that, if Mohammed is the Seal of the Prophets, the one who revealed the ultimate truth, Jesus cannot be the Redeemer of mankind. We should not forget that the Koran is not about Jesus, but about Mohammed's revealed teachings; Jesus finally has a subordinate position in Islam. He is a honoured person, adopted by Islam as an exceptional person worthy of veneration. Yet, at the same time, he is divested of almost all that is central to orthodox Christian teaching.

We should also not forget that it was Mohammed's opinion that the Christian Church had adulterated the original teachings of Jesus, just as Judaism was not what Abraham and Moses had taught. Jesus was by no means as important to Islam as Abraham who was considered the true founder of monotheism and the initiator of the Ka'aba cult. [63]

19. First encounters with Christians

The first encounters of some importance with Christians took place when Mohammed lived at Medina; the exact date is not known. A delegation from the Christian community at Najran came to visit the Prophet; Najran is situated in the south of Arabia, more than seven hundred kilometers from Medina. Mohammed's fame had already spread very far. The deputation consisted of seventy men on horseback, among them fourteen notables, one of these being the leader of the community and another their bishop, Abu Haritha, a very learned man and a favourite of the court in Constantinople. They were all richly attired. Having entered Medina at the time of the afternoon prayer, they went to the mosque and prayed there, facing east, with the Prophet's consent. They are described as Christians of the Byzantine rite, "though they differed among themselves in some points."

Two of the leaders had a conversation with Mohammed. The Prophet asked them to accept Islam to which they answered that they had done so long ago. What they insinuated was not that they had already become Muslims in Najran but that Islam was in fact an epiphenomenon of Christianity. This nettled Mohammed of course, and he said : "You lie. Your assertion that God has a son, your worship of the cross, and your eating pork hold you back from submission [to Islam]." Thus the discussion had hardly begun when the main points of disagreement were already stressed.

The rest of the argument was about the status of Jesus and seems to have run along the lines to be found in the first eighty verses of the third *sura*. The Prophet argued that Jesus could not possibly be the Son of God, since God is eternally living, whereas Jesus died a human death on the cross. How could God ever have been a child? Mary carried him in her womb as all mothers do; her son had to eat and drink as every other person. "How can it be then as you said? Whereupon the Christians were silent." Dikken rightly concludes that "here the conviction of the Christians that Jesus is the Son of

God is the great obstacle for Muhammad." [64] The divergence of opinion proved to be insuperable. Other ancient Muslim traditions confirm this.

The German scholar Schumann makes a very apt remark with respect to Mohammed's idea of Jesus. "He could not comprehend that a man, who is *per definitionem* a created being, would participate in the godhead ... He was rather concerned to present the invincible distance between God and man that could not be bridged by any mediator. God is the One and Only and stands opposite the creation and all that is in it, as the Creator and Lord." Every attempt to diminish this distance was the sheerest disbelief in his eyes. [65]

20. Mohammed's attitude towards Christians

At first Mohammed's attitude towards Christians in Mecca and Medina was tolerant. This tolerance also extended to the important Christian community at Najran. Mohammed agreed to leave them in peace, if only they paid him two thousand pieces of clothing each year - obviously the earliest form of the *jizya*. They had also to assist him in his wars, not with soldiers, but with armour and mounts. In recompense they would enjoy the Prophet's protection. [66]

The policy of tolerance had its limits. The Arabian chronicler Wahidi relates how a Medinan Christian said that the mu'addhin (the man who announced the hour of prayer) who cried aloud that Mohammed was the messenger of Allah, was a liar who should be burnt. Instead, he and his family were burnt, when his house was set alight during the night. [67] The Koran commands : "Fight those who believe not in God nor the Last Day." In case one thinks that this does not refer to Jews and Christians, because they believe in God, it is added : "Nor acknowledge the Religion of Truth, [even if they are] the People of the Book, until they pay the *jizya* with willing submission and feel themselves subdued." [68] In accordance with this, the second caliph, Umar I, expelled all Christians who were not ready to pay the *jizya* from Arabia; they emigrated to Syria and Iraq. 'Submission, subdued', these are the key-words here that prove that Muslim-Christian relationship was dualistic.

21. The effects of islamization

One question still remains. Why did the majority of the Christians in the countries of the Middle East and North Africa that came under Muslim rule in the centuries after Mohammed's death convert to Islam? Not immediately, not all together, but in the course of time, most of them became Muslims. I spoke of the Middle East and North Africa, because in Spain and Portugal, countries that were under Muslim rule for some centuries, there was no general trend. The same applies to the Balkans, which were under Turkish rule for a long time, but much later, from the thirteenth century onward, although many Muslims live in Albania, Kosovo, Serbia, Montenegro, Bosnia, Croatia, Macedonia, and Bulgaria, but not in Greece and Slovenia. [69] It is also true that there were, and still are, pockets of Christianity in the Middle East; there are even Christian Arabs. Ten percent of the Egyptian population are Coptic (Monophysite) Christians; one may also think of the (non-Christian) Mandaeans in southern Iraq. [70]

The question is all the more pressing since the Christians were not forced to convert with a knife at their throats. The official policy was, as I wrote already, to leave them in peace as long they paid the *jizya*. Every-day reality, however, did not always concur with the lines of official policy. The taxes paid by the Christians, mainly the *jizya*, were always higher than those asked from the Muslims; those who converted to Islam became financially better off. Many did not resist this temptation. Jews and Christians often had to suffer from the rapacity of Muslim soldiers, while they themselves were forbidden to carry arms. Officially non-Muslims were not allowed to fulfil public functions, but since the rulers were often short of capable personnel, infidels were sometimes appointed to important functions. However, they were liable to be fired at any moment. Sometimes government employees embraced Islam in order to keep their posts. In lawsuits non-Muslims were not allowed to testify against a Muslim; a Muslim could not be condemned to death because of an offense committed against a *dhimmi*. The gravest crime an infidel could commit was blaspheming the Prophet; the culprit could only escape capital punishment by converting to Islam.

There were restrictions on the freedom of religion. Erecting new churches, monasteries, and synagogues was forbidden. Existing buildings were not always spared brutal attacks so that many of them looked poor and delapidated. Entering a mosque was strictly fordbidden to Jews and Christians; this was punishable by death. It goes without saying that no Jew or Christian was ever allowed to set a foot on the hallowed ground of the *haram* at Mecca where the Ka'aba stood; might such a person be discovered there, his fate was not to be envied. Showing religious objects, such as crosses and icons, outside the temples, was strictly forbidden, while the sounds of the cult should not be heard beyond their walls. The peace of Jewish and Christian cemeteries was not always respected. Although the Koran does not permit forced conversions, there are many instances where they occurred. It also happened that Jews and Christians were simply massacred.

In many places the *dhimmi* were deliberately humiliated. They might, for instance, not employ Muslim servants nor were they allowed to possess such noble animals as camels and horses. There were cities where Jews were not permitted to enter Muslim quarters. Often the infidels were subjected to special rules regarding their exterior and clothing; Christians had to shave their foreheads. There can be no doubt that the *dhimmi* were the victims of disdain and oppression; in the eyes of a Muslim they could never be his equals. [71]

This general climate of repression, humiliation, and segregation was, of course, an important cause of defection. The Jews too were the victims of oppressive measures, but on the whole they withstood the urge to become Muslims successfully. The reason for this is that they lived in closely knit communities, bound together by strong family ties, and sustained by their own peculiar habits and way of living. The knowledge that their religion was so much older than Islam may also have played a part. It is also important that their community was an ethnic one, different from the Arabs and all other peoples among whom they lived. But Christianity almost totally disappeared from the countries where it had begun its existence and which in the course of the first six centuries had been successfully christianized.

I feel that the main reason for the fairly general apostasy must be sought in the christological and other theological battles that had been fought in the first centuries and that had raged, often with fanatical fierceness, in exactly those countries where the Muslim religion later triumphed. These struggles were amply recorded in my Volume XIII. Judaism did not experience a similar divergence of opinion. Many Christians must have become weary of the interminable squabbles, of all those councils and synods, of the condemnations and excommunications, of the solemn statements and the banishments, of the often vitriolic polemics. Even if they did not read the tractates and the pamphlets, they heard what was going on in often vehemently partisan sermons.

Numerous Christians will have seen in Islam the best solution to their problems. It claimed to combine the best of Judaism and Christianity. And, compared to the Christian creed, it is a simple one without such difficult doctrines of the three-in-one of the Trinity, of the God-man Jesus Christ - wholly God and wholly man -, of the virgin birth - Jesus born without male intervention -, and of a death on the cross through which all mankind was redeemed. Finding themselves in a far from enviable social position, many Christians were incapable of withstanding the lure of a religion that was as promising as it was powerful.

NOTES TO CHAPTER IX

1. Schoeps, *Theologie und Geschichte des Judenchristentums* 342.
2. Adang, *Muslim writers on Judaism* 196, note 23.
3. *Sura* 6.82.
4. Geiger, *Was hat Mohammed aus dem Judenthume aufgenommen?* 15/16.
5. *Sura* 6.67.
6. Geiger, *Was hat Mohammed aus dem Judnethume aufgenommen?* 13.
7. *Sura* 2.71.

8. Quoted from Ibn Hisham by Hamidullah, *Le Prophète de l'Islam* I, 382.
9. This story is told by Ibn Hisham, quoted by Hamidullah, *Le Prophète de l'Islam* 382.
10. Related by Ibn Hisham, quoted by Hamidullah, *Le Prophète de l'Islam* 382/383.
11. Ibn Ishaq, *The Life of Muhammad* 568/569, ed. Guillaume 363.
12. Dikken, *Muhammad, Jews and Christians* 55-57. See for a general overview of Muslim-Jewish relations in this period Jansen, *Early History and Background of the Jews of Islam*, in *Jews and Islam* (see Bibliography). Also Wensinck, *Mohammed en de Joden te Medina* (see Bibliography).
13. Ibn Ishaq, *The Life of Muhammad* 657, ed. Guillaume 440.
14. Related by Ibn Hisham, quoted by *Hamidullah,* Le Prophète de l'Islam 385.
15. Ibn Ishaq, *The Life of Muhammad* 652-661, ed. Guillaume 437-445.
16. Watt, *Muhammad at Medina* 213.
17. Watt, *Muhammad at Medina* 214.
18. Ibn Ishaq, *The Life of Muhammad* 684-693, ed. Guillaume 461-466.
19. Watt, *Muhammad at Medina* 215.
20. Watt, *Muhammad at Medina* 328.
21. Watt, *Muhammad at Mmedina* 217.
22. Ibn Ishaq, *The Life of Muhammad* 745-776, ed. Guillaume 510-523.
23. Cl. Cahen s.v. 'dzjiya', *Enc. of Islam* II.
24. *Sura* 9.29.
25. Cl. Cahen s.v. 'Dhimma', Enc. of Islam II (1965); Jansen, *Early History and Background of the Jews of Islam*, in *Jews under Islam* 15-19.
26. Hayek, *Le mystère d'Ismaël* 160 : "Fidèle à lui-même et à sa doctrine Mahomet a projeté rétrospectivement sur son ancêtre [Abraham] ses propres convictions religieuses ses préoccupations cultuelles. Ayant conscience de récupérer la vocation des prophètes antérieurs et de prolonger leur message, il découvre dans sa propre vie les grands épisodes de la leur ... De ceux-là Abraham fut le modèle par excellence dont il a voulu être l'exacte réproduction."
27. *Sura* 3.67.
28. *Sura* 3.68.

29. Watt, *Mohammed at Medina* 205; for the resemblances between the two religions see Geiger, *Was hat Mohammed aus dem Judenthume aufgenommen?* 93 sqq.
30. Sura 2.127.
31. Sura 2.129.
32. Sura 2.42.
33. Sura 7.161.
34. Sura 2.157.
35. Sura 2.162.
36. Sura 3.184.
37. Sura 2.109.
38. Watt, *Muhammad at Medina* 208.
39. Thirty-two years after Schoeps, the controversial author Lüling, *Die Wiederentdeckung des Propheten Muhammad* 223, adopted Schoeps's thesis : "Das theologische Denken und Wirken des Propheten Muhammad ist zweifelsfrei die ungebrochene Fortsetzung einer ur- und judenchristlichen Tradition, also eine Tradition die weder christlich im abendländischen Sinne [= hellenistisch-christlich] noch jüdisch gewesen ist."
40. Katsh, *Judaism in Islam* XVII.
41. Sura 61.6.
42. The afore mentioned scholar Lüling, *Die Wiederentdeckung des Propheten Muhammad* 21, is definitely at one with Mohammed; he speaks of 'das erkennbare Recht des Propheten Muhammad in seiner Verteidigung urchristlicher Theologie gegenüber dem hellenistisch-christlichen Dogma des Abendlandes' and of 'die Fehlentwicklung des hellenistisch-christlichen Dogmas'. In his opinion Mohammed's fight was essentially a fight against 'das hellenistische Christentum'.
43. Sura 4.171.
44. As remarked earlier, Muslims suspect, or even accuse, Christians of having three gods. Schedl, *Muhammad und Jesus* 471, points to an Alexandrinian theologian, who was Mohammed's contemporary (he died ca. 600), Johannes Philoponos. This author held that there were really three gods, Father, Son, and Holy Ghost; his system is called 'tritheism'. There was a Syrian translation of his *oeuvre*. It could be that some of this was known among the Arabs. If it had reached Mohammed's ears, it could have fortified him in his opinion that the Christians were wrong.
45. All the places are given by Parrinder, *Jesus in the Qur'an* 18-20.

46. Parrinder, *Jesus in the Qur'an*, Ch. 4.
47. *Sura* 5.79.
48. Parrinder, *Jesus in the Qur'an* 30.
49. Parrinder, *Jesus in the Qur'an* 37.
50. Parrinder, *Jesus in the Qur'an* 60.
51. *Sura* 19.17-21 and 3.38-42.
52. *Sura* 21.91 and 66.12.
53. Ibn Ishaq, *The Life of Muhammad* 409, ed. Guillaume 276/277.
54. *Sura* 3.52.
55. *Sura* 19.23-26.
56. *Sura* 3.43
57. *Sura* 19.34.
58. *Sura* 4.154-156.
59. Parrinder, *Jesus in the Qur'an* 108/109.
60. Parrinder, *Jesus in the Qur'an* 109.
61. Parrinder, *Jesus in the Qur'an* 111.
62. Parrinder, *Jesus in the Qur'an* 121.
63. Schumann, *Der Christus der Muslime* 25.
64. Ibn Ishaq, *The Life of Muhammad* 401-405, ed. Guillaume 270-273; literal texts from sources also in Dikken, *Muhammad, Jews, and Christians* 97-99; quotation on p. 99.
65. Schumann, *Der Christus der Muslime* 28.
66. Dikken, *Muhammad, Jews, and Christians* 105/106.
67. Quoted by Dikken, *Muhammad, Jews, and Christians* 110.
68. *Sura* 9.29.
69. Nobody knows how many Muslims there still are in Serbia, Croatia, and Bosnia, since in 1991 the period of 'ethnic cleansing' began that led to the death of thousands and thousands of Muslims, mainly men, and to large-scale deportations.
70. This is another threatened group. The marshes of southern Iraq where they live are being drained which deprive these people who live from boat building and fishing of their livelihood; many of them have emigrated to Iran.
71. Ye'or, *Le dhimmi* 71.

CHAPTER XI

'RELIGIOUS IMPERIALISM'

1. Muslim imperialism

Some scholar - I cannot remember which - said that Islam knows three inequalities : between men and women, between masters and slaves, and between Muslims and infidels. As the foregoing chapter doubtless will have illustrated, non-Muslims were definitely held in low regard in Muslim opinion. As far as Muslim power would reach - and in principle there was no limit to it - disbelievers needed to be subjected to Muslim rule and, if possible, be converted. In practice, their countries had to be conquered with sword in hand. This meant that non-Muslim political communities were denied the right to independent political existence; they could exsist only under the *aegis* of Islam. In this context we can speak of 'religious imperialism'. [1] All forms of imperialism are dualistic, religious imperialism as much as any other.

2. The Holy War concept

This Muslim imperialism is closely linked to a well-known Islamic concept, that of Holy War. Since this is surrounded by many misunderstandings, we must proceed very cautiously. [2] Professor Johnson, who is an expert on these matters, lists ten meanings associated with Holy War; these demonstrate that this concept is by no means restricted to Islam alone. 1. Holy War is fought at God's command. As such it was fought in ancient Israel, during the Crusades - *Dieu le veult!* -, and by the English Puritans in the seventeenth century. 2. It is fought on God's behalf by his duly authorized representative. One could think here of the Pope authorizing the Crusades. 3. It is fought by God himself. In this way it is presented by the prophets of the Old Testament.

4. It is waged to defend religion against its enemies, within and without. This was and is a common idea in Jewish, Christian, and Islamic traditions. 5. It is waged to propagate correct religion or to establish a social order in line with divine authority. This idea is not found as often as the latter one. 6. It is waged to enforce religious conformity and/or to punish deviation. This was, for instance, the *ratio* for the crusade against the Albigensians. 7. It is a war in which the participants are themselves ritually and/or morally 'holy', for instance, by abstaining from sexual intercourse during a campaign. 8. It may also be understood as an inner struggle to lead the good life. 9. It is a war under religiously inspired (charismatic) leadership. One could think here of the Mahdi revolt in the Sudan (1881-1885). 10. It is a phenomenon recognized during and after the fact as an 'absolute miracle'. Instances are the surprising victories of small Jewish forces led by the Maccabees, over much larger Syrian armies. [3]

Neither Jews nor Christians fight Holy Wars any longer. The last wars of this kind were the wars of religion in the seventeenth century; since then the very idea has become repellent to the western mind. However, many armed conflicts since then resemble a secularized Holy War, for instance the struggle against Nazism and the Third Reich during the World War II. Not without reason did General Eisenhower, the supreme commander of the Allied forces in Western Europe, give his memoirs of this period the title of 'Crusade in Europe'.

3. The 'two worlds'

Christian and Islamic traditions make a decisive, even dualistic difference between two worlds, 'one ordered toward God and the other not'. Whereas in Christian thought, for example in Saint Augustine, the distinction is of a theological nature, in Islamic thinking it is juridical. Two spheres are distinguished. The first is the *dar al-Islam*; this is the world of Islam where things are ordered as God wills them, so that peace prevails there. The second is the *dar al-harb*, the territory of war. In this sphere war, conflict, strife is the normal situation, internally and externally, very much contrary to God's will.

The *dar al-harb thus* has to be subjected and turned into the *dar al-Islam*. This is the sacred duty of all Muslims as an essential element of their obedience to Allah. Is there a limit to the extension of the dar al-Islam? There is not! Or maybe its limit should be the very frontiers of the earth, for the final aim is the establishment of the universal reign of peace. [4] It should be noted that Islam is not only a religion but also, and by the same token, a socio-political community, the *umma*, with political aims and employing political and military means. [5]

There is a fundamental distinction between medieval Islamic and Christian conceptions in this field. The *civitas Dei*, the City of God - the term goes back on Saint Augustine, of course - is something ideal, never to be fully realized on earth; it is an adumbration of what exists in heaven. Not even the Church, imperfect as it is in its terrestrial form, is this *civitas*. Still less is it any political community. Political or military means cannot bring it about. It can be realized by grace only, by the spiritual transformation of individual Christians that may lead to a less imperfect society. The history of the *civitas Dei* is, therefore, not a history of power and conquest but of salvation.

In Islamic thought, however, the distinction between the two spheres is not of a theological but of a juridical nature. What is to be brought about is a situation of "right behavior rather than right motivation; it defined the world in terms of control of territory rather than the invisible progress of divine grace, and it defined membership in the two spheres by behavior (submission to God's will, *islam*, whether or not this was accompanied by faith, *iman*) and not the invisible presence of divine grace." [6] In practice, the basic Muslim concept of the all-comprising *umma* has proved to be just as *idealtypisch* as the Christian idea of the *civitas Dei*. It was considered a sign of hopeless imperfection that the non-Muslim world was and is divided into several states. But soon enough there was no longer the one *umma*; Islam too has its separate states.

One final remark is necessary before we embark on the history of the Arab conquests. The Arab word for Holy War is *jihad*; those who fight in it are called *mujahidum*. *Jihad*, however, has two meanings, the first being that of fighting for Islam arms in hand; the other is that of 'striving in the path of

God', i.e. of attempting to be a good Muslim. Not wanting to be seen as aggressive and belligerent, many modern Muslims prefer this second meaning. [7]

4. Mohammed's struggle with the Meccans

One should realize that Mohammed's position in Medina was an isolated one, the rest of the Arab world looking with less than friendly eyes on his movement. Even the transformation of Medina itself into a Muslim bulwark had proved a hard task. Soon the Prophet, the religious leader, began acting as a warlord. The first feats of arms were razzias during which caravans were plundered, mainly under the leadership of Abu Bekr. These razzias served three aims : enhancing the Prophet's prestige, ameliorating the economic situation of the Muslim community of Medina, and cementing together the Meccan immigrants and the native Medinan Muslims through their common exploits.

One of these razzias led to the first pitched battle the Muslims fought; it took place in March 624 under the command of the Prophet himself. The Medinans had got wind of a rich Syrian caravan coming from Gaza that was heading towards Mecca. Mohammed assembled a force of three hundred volunteers to attack it, but the caravan leaders were informed of the preparations and began travelling along the coast. A courier was dispatched to Mecca, so that when Mohammed intercepted the caravan near Badr, on the coast to the south-west of Medina, he saw himself confronted with an army of some nine hundred to a thousand Meccan warriors. He had some difficulty in persuading his own men to begin the fight, but when they obeyed, they could celebrate a resounding victory. The Meccans were completely routed; their losses were considerable. But there arose much wrangling over the booty. [8]

Chafing under the defeat, the Meccans brooded on revenge, the more so because the razzias continued. They prepared the next encounter by concluding an alliance with the men of the Ta'if oasis and with some Bedouin tribes. In this way they were able to raise a force of three thousand men with as many camels and seven hundred horses. In January 627, they marched out and, circumventing Medina, chose a position near the mountain Ochod to the north of the oasis, although close to it. Instead of awaiting the attack in Medina, Mohammed marched out and joined battle with the superior forces of the enemy. This time the Muslims were beaten, and Mohammed was slightly wounded. The victor did not attack Medina, but returned.

At this juncture, the issue between Medina and Mecca was still undecided. The Meccans succeeded in mobilizing an enormous force of some ten thousand men. They appeared like lightning near Medina in March 627. Mohammed did not have much time to preparing a defence; he only had three thousand warriors at his disposal. Because the northern flank of the oasis lay entirely open, he had it covered by a broad trench. Hence the name of the ensuing battle, the 'Battle of the Ditch' (the *khandaq*). There was, however, hardly a battle, only a series of skirmishes. It proved impossible for the Meccans to cross the ditch. Tired and hungry they departed. The Battle of the Ditch led to the destruction of the Qurayzah Jews who were accused of having made common cause with the aggressors.

Somewhat later, in May 628, Mohammed captured, as related already in Chapter IV, Khaibar, to the north of Medina, and expelled the Jews from there. Still more to the north lay the oasis of Fadak, which surrendered peacefully to the Muslims. A considerable part of the Hedjaz was in their hands now, but the Prophet's real goal was the conquest of Mecca, or rather the possession of the Ka'ba. A second, more distant goal was the conquest of the whole of Arabia in order to stamp out all paganism in the peninsula.

After protracted negotiations with the pagan Meccans, Mohammed was allowed to make the pilgrimage, the *umra*, to the holy places. Seven years after he had left it, in 629, he entered his native city again to stay there for three days unmolested by the pagans. He performed all of the customary rites; the Meccans, who had probably been led to believe that he had become an enemy of religion, were much edified by his pious behaviour. Two influential Meccans, Khalid ibn al-Walid, the general who had won the battle of Ochod, and Umayyah 'Amr ibn al-'As, who was to become governor of Egypt, went to Medina once the Prophet had returned there and made their profession of faith to him. Khalid put his soldierly prowess at the disposal of the Muslims and came to be called 'the Sword of Islam'.

The position of his Meccan adversaries having been much weakened now, Mohammed did not need much of a pretext to submit the holy city to his control. An incident between Bedouins who were his allies and some Meccans provided him with the ideal opportunity. In the beginning of 630 the Prophet left Medina with an army of ten thousand Medinans and Bedouins, the greatest force he had levied so far. On their way south, they were joined by a crowd of armed Meccans, led by Mohammed's uncle 'Abbas, once his fiercest opponent. When they pitched camp at the outskirts of the city, the leader of the pagan opposition came and converted to Islam. He presented the keys of the city to Mohammed. There was only a short skirmish before he could triumphantly enter Mecca. The conquest did not occur without bloodshed : Khalid had twenty-eight people killed, while four others were executed on the orders of the Prophet himself, two of them being single females, who had sung songs mocking him.

The Prophet was acknowledged as the ruler of the city he had fled as a fugitive in 622. Most of the inhabitants adopted the new faith. Mohammed used his newly won power first and foremost to cleanse the town of all idolatry. The three hundred and sixty idols in the Ka'aba were smashed to the ground; only the Black Stone was spared. Then he rode around the sanctuary seven times, each time passing the Black Stone and touching it with his staff.

5. The capture of Ta'if

Mohammed remained in his native town for no longer than two weeks since there was more fighting to be done. The inhabitants of Ta'if, the town to the south-west of Mecca, that had once shown him the door, had concluded an alliance with Bedouin tribes in the Najd, enabling the enemies of Islam to muster a force of thirty thousand men. A Muslim army of twelve thousand met them in the Valley of Hernayn, between Ta'if and Mecca; it was commanded by the Prophet in person, riding on a white mule. The Muslim army came on the brink of defeat; Mohammed himself barely escaped death,

VII ARAB CONQUESTS 632-732

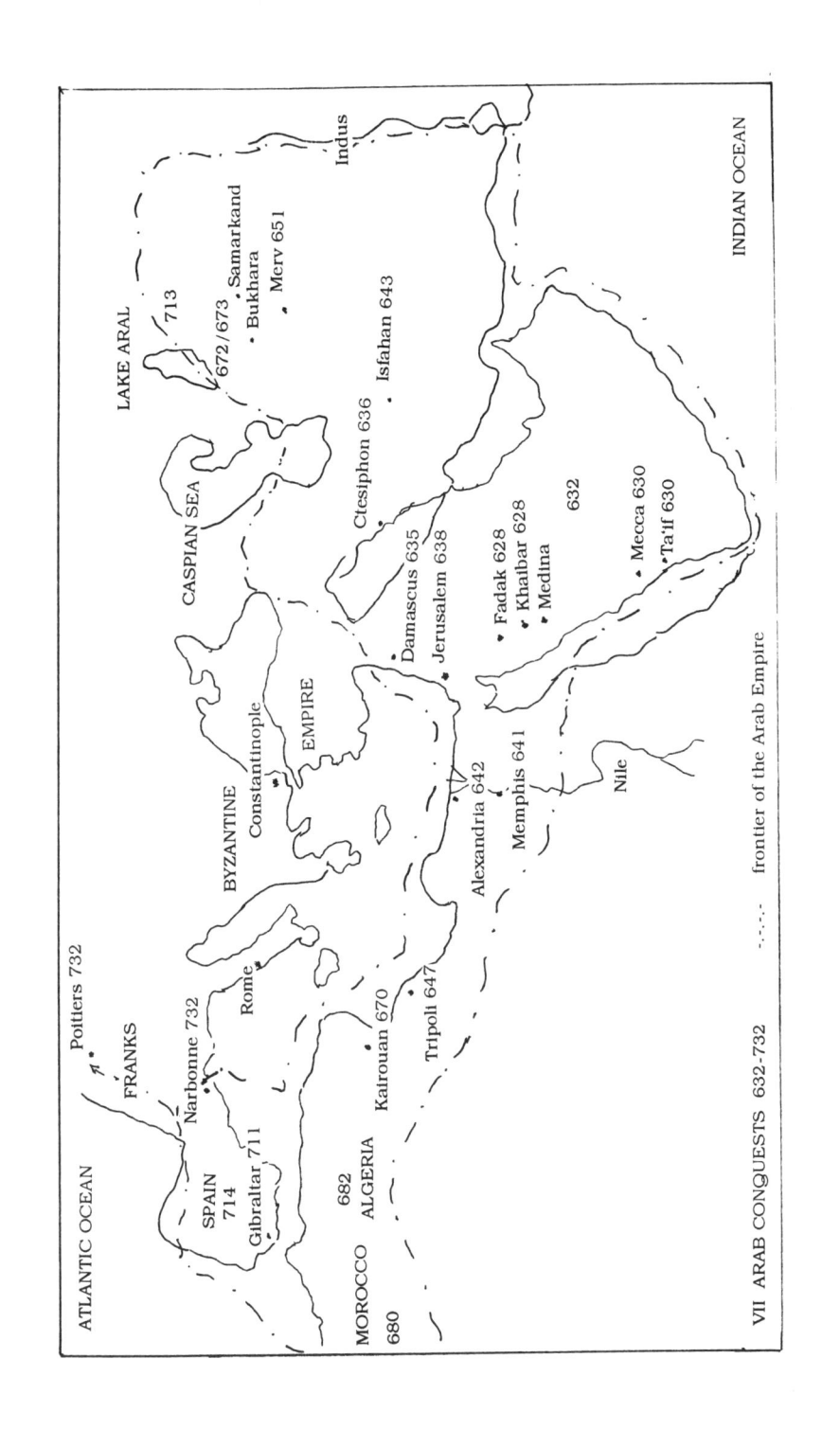

- Atlantic Ocean
- Poitiers 732
- Franks
- Narbonne 732
- Rome
- Spain 714
- Gibraltar 711
- Morocco 680
- Algeria 682
- Kairouan 670
- Tripoli 647
- Byzantine Empire
- Constantinople
- Alexandria 642
- Memphis 641
- Nile
- Caspian Sea
- Lake Aral
- 672/673
- 713
- Samarkand
- Bukhara
- Merv 651
- Ctesiphon 636
- Isfahan 643
- Damascus 635
- Jerusalem 638
- Fadak 628
- Khaibar 628
- Medina
- 632
- Mecca 630
- Ta'if 630
- Indus
- Indian Ocean

-·-·-· frontier of the Arab Empire

while several companions were killed at his side. Finally, victory was won after which there was much slaughter of defeated and flying enemies.

Ta'if was besieged and captured; the booty was enormous. Its inhabitants converted to Islam, but not all of them of their own free will. A large part of western Arabia was under Muslim control now, namely the region stretching from Fadak in the north to Najran in the south (the Christian community of Najran steadfastly refused to abandon its faith.)

6. Byzantine nervousness

It needs no argument that the Byzantines began to feel somewhat nervous; a new power was arising on the frontiers of Egypt, Palestine, and Syria, countries they had only recently reconquered from the Persians. [9] The governor of Egypt, Cyrus, attempted to assuage the belligerent impulses of the Prophet by sending him, along with more gifts, two beautiful slave girls; he must, writes Brockelmann, "have been well informed concerning his tastes." The sixty-year old Prophet kept one of them for himself and presented the other to his court poet. [10]

The first armed conflict between the Muslims and a Byzantine force ended disastrously. On the Byzantine-Arab frontier in Palestine, an Arab courier was taken prisoner by the Byzantines and killed. This happened in 629. Mohammed sent a contingent of three thousand men northward under the command of his adopted son Zaid. The Byzantines, however, reacted quickly; pushing deeply into Arabian territory, they engaged the Muslims north of Medina. The Muslims gained the victory. A new Byzantine army raided the whole coast until the extreme south-western tip of Arabia. Zaid pursued them but was defeated and killed; Khalid led the disheartened forces back to Medina. These were the first military encounters between Muslims and Christians; they would face each other in battle for many centuries to come.

7. Mohammed's death causes a crisis

Mohammed would not have been a true Arab, if he had not planned new raids. In the glaring summer heat of 630 he marched north with thirty thousand men, but got no farther than the oasis of Tabuk in the most north-westerly region of Arabia. He no longer had his old vigour. He felt unable to harass the Byzantines as his intention was, but could accept the submission of many Jewish and Christian communities in the north of the peninsula; they were all forced to pay the *jizya*, because they, with a few exceptions, failed to embrace Islam. The indefatigable Khalid brought about the subjugation of numerous pagan tribes of Bedouins in the boundless desert. The Prophet was planning a new campaign against the Byzantines, when he died, probably of malaria, in Medina on July 7th, 632.

The Prophet's death resulted in a dangerous crisis. Many important Bedouin tribes rose in revolt against the Muslims. They did not want the Muslims levying taxes on them, and having always cherished their independence, they chafed at the rule of the Medinans whom they did not love. The new leader of Islam became Abu Bekr, Mohammed's father-in-law; he is called the *khalifah*, the successor or 'caliph', combining the religious, political, and military leadership in his person. The task of beating down the rebellions was entrusted to Khalid who performed it with his usual thoroughness and unscrupulousness. On both sides there were bloody losses. After heavy fighting Arabia fell once again under the control of the Muslims in 633. There was one exception : Oman, the region at the south-eastern tip of the peninsula, remained independent; even today it does not form part either of Saudi Arabia or the United Arab Emirates along the coast of the Persian Gulf.

8. Arabian unity

Gaudefroy-Demombynes lists the reasons why, all counted, it had been not so hard to unite all Arabs under the green banner of the Prophet. It is true that there were separatist movements, while Medinan rule was not very popular with the Bedouins of the desert. However, the divisions among their tribes had been too great to present a common front against Islam. Soon enough they came to realize the great advantages that Arab unity had for them : boons of a material kind, especially a share in the booty, solidarity as a result of having a common war-aim, the continuation of their age-old existence as marauders, and the great victories that were to be won. [11]

9. War on two fronts

According to Muslim opinion, the Bedouin rising was only an incident. The dominating idea was that the world outside Arabia, with its Jewish, Christian, and pagan populations, had to be brought under the green banner of Islam. Leading the Muslim forces beyond the boundaries of the homeland would have the additional advantage of depriving the warlike Bedouins of the chance to cut one another's throats. For the time being the Byzantine Empire had proved too strong, but perhaps its eternal rival, the Persian Empire, offered a better opportunity for extending Muslim power. Khalid discovered how weak it had become when he was able to conquer Hirah, a frontier town on the Middle Euphrates, in 633. But it did not yet prove possible to penetrate beyond the river into Babylonia, the more so because Khalid was transferred to the Syrian front. In 634 Abu Bekr decided to wage war in Syria. Yet the war against Persia had also to continue on, which meant that the Muslims were attacking two Empires simultaneously. This demonstrated that they must have possessed a very great faith in their own cause and an extremely solid self-reliance. On the other hand, it may be asked whether they had had the intention to conquer both Empires right from the start.

In the spring of 634, two Arab armies attacked Palestine, one in the south, the other more to the north. The Byzantines were slow in reacting, but when they came they stopped the advance of the southern army. Khalid, however, arrived in time from the region of Hirah to defeat the Byzantines in the Battle of Ajnadayn. [12] The Arab commander, who had made a daring crossing of the swollen river Jordan, pushed his enemy northward towards Damascus, defeating the Byzantines again, laying siege to the city, and capturing it in September 635. This is the first really important Muslim conquest outside of Arabia. The Byzantines mounted an enormous counter-offensive, but their army was crushingly defeated just south of Lake Tiberias at the river Yarmuk (now the frontier between the Israel occupied part of Palestine and Jordan.) The battle took place on August 20th, 636.

10. The Persians lose their capital

Simultaneously the offensive against Persia gathered momentum. The man behind it was the second caliph, Umar I. Abu Bekr having died in July 634, the energetic Umar succeeded him (634-644). He is considered to be the real founder of the Muslim Empire. Immediately he sent reinforcements to the Euphrates front. The Arabs crossed the river on a pontoon bridge, only to be defeated by a Persian army. Their belief in their own invincibility was so unshakeable that they had already begun to demolish the bridge; for this reason it was difficult for the vanquished detachments to reach the safe side.

Much encouraged by this success, the Persians approached in June 636 under their supreme commander, Rustam. In a long and confused battle near Kufa the Persians suffered a bloody defeat and retreated eastward through Babylonia. Although the Arabs had also had severe losses, they followed their enemy and occupied Babylonia. They then crossed the Tigris and occupied the Persian capital Ctesiphon without having met serious resistance. This was the second great triumph of the Muslims. The booty was enormous. Soon enough a mosque was built, the first in non-Arab territory. The Muslims were there to stay!

The new Persian capital became Hulwan, in the region where the passes through the Zagros Mountains begin. Here the Persian Emperor Yezdegerd III, the grandson of Chosroes II, assembled a new army, calling up reinforcements from all over his territory. However at the end of 637 an Arab army defeated it in the valley of the river Diyala, north of Ctesiphon. The Persians realized that they would never return to their capital.

11. Jerusalem in Muslim hands

Returning now to Syria, we bear witness to caliph Umar arriving in 637 at Jabiya, south of Damascus. A great army assembly took place there, called the 'Day of Jabiya', with as its most important result that all those who took part in the campaigns would have their share in the proceeds of the conquered territories - a powerful incentive for Arab warriors! From Jabiya Umar sent an army to the south, which invested Jerusalem and after an incredibly short siege took it in 638 - the third great Muslim prize in no more than three years. The Christians were left in peace following payment of the *jizya*. Umar came in person, had the rock on which the Temple once stood purified, and prayed there. To this day the site remains in Muslim hands. Soon enough the great Mosque of Umar would arise on it. For Jews and Christians alike the fall of the Holy City was a dramatic loss.

From Syria, now firmly in Muslim hands, the Arabs staged an offensive against Assyria, the northern part of Mesoptamia; the campaign lasted only one and a half year during which all the Byzantine strongholds were captured (639-641).

12. Egypt conquered

The Byzantine Empire had already suffered irreparable losses - Assyria, Syria, and Palestine -, when it was Egypt's turn. The attack, starting from southern Palestine, began in December 639. Its first result was the capture of the old frontier fortress of Pelusium. Disorderly marauding Muslims even reached the Nile. In June 640, the Arabs defeated the Byzantines at Heliopolis, at the southern tip of the Delta. On Easter Monday, April 9th, 641, the Muslims entered the ancient capital of the Pharaohs, Memphis. Having by then lost all hopes of being able to keep Egypt, the Byzantines peacefully surrendered their own capital Alexandria to the Muslims on September 17th, 642 - their fourth great prize! [13] A mosque was built in the army camp near Fustat, the first with some sort of minarets; it is the Mosque of 'Amr, which now forms part of Old Cairo.

13. The end of the Sasanian Empire

In Persia the court left Hulwan, its position having become hopeless, and retreated eastward in 640. A large Muslim army followed the Persians on their heels and penetrated into Persis, their ancient heartland. In 642 they defeated their adversaries near Nihawend in a battle lasting several days. In 643 the victors appeared in Isfahan. Always fleeing eastward, Yezdegerd hoped to stage a last desperate stand in the extreme north-east of his realm. But the tribes there judged the situation hopeless and did not give him any help. Finally, the unfortunate ruler reached Merv, only to find its gates closed to him. The last Sasanian ruler found a refuge in a hospitable mill, but one of his satraps had him murdered there in 651. Who is not reminded here of the fate that befell, a thousand years earlier, another Persian ruler, Darius III Codomannus, whilst fleeing from Alexander?

The once so powerful Persian Empire, the curse of the Greeks, the Seleucids, the Romans, and the Byzantines, had come to an end. And this in such an incredibly short time! The succesive Persian Empires - the Achaemenid, the Arsacid, and the Sasanian - had all weighed like an incubus on the western world. Now the Persian menace had definitely disappeared, but the West did not profit from it.

14. The organization of the Muslim Empire

We should pause for a moment to examine how the so rapidly assembled conquests were organized. In 643 the new empire stretched from the Nile to the foothills of the Hindu Kush. Permanent garrisons were needed to keep the subjected nations in check; military colonies were founded. The Arabs were only a minority in their own empire. It was necessary, therefore, that all male Arabs capable of bearing arms, were permanently ready to be called up. Many of them were settled in the newly won territories; they were called *muhajirs*, emigrants. All the governors of the new provinces were Arab military commanders. Brockelmann calls the Arab nation as such the 'military caste', proud and privileged.

Opposite it, and far below it, at a dualistic distance, stood the subjects (not the citizens!), the non-Arabs, for the time being still the non-Muslims, the ra'ayah', the plural of which is ra'aya; this word signifies 'herd', which says in itself enough. They paid the jizya, a very important source of income for the Muslim state. Towns that had had to be taken *manu militari* became the gains of the victors, one fifth of which fell to the state, while the rest was divided among the conquerors; towns and regions that had surrendered without offering resistance might keep what they possessed.

In Arabia itself, the cradle of Islam, no non-Muslims were henceforward tolerated; Umar I had all Arabian Jews deported to Syria. Elsewhere a slow process of islamization began. [14]

15. Problems of the succession

Umar was murdered by a Christian slave on November 23[d], 644. A small board of electors coopted one out of their midst as the third caliph, 'Uthman (644-656), a son-in-law of the Prophet. The new ruler was a member of one of the wealthiest and most influential Meccan clans, the Umayyah. With 'Uthman the Umayyah period began, for he nominated members of this clan for leading positions. This was understandably not well received by other clans; in Medina 'Ai'sha, the Prophet's youngest widow, vigorously intrigued against him. 'Uthman ordered a definite version of the Koran to be made, since there circulated several versions of it which had led to quarrels and blows. The new version was made by a committee and was finally accepted as canonical.

'Uthman's autocratic and nepotistic rule led in the end to a civil war. Rebelling Egyptian troops marched on Medina; the majority of its inhabitants, fed up with 'Uthman's rule, chose their side. When he attacked them with an aggressive sermon in the mosque, he was pelted with stones and carried home unconsciously. The Egyptians laid siege to his house, together with the Medinans. On Friday June 17th, 656, they invaded it and killed 'Uthman; his blood streamed over the copy of the Koran that he sat reading. He was the second caliph in succession to meet with a violent end.

On that same day Mohammed's other son-in-law, 'Ali, was proclaimed caliph. He immediately encountered strong opposition, from the Umayyah, of course, and others, but also from 'Ai'sha who did not love 'Ali better than she had loved 'Uthman. Two military colonies on the Euphrates became the respective strongholds of the two parties, the anti-'Ali group assembling considerable forces at Basra, while 'Ali and his adherents had the support of the garrison of Kufa. Somewhere between these towns the two armies collided. This battle of December 4th, 656, is called the Battle of the Camel, since the warlike 'Ai'sha, seated on a camel, spurred those of Basra on. 'Ali remained victorious; Mesopotamia acknowledged him as its caliph. His victory had important consequences, because Iraq now became one of the centres of gravity of Islam. The days of Medina were over.

The Umayyah party, now headed by Mu'awiyyah, the governor of Syria, did not give in : it demanded the extradition of 'Uthman's murderers. In the spring of 657 two enemy armies confronted each other in the region where the Euphrates was the frontier of Syria. Weeks of negotiating followed, interrupted by a period of desultory fighting. Ultimately it was decided that the matter should be referred to a court of arbritration, which met at Adhruh in southern Palestine. This court declared both Mu'awiyyah and 'Ali unfit for the succession. Yet, although 'Ali had sworn on oath that he would respect the court's decision, he did not step back. This breaking of a solemn oath weakened his position considerably. He had not only to cope with Mu'awiyah's troops, but also with a rebellion amongst his own ranks. On January 24th, 661, this fourth caliph was murdered as an act of vengeance in the mosque of Kufa.

Meanwhile, Mu'awiyyah had been constantly strengthening his position. He had made sure of Egypt and had been acknowledged as caliph in Jerusalem in May 660. He was already on his way to Kufa when he heard that his rival was dead. 'Ali's son Hasan waived his claims in return for a large sum of money. Mu'awiyah was lucky in having some very capable and absolutely loyal collaborators. Concentrating on the western half of the Muslim Empire, he left the control of the eastern half to his (illegitimate) half-brother Ziyad. Using a hard hand, this man effectively put an end to all rebellious movements in Iraq.

16. Peace with Byzantium

Mu'awiyyah, who was a wise and prudent ruler, chose Damascus as his residence. His great design was to definitely destroy the Byzantine Empire, but in this he failed. In 649 an attack on Cyprus misfired. It proved equally impossible to penetrate far into Asia Minor; the Byzantine defences held firm there. In the years 674-682 the Arabs had a naval base in Cyzicus, almost opposite Constantinople. Year after year attacks were made on the capital, but the defenders used their Greek fire with devastating success. In the end a peace was concluded that left Asia Minor in Byzantine hands.

17. North Africa conquered

Great successes, however, were achieved in North Africa. Tripoli, now the capital of the Republic of Libya, was in Muslim hands since 647. A generation later, Muslim forces under the very capable command of 'Uqbah ibn-Nafi', broke through the Byzantine lines of defence and penetrated into Tunisia, where in 670 the military colony of Quyrawan (now the city of Kairouan) was founded. In 682 a vigorous campaign brought Algeria and Morocco into 'Uqbah's hands; the Atlantic Ocean was reached on the western coast of Morocco. The victorious general rode his horse into the waves of the sea as far as possible; he is reported to have cried : "Allah! You see I can go no farther!" The whole of North Africa was now lost to Byzantium.

18. New succession problems

Mu'awiyyah could not rejoice in this great news, for he died on April 18th, 680. The reign of his son Yazid was only short (680-683), while Yazid's son Mu'awiyyah II, who had succeeded his father, died already in 684. The then head of the Umayyah house, Marvan, became caliph, but in 685 he fell victim to the plague. The fifth Umayyah caliph in so short a time was 'Abd al-Malik, who reigned until 705.

Of course, this period of confusion and uncertainty gave many opportunists and adventurers a chance. In some places there were even counter-caliphs, for instance one in Mecca. 'Abd al-Malik had many years of very hard internecine warfare behind him before he had the monopoly of power at last. Just as after the death of the Prophet in 632 and that of 'Uthman in 656, the *umma*, the community of the Muslims in which nobody was better than another, proved an illusion. Rebellion after rebellion had to be beaten down, mainly in Syria and Iraq. In the latter, a certain al-Mukhtar operated, a charismatic leader; he foretold the coming of the *Mahdi*, a Messiah-like figure who would appear at the end of time and wipe out all evil and establish a reign of justice; it was not the last time that the world would hear of a *Mahdi*. Mukhtar met his end in Kufa on April 4th, 687. The pseudo-caliph of Mecca withstood a long siege of the Ka'aba quarter, but was killed in October 692.

19. Fresh conquests in the East

It was only then that al-Malik could resume the strategy of conquest. Since Byzantine influence was still strong in Syria and Palestine, al-Malik set out to diminish it. The Byzantine currency, which was still in use was replaced by Arab coins, minted in Damascus. After the death of this autocratic ruler he was succeeded by his son Walid (705-715). Already in 672-673 the Arabs had added yet another province to their empire, the region of the Hindu Kush stretching onto the Amu Dar'ya, now the frontier between Turkmenistan and Uzbekistan. Beyond this river lay Bukhara, the Turkish ruler of which city became a Muslim; Samarkand had to accept an Arab garrison. This happened around 710. In 713 the Syr Dar'ya was reached, still more to the north in what is now Kazakhstan. Farther south, in present-day Afghanistan and along the coast of the Indian Ocean, the Muslim armies pushed relentlessly on until they could plant their green banners on the banks of the Indus. It must be stated, however, that the Muslim grip on these regions, so immeasurably far from the centre of power, was never very firm.

20. Conquests in the West

In the West, some important events occurred in Walid's reign. In July 711 the Arabs crossed the Straits of Gibraltar. The first Arab detachments to appear in Europe came ashore near a promontory that was given the name of the Muslim commander Tariq ibn-Ziyad; it was called *Jabal Tariq after him*, the Rock of Tariq = Gibraltar. A Visigoth army attempting to stop the Arab advance was defeated in a two-day battle on July 25th and 26th 711, in which the last Visigothic king, Roderick, lost his life. After this success, the Arab onrush was rapid. In three years' time the whole Iberian peninsula was occupied, with the exception of Asturia, the region in the extreme north-west along the coast of the Atlantic, which remained in Christian hands.

Walid having died, only forty years old, in 715, he was succeeded by his brother Sulayman I whose short reign ended already in 717, when he too died a premature death. The reign of Umar II was equally short (717-720); he was succeeded by Yazid II (717-724) and he by his brother Hisham (724-743). With him we are at the tenth caliph with whom we conclude this chapter and this volume.

His choice as governor of Spain was 'Abd-ar-Rhaman, an energetic man who carried the Muslim banners into France. Duke Eudo of Aquitaine was defeated near Bordeaux, after which the Muslim troops pushed relentlessly northward. They had almost reached the Loire, when a Frankish force under Charles Martel, the mayor of the palace, intercepted them. Near Poitiers the Muslims suffered a bloody defeat. 'Abd-ar-Rahman fell, and the Arabs retreated to Spain. Only a bridgehead near Narbonne remained in their hands. This happened in October 732. This again was a fact of great historical importance. France and the rest of Europe were spared Arab occupation and subsequent islamization. [15]

21. The results

Let us now look at the results, if our gaze is capable of embracing such an enormous expanse of land. [16] In 732 Muslim power stretched from the Pyrenees all through North Africa and the Middle East onto the Indus and the Syr Dary'a. In one single century of warfare (632-732) the Arabs had assembled an empire as large or perhaps even larger than that of the Romans. They did not have Gaul, Italy, the Balkans, and Asia Minor, but instead they possessed Arabia and the immense, almost endless stretch of land between the Tigris and the Indus, regions that had never seen a Roman. One great Empire, that of Sasanians, had quickly succumbed to the Muslim onslaught, while the other one, the Byzantine Empire, after suffering great losses and after losing the heartlands of Christianity, with great difficulty succeeded in keeping Asia Minor.

Natura non facit saltus, says the proverb. But history does. If we view history as presenting more or less regular patterns, the Muslim outburst was an a-historical event. Who could have foretold that a barely literate Arab would set in motion such a race of conquerors, that these desert dwellers, always fighting with one another, would form regular armies that were more than a match for the Byzantine and Persian generals, steeped in the art of war, and that these nomads living in tents and huts would be able to become settlers in foreign countries and even capable administrators?

How must we explain this curious phenomenon? There was first of all the religious impulse, of course, implanted by the Prophet into his countrymen. It gave them a sense of destiny and unity and filled them with an almost inexhaustible energy. But this impulse was fortified by more mundane motives. Arabs had always been warriors. Now they got the chance to gain fame and renown in wars on a much greater scale, and not only fame but booty too, more loot than any marauding Bedouin had ever brought home from his forays in the mother country. Later there was land to be had, and houses, and all kinds of functions, plus the chance to lord it over the subjected nations. And then, to crown it all, there was the promise that fallen warriors would go straight to heaven.

The Greek, Hellenistic, Roman, and Byzantine worlds had always felt the threat from the East, incorporated in the successive Persian Empires. Persia no longer presented a threat now, but a far greater danger confronted the Christian world. The Muslims stood where the Persians had never been, or only very temporarily, on the shores of the Mediterranean and at the Pyrenees. In past volumes, I characterized the East-West tension as dualistic. The Christian-Muslim relationship would be just as dualistic.

NOTES TO CHAPTER XI

1. I borrow this term from the famous French series edited by Henri Berr, *L'évolution de l'humanité, deuxième section, Origines du Christianisme et Moyen Age*, Part III of which is called *L'impérialisme religieux*.

2. For this section I am relying on Johnson, *The Holy War Idea* (see Bibliography).

3. Johnson, *The Holy War Idea* 37-42.

4. Johnson, *The Holy War Idea* 48.

5. Johnson, *The Holy War Idea* 51.

6. Johnson, *The Holy War Idea* 51.

7. See for this subject Peters, *Jihad in classical and modern Islam*. Ch 8 *The doctrine of Jihad in modern Islam*. There is a distinction between *jihad* with a mobilizing character (instances of which still exist) and with an instructive character, 'the struggle against one's evil inclinations.' The difference is sometimes described as that between the '*jihad* of the sword', the 'smaller *jihad*', and the peaceful form, the 'greater *jihad*'.

8. Extensive description of this battle in Gaudefroy-Demombynes, *Mahomet* 124-132.

9. See for this Vol. XV, Ch. IV, § 17.

10. Brockelmann, *Geschichte der islamischen Völker* 27.

11. Gaudefroy-Demombynes, *Mahomet* 217.

12. There is no modern town of this name, but it seems to have been situated near Ramallah, north of Jerusalem.

13. There is a story about the conquest of Alexandria. At the time of the capture of the town by the Arabs one of its inhabitants was John the Grammarian, John Philoponus, a defrocked Coptic priest. This man made the acquaintance of 'Amr ibn al-'As, the conqueror of Egypt.

John remarked to him that of all the booty some things might perhaps not be of any value to the Muslims; he made it clear that he was referring to the books of the library. 'Amr answered that he could do nothing without the consent of caliph Umar I. The caliph's opinion was negative. "Touching the books you mention, if what is written in them agrees with the Book of God [the Koran], they are not required; if they disagree, they are not desired. Destroy them therefore." In consequence, the books were used as fuel for the furnaces of the Alexandrian baths; they were sufficient in bulk to keep them burning for six months. Thus far the story.

It became *gefundenes Fressen* for those western authors, who are not rare, who see it as an instance of the barbarous bigotism of the Muslims. I must admit that I myself, in my first years as a history teacher, told it to my pupils. It did not occur to me that there is an improbable element in it. How could the four thousand furnaces of the town have been kept burning for so long on books? An incredible amount of papyrus would have been needed for this! The story has been carefully analysed by Alfred J. Butler, *The Arab conquest of Egypt and the last thirty years of Roman dominion*. Edited by P.M. Fraser, Oxford, 1978^2 (1902^1), Ch. XXV *The Library of Alexandria*. I present his findings as an *amende honorable* for what I wrongly told my pupils.

The story is to be found only in the second half of the thirteenth century by an author called Abu 'l Faraj, who does not mention his sources. It must make us think that the story emerges six centuries after the event. An almost contemporary author writing in Greek, John of Nikiou, who published a detailed account of the capture of Alexandria, makes no mention of the fate of the library. What makes the story still more improbable is that John the Grammarian died thirty years before the arrival of the Arabs.

It is far from clear to which library the story is referring. In ancient days there were two of them in the Egyptian capital, the Museum Library and the Serapeum Library. The Museum Library went up in flames at the time of Julius Caesar during the Alexandrian War; the Roman set his own fleet on fire, the flames sped to the dockyards, and from there to the library. Several ancient authors mention this, estimating the loss of books at four hundred thousand to seven hundred thousand volumes. What was left or rebuilt of the Museum totally disappeared in 273. The Serapeum Library was in fact the university library. Butler argues that, when the Christians destroyed the Serapis Temple in 391, the library perished with it. Or its contents were removed earlier. In any case, no text of the fifth, sixth, or seventh century makes mention of it. Butler's conclusion (p. 425) is : "One must pronounce that Abu 'l Faraj's story is a mere fable, totally destitute of historical foundation." It may be added that Abu 'l Faraj was not a Muslim, but an Armenian Jacobite Christian who may have had his own reasons to vilify the Muslims.

14.   Brockelmann, *Geschichte der islamischen Völker* 55-57.

15. Almost all historians agree in this, but for objectivity's sake I mention the dissident voice of the French historian Charles Seignobos, *Histoire sincère de la nation française. Essai de l'évolution du peuple français.* Paris, 1939[54], p. 58 note, who says that the sources about this event are rather untrustworthy. The Muslims had been plundering near Tours; it does not appear that they would establish themselves farther north than the Midi. "Il n'est pas certain, comme on dit, qu'elle (the Battle of Poitiers) a sauvé l'Europe de l'invasion des Arabes." Anyhow, as a result of their defeat the Arabs did not settle even in the Midi but withdrew behind the Pyrenees.

16. Scholarly literature on the period of the great Arab conquests has flowed profusely. 1. Laura Veccia Vaglieri, *The Patriarchal and Umayyad Caliphates. The Cambridge History of Islam.* Vol. I, 57-103. Cambridge, 1970. 2. Francesco Gabrieli, *Geschichte der Araber.* Urban Bücher 73, 43-93. Stuttgart, 1963. Translation of *Gli Arabi.* Florence, 1957. 3. *Geschichte der Araber von den Anfängen bis zur Gegenwart. Band 1 Voraussetzungen, Blüte und Verfall des arabisch-islamischen Feudalreiches.* Verfaßt von einem Autorenkollektiv der Karl-Marx-Universität Leipzig. Kap. II und III. Berlin, 1971. 4. Philip K. Hitti, *History of the Arabs from the earliest times to the present.* Chs. XI-XX. New York, 1967[9] (1939[1]). And still others.

CHRONOLOGY

EMPERORS	POPES	RELIGIOUS EVENTS
Zeno 474-491	468-483 Simplicius 483-492 Felix II	451 Council of Chalcedon : the two natures of Christ
Anastasius I 491-518	492-496 Gelasius I 496-498 Anastasius I 498-514 Symmachus	475 anti-Chalcedonian policy of Basiliscus 482 the *Henotikon* 484 schism Rome-Const.
Justin I 518-527	514-523 Hormisdas 523-526 Johannes I 526-530 Felix III	512 Severus Monophysite leader 518 anti-Monoph. action by Justin I 519 schism healed 526 Pope Hormisdas visits Const.
Justinian I 527-565	530-532 Bonifatius II	527 decree against all heretics; Justinian orth., Theodora Monoph.
532 Nika revolt in Constantinople	533-535 Johannes II 535-536 Agapitus I 536-537 Silverius 537-555 Vigilius	536 Pope Agapitus I visits Const.
556 Samaritan revolt		
Justin II 565-578	555-561 Pelagius I 561-574 Johannes III	
Tiberius II 578-582	574-579 Benedictus I 579-590 Pelagius II	
Maurice 582-602	590-604 Gregorius I	Under Maurice Monoph. harassed
Phocas 602-610	604-606 Sabinianus 607 Bonifatius III 608-615 Bonifatius IV	Under Phocas orthodox persecuted
610 Samaritan-Jewish revolt		
Heraclius I 610-641	615-618 Deusdedit 619-625 Bonifatius V 625-638 Honorius I 638-640 Severinus 640-642 Johannes IV	
614/615 Jews and Christians slaughter each other in Jerusalem		

CHRONOLOGY

CAMPAIGN IN THE WEST	SLAVS AND AVARS	WARS WITH PERSIA
	First half of 5th century frequent Slav invasions of Balkans	
533 Byz. offensive against Vandal kingdom 535 Byz. conquer Dalmatia and Sicily 536 Byz. landing in Italy; Rome occupied 540 Ravenna occupied 546 Ostrogoths reconquer Rome 548 campaign in North Africa concluded 563 It. campaign concluded after 563 southern Spain conquered 568 Lombard invasion of It.	after 560 Avar threat 581 Avars capture Sirmium 619-629 Avars threaten Const.; Avars thrown back beyond the Danube	527-532 war with Persia 531-579 Chosroes I 540-545 war with Persia; Persian invasion of Byz. territory 549-555 war with Persia 562 peace treaty 572 fighting again 575 peace treaty 579-590 Hormisdas IV 591-628 Chosroes II 604 great Persian offensive; 613/614 Damascus taken 614/615 Jerusalem taken; Egypt conquered 622 Byz. counter-offensive; lost territories recovered by Her. I 626 Byz. invasion of Persia 628 Kavad Persian Emperor; peace with Byzantium

CHRONOLOGY

ca. 570	Mohammed born in Mecca
595	Mohammed caravan leader and commercial agent; marries Khadija who gives him five children
ca. 610	Mohammed's mystical experience in the cave of Hira; public preaching and first converts
619	death of Khadija; marriage to Sauda bint Zamara
619	attempt to convert the town of Ta'if fails
622	Mohammed leaves Mecca and establishes himself at Medina; marries A'isha; problems with the Jewish community of Medina
624	victory over the Meccans near Badr
627	Muslims defeated by the Meccans near Mount Ochod; Battle of the Ditch saves Medina
628	Mohammed captures Khaibar; oasis of Fadak surrenders to him
629	armed clashes with a Byzantine force
630	Mohammed captures Mecca and Ta'if
631, 632	pilgrimages of Mohammed to Mecca; stays at Medina
632	death of Mohammed

CHRONOLOGY

624	First clashes between Medinans and Meccans
627, Jan.	Battle near the mountain Ochod
627, March	Battle of the Ditch
628	Khaibar and Fadak captured
629	First clashes with the Byzantines
630	Conquest of Mecca; Ta'if captured
633	Hirah on the Euphrates captured
635	Damascus captured; Syria occupied
636	Byzantine defeat at the Yarmuk; Babylonia occupied; Ctesiphon in Arab hands
638	Jerusalem captured; Palestine occupied
639-641	Assyria occupied
641	Memphis captured
642	Surrender of Alexandria; Egypt occupied; Persians defeated at Nihawend
643	Isfahan captured; Persia occupied; end of Sasanian Empire
647	Libya and Tripoli occupied
670	Tunisia occupied
672-673	Hindu Kush region occupied
682	Algeria and Morocco occupied
711-714	Iberian peninsula occupied
713	Arabs reach the Syr Dar'ya and the Indus
732	Arabs in France; defeated at Poitiers; France not occupied

BIBLIOGRAPHY

I ORIGINAL SOURCES

A COLLECTIONS

CODEX IUSTINIANUS. Corpus iuris civilis. Ed. P. Krueger. Berlin, 1963 (photostatic reprint of edition Berlin, 1877).

CORPUS SCRIPTORUM CHRISTIANORUM ORIENTALIUM (CSCO).

CORPUS SCRIPTORUM ECCLESIASTICORUM LATINORUM (CSEL).

CORPUS SCRIPTORUM HISTORIAE BYZANTINAE.

MONUMENTA HISTORIAE GERMANICA (quoted as MGH). Hannover.

PATROLOGIA GRAECA (quoted as PG).

SACRORUM CONCILIORUM COLLECTIO. Ed. J.D, Mansi. Florence (quoted as Mansi).

THE HOLY QUR-AN. Text, Translation, and Commentary by Abdullah Yusuf Ali. New York, 1946.

B INDIVIDUAL AUTHORS

AGATHIAS MYRINAEUS
 Historiae. In : Prokops Werke II. Griechisch-deutsch. Ed. Otto Veh. München (1966).

ARISTOTLE
1. Nicomachean Ethics. Ed. H. Rackham. Loeb Classical Library 73. Cambridge (Ms)/London, 1926.
2. Metaphysica. Ed. Hugh Tredennick. Loeb Classical Library 271 and 287. Cambridge (Ms)/London, 1975 and 1969.

CHRONICON PASCHALE
Vol. I Corpus Scriptorum Historiae Byzantinae. Ed. B.G. Niebuhr. Berlin, 1882.

CORIPPUS, FLAVIUS CRESCONIUS
Iohannidos seu De bellis Lybicis Libri XVIII. Eds. Iacobus Diggle et F.R.D. Goodyear. Canterbury, 1970.

DIO CASSIUS
Roman History. 9 vols. Translated by Earnest Cary. Loeb Classical Library. Cambridge (Ms)/London.

EVAGRIUS
Historiae ecclesiasticae. PG 86bis. Paris, 1863.

FREDEGARIUS
Chronicarum libri quattuor. Ausgewählte Quellen zur deutschen Geschichte des Mittelalters. Quellen zur Geschichte des 7. und 8. Jahrhunderts. Bd IVA, übertragen von Andreas Kusternig. Darmstadt, 1982.

GEORGIUS PISIDAE
1. Bellum avaricum. Giorgia di Pisidia, Poemi I. Panegyrici epici. Edizione critica, traduzione e commenta a cura di Agostino Pertusi. Studia patristica et byzantina. 7. Heft. Eital, 1959.
2. Expeditio persica. See 1.
3. Fragmenta. PG 92. Paris, 1982 (reprint of Paris, 1868).

HESYCHIUS ILLUSTRIUS
Patria Constantinopolis. Scriptores originum Constantinopolis I. Ed. Theodorus Preger. New York, 1975 (photostatic reprint of the Taubner edition, Leipzig, 1901).

JOHANNES EPHESINUS
Historia ecclesiastica. John of Ephesus, Ecclesiastical history. Ed. and translated by E.W. Brooks. CSCO 106. Scriptores syriaci 55. Louvain, 1952 (reprint of 1936[1]).

JORDANES
Romana. Recensuit Theodor Mommsen. MGH Va. (Photostatic reprint 1961 of the edition Berlin, 1882).

MALALAS, Ioannes
Chronographia. Ed. Ludovicus Dindorfius, Corpus Scriptorum Historiae Byzantinae. Bonn, 1881.

MARCELLINUS
The Chronicle of Marcellinus. Ed. with translation nd commentary by Brian Coke. Australian Association for Byzantine Studies. Byzantina australiensia 7. Sydney, 1995.

MENANDER PROTECTOR
Excerpta de legationibus barbarorum ad Romanos. PG 113. Paris, 1864.

NIKEPHOROS
Nikephoros, Patriarch of Constantinople, Short History. Text, translation, and commentary by Cyril Mango. Corpus Fontium Historiae Byzantinae. Volume XIII. Washington, 1990.

PAULUS DIACONUS
Historia Langobardorum. MGH 48 (in usum scholarum separatim edita). Hannover, 1978 (unveränderter Nachdruck der Ausgabe 1878).

PHILOSTORGIUS
Kirchengeschichte. Herausg. Joseph Bidez. Die griechischen christlichen Schrifsteller der ersten drei Jahrhunderte. Berlin, 1972².

PROCOPIUS
1. Anecdota. Geheimgeschichte des Kaiserhofs von Byzanz. Griechisch-deutsch. Ed. Otto Veh. München (1961).
2. De bello gotico. Prokops Werke II. Griechisch-deutsch. Ed. Otto Veh. München (1966).
3. De bello persico. Prokops Werke IV. Ed. Otto Veh. München (1971).
4. De bello vandalico. Vandalenkriege. Prokops Werke IV. Griechisch-deutsch. Ed. Otto Veh. München (1971).

THEOPHANES
Chronographia. The Chronicle of Theophanes Confessor. Byzantine and Near Eastern History A.D. 284-813. Translated by Cyril Mango and Roger Scott. Oxford, 1997.

THEOPHYLACTUS SIMOCATTA
The History of Theophylactus Simocatta. An English translation with introduction and notes by Michael and Mary Whitby. Oxford, 1986.

ZOSIMUS
Historia nea. Histoire nouvelle. Texte établi et traduit par François Pachoud. Paris, 1971.

II CONTEMPORARY WORKS

A COLLECTIONS

L'Arabie antique de Karib'Il à Mahomet. Nouvelles données sur l'Histoire des Arabes grâce aux inscriptions, pp. 45-54. Revue du monde musulman er de la Méditerranée 61. Aix-en-Provence, 1992.

Jews under Islam, a culture in historical perspective. Ed. Julie-Marthe Cohen. Zwolle (NL), (1993).

Mithraism in Ostia. Mystery religion and Christianity in the ancient Port of Rome. Ed. Samuel Laeuchli (1967).

B WORKS OF REFERENCE

ENCYCLOPAEDIA OF ISLAM. Leiden/New York. (Quoted as Enc.Isl.)

LEXIKON FÜR TTHEOLOGIE UND KIRCHE.
THE OXFORD DICTIONARY OF BYZANTIUM. New York/Oxford.

THEOLOGISCHE REALENZYKLOPÄDIE (quoted as TRE).Berlin.

C MONOGRAPHS

ABBOTT, Nabia, Aisha, the Beloved of Mohammed. New York, 1973 (reprint of Chicago, 1942).

ADANG, P.W.M., Muslim Writers on Judaism and the Hebrw Bible from Ibn Rabbas to Ibn Hazm. Doctoral thesis Catholic University of Nijmegen, 1960.

AHMAD, Hazrat Mirza Bashir-ut-Din Mahmud, The Life of Muhammad. Rabwah (Pakistan), w.d.

ALMOND, Philip C., Heretic and hero. Muhammad and the Victorians. Studies in Oriental Religions no. 18. Wiesbaden, 1989.

AVANZINI, Alessandra, Remarques sur le 'matriarchat' en Arabie du Sud. In: L'Arabie antique.

AVENARIUS, Alexander, Die Awaren in Europa. Amsterdam/Bratislava, 1974.

AVI-YONAH, Mordechai, The Jews under Roman and Byzantine Rule. A Political History of Palestine from the Bar Kokhba War to the Aran Conquest. Jerusalem, 1984 (original Hebrew edition, 1946, first English version 1976).

BARKER, John W., Justinian and the Later Roman Empire. Madison/Milwaukee/London, 1966.

BIRKELAND, Harris, The Legend of the Opening of Muhammad's Breast. Avhandlinge utgitt av Det Norske Videnskaps Akademi i Oslo. II. Historisch-Filosofische Klasse. 1955. no. 3. Oslo, 1955.

BLACHèRE, Régis, Le problème de Mahomet. Essai de biographie critique du fondateur de l'Islam. Paris, 1952,

BOEHM, Rudolf, Kritik der Grundlagen des Zeitalters. Den Haag, 1974.

BRAVMANN, M.M., The spiritual Background of Early Islam. Series: Studies in Ancient Arab Concepts. Leiden, 1972.

BRÉHIER, Louis, Vie et mort de Byzance. Collection 'Évolution de l'humanité. Le monde byzantin I'. Paris, 1948.

BROCKELMANN, Carl, History of the Islamic Peoples. London (1949). (Original German version 'Geschichte der islamischen Völker und Staaten', 1932).

BROWNING, Robert, Justinian and Theodora. London (1971).

BUHL, Frants,
  1. The historical Muhammad. In: Enc.Isl. Vol. VII (1993).
  2. Muhammad, the prophet of Islam (revised by A.T. Welch). In: Enc.Isl. Vol. VII (1993).

BURY, J.B., A History of the Later Roman Empire from Arcadius to Irene (395 A.D to 800 A.D.). Vol. II. Amsterdam, 1966 (unchanged reprint of edition London, 1889).

CAMERON, Alan, Circus Factions. Blues and Greens at Rome and Byzantium. Oxford, 1976.

COOK, Michael, Muhammad. Series: Past Masters. Oxford/New York, 1983.

DIEHL , Charles
  1. L'Afrique byzantine. Histoire de la domination byzantine en Afrique (533-709). New York (photostatic reprint w.d. of edition Paris, 1896).
  2. Justinien et la civilisation byzantine au VIe siècle. 2 Vols. New York (1969, photostatic reprint of first edition 1901).
  3. Théodora. Impératrice de Byzance. Paris (1937).

DIKKEN, Berend-Jan, Muhammad, Jews and Christians. A short survey of the position of the Jews and the Christians in Arabia in early islam according to Muslim traditions. Paper for the Dutch doctoral degree. Utrecht State University, 1993.

DRAGON, Gilbert, Naissance d'une capitale. Constantinople et ses institutions de 330 à 451. Bibliothèque byzantine. Études-7. Paris, 1974.

FREND, W.H.C., The Rise of the Monophysite Movement. Chapters in the history of the Church in the fifth and sixth centuries. Cambridge, 1972.

GABRIELI, Francesco, Mahomet. Présentation de Mahomet. Série: Le mémorial des siècles. Paris (1965).

GAUDEFROY-DEMOMBYNES, Maurice, and PLATONOV, Sergej Fedorovic, Le monde musulman et byzantin jusqu'aux croisades. Série: Histoire du monde. Tome III. Paris, 1931.

GAUDEFROY-DEMOMBYNES, Maurice, Mahomet. Série: L'évolution de l'humanité. Paris, 1957.

GEIGER, Abrham, Was hat Mohammed aus dem Judenthume aufgenommen? Leipzig, 1833, revised edition Wiesbaden, 1902. English translation under the title 'Judaism and Islam', New York, 1970.

GIBBON, Edward, The Decline and Fall of the Roman Empire. Vol. II 395 A.D.-1185 A.D. New York (w.d.).

GLUBB, John Bagot (Glubb Pasha), The Life and Times of Muhammad. London, 1970.

GOLDZIHER, Ignaz, Vorlesungen über den Islam. Fotomechanischer Nachdruck der 2. von Franz Babinger umgearbeitete Auflage. Heidelberg, 1963 (1925^2, 1910^1).

GROHMANN, Adolf, Arabien. Reihe: Kulturgeschichte des Alten Orients. 3. Abschnitt, 4. Unterabschnitt. Handbuch der Altertumswissenschaft. 3. Abteilung, 1. Teil, 3. Band. München, 1963.

GUILLAUME, Alfred, New Light on the Life of Muhammad. Journal of Semitic Studies. Monograph no. 1. Manchester University Press (w.d.).

HAMIDULLAH, Muhammad, Le prophète de l'Islam. Paris, 1959.

HAYEK, Michel, Le mystère d'Ismaël. Paris, 1964.

HAYKAL, Muhammad Husayn, The Life of Muhammad. North American Trust Publications. 1976.

HÖFNER, Maria, Die vorislamitischen Religionen Arabiens. In: Die Religionen Assyriens, Altarabiens und der Mandäer. Reihe: Die Religionen der Menschheit. Band 10.2. Stuttgart/Berlin/Köln/Mainz (1970).

ISHAQ, Ibn, The Life of Muhammad. A translation of Ishaq's Sirat Rasul Allah. With introduction and notes by A. Guillaume. London/New York/Toronto, 1955. The Life of Muhammad, Apostle of Allah. Ed. Michael Edwards. London, 1964.

JANSEN, Johannes J.G., Early History and Background of the Jews of Islam. In: Jews under Islam.

JOHNSON, James Turner, The Holy War Idea in Western and Islamic Traditions. The Pennsylvania State University Press (1997).

KATSH, Abraham I., Judaism in Islam. Biblical and Talmudic Backgrounds of the Koran and its Commentaries. Sura II and III. New York, 1954.

KELLERHALS, Emanuel, Der Islam. Seine Geschichte, Seine Lehre, Sein Wesen. 2. durchgesehene Auflage. Stuttgart, 1956 (1945[1]).

KITCHEN, K.A., Documentation for Ancient Arabia. Part I. Chronological framework and historical sources. The World of Ancient Arabia Series. Liverpool University Press, 1994.

KNECHT, August, Die Religions-Politik Kaiser Justinians I. Würzburg, 1896.

LAEUCHLI, Samuel, Mithraic dualism. In : Mythraism in Ostia.

LINGS, Martin, Muhammad. His life based on the earliest sources. London, 1983.

LÜLING, Günter, Die Wiederentdeckung des Propheten Muhammad. Eine Kritik am 'christlichen' Abendland. Erlangen, 1981.

MORSY, Magali, Les femmes du Prophète. Paris, 1989.

MOSCATI, Sabatino, Ancient Semitic Civilizations. London (1957).

OHM, Thomas, Die Gebetsgebärden der Völker und das Christentum. Leiden, 1948.

PARRINDER, Geoffrey, Jesus in the Qur'an. London, 1965.

PETERS, F.E., Muhammad and the Origins of Islam. New York (1994).

PETERS, Rudolph, Jihad in Classical and Modern Islam. Princeton, 1996.

PREVITÉ-ORTON, C.W., The Shorter Medieval Cambridge History. Vol. I The Later Roman Empire to the Twelfth Century. Cambridge, 1952.

RABELLO, Alfredo M., Giustiniano, Ebrei e Samaritani all luce delle fonti storico-letterarie, ecclesiastiche e giuridiche. Vol. II. Milano, 1988. Monografie del vocabulario di Giustiniano, Vol. 2.

RINNGREN, Helmer, Studies in Arabian fatalism. Uppsala Universitets Årskrift 1955:2. Acta Universitatis Upsaliensis. Uppsala/Wiesbaden (1955).

ROBIN, Christian
1. Cités, royaumes et empires de l'Arabie avant l'Islam. In: L'Arabie antique.
2. Du paganisme au monothéisme. 3. La diffusion des religions monothéistes en Arabie du Sud avant l'Islam. In; L'Arabie antique.

RODINSON, Maxime, Mahomet. (1961).

RUBIN, Berthold, Das Zeitalter Justinians. Zweiter Band. Aus dem Nachlaß herausgegeben von Carmelo Capizzi. New York, 1995.

SCHEDL, Claus, Muhammad und Jesus. Die christologisch relevante Texte des Korans neu übersetzt und erklärt von -. Wien/Freiburg/Basel (1978).

SCHIMMEL, Annemarie,
1. Deciphering the signs of God. A Phenomenological Approach to Islam. (Edinburgh, 1994).
2. Und Muhammad ist sein Prophet. Die Verehrung des Propheten in der islamischen Frömmigkeit. Düsseldorf/Köln, 1981.

SCHUMANN, Olaf H., Der Christus der Muslime. Christologische Aspekte in der arabisch-islamischen Literatur. Gütersloh, 1975.

SEIGNOBOS, Charles, Histoire sincère de la nation française. Essai d'une histoire de l'évolution du peuple français. Paris, 1939[54].

SLIMAN BIN IBRAHIM, Het leven van Mohammed, Allah's profeet. Amsterdam, w.d. (Translation by Jan Prins of the French edition La vie de Mahomet, Prophète d'Allah. 1939).

SCHOEPS, Hans-Joachim, Theologie und Geschichte des Judenchristentums. Tübingen, 1949.

SZADECZKY-KARDOSS, Samuel, Über die Wandlungen der Ostgrenzen der awarischen Machtssphäre. Szeged, 1986.

VASILIEV, A.A.
 1. History of the Byzantine Empire 324-1453. Madison, 1952.
 2. Justin the First. An Introduction to the Epoch of Justinian the Great. Cambridge (Ms.), 1950.

WATT, W. Montgomery,
   1. Muhammad at Mecca. Oxford, 1953.
   2. Muhammad's Mecca. History in the Qur'-an. Edinburgh (1988).
   3. Muhammad at Medina. Oxford, 1956.
   4. Muhammad. Prophet and Statesman. Oxford, 1961.

WENSINCK, J.A., Mohammed en de Joden te Medina. Leiden, 1928².

YE'OR, Bat, Le dhimmi. Profil de l'opprimé en Orient et en Afrique de Nord depuis la conquête arabe. Paris (1980).

GENERAL INDEX

Al-'Abbas, uncle of Mohammed, 233, 317
Abassids, 256
Abbott, Nabia, 261
'Abd-al-Muttalib, Mohammed's grandfather, 234
'Abd Allah bin Ubayy, chief in Medina, 250-251, 252, 291
'Abd al-Malik, Umayyah caliph, 327
'Abd-ar-Rahman, Arab governor of Spain, 328
Abdullah ibn Arqat, freedman of Abu Bekr, 247
Abdullah Yusuf Ali, Islamic scholar, 258
Abraham, 233, 251, 269, 272, 296, 298, 303, 304, 309
Abu Bekr, friend and successor of Mohammed, 241, 242, 246, 247, 249, 250, 255, 289, 315, 319, 320, 321
Abu 'l Faraj, Muslim historian, 331
Abu Haritha, bishop of Najran, 304
Abu Lahab, uncle of Mohammed, 233, 241, 242, 244, 248, 259
Abu Lababa, a Muslim, 293
Abu Talib, uncle of Mohammed, 233, 234, 240, 243
Abyssinia(n), 242, 259
Acacius, Patriarch, of Constantinople, 197, 198, 199, 200, 201, 202
Academy of Athens, 43, 51, 185
Achaemenid Empire, 323
Adam, 50, 233, 269, 296, 299, 301-302
Adang, C.P.W.M., 287, 308
Adoptionism, Adoptionist(s), 28-30
Adrianople, 114
Adhruh, town in Palestine, 325
Adriatic (Sea), 78, 88, 90, 94, 98, 103, 104, 117, 209
Aegean Sea, 64, 65, 75, 138
Aeneas, 87
Afghanistan, 327
Agapitus I, Pope, 91, 214
Agathias, Byzantine historian, 95, 108, 109, 218
Ahmad, for Mohammed, 300
Ahmad, Hazrat Mirza Bashir-ut-Din Mahmud, 262
Ahra Mainyu see Angra Mainyu
Ahriman, 37
Ahura Mazda, 7, 37
'A'isha, Mohammed's third wife, 238, 249-250, 254, 261, 262, 324, 325
Ajax, Dutch football club (Amsterdam), 159, 161
Akkad, 63, 76
Alaric, King of the Visigoths, 77

Albigensians, 313
Albania(n), in the Balkans, 78, 306
Albania, region in the Caucasus, 141
Alboin, Lombard king, 102, 103
Alcinous, 17
Alemanni, 2
Alexander the Great, 15, 39, 65, 120, 131, 139, 145, 147, 223, 323
Alexandria(n)(s), 20, 32, 80, 137, 156, 171, 194, 195, 196, 197, 202, 204, 207, 212, 214, 310, 330, 331
Alexandrian War, 331
Algeria, 326
'Ali ibn Abu Talib, nephew and adopted son of Mohammed, caliph, 240, 248, 255, 277, 325
Aligern, brother of the Ostrogothic King Teja, 99
Allah, 237
Allat, al-Lat, Arab goddess, 228, 263
Allen, Pauline, 187, 219
Allies, 91
Almond, Philip C., 258, 261
Alogoi, 29
Alps, 97, 100, 103
Altai, 127
Amalasuntha (Amalaswintha), 89, 92
Amantius, Byzantine comes, 173
Ambrosius, Father of the Church, 181
Amida, town in Mesopotamia, 133, 142, 200
Amina, mother of Mohammed, 233, 234
'Amr ibn al-'As, Meccan leader, conqueror of Egypt, 316, 330-331
Amsterdam, 109, 161, 249
Amu Dary'a, river in Central Asia, 64, 123, 127, 327

Anastasius I, Byzantine Emperor, 78, 111, 201, 202, 203, 205, 206
Anastasius, late Latin author, 108, 187
Anastasius, Patriarch of Antioch, 177
Anastasius, presbyter in Constantinople, 188-189
Anatolia, 62, 63
Anaximander, 38
Anchialus (Pomorie) (Byzantine town in Bulgaria, 114, 115
Androgynity, 57
Anglo-Saxon, 2
Angra Mainyu, 7, 37
Anonymus Valesianus, 105
Antai see Wends
Anthropology, anthropological, 4, 31, 34
Anthropomorphism, 17
Anthimus, Patriarch of Constantinople, 214
Antioch, 124, 128, 134, 135, 156, 171, 174, 177, 195, 196, 197, 200, 204, 205, 207, 211, 213, 214, 215
Anti-Semitism, 159
Antonina, wife of Belisarius, 93
Apamea, town in Syria, 128
Aphrodite of Cnidus, 196
Apocalypses, Jewish, 179
Apollinaris fils, 34, 190, 213
Aquileja, 103, 129
Aquitaine, 328
Arabia, Arab(s)(ian), Arabic, 150, 152, 173, 217, Ch. VII passim, 232, 233, 236, 237, 238, 240, 247, 250, 251, 255, 257, 263, 282, 283, 285, 288, 289, 291, 294, 296, 302, 304, 305, 306, 307, Ch. XI passim
Arabia felix, 224, 310
Arabian Gulf, 225
Aramaic, 224
Araxes (Araks) river in Azerbaijjan, 140, 142
Arbela (Arbil), town in Mesopotamia, 145
Ardashir I, Partian emperor, 120-121

Ariadne, wife of the Emperors Zeno and Anastasius, 201
Arianism, Arian(s), 32-34, 34, 77, 78, 81, 88, 90, 91, 183, 186, 187, 190, 201
Ariminium (Rimini), 94
Aristotle, Aristotelian, 15, 34, 46-49, 70, 71
Arius, 32-34, 187, 190
Armenia(n), 63, 77, 121, 122, 123, 124, 127, 129, 133, 138, 140, 141, 142, 207, 216
Armenian Jacobite, 331
Arsacid Empire, 323
Aryans, 10, 54
Ascetic, asceticism, 30-32, 53
Ascona, 104
Asia(tic), 76, 126, 133, 135, 150, 215
Asia Minor, 31, 63, 64, 65, 66, 77, 115, 137, 138, 139, 140, 143, 186, 200, 202, 207, 215, 326, 329
Asones, unidentified Asiatic tribe, 131
Assyria(n)(s), 63, 64, 77, 145, 224, 322
Assyrian Empire, 76
Asturia, 328
Athalaric, Ostrogothic king, 89
Athanasius, Father of the Church, 183, 192
Atheism, 268
Athens, Athenian, 43, 54, 55, 56, 165
Atlantic Ocean, 326, 328
Atomism, 40-41, 41
Atticus, 18
Attila, King of the Huns, 77
Augsburg, 109
Augustine, Father of the Church, 179, 181, 199, 313, 314
Augustus, 81

Aurelian, Roman Emperor, 225
Aurès mountains, 85
Aus, Jewish tribe in Medina, 250
Austria, 2, 102
Authari, Lombard king, 104
Avanzini, Alessandra, 230
Avar(s), 102, 103, 110, 112-118, 127, 135, 138, 140, 143, 144, 150, 197, 207-208, 208, 211
Avenarius, Alexander, 118, 119
Avi-Yonah, Mordechai, 172, 175, 176, 217, 218
Aya Sofia, 81, 165, 167, 201, 276
Azerbaijjan (Media), 140

Babylon, 63, 65
Babylonia(n)(s), 63, 64, 224, 320, 321
Babylonian Empire, 76
Babylonian Captivity, 10
Badr, town in Arabia, 290, 315
Baian, Bagan, Avar king, 113, 114, 117, 119
Balearic islands, 85
Baladhuri, Arabian chronicler, 241, 242, 260
Balkans, 64, 65, 77, 78, 95, 98, 110, 111, 113, 114, 117, 306, 329
Banu Qaynuga', Jewish tribe in Medina, 290-291
Banu Qurayza, Jewish tribe in Medina, 292-294
Baram (Varahram), Persian emperor, 130, 132
Barbelo-Gnostics, Gnostic sect, 24, 57
Barker, John W., 107, 109
Basilidians, Gnostic sect, 24-25
Basiliscus, Byzantine Emperor, 196-197
Basra, town in Iraq, 325
Battle of Ajnadayn, 320
Battle of the Camel, 325
Battle of the Ditch, 316
Battle of Poitiers, 328, 332
Bayle, Pierre, 3
Bederiana (Bader), town in Serbia, 205-206

Bedouin(s), 224, 247, 315, 317, 319, 320, 329
Beidawi, Arab author, 289
Belgium, 2
Belisarius, Byzantine general, 83-85, 87, 90-96, 97-98, 99, 123, 124, 143, 165, 167
Benevento, 103
Berbers, 85-87
Bergengrün, Werner, 118
Berlin, 118
Berr, Henri, 330
Berytus, town in Syria, 202
Bessos, Byzantine general, 125-126
Beverwijk, town in the Netherlands, 161
Bible, 44, 50, 59, 141, 179, 199, 202, 240, 269, 277, 282, 284, 288
Birkeland, Harris, 235, 257
Bisexuality see Androgynity
Bithynia(n), 124
Blachère, Régis, 256
Black Sea, 75, 77, 114, 124, 125, 126, 127, 138
Blixen, Karen, novelist, 7
Boehm, Rudolf, scholar, 46, 70, 71
Boethius, 88
Book of Daniel, 179
Bordeaux, 328
Borion, town in Cyrenaica, 175
Bosnia, 78, 306, 311
Bosporus, 76, 116, 132, 133, 143
Bowman, Stephen B., 217
Brahmanic religion, 11
Brahmans, 11
Bravmann, M.M., 230
Bréhier, Louis, 81, 106, 152
Brescia, 100
Brindisi, 209
Britain, British, 2, 169
Brockelmann, Carl, 227, 230, 318, 323, 330, 331
Browning, Robert, 79, 105

Bruges, 109
Buddha, 55
Buddhism, Buddhist, 11, 13-14, 55
Buhl, Frants, 232-233, 256, 259
Bukhara, town in Uzbekistan, 327
Bulgarian(s), 110, 111, 114, 116, 117, 306
Burgundians, 2, 94-95
Butler, Alfred J., 331
Bury, J.B., 101, 109, 111, 114, 118, 119, 126, 127, 128, 130, 144, 151, 153, 154, 181, 199, 218, 219, 220
Byzantine(s), 2, from Ch. II -Ch. VI passim, 223, 247, 258, 318, 319, 321, 322, 326, 327, 329, 330
Byzantine Empire, 2, 77, 81, 156, 158, 166, 171, 174, 183, 196, 197, 198, 205, 215, 320, 322, 326, 329
Byzantine Senate, 162, 196, 201, 206, 210
Byzantium, Greek town, 74, 75, 76

Caesar, Julius, 81
Caesarea, town in Cappadocia, 133
Caesaropapism, 178-183, 195-197
Cahen, Cl., 309
Cairo, 322
Calabria, 104
Cambyses, King of Persia, 64
Canaanite, 61
Cappadocian(n), 124, 133, 139
Capua, 100
Caput Vada (Rass Kaboudia), cape in Tunisia, 83
Cadiz, 100
Caesarea, Palestine, 173
Cameron, Alan, 157, 158, 161, 169
Carpocratians, Gnostic sect, 23
Cartagena, 100
Carthage, 82, 83, 84, 118, 175
Caspian Sea, 141
Cassiodorus, 88
Caucasus(ian), 122, 124, 125, 141, 142, 193
Celts, 76

Cerinthus, Gnostic prophet, 23
Chalcedon, town opposite, Constantinople, 132, 133, 137, 138, 139, 140, 142, 143, 144, 145, 146, 171, 199, 203, 304
Chalcedonian(s), anti-Chalcedonian(s), 188, 190, 194, 195, 197-217
Charlemagne, 117
Charles Martel, 328
Chiesa, Bruno, 229
China, Chinese, 6, 10, 12, 60, 127
Chosroes I Nushirvan, Persian emperor, 122-129, 185, 216
Chosroes II, Persian emperor, 130-149, 149, 152, 321
Christianity, Christian(s), 7, 11, 12, 27-36, 44-45, 50, 52, 53-54, 59-60, 61, 75, 81, 88, 104, 117, 125, 127, 128, 136, 138, 141, 148, 152, 156, 172, 173, 174, 175, 176, 177, 178, 179, 180, 183, 185, 189, 192, 193, 198, 201, 202, 218, 228, 232, 234, 237, 238, 239, 240, 248, 249, 251, 257, 258, 260, 263, 264, 267, 269, 274, 276, 277, 278, 279, 280, 281, 282, 283, 284, 285, 287, 288, 295, 296, 297, 298, 299, 299-308, 310, 313, 314, 318, 319, 320, 322, 328, 329, 330, 331
Church of Justice (Manichaeism), 27
Churchill, Winston, 91
Cicero, 41
Cilicia, 138, 142
Circumcision, 271
Circus Maximus, Rome, 156
Clovis, 94
Colchis see Lazica

Constantine I the Great, 74-75, 75, 168, 180, 183
Constantinople, 2, 35, 74-75, 77, 80, 84, 91, 95, 98, 99, 102, 110, 111, 113, 114, 116, 118, 124, 127, 129, 131, 133, 134, 137, 138, 139, 140, 143, 149, Ch. V passim, 181, 183, 185, 194, 196, 202, 211, 214, 276
Cook, Michael, 256
Coptic Church, Coptic, 197, 330
Cordoba, 100
Corpus Hermeticum, 22
Corippus, Flaccus Cresconius, North African poet, 85, 87, 107
Corsica, 85, 100, 104
Council of Chalcedon, 35, 36, 171, 172, 182, 187, 189, 191, 192, 193, 194, 197, 198, 199, 200, 201, 203, 204, 205, 207, 210, 213
Council of Constantinople of 381, 34, 190, 197, 198, 207
Council of Ephesus in 431, 189, 198, 207
Council of Ephesus in 449 (the Robbers' Council), 191, 197, 198
Council of Nicaea, 33, 44, 190, 192, 197, 198, 207
Covenant (of God with Israel), 60
Creed of Nicaea, 36
Cremona, 104
Crete, 54
Crimea, 195, 196
Croatia, Croats, 78, 90, 117, 306, 311
Crusades, 312, 313
Ctesiphon, the Persian capital, 129, 141, 146, 147, 321
Cumae, ancient town near Naples, 99
Cunimund, Gepid prince, 102, 103
Cyprus, 326
Cyrenaica, 77, 137
Cyrillus, Patriarch of Alexandria, 189, 192, 193
Cyrillus of Jerusalem, Christian author, 187
Cyrus II, King of Persia, 64, 120, 125, 130, 137

Cyrus, Byzantine governor of Egypt, 318

Dacia, 78
Dagobert I, king of the Franks, 136
Dalmatia, 78, 90, 214
Damascius, Greek philosopher, 185
Damascus, 135, 156, 320, 322, 326, 327
Danish, 232
Danube, 64, 65, 77, 78, 81, 98, 101, 102, 110, 111, 112, 113, 114, 115, 117, 120, 144, 150
Daoism, 6
Dara, town in Mesopotamia, 122, 123, 128, 132, 133
Darius III Codomannus, King of Persia, 65, 323
Dastargherd, Persian royal residence, 146, 147
Dead Sea, 21, 225
Decimum, town in Tunisia, 84
Declaration of Independence, 50
Delta (in Egypt), 10, 322
Delta (of the Euphrates and Tigris), 62
Demiurge, 265
Democritus, 40, 41
Diadochi, 223
Diaspora, 171, 172
Dikken, Berend-Jan, 304, 309, 311
Diocletian, Roman emperor, 121
Dioscurus, Patriarch of Alexandria, 191, 192, 193, 194
Diehl, Charles, 83, 84, 105, 106, 107, 150, 169, 170, 173, 217, 218, 219
Dio, Cassius, 105
Diocletian, 11
Diyala, river in Persia, 321
Dobruza, 111

Docetism, Docetist, 28, 303
Domentziolos, nephew of the Emperor Phocas, 133
Domitian, bishop of Melitene, 175
Donatism, Donatists, 31, 53, 186
Dorkon, the horse of Heraclius I, Byzantine Emperor, 145, 171, 247
Dorotheus, bishop of Thessalonica, 210
Dragon, Gilbert, 105
Drava, river in the Balkans, 117
Dualism, dualist(ic), Chapter I passim, 75, 81, 96, 100, 109, 112, 113, 117, 118, 120, 126, 131, 142, 160, 169, 173, 176, 179, 182, 217, 229, 235, 252, 264, 265, 268, 269, 273, 278-283, 297-298, 330
Dutch, 109, 123, 278, 284, 286
Dyrrhachium (Dürres), town in Albania, 78

Edessa (Urfa), 124, 133
Egypt(ian)(s), 10, 12, 22, 23, 54, 60, 63, 64, 65, 66, 76, 134, 136, 137, 149, 192, 193, 194, 195, 196, 198, 207, 211, 211-212, 213, 214-215, 215, 217, 316, 318, 322, 324, 326, 330, 331
Eisenhower, Dwight D., 313
Elam, 63
Elbe, 102
Eleatic school, 41
Elias, Patriarch of Jerusalem, 203
Empedocles, 6
Encratism, Encratist(s), 30-31, 53
English, 284, 286, 312
Ephesus, 197
Ephraim, Patriarch of Antioch, 215
Epictetus, 42
Epicurus, 46, 51
Epiphanius, bishop of Tyre, 209, 211
Epiphanius, Father of the Church, 209
Epiphanius, Patriarch of Constantinople, 211, 214
Essenes, 21
Essentialism, 34
Ethiopia, 137, 215-216

Eudo, Duke of Aquitaine, 328
Eudocia, wife of the Vandal King Huneric, 106
Eudocia, first wife of Heraclius I, 140
Eudocia, daughter of Heraclius I, 153
Eudocia, wife of Theodosius II, 193
Euphemia, first wife of Justinian I, 81, 95, 110, 112
Euphemius, Patriarch of Constantinople, 201, 202
Euphrates, 65, 66, 77, 81, 110, 120, 121, 133, 140, 143, 150, 189, 320, 321, 325
Europe(an), 2, 65, 76, 109, 118, 135, 137, 182, 223, 259, 293, 328
Eusthatius, bishop Berytus, 192
Eutyches, 35, 188, 191, 213
Eutychian, 201
Evagrius, Christian historiographer, 151, 206, 219, 220, 221, 222
Eve, 58
Exarchate of Ravenna, 100, 104

Fadak, oasis in Arabia, 316, 318
Fascist, 169
Fathers of the Church, 32, 59-60, 202, 219, 277
Fatima, daughter of Mohammed, 240, 255
Fatimids, 255
Fegelein, Hermann, SS-commander, 136
Felix III, Pope, 199, 200, 201
Feyenoord, Dutch football club (Rotterdam), 159, 161
Flavian, Patriarch of Constantinople, 197
France, 2, 328

Franks, Frankish, 2, 90, 92, 94, 95, 96, 98, 100, 101, 111, 328
Fredegarius, 153
French, 81, 332
Frend, W.H.C., 182, 193, 195, 197, 198, 200, 201, 202, 204, 210, 214, 215, 217, 218, 219, 220, 221, 222
Fustat, town in Egypt, 322

Gabriel, archangel, 238, 257, 258, 289, 291, 292, 301, 332
Gabrieli, Francesco, 260, 261
Galatia(n), 124
Galen, 59
Gallia, 90
Gangra (Çankiri), town in Paphlagonia, 195
Ganzaca (Takht-i-Soleima?), town in Media, 140, 141
Gaudefroy-Demonbynes, Maurice, 230, 231, 257, 258, 319, 330
Gaugamela, Battle of, 145
Gaul, 329
Gaza, town in Palestine, 193, 315
Gelasius I, Pope, 199, 202, 220
Geiger, Abraham, 308, 310
Gelimer, Vandal king, 82, 83-85
Genesis, Book of, 44, 54
Genoa, 103, 104
Genseric, Vandal king, 181
Gentiles (Goyim), 60
Georgius Pisidae, 119, 138, 139, 140, 152, 153
Gepids, 98, 101, 102-103
German(s), 1, 109, 284, 285
Germanic, 1, 2, 76, 77, 81, 92, 94, 95, 96, 99, 100, 101, 102, 103, 104, 122, 176
Germanica, town in Cilicia, 143
Germany, 2, 66, 109, 118
Gibbon, Edward, 77, 80, 94, 96, 105, 106, 108, 118, 122, 125, 134, 149, 150, 151, 152, 153, 154, 180, 218, 261
Gibraltar, 328
Glubb, John Bagot (Glubb Pasha), 240, 243, 245, 247, 256, 258, 259, 260

Gnosis, Gnostic, 5, 6, 14, 20, 22-27, 23-27, 36, 43-44, 49-50, 52, 53, 56-58, 179, 212, 265, 268
Gödel, Kurt, 8
Golden Horn, 116, 164, 171
Goldziher, I., 258
Gospel of John, 29, 32
Goths, 75
Gospel of Philip, 57
Gospels, 28, 54, 270, 302
Gourgaud, Gaspar, 261
Greece, 10, 22, 64, 65, 98, 112, 306
Greek(s), 10, 14, 16, 17, 20, 35, 38, 39, 40, 41, 45, 55, 58, 61, 64, 77, 78, 79, 91, 98, 99, 122, 126, 137, 146, 160, 178, 199, 203, 204, 214, 226, 257, 323, 330
Gregory of Nyssa, 45
Grelling, Kurt, 8
Grillmeier, A., 219
Grohmann, Adolf, 230
Guillaume, A., 256, 258

Halys (Kizil-Irmak), river in Asia Minor), 143
Hamidullah, Muhammad, 253, 257, 259, 261, 262, 309
Hamza, uncle of Mohammed, 233, 242
Hammurabi, King of Babylon, 63
Hattusilis, King of the Hittites, 63
Hayek, Michel, 309
Haykal, Muhammad Husayn, 260
Hebrew, 3, 60, 224, 257, 283
Heisenberg, Werner, 9, 38
He(d)jaz, region in Arabia, 247, 316
Heliopolis, 322
Hellenic see Greek
Hellenistic, 20, 39, 178, 330
Heraclitus, 6

Heraclius I, Byzantine Emperor, 115-116, 134-149, 176, 216-217
Hermas, Christian author, 28
Hermetic, 57
Heruli, 99
Hesiod, 56
Hesychius, Christian author, 75, 105
Hieropolis, town in Syria, 133
Hilderic, Vandal king, 82, 106
Hindu, 10, 13, 55, 56, 122
Hindu Kush, 323, 327
Hippodrome of Constantinople, 156, 162, 163, 164, 166, 167, 200, 206
Hippolytus, Christian author, 179
Hira, cave on Mount Nur near Mecca, 237, 238
Hirah, town on the Euphrates, 320
Hisham, Umayuyah caliph, 328
Hisham, Ibn, 309
Hitler, Adolf, 136
Hitti, Philip K., 332
Hittites, Hittite Empire, 63, 76
Höfner, Maria, 230, 231
Holy Cross, 135, 137, 141, 149, 176, 177
Holy War, 267, 312-313
Homer, 45
Hormisdas IV, Persian emperor, 129-130
Hormisdas, Pope, 205, 209, 210, 211
Hulwan, town in Persia, 321, 323
Hume, David, 275
Huns, 110
Huneric, Vandal king, 106
Hungary, Hungaria(ns), 101, 102, 112
Hunnic Empire, 77, 102, 112
Huns, 99, 101
Hyde, Thomas, scholar, 3
Hypation, Byzantine prince, 166, 167

Iamblichus, 20
Iberian peninsula, 328
Iberians, 76

Ibn Isham, Islamic chronicler, 260, 309
Iliad, 196
Illus, Byzantine general, 200
Illyria(n), 78, 113
Imperialism, imperialistic, 62-66, 312
India(n), 6, 10-11, 13-14, 37, 54-55
Indian Ocean, 224, 327
Indus, 65, 327, 329
Iohannes Ephesius, Christian historiographer, 151, 185, 218
Iran(ian), 4, 6, 22, 37, 63, 121, 295
Iraq, 26, 295, 305, 311, 326, 327
Isauria, town in Asia Minor, 200
Isaurian, 77
Isdiguce, Persian diplomat, 124-125
Ishaq, Ibn, Arabian historian, 236, 245, 256, 257, 259, 260, 261, 262, 292, 294, 309, 311
Isis Temple on Philae Island, 185
Islam(ic), 177, 228, 232, 241, 244, 245, 252, 253, Ch. IX and Ch. X passim
Ismael, son of Abraham, 296
Ispahan, town in Persia, 323
Israel (kingdom), 10, 178
Israel (people), 54, 60, 61
Ister see Danube
Istria, 90
Italy, Italian, 2, 77, 78, 83, 88-100, 110, 111, 115, 117, 124, 285, 329

Jabiya, town in Syria, 322
Jainism, Jainists, 13
James Bar'Addai, Monophysite bishop, 215
Jansen, Johannes J.G., 309
Jerome, Father of the Church, 199
Jerusalem, 64, 84, 135, 136, 141, 149, 152, 175, 176-177, 177, 193, 196, 214, 252, 296, 322, 325, 330
Jesus of Nazareth, 12, 27, 28, 29, 31, 32, 34, 35, 36, 50, 59, 138, 187, 188-189, 190, 192, 196, 199, 203, 204, 261, 269, 280, 283, 287, 298, 299-305, 308
Jews, Jewish, 10, 11, 12, 20, 21, 24, 52, 61, 66, 134, 136, 138, 149, 152, 159, 163, 171-172, 172, 173, 174-177, 179, 203, 204, 212, 218, 228, 237, 244, 248, 250, 251-252, 253, 257, 261, 268, 271, 274, 276, 278, 279, 280, 283, 284, 287, 287-298, 303, 305, 306, 307, 313, 316, 319, 320, 322, 324
Johannes of Beith-Aphthonia, Byzantine author, 221
Johannes Philoponos, John the Grammarian, ancient author, 283, 310, 330-331
John Patriarch of Constantinople, 207-209, 209-210, 211
John, Patriarch of Jerusalem, 209
John I, Pope, 211
John II, Pope, 213
Johannes Troglita, Byzantine general, 87
John of Nikiou, Byzantine scholar, 331
John the Sanguinary, Byzantine general, 94
John the Cappadocian, Byzantine praefectus praetorio, 82
John of Ephesus, Byzantine author see Iohannes Ephesius
John Lydus, Byzantine historiographer, 206
Johnson, James Turner, 312, 330
Jordan (the river), 285, 320
Jordan (kingdom), 321
Jordanes, Byzantine historian, 77, 93, 105, 107, 108
Juda (kingdom), 10
Judaeo-Christians, Judaeo-Christianity, 237, 283, 287, 298-299, 310
Judas, 303

Judaism, 12, 27, 52, 168, 175, 176, 177, 180, 228, 239, 240, 249, 251, 258, 263, 269, 274, 277, 279, 283, 284, 287, 296-297, 298, 299, 300, 303, 307
Julian the Apostate, 121, 180
Julianus, Samaritan rebel, 172-173
Julius Caesar, 331
Justin the Martyr, 44
Justin I, Byzantine Emperor, 80, 205-207, 209, 210, 211, 212
Justin II, Byzantine Emperor, 103, 112, 113, 127-128, 128-129, 174, 216
Justinian I, 78, 80-81, 81-82, 82-83, 85, 86, 87, 88, 89, 90, 97, 98, 99, 100, 101, 102, 106, 121-122, 123, 125, 126, 127, 140, 151, 158, 162, 163-168, 172, 173, 174-175, 182-183, 183, 184, 185, 186, 187, 206, 207, 209, 212, 213, 214-215, 216, 217, 218
Justinian, Byzantine general, 128, 129
Juvela, bishop of Jerusalem, 193

Ka'aba, Mecca, 227, 228, 241, 272, 276, 296, 307, 317, 327
Ka'b ibn Assad, Jewish leader, 293
Ka'b al Ashraf, Jewish poet, 291
Kairouan, town in Tunisia, 326
Katsh, Abraham, 298-299
Khaibar, town in Arabia, 316
Khadija, first wife of Mohammed, 235-236, 240, 243, 254, 255, 261, 262
Khalid ibn al-Walid, Meccan leader, 316, 319, 320

Khalid ibn Zaid, second host of Mohammed in Medina, 248
Khazraj, Jewish tribe in Medina, 250
Kahzdan, Alexander, 192, 219
Kallopodios, first a Green, later a Blue, 163
Katholikos of the Nestorian Church, 189
Kavad-Shiryua, Siroes, son of Chosroes II, his successor, 148-149, 247
Kazhan, Alexander P., 109
Kellerhals, Emanuel, 258, 282-283, 286
Kemal Ataturk, 273
Khagan, title of the Avar king, 113, 114-115, 115-116, 116, 117
Khan, title of the Turkish ruler, 127, 128
Khaybar, town in Arabia, 292, 294-295
Kingdom of the Germans in Italy, 2
Kitchen, K.A., 229
Knecht, August, 184, 217, 218
Koran, 238, 241, 242, 256, 265, 266, 267, 270, 271, 276, 277, 279, 283, 284, 285, 286, 288, 295, 297, 299, 300, 301, 302, 303, 305, 307, 324, 331
Kosovo, 306
Koukosor (Gogsyn?) in Cappadocia, 196
Kufa, town in Iraq, 321, 325, 327
Kuhn, Thomas, 8
Kurdistan, 63

Laeuchli, Samuel, 4, 67
Lake Aral, 64
Lake Tiberias, 321
Lake Van, 129
Langobards (Lombards), 98, 99, 101-104, 109, 111, 115
Last Supper, 302
Latin(s), 2, 78, 85, 90, 91, 92, 103, 203, 204, 211, 214, 228, 248, 257
Lausus palace in Constantinople, 196

Lazi, inhabitants of Lazica, 125, 126
Lazica (Colchis = Georgia), in the Caucasus region, 124, 125, 140, 144
Leibniz, Gottfried Wilhelm, 3
Leo I, Pope, 181, 191, 194, 197, 199, 204, 209, 213, 220
Leo I, Byzantine Emperor, 182, 194, 195, 206
Leontius, Byzantine Emperor (usurper), 200
Liberatus, Byzantine author, 108
Libya, 83, 135, 137, 326
Liguria, 94, 95, 104
Lings, Martin, 256
Loire, 1, 328
Lombards see Langobards
Lombardy, 104
Long Walls of Constantinople, 111, 114, 116, 118, 143
Longinus, exarch of Ravenna, 103
Lucretius, 41
Luke, 301
Lüling, Günter, 283, 310
Luxemburg, 2
Luzalzagissi, King of Sumer, 62
Lydia, 64

Maccabees, 313
Macedonian Empire, 64-65
Macedonia(n)(s), 11, 64-65, 66, 131, 306
Madin, town on the Persian frontier, 200
Magi (Persian), 125
Mahdi, 327
Mahdi revolt in Sudan, 313
Maiuma, town in Palestine, 193, 203
Malaga, 100
Malalas, 168, 169, 170, 172, 217, 218

Manat, Arab goddess, 228, 263
Mandaeans, Gnostic sect, 26, 58
Mani, 26, 213
Manichaeism (Church of Justice), Manichaean(s), Manichee, 27, 58, 163, 173, 185-186, 201, 205, 207, 212
Mansi, 218, 219, 221
Marcian, Byzantine Emperor, 182, 191, 194
Marcion, Gnostic prophet, 26, 58
Marcionite Church, 26, 58
Marcus Aurelius, 42
Maritain, Jacques, 46
Martina, second wife of Heraclius I, 140
Martyrius, Patriarch of Constantinople, 198
Martyropolis, town in Persia (Silvan), 132, 142
Marusians see Berbers
Marvan, Umayyah caliph, 326
Mary, mother of Jesus, 35, 188-189, 299, 300, 301-302, 303, 304
Matasuntha, Ostrogothic queen, 92
Materialism, 41
Maurice, Byzantine Emperor, 114, 115, 129-132, 133, 136, 175, 216, 262
Maximus, Roman Emperor, 181
Mecca(n)(s), 223, 227, 228, 231, 233, 237, 241, 243, 244, 246, 248, 249, 250, 252, 254, 255, 256, 257, 258, 259, 260, 272, 276, 281, 283, 284, 288, 290, 292, 298, 299, 305, 307, 315, 316, 317, 324, 327
Medes, Media, 64, 131, 140
Medina(n)(s) (Yathrib), 223, 228, 234, 236, 244, 245, 246, 247, 248, 249, 250-254, 254, 255, 257, 260, 261, 262, 283, 288, 289, 290, 291, 292, 294, 295, 296, 298, 299, 304, 305, 315, 316, 318, 324, 325
Mediterranean Sea, 100, 330
Megara, Greek town, 74
Melitene, 175
Memphis, 322
Menander, Gnostic prophet, 23

Menander, Byzantine author, 119, 151
Menas, Patriarch of Constantinople, 214
Meredith-Owens, G.M., 256
Merv, town in Turkmenistan (also called Mary), 323
Mesopotamia(n), 62, 63, 66, 77, 121, 123, 124, 128, 132, 133, 144, 200, 230, 322, 325
Messiah, 297, 300, 302, 303
Messina, 91
Michael, archangel, 289
Michael III, Byzantime Emperor, 157
Middle Platonism, 6, 17-18
Milan, 94-95, 97, 103
Mina, township near Mecca, 272
Mithridates I, Parthian emperor, 120
Modalism, Modalists, 28-29, 29
Mohammed, Muhammad, 227, 229, 231, Chs. VIII, IX and X, passim, 309, 310, 315-319, 324, 325, 327, 329
Monarchianism, Monarchianists, 28, 29
Mongolians, 77, 102, 112
Monism, monistic, 6, 7, 37, 42
Monophysitism, Monophysites, 35, 80, 134, 36, 158, 171, 174, 187-217
Monotheism, monotheists, monotheistic, 172, 228, 231, 237, 249, 251, 263, 299, 304
Mons Lactarius, mountain near the Vesuvius, 100
Montanism, Montanist(s), 31, 53, 186, 212
Montanus, heterodox Christian author, 31
Montenegro, 306
Morocco, 326

Morsy, Magali, 259, 261, 262
Moses, 296, 297, 298, 299, 303
Mosaic Law, 10
Moscati, Sabatino, 230
Mosque of 'Amr in Cairo, 322
Mosque of Umar in Jerusalem, 322
Mount Arafat, near Mecca, 272
Mount Gerizim, in Palestine, 172
Mount Nur, near Mecca, 237
Mount Thaur, near Mecca, 247
Mu'awiyyah I, Umayyah caliph, 325-326
Mu'awiyyah II, Umayyah caliph, 326
al-Mukhtar, Arab rebel leader, 327
Museum Library in Alexandria, 331
Muslims, 228, 232, 233, 234, 240, 241, 244, 246, 248, 250-254, 255, 257, 259, 260, 261, 262, Ch. IX and Ch. X passim
Mycene, 54
Mysogyny, 21

Nabataean kingdom, 225
Nablus, town in Palestine, 172
an-Nadir, Jewish tribe in Medina, 291, 291-292
Najd, central plateau of Arabia, 223, 317
Najran, town in Arabia, 304, 305, 318
Naples, 91, 92, 97, 104
Napoleon I, 261
Narbonne, 328
Narses, Byzantine general, 99-100, 103, 109, 133
Nazareth, 301
Nazism, 313
Neapolitans, 91
Near East, 80
Nebuchadnessar II, King of Babylonia, 64
Neo-Arianism, 33-34
Neoplatonism, Neoplatonist, 6, 15, 16, 18-20, 42-43
Neopythagoreanism, 6, 16
Nero, 157

Nestorian(ism), 136, 140, 189, 190, 192, 212
Nestorian Church, 189-190
Nestorius, Patriarch of Constantinople, 35, 188-189, 189, 198, 213
Netherlands, 2, 109, 272
New Testament, 26, 29, 53, 59, 61, 237, 257, 270, 279, 283, 287, 301, 303
Nicomedia, 140
Nihawend, town in Persia, 323
Nikephoros, Byzantine author, 119, 135, 152, 154
Nile, 10, 215, 322, 323
Nineveh, 145
Nirvana, 14
Nisibis, 77, 121, 123, 128, 132
Noach, 269, 296
Noetus, heterodox Christian author, 28
Nominalism, 29-30
North Africa(ns), 2, 31, 65, 76, 77, 80, 82-87, 88, 91, 110, 111, 117
Norwegian, 235
Nubian, 215
Numenius, 16-17
Numidia, 85, 86

Ochod, mountain near Medina, 316
Odoacer, King of the Germans in Italy, 1, 2, 78
Odyssee, 196
Oestrup, J., 281, 287
Ohm, 280, 285, 286
Old Testament, 12, 21, 26, 44, 53, 54, 59, 172, 175, 237, 257, 270, 276, 283, 287, 296, 312
Olympian religion, 41
Olympic Games, 180
Oman, 319
Ophites, Gnostic sect, 24
Origen, 32, 44, 45, 53, 179
Ormuzd, 37

Orphic religion, 6
Osiris, 192
Ostrogoth(s), Ostrogothic, 77-78, 88-100, 103, 111, 123, 212, 214
Oxford University, 3
Oxus see Amu Dary'a

Pagan(ism), 35, 59, 128, 173, 176, 180, 183, 184-185, 212, 235, 264, 269, 320
Pakistani, 262
Palestine, Palestinians, 61, 63, 64, 65, 66, 77, 137, 171, 172, 174, 193, 203, 207, 224, 228, 318, 320, 321, 322, 325, 327
Palmyra, Kingdom of, 225
Pandora, 56
Pantheism, 6-7
Paphlagonia, 195
Parmenides, 6, 38, 40
Parrinder, Geoffrey, 300, 301, 310, 311
Parthia, Parthian Empire, 65, 66, 120, 131
Patriarchical, patriarchate, 54, 56
Patricius, 2
Paul, apostle, 59
Paul of Samosata, heterodox Christian author, 29, 30
Paulus Diaconus, historian, 103, 109, 220
Paulinians, 29
Pavia (Ticinum), 103
Pax Romana, 39
Pelusium, town in Egypt, 137, 322
Perozen, Persian general, 123
Persepolis, 147
Perscennius Niger, Roman emperor (usurper), 95
Persian(s), Persian Empire, 10, 64, 65, 76, 82, 88, 97, 110, 113, 115, 116, 118, Ch. IV passim, 167, 173, 177, 185, 186, 206, 215, 216, 230, 318, 320, 321, 323, 329, 330
Persian Gulf, 319
Persis, 323
Perugia, 99, 104
Peter, Byzantine diplomat, 89-91

Peter the Fuller, Patriarch of Antioch, 195, 196
Peter the Iberian, bishop of Maiuma, 193
Peters, F.E., 257, 330
Petra, town on the Black Sea coast, 124, 125-126
Petra, town in Palestine, 225
Pharaohs, 322
Philae Island, in the Nile, 185
Philip II, King of Macedonia, 65
Philo, 20-21, 27, 57
Philostorgius, Church historian, 74, 104
Phocas, Byzantine emperor, 132-134, 135, 157, 175-176, 177
Phoenician, 135
Photius, an enemy of Phocas, 134, 216
Phrygia, 31, 186
Pilate, Pontius, 303
Pinechas, Jew of Medina, 289
Pisidia, 202
Plato, Platonic, Platonist, 6, 15, 17, 18, 51, 91, 122, 185
Platonov, Sergej Fedorovic, 230, 231
Plotinus, 6, 18-19, 20, 42
Plutarch, 17-18
Po, 97
Poitiers, 328
Polygamous, polygamy, 54
Polytheism, polytheistic, 237, 240, 241, 252, 264
Pompeius, Byzantine prince, 167
Pontus, 140
Porphyry, 19
Porta Asinaria in Rome, 92
Porta Flaminia in Rome, 92
Praxeas, heterodox Christian author, 29
Presocratics, 37-38
Previté-Orton, C.W., 121, 150

Priscillian, heterodox Christian author, 31, 53-54, 181
Priscillianism, Priscillianists, 31-32
Priscus, Byzantine general, 115
Probus, Byzantine prince, 166
Proclus, 39, 43
Procopius, Byzantine historian, 78-81, 82, 83, 84, 86, 87, 89, 92, 94, 96, 97, 99, 105, 106, 107, 108, 109, 123, 124, 124, 150, 151, 158, 159, 160, 169, 172, 175, 205, 206, 217, 221
Proterius, arch-priest in Alexandria, 194, 195
Provence, 90, 92
Punic, 224
Puritans, Puritanism, 274, 312
Pyrenees, 329, 330, 332
Pythagorean(ism), 6, 16, 51
Pythagoras, 16, 22, 29, 39

Qoba, village in the Medina oasis, 248
Queen of Sheba, 145
Qulthoom ibn Hidm, Mohammed's first host in Medina, 248
Qumran, 21
Quraysh, clan of Mohammed, 236, 241, 246, 256
Qurayzah, Jewish tribe in Medina, 292-294, 316
Quyrawan (Kairouan), town in Tunisia, 326

Rabello, Alfredo M., 218
Ragusa, Balkan town, 117
Ramadan, Muslim month of fasting, 237, 238, 272, 276
Ramallah, town in Palestine, 330
Ratchis, Lombard Duke, 103
Ravenna, 78, 79, 88, 92, 94, 95-96, 97, 100, 104, 211
Razates, Persian general, 145-146
Realm of Syagrius, 1
Red Sea, 223
Reggio di Calabria (Rhegium), 91, 104
Revelation of John, 179

Rhine, 65, 81
Rimini, 94, 104
Ringgren, Helmer, 228, 229, 231
Riviera (French), 90
Robin, Christian, 230
Roderick, Visigothic king, 328
Rodinson, Maxime, 262
Roman(s), 1, 2, 11, 16, 39, 55-56, 58-59, 61, 66, 76, 78, 81, 88, 89, 93, 105, 111, 121, 126, 149, 156, 178, 223, 226, 303, 331
Roman Catholic Church, liturgy, religion, 2, 8, 31, 33, 36, 59, 171, 179, 181, 183, 278, 279, 280, 285, 287, 303
Roman Empire, 1, 2, 9, 17, 34, 36, 39, 43, 65-66, 75, 76, 77, 81, 120, 179, 180, 190, 191, 225, 287
Roman Law, 2
Roman Republic, 58, 66, 88
Roman Senate, 2, 88, 89
Romania, 78, 101, 102
Roman(s), 329, 330
Rome (city), 1, 2, 16, 65, 74, 75, 77, 78, 84, 85, 88, 91, 92, 93-94, 97, 98, 104, 137, 168, 181, 183, 189, 199, 209, 210
Romulus Augustulus, 1, 157
Royal Library in Constantinople, 197
Rubin, Berthold, 106, 107
Russell, Bernard, 8
Russian Orthodox Church, 280
Rustam, Persian general, 321

Saba, 224-225
Sabbath, 293, 296
Sa'd ibn Mu'adh, a Muslim, 293
Saddam Hussein, 136
Sádeckzy-Kardoss, Samuel, 118
Safa, hill in Mecca
Sain (Saes), Persian general, 144
Sahara, 81
Saint Peter in Rome, 97, 168
Samaritans, 10, 66, 163, 172-174, 174, 177, 212
Samarkand, town in Uzbekistan, 327
Sampson Hospital, Constantinople, 165
San Vitale, church in Ravenna, 79
Sarabanglas, Persian general, 142
Sarban, town in Armenia, 142
Sardinia, 83, 84, 85, 100, 104
Sargon, King of Akkad, 63
Sasanian (Empire), 66, 77, 120, 122, 123, 125, 189, 323, 329
Satan, 31, 57, 274, 289
Saturnilos, Gnostic prophet, 23
Sauda bint Zamara, second wife of Mohammed, 243, 254, 259
Saudi Arabia, 319
Sava, river in the Balkans, 78, 117
Schall, Anton, 283
Schedl, Claus, 310
Schimmel, Annemarie, 232, 256, 275, 282, 283, 285, 286, 287
Schoeps, Hans-Joachim, 283, 287, 298-299, 308, 310
School of the Garden, 51
Schoolmen, 49, 188, 277
Schumann, Olaf H., 305, 311
Sciri, 1
Scythia, 77
Sea of Marmora, 74
Sebeos, Armenian historian, 138
Seignobos, Charles, 332
Seleucia, town in Mesopotamia, 147
Seleucid Empire, emperors, 65, 66, 179, 323
Semites, Semitic, 224, 227
Senate House in Constantinople, 165
Seneca, 41-42, 42
Septimius Severus, Roman emperor, 74
Septuagint, 175

Serapeum, Serapis Temple and Library in Alexandria, 194, 331
Serbia, Serbs, 78, 117, 205, 306, 311
Sergius, governor of North Africa, 86
Sergius, patriarch of Constantinople, 136
Sergius, bishop of Caesarea, 173
Sethians, Gnostic sect, 23-24, 57
Severians, Gnostic sect, 57
Severus, Monophysite author, bishop of Antioch, 202-205, 207, 209, 210-211, 213, 214, 220, 221
Sexuality, 27, 30, 56-60, 284, 286
Shapur I, Parthian emperor, 121
Shahr Barz, Persian general, 135, 139, 140, 141-144, 146
Sicily, 83, 90, 91, 97, 100, 104, 214
Shi'ite Muslims, 277
Silverius, Pope, 92, 93
Simon the Magus, 23
Simplicius, Greek philosopher, 185
Simplicius, Pope, 199
Sirmium, town on the Danube, 101, 112-114
Siroes see Kavad-Shiryua
Sisibut, king of the Visigoths, 136
Skupic (Skopje), town in Serbia, 205
Slav tribes, 110-112, 115, 116, 117
Slavery, slaves, 61-62
Slavonic, 111, 113
Sliman bin Ibrahim, biographer of Mohammed, 262
Slovenia, Slovenes, 117, 306
Socrates, 29, 178
Solomo, king of Israel, 145, 225
Solomon, Byzantine general, 85, 86
Somme, 1
Sophia, wife of the Emperor Justin II, 216
Sozopolis, town in Pisidia, 202
Spain, 31, 100, 111, 136, 328
Spartans, 129
Spenta Mainyu, 7, 37
Split (Spalato), Balkan town, 117
Spoleto, 99, 103
Stalin, Joseph, 136
Stoa, Stoic(s), 7, 16, 40, 41, 42
Straits of Gibraltar, 328
Sudan, 215, 313
Sulayman I, Umayyad caliph, 328
Sumer, 62-63, 76
Swedish, 228
Switzerland, Swiss, 2, 282
Syagrius, Roman general, 1
Sykai, part of Constantinople, 200
Symeon the Stylite, 195
Syracuse, 90
Syr Dar'ya, river in Kazakhstan, 327, 329
Syria(n)(s), 63, 64, 65, 66, 77, 123, 124, 128, 133, 134, 135, 136, 138, 188, 192, 193, 196, 198, 200, 207, 212, 215, 216, 217, 224, 225, 228, 234, 235, 237, 255, 305, 310, 313, 315, 318, 320, 322, 325, 327

'Al-Tabari, biographer of Mohammed, 238, 259
Tabuk, oasis in Arabia, 319
Taginae, village in Umbria, 99
Ta'if, town in Arabia, 244, 315, 317-318
Tarento, 104
Tariq ibn-Ziyad, Arab general, 328
Tartars, 112
Tatian, heterodox Christian author, 30-31, 53
Taunus mountains, 77
Taurus mountains, 142
Teja, Ostrogothic king, 99-100
Temple of Jerusalem, 84, 177, 178, 322

Tertullian, 59
Thebarmes, town in Media, 141
Thebes, 171
Theodebert I, King of the Franks, 94-95, 98
Theodahad (Theodatus), Ostrogothic king, 88-92, 93, 214
Theodora, Byzantine Empress, 78-81, 89, 93, 140, 165, 166, 167, 215
Theodore of Mopsuestia, 34-35
Theodore, brother of Heraclius I, 144
Theodoric, King of Italy, 77-78, 78, 88, 89, 92
Theodosius I the Great, 115, 180
Theodosius II, 168, 181, 188, 191, 193
Theodosius, Patriarch of Alexandria, 214, 21
Theodosopolis, town in Armenia, 133
Theophanes, Byzantine author, 109, 119, 133, 141, 142, 143, 144, 145, 147, 149, 152, 153, 154, 163, 166, 167, 169, 170, 195, 199, 201, 218, 219, 220, 258
Theophilos, Byzantine Emperor, 157
Theophylactus, Byzantine author, 114, 119, 129, 130, 151, 152
Thermopylae pass, 112
Thessalonica, 111, 114, 156, 210
Third Reich, 313
Thomas of Aquinas, 277
Thora, 270
Thrace, 111, 112
Tiber, 65
Tiberius II, Byzantine Emperor, 114, 129-130, 216

Tiflis (Tblisi), town in Georgia, 144
Tigris, 65, 130, 132, 133, 142, 145, 146, 147, 321, 329
Timothy IV the Cat, bishop of Alexandria, 195, 196, 197, 211, 212, 213, 214
Tisza (Theiss), river in Hungaria, 101
Titus, Roman Emperor, 84
Torah, 296-297, 300
Toth-Hermes, 22
Totila, Ostrogothic king, 97-99
Tours, 332
Trapezus (Trabzond), town in Asia Minor, 77
Tricameron, town in Tunisia, 84
Tripoli(s), town in Libya, 83, 137, 326
Tunisia, 78, 326
Turisund, Gepid king, 102, 103
Turkmenistan, 327
Turkey, Turks, Turkish, 127-128, 128, 129, 144-145, 153, 273, 306, 327
Tuscany, 92, 103, 104
Tyre, 209

Ukaz, town in Arabia, 237
Ukraine, 102
Umar I, caliph, 289, 295, 305, 321, 322, 324, 331
Umar II, caliph, 295, 328
Umayyah dynasty, 324, 325
'Uthman, caliph, 324, 325, 326, 327
Umbria, 99
Umma, Sumerian city, 62
United Arab Emirates, 319
'Uqbah ibn-Nafi, Arab general, 326
Usayr, Jewish leader, 292
al-'Uzza(h), Arab goddess, 228, 263
Uzbekistan, 327

Varahram see Baram
Valencia, 100
Valentinians, Gnostic sect, 25
Valentinianus III, Roman Emperor, 106
Valley of Hernayn, in Arabia, 317

Valley of the Nile, 10
Valley of the Po, 95, 103
Vandals, 78, 82-87, 88, 106, 111, 118, 181
Vasiliev, A.A., 104, 105, 106, 205, 207, 208, 212, 221
Vecca Vaglieri, Laura, 332
Veklal, Park of, 146
Venice, 98, 103
Verina, wife of Leo I, 196, 200
Verona, 97, 100, 103
Vesuvius, 99
Via Egnatia, in Italy, 209
Vigilius, Pope, 93, 97, 98
Viminacium (Byzantine town on the Danube), 114
Visigoths, 2, 77, 100, 111, 136, 328
Vitiges, Ostrogothic king, 123
Vitalian, Byzantine patricius, 212
Vulgata, 199

Wahidi, Arabian chronicler, 305
Walid, Umayyah caliph, 327-328
Waraqa ibn Nofal, cousin of Mohammed, 240
Watt, W. Montgomery, 256, 257, 259, 260, 261, 262, 292, 293, 294, 296, 297, 309, 310
Welch, A.T., 256
Welfare Party, 273
Wellhausen, J., 253
Wend(s), 111, 118
Wensinck, A.J., 261, 309
Wittigis, Ostrogothic king, 92-96
Wolff, Christian, scholar, 3
World War II, 313

Xenocrates, 15
Xerxes I, King of Persia, 64, 120, 137

Yarmuk, river in Palestine, 321
Yathrib see Medina
Yazid I, Umayyah caliph, 326
Yazid II, 328
Yemen(initic), 223-224, 224, 228, 283, 288
Yezdegerd III, Persian emperor, 321, 323
Yin & Yang, 12
Yoga, 6, 13

Zaandam, Dutch town, 249
Zab, Great (Zei Badinan), tributary of the Tigris, 146
Zab, Lesser (Zei Koya), tributary of the Tigris, 146
Zacharias, Patriarch of Jerusalem, 177
Zacharias Rhetor, Byzantine historian, 194, 219
Zagros mountains, 147, 321
Zaid ibn Harithad, Mohammed's slave and adopted son, 240, 244, 318
Zeno, Byzantine Emperor, 2, 76-77, 174, 195-197, 197, 198, 199, 200, 201
Zeno, the philosopher, 7
Zenobia, Queen of Palmyra, 225
Zenonis, wife of the Emperor Basiliscus, 196
Zervan, 37
Zervanism, 5, 37
Zeuxippos Baths, Constantinople, 165
Ziebel, Turkish commander, 153
Ziyad, governor of Iraq, 326
Zoroaster, 7, 22, 141
Zoroastrian(s)(ism), 4, 6, 37, 125, 129, 295
Zosimus, Church historian, 75, 105

3483/029